of Vicious Circle of Conflict & lack of environmental Reg

Need for dispute res syst. ?
Env.

11 & HR
less than stellar
intnl response to HR
calls into q. its utility in
envr Reg

Water & GCC as HR issues

P 104
poor envr + Conflict
perform

AN UNFINISHED FOUNDATION

The United Nations and Global Environmental Governance

Env. Security agenda
post C.W.

P 193
Call to
action

Chapt p 90

96
— statement —

SL vs Bots
Resource issue
+ Doubts

Ken Conca

Pro active vs
current reactive + barriers
to
Prevention
Conflict policy
Conflict Prevention vs
Conflict Resolution

producer state human cost
of overconsumption
in importing states
Nigeria / Calif.

econ globalization
challenges ability of
why one to

OXFORD
UNIVERSITY PRESS

social
disrupti

D0910862

OXFORD
UNIVERSITY PRESS

Oxford University Press is a department of the University of
Oxford. It furthers the University's objective of excellence in research,
scholarship, and education by publishing worldwide.

Oxford   New York
Auckland   Cape Town   Dar es Salaam   Hong Kong   Karachi
Kuala Lumpur   Madrid   Melbourne   Mexico City   Nairobi
New Delhi   Shanghai   Taipei   Toronto

With offices in
Argentina   Austria   Brazil   Chile   Czech Republic   France   Greece
Guatemala   Hungary   Italy   Japan   Poland   Portugal   Singapore
South Korea   Switzerland   Thailand   Turkey   Ukraine   Vietnam

Oxford is a registered trademark of Oxford University Press
in the UK and certain other countries.

Published in the United States of America by
Oxford University Press
198 Madison Avenue, New York, NY 10016

Library of Congress Cataloging-in-Publication Data
Conca, Ken.
An unfinished foundation : the United Nations and global
environmental governance / Ken Conca.
pages cm
Includes bibliographical references and index.
ISBN 978-0-19-023285-6 (hardcover : acid-free paper)—ISBN 978-0-19-023286-3
(pbk. : acid-free paper)   1. Environmental justice—International cooperation.   2. Human
rights—International cooperation.   3. Sustainability—International cooperation.
4. United Nations—Environmental policy.   I. Title.
GE220.C66 2015
363.7'0526—dc23
2015004028

9 8 7 6 5 4 3 2 1
Printed in the United States of America
on acid-free paper

CONTENTS

LIST OF FIGURES AND TABLES

FIGURES

TABLES

PREFACE

Intellectually, I came of age during heady times for global environmental politics. I finished my doctoral degree in 1992, the year of the Earth Summit in Rio de Janeiro. It was an era brimming with bold new concepts—global change, sustainability, earth systems, global governance—and efforts to create better environmental law between nations and more sustainable economic development within them. Readers familiar with my past research and writing will know that I have long been skeptical about the formal institutions and codified arrangements among governments that constitute the mainstream quest for global sustainability. In 1993, my graduate-school colleague Ronnie Lipschutz and I published an edited collection of essays, *The State and Social Power in Global Environmental Politics*, which was an early articulation of the skeptics' position on whether a path to sustainability could be charted mainly through new international law and improved development practice.

I then spent several years working on another book, *Governing Water*, which pleaded for a broader view of what it means to "institutionalize" global environmental governance. That work argued that transnational processes of contentious social politics, rooted in transnational movement activism and the responses to it, had come to be a more robust source of new social practices and governing approaches to water than the more formal "stuff" of international relations (specifically, international law and expert science). That book, and much else that I have written, was informed by a few key elements: strong skepticism about formal political processes, an effort to see and hear institutional politics beyond the state, and a belief that good (if sometimes messy) things happen when marginalized actors can push their way into political processes at all levels. Metaphors about letting a hundred flowers bloom, letting the grass grow up through the cracks in the concrete, and would-be eco-emperors in various states of disrobe find their way into my teaching and public speaking on a regular basis.

It may seem odd, then, to find my name on a book about that most formal and conventional of international institutions, the United Nations. Why write a book about Stockholm, Rio, Brundtland, UNEP, *Agenda 21, The Future We Want*, COPs and POPs, MDGs and SDGs? Why a book about a system that seems to specialize in unimaginatively spitting out the same ineffectual institutional forms, while missing the creative political possibilities all around it? Well, for exactly that reason. As I have tried to make the case herein, global environmental governance takes place on a built institutional landscape, and the unevenness of that landscape has important consequences for how we see and act on environmental challenges. Understanding where that landscape came from, how it matters, and its possibilities for change seems to me a prerequisite for effective action, inside and outside the UN, and thus an important intellectual project.

A second reason is that, much like the UN itself, a good deal of the scholarship produced about global environmental governance and the UN has made assumptions about the supposedly "natural" character of that built landscape. We have strong tendencies to recount the history, gauge the current mood, and chart the prospects for progress in terms of treaties ratified and sustainable development projects implemented. We spend much time inspecting the strength, health, and overall fitness of the UN's "legs" of environmental law and sustainable development. In assuming that the environment is, inherently, the stuff of law and development, we have spent almost no time asking why the UN—a four-legged creature with a mandate for peace, human rights, international law, and development—has come to stand on only two of the legs at its disposal, and whether things could be different. This book tells a different story about that history, stressing the curious nature of an institutional landscape and an issue construction that we tend to take for granted.

Writing a book can be a solitary exercise, but books are never written alone. I owe an unpayable debt to several people for helping me get these ideas on paper. I was fortunate to have several able research assistants over the course of the project, including Lakhpreet Dhariwal, Courtney Greenley, Namalie Jayasinge, Tim Kovach, Goueun Lee, Brett Lingle, Isabelle Rodas, Tristan Slusser, Joe Thwaites, and Jennifer Wallace. Colleagues in the School of International Service (SIS) at American University, and particularly those active in the Global Environmental Politics Program, have created a warm and supportive intellectual environment. I owe a particular debt to David Bosco, my co-conspirator on the SIS Roundtable on the United Nations, and David Jensen of the UN Environment Programme. They have helped me to think about the UN in new and different ways.

Thanks are also due to the many people who offered comments on various portions of the manuscript or the ideas therein. Several presentations of various portions of the work, including those at American University, the Center for International Climate and Environmental Research (CICERO), Columbia University, the Monterey Institute of International Studies, the Norwegian Association of Development Research, Tufts University, and the annual meetings of the International Studies Association, helped me to sharpen the message. I'm grateful to the audience members, discussants, and fellow panelists who offered comments at these sessions. A portion of the material in chapter 4 appeared in earlier form as a chapter in *Handbook of Global Environmental Politics* (Edward Elgar, 2012; Peter Dauvergne, editor) and benefited from that project's editorial process. The three anonymous reviewers at Oxford University Press each gave me a wonderfully thorough reading and some very helpful advice. And special thanks to my crack editorial team at Oxford University Press: Angela Chnapko, Princess Ikatekit, Suvesh Subramanian, and Richard Isomaki.

Also important to the process of bookmaking are the people who help a writer keep in rhythm while maintaining the outward appearance of a normal life. I spent many hours writing at the Howard County Public Library; its cheerful and efficient staff oversee a wonderful environment for thinking and writing. I could never have written this book while also directing the Global Environmental Politics (GEP) Program at American University without the help of Vicki Fulton, Judy Shapiro, and all my GEP colleagues. Family, friends, students, and colleagues were patient with my need to be left alone in the morning to write. I thank them for all they have done to help me along the way.

LIST OF ACRONYMS

Note: The UN uses British spelling in the official English-language name of bodies and organs such as the United Nations Environment Programme, International Labour Organization, and United Nations Development Programme.

AIDS	acquired immune deficiency syndrome
ASEAN	Association of Southeast Asian Nations
BCPR	Bureau of Crisis Prevention and Recovery, UN Development Programme
CAR	Central African Republic
CBD	Convention on Biological Diversity
CERD	Committee on the Elimination of Racial Discrimination, United Nations
CESCR	Committee on Economic, Social and Cultural Rights, United Nations
CITES	Convention on International Trade in Endangered Species of Wild Fauna and Flora
COP	conference of the parties
DEWA	Division of Early Warning and Assessment, UN Environment Programme
DPA	Department of Political Affairs
DPKO	Department of Peacekeeping Operations, United Nations
DRC	Democratic Republic of the Congo
ECOSOC	Economic and Social Council, United Nations
EITI	Extractive Industries Transparence Initiative
ENVSEC	Environment and Security Initiative
EU	European Union

FAO	Food and Agriculture Organization
G-77	Group of Seventy-Seven
GDP	gross domestic product
HIV	human immunodeficiency virus
IACHR	Inter-American Commission on Human Rights
ICC	International Criminal Court; or, Inuit Circumpolar Conference
ICCPR	International Covenant on Civil and Political Rights
ICESCR	International Covenant on Economic, Social and Cultural Rights
ICJ	International Court of Justice
ICSU	International Council for Science; previously, International Council of Scientific Unions
IGO	intergovernmental organization
IISD	International Institute for Sustainable Development
ILC	International Law Commission
ILO	International Labour Organization
IMO	International Maritime Organization
IPCC	Intergovernmental Panel on Climate Change
IUCN	International Union for Conservation of Nature; previously known as the World Conservation Union, the International Union for the Conservation of Nature and Natural Resources, and International Union for the Preservation of Nature (IUPN)
IUPN	International Union for the Preservation of Nature
MARPOL	International Convention for the Prevention of Pollution from Ships
MDG	Millennium Development Goal
MONUC	United Nations Organization Mission in the Democratic Republic of Congo
NAM	Non-Aligned Movement
NAFTA	North American Free Trade Agreement
NATO	North Atlantic Treaty Organization
NGO	nongovernmental organization
NIEO	New International Economic Order

OECD	Organisation for Economic Co-operation and Development
OHCHR	Office of the High Commissioner for Human Rights, United Nations
OPEC	Organization of the Petroleum Exporting Countries
OSCE	Organization for Security and Co-operation in Europe
PBC	Peacebuilding Commission, United Nations
PBSO	Peacebuilding Support Office, United Nations
PCDMB	Postconflict and Disaster Management Branch, UN Environment Programme
PCNA	postconflict needs assessment
PCOB	Postconflict Branch, UN Environment Programme
POP	persistent organic pollutant
PSNR	permanent sovereignty over natural resources
R2P	responsibility to protect
REDD	Reducing Emissions from Deforestation and Forest Degradation in Developing Countries
SDG	Sustainable Development Goal
UDHR	Universal Declaration of Human Rights
UNAMSIL	United Nations Mission in Sierra Leone
UNCED	United Nations Conference on Environment and Development (1992)
UNCESCR	United Nations Committee on Economic, Social and Cultural Rights
UNCHE	United Nations Conference on the Human Environment (1972)
UNCHR	United Nations Commission on Human Rights
UNCLOS	United Nations Conference on the Law of the Sea
UNCSD	United Nations Commission on Sustainable Development; or, United Nations Conference on Sustainable Development (2012)
UNCTAD	United Nations Conference on Trade and Development
UNDESA	United Nations Department of Economic and Social Affairs
UNDG	United Nations Development Group
UNDP	United Nations Development Programme
UNECE	United Nations Economic Commission for Europe

UNEP	United Nations Environment Programme
UNESCO	United Nations Educational, Scientific and Cultural Organization
UNFCCC	United Nations Framework Convention on Climate Change
UNFPA	United Nations Population Fund
UNGA	United Nations General Assembly
UNHRC	United Nations Human Rights Council
UNICEF	United Nations Children's Fund
UNISDR	United Nations International Strategy for Disaster Reduction
UNITAR	United Nations Institute for Training and Research
UNMIL	United Nations Mission in Liberia
WCED	World Commission on Environment and Development
WCS	World Conservation Strategy
WEHAB	water, energy, health, agriculture, and biodiversity
WEO	World Environment Organization
WHO	World Health Organization
WMO	World Meteorological Organization
WRI	World Resources Institute
WSSD	World Summit on Sustainable Development (2002)

An Unfinished Foundation

CHAPTER 1

The Global Environment and the Four Pillars of the UN System

WE THE PEOPLES OF THE UNITED NATIONS DETERMINED

to save succeeding generations from the scourge of war, which twice in our lifetime has brought untold sorrow to mankind, and to reaffirm faith in fundamental human rights, in the dignity and worth of the human person, in the equal rights of men and women and of nations large and small, and to establish conditions under which justice and respect for the obligations arising from treaties and other sources of international law can be maintained, and to promote social progress and better standards of life in larger freedom . . .

Preamble to the Charter of the United Nations

THE UN ROLE IN GLOBAL ENVIRONMENTAL GOVERNANCE

We live in an era of extraordinary environmental change. A recent assessment in the influential journal *Science* noted that "human activities are moving several of Earth's sub-systems outside the range of natural variability typical for the previous 500,000 years."[1] Put more bluntly: we are altering the planet's life support systems at a rate and to an extent that is unprecedented in human history. Scientists studying the loss of global biodiversity refer to the current era as the "sixth extinction," comparable in scale and scope only to a handful of abrupt shifts in the planet's history. The amounts of carbon and nitrogen liberated by human activities rival natural background flows of these elements through the global carbon and nitrogen cycles. Human beings use almost half of the available runoff of fresh water, with dire consequences for critical freshwater ecosystems around the world.[2] If greenhouse-gas emissions proceed on their current course, instability in the Greenland Ice Shelf could increase sea level by as much as seven meters over the next millennium.[3]

Disruptive environmental change is not a global abstraction; nor is it a speculative problem for the future. Quite the contrary: it has profound consequences for the lives of people today, across the planet. The World Health Organization estimates that more than three million people annually die prematurely due to air pollution.[4] More than two billion people lack a sanitation system of the sort that was introduced at the height of the Roman Empire, two thousand years ago.[5] As much as one-third of the world's population extracts its living and its food supply from degraded land that has suffered a long-term loss of ecosystem functions and services.[6] For far too many people, the water, land, and air that should sustain them pose threats to health and well-being.

Environmental change also takes an enormous economic toll. To be sure, resource extraction, productive uses of land, energy use, water withdrawals, and other activities that transform the environment produce economic gains. But those gains must be weighed against not only the aforementioned human toll but also the loss of "natural capital"—the forests, wetlands, grasslands, fisheries, and other natural systems that, when intact and functioning, provide people with a continuous flow of benefits. Such losses may total US$2.0–US$4.5 trillion annually, according to one estimate.[7] The UN Environment Programme reports that "deforestation and forest degradation alone are likely to cost the global economy more than the losses of the 2008 financial crises."[8]

Our ability to address these profound planetary environmental challenges is one of the great political questions of the day. It is difficult to imagine a world of peace and prosperity unless the problems of climate change, water shortages, the loss of forests, and the destruction of critical ecosystems are addressed. It is also hard to imagine effective responses to these problems without a strong role for the UN. For all its flaws—many of which will be discussed in the pages that follow—the UN remains the only plausible forum for engaging broadly global challenges. It is the only venue in which a sufficiently wide range of voices may be heard as we seek to forge a robust consensus on difficult environmental problems. It has been the most important catalyst for negotiating international environmental agreements among nations, and the most important focal point for disseminating new ideas and practices for better environmental stewardship. Indeed, the most important environmental accomplishments of the past forty years—the rise of global environmental awareness, the birth of key ideas such as sustainability, the negotiation of important treaties for environmental protection—all bear the UN stamp in one way or another.

Certainly, the environment has become a central part of what the UN does. UN Secretaries-General routinely include the environment when identifying the most important global challenges. The UN General Assembly devotes a good portion of its annual agenda to environmental issues. Nearly all of the UN's commissions, programs, funds, and specialized agencies now recognize a "green" dimension to their mandate. The UN has conducted four major global environmental summits: at Stockholm in 1972, Rio de Janeiro in 1992, Johannesburg in 2002, and Rio again in 2012. Several UN organs have been created to catalyze and coordinate environmental activities, including the UN Environment Programme (UNEP), the UN Commission on Sustainable Development (UNCSD), and, most recently, the High-Level Political Forum on Sustainable Development. Dozens of conventions, protocols, and other instruments of international environmental law have been negotiated under UN auspices.

The UN has also championed important conceptual shifts. A series of UN General Assembly declarations has sharpened and defined both the natural-resource rights and the environmental responsibilities of UN member states.[9] The World Commission on Environment and Development (WCED), appointed by the General Assembly, articulated a new, environmentally sensitive, "sustainable" approach to development.[10] Kofi Annan's High-Level Panel on Threats, Challenges, and Change flagged the environment as a serious challenge to international security in the twenty-first century.[11] Several accords negotiated under UN auspices have brought forth important new concepts, such as the idea that the global commons are "the common heritage of humanity" (United Nations Convention on the Law of the Sea) or the notion that governments bear "common but differentiated" responsibilities for environmental protection (*United Nations Framework Convention on Climate Change* [UNFCCC]).

Unfortunately, these acknowledged gains have not been enough. Arrayed against them, we also find a UN record of failure, inaction, and disappointment. The fabric of international environmental law, though not entirely threadbare, contains many tears and missing strands. International law on toxic substances, for example, is a jumble of poorly integrated treaties—addressing some chemicals but not others, lacking ratification by some of the world's most important economic powers, and addressing only some parts of the cradle-to-grave cycle of toxic substances that courses through modern life. International water law remains largely hortatory and symbolic, despite the fact that nearly all of the world's major rivers cross or form national borders. International climate law has been an exercise in codifying weak aspirations, only to see them weakened further by loopholes and dubious "flexibility" mechanisms.

Progress toward "sustainable development" has also been uneven, to put it charitably. The concept of sustainability was widely embraced at the 1992 Rio Earth Summit, and the dire need for more sustainable forms of economic development amply documented there (albeit with a selective gaze that focused on the global South but ignored the core of the world economy). But development assistance for sustainability initiatives would fail to match even the modest commitments made at Rio. A decade later, at the "Rio+10" summit in Johannesburg, the intergovernmental dialogue focused so little on the environmental side of "environment and development" that activists ruefully dubbed the event "Rio minus 10."[12] A few environmental considerations were included in the UN's Millennium Development Goals, adopted in 2000, but they were defined with such vagueness as to be little more than hortatory.[13] The post-2015 Sustainable Development Goals (SDGs) are more ambitious in their environmental aspirations—but it is difficult to know what to make of goals as vague as "By 2030, achieve the sustainable management and efficient use of natural resources," or as wildly optimistic as "By 2020, sustainably manage and protect marine and coastal ecosystems to avoid significant adverse impacts."[14]

Nor has the UN been able to muster a robust organizational framework commensurate with the problem. UNEP exists, in theory, to coordinate and catalyze UN activities on the issue. Yet its annual budget is smaller than that of a decent liberal-arts college, and UNEP routinely struggles just to collect the paltry amounts of funding promised by member states. UNEP's budget for 2013 was $207.7 million; for comparison, the budget for my university alone (which is midsize by US standards) was $548.8 million that same year.[15] Moreover, the funds available to UNEP included only $4 million from the UN regular budget; the rest came as targeted "earmarks" from donors and voluntary contributions by member states.[16] The UNCSD, another byproduct of the 1992 Earth Summit, proved so ineffectual in engaging governments that it was scrapped twenty years later, at the "Rio+20" summit of 2012.

THE REFORM DEBATE AND THE DEEPER PROBLEM

Concern about the lack of progress on so many pressing environmental challenges is voiced frequently in and around the UN—by member states, the Secretary-General, UN agencies, and civil-society groups. Typically, these concerns express themselves in calls for better management and coordination, or more effective implementation of existing initiatives. In 2006, for example, Secretary-General Annan's High-Level Panel on United Nations System-Wide Coherence reached the following conclusion:

> We possess fairly comprehensive knowledge and understanding of what we individually and collectively need to do to reverse [environmental] trends—all spelled out in reports, declarations, treaties and summits since the early 1970s. While we have made significant advances within the United Nations framework, what is needed now is a substantially strengthened and streamlined international environmental governance structure, to support the incentives for change required at all levels.[17]

A similar tone was struck when the General Assembly authorized an informal consultative process on how to improve the institutional framework for environmental activities.[18] The ensuing debate centered on problems of institutional complexity and fragmentation among UN organs, a poorly coordinated patchwork of multilateral environmental agreements, lack of funding, and poor implementation of existing obligations and commitments. Recommendations included strengthening UNEP, enhancing cooperation among UN agencies, improving coordination among existing multilateral agreements, strengthening implementation, and bolstering key support functions such as financing, capacity building, and technical assistance.[19]

Governments and activists dissatisfied with this incremental, managerial agenda have called for the UN to embrace bolder reforms, centered on the creation of a World Environment Organization (WEO).[20] They argue that a more powerful entity is needed to engage the UN's specialized agencies and other key multilateral organizations such as the World Bank and the World Trade Organization—political tasks well beyond the reach of the current UNEP. The Rio+20 summit failed to find consensus on the question, with European and African nations supporting the WEO idea, while the United States and others strongly opposed it. In the end, Rio+20 settled for adjusting UNEP's organizational structure.[21]

To be sure, UN administrative reforms are needed: coordination is often poor; implementation, hesitant; and effective management, lacking. Better funding and more consistent political support would also help. Effective environmental action is also held hostage to some of the larger disputes swirling around the UN: how to reform the Security Council to make it a more effective and legitimate body; how to modernize, professionalize, and monitor the bureaucracy's performance; and how to place the organization's budget on a more stable long-term footing.[22]

Yet, as a longtime observer of the UN's environmental landscape, I have been struck by the narrowness of the reform debate. Both the incremental and bolder approaches to administrative reform have overlooked a deeper and more troubling concern. The core problem is that the UN has institutionalized a highly selective approach to environmental challenges—one that defines the task too narrowly, fails to connect it to key elements of the organization's mandate, and leaves unused some of the UN's most important tools. The UN Charter sets out powerful aspirations for the world's nations and peoples, and it provides the global organization with an array of means for building that better world. When it comes to the environment, however, the UN approach engages only some of those aspirations, and has not used the full means at its disposal.

What, then, is the UN's approach to environmental challenges, and which of the organization's available tools does it use? One key element is international law: or, more specifically, the negotiation of binding treaties on a number of specific issues, including climate change, biodiversity, desertification, ocean protection, toxics management, wetlands preservation, the ozone layer, and trafficking in endangered species. The second key element is sustainable development—famously defined by the WCED as development that "meets the needs of the present without compromising the ability of future generations to meet their own needs."[23] Combining these two elements, the UN's grand strategy for global environmental governance consists, essentially, of better law between nations and better development within them.

This way of framing the problem is linked to important parts of the UN mandate, set out in the powerfully idealistic language of the UN Charter. The quest for better environmental law between nations reflects, and draws upon, the UN's mandate "to establish conditions under which justice and respect for the obligations arising from treaties and other sources of international law can be maintained." The quest for more sustainable development within nations channels the charter mandate "to promote social progress and better standards of life in larger freedom."

But the Charter of the United Nations stands on four legs, not two. The strategy of better law between nations and better development within them overlooks almost entirely the charter mandate on peace: "to save succeeding generations from the scourge of war." It is also mostly silent on the charter mandate to promote human rights and thereby realize "the dignity and worth of the human person." By framing the problem as one of law and development, the UN has, for the most part, failed to understand or act on environmental problems as matters of peace and international security, or as a core component of human rights.

This failure, which goes largely unnoticed in day-to-day UN activities and episodic moments of political summitry, has profound consequences. I will argue that it prevents the UN from making progress on several of today's thorniest environmental problems—including climate change, the loss of the world's forests, water resources management, and the control of toxic pollution. Such challenges—often dubbed as "wicked" or even "super wicked" problems because of their complexity—cannot be addressed, or even contained, through the current UN approach.[24]

Worse, the failure to focus on peace and human rights not only stymies environmental progress but also makes it harder for the UN to realize those foundational elements of its mandate. Environmental degradation and natural resource plunder are part and parcel of a wide swath of conflict episodes and human rights abuses. Ineffectual responses to those problems hurt the quest for peace and the realization of human rights just as much as they do the effort to create a sustainable world and a healthier planet.

If the UN's core problem on environmental governance is the failure to stand on two of its four legs, then what is needed is not simply a managerial reorganization but a conceptual revolution—one that acts on environmental challenges in a manner consistent with the full range of the organization's four-part mandate.

A SELECTIVE AGENDA AND ITS CONSEQUENCES

Early in my effort to wrestle with the ideas at the heart of this book, a quick perusal of the UN's website revealed the highly selective manner in which environmental challenges are framed in UN circles. Visiting the organization's home page, I found thematic tabs related to the four mandate areas: peace and security, development, international law, and human rights.[25] Exploring these web pages, I found environmental issues flagged here and there under the mandate domains of development and international law. While the limited attention was discouraging, more telling was the complete absence of environmental content in the pages on peace and security and on human rights. The peace and security page flagged a strikingly wide array of themes—peacekeeping, peacebuilding, disarmament, children and conflict, terrorism, electoral assistance—but made no mention of the links between natural resources and violent conflict, or of the tight coupling between environmental degradation and human insecurity, or of the calamitous environmental consequences of war. The human rights tab listed an equally wide array of vital challenges, including genocide, indigenous peoples' rights, disabilities, violence against women, children's rights, and the Holocaust—but omitted any reference to a right to safe water, breathable air, a stable climate, or protection from toxic exposure.

Unfortunately, this selective attention runs far deeper than the UN's website. It pervades how the UN acts: the programs of its specialized agencies, the way the organization works with member states, and the role it plays in legitimizing and implementing policy agendas in the global system. The imbalance is evident when comparing activities of the UN's two central councils, the Economic and Social Council (ECOSOC) and the Security Council.[26] ECOSOC has made the environment a central part of its mandate. It created a Commission on Sustainable Development, has accredited scores of environmental NGOs with consultative status, and has launched ambitious initiatives on everything from forest dialogue to labeling hazardous chemicals. The Security Council, in contrast, has been both very late to the game and not much interested in playing. It has acknowledged a link between natural resources and conflict in a few resolutions, implemented economic sanctions on "conflict resources" in a handful of cases, and included environment and natural resource management in the mandate of a few peacekeeping missions. The Security Council has taken up the question of climate change—for two single-day sessions, with much of the discussion dominated by fractious debate over whether it was suitable for the Council even to discuss climate.[27] While a number of member states called for (often unspecified) action on the climate problem, many objected that climate was a "development" issue, not a matter of peace and security.

A similar imbalance is found in the UN's legal responses to environmental challenges. Clearly, international law is a fundamental part of global environmental governance. In UN circles, however, "international environmental law" is almost universally taken to mean treaty-based regimes to regulate specific environmental issues. Almost entirely missing from the conversation is another seminal body of international law for which the UN is primarily responsible: the law of human rights. The major human rights covenants do not articulate a right to a healthy or life-sustaining natural environment. Indeed, in a 2009 report on climate change, the Office of the High Commissioner for Human Rights (OHCHR) found that there is no direct basis for treating the environment as a human right in international law, beyond highly general and nonbinding "soft-law" instruments such as the declarations of global summits.[28] The UN Human Rights Council has begun to engage the question of a human right to the environment—but achingly slowly, in a patchwork manner, and with little tangible progress. When it comes to international law, the UN has made far more progress in codifying the environmental rights and responsibilities of nations than in naming the environmental rights of people.

FROM STOCKHOLM, TO RIO TO STALLED

Global summit meetings provide useful moments with which to bracket the UN's evolution on environmental matters. Viewed through the lens of global summitry, the high-water mark for the UN's environmental efforts was clearly the 1992 UN Conference on Environment and Development (UNCED), held in Rio de Janeiro and popularly dubbed the Earth Summit. The law-and-development approach to global environmental governance suffused UNCED. First, law: The summit witnessed the signing of global treaties on climate change and biodiversity, made recommendations that led to a treaty on desertification, and produced a "soft-law" declaration on forest principles. Also, development: The Earth Summit embraced as its central organizing principle the Brundtland Commission's formulation of "sustainable development," which was largely credited with transcending the North-South political paralysis that flared at the Stockholm Conference two decades earlier. The Rio summit endorsed *Agenda 21*, a lengthy blueprint for achieving sustainability.

Twenty years later, when nations returned to Rio in June 2012 for the UN Conference on Sustainable Development, or "Rio+20," it was the limits of the UN's abilities that were most prominently on display. At Rio+20, the world's governments were unable to reach meaningful agreement on any of the conference's core agenda items—how sustainable development relates to the transformation to a "green economy," what institutional reform of the UN system should actually look like, how to structure a high-level body to replace the ineffectual Commission on Sustainable Development, whether a major new treaty is needed for the world's oceans, what to include in a new set of SDGs, or how any of the preceding should be funded. In the end, the meeting simply kicked the key agenda items forward, referring them back to the General Assembly with little or no substantive guidance. The irony, of course, is that the General Assembly is made up of the very same governments that could not agree at Rio.

Unable to agree on policy, the UN member states assembled at Rio also struggled to adopt a collective statement of their aspirations. On the eve of the meeting, most of the proposed language for the summit's "outcome document" remained contested, as governments found themselves unable to agree on language in dozens of key passages (and many trivial ones, as well). It took some adept eleventh-hour diplomacy from host nation Brazil—consisting mainly of cutting out anything controversial and retreating into least-common-denominator generalities—to salvage an outcome statement at all. The resulting text, titled *The Future We Want*, was a jumbled amalgam of past commitments and vague ambitions. Gro Brundtland, who three decades earlier had chaired the WCED and its pathbreaking report, *Our Common Future*, found the forty-nine-page product wanting: "We can no longer assume that our collective actions will not trigger tipping points, as environmental thresholds are breached, risking irreversible damage to both ecosystems and human communities. These are the facts—but they have been lost in the final document."[29] A prominent activist, Kumi Naidoo of Greenpeace International, put it more succinctly, tweeting, "longest suicide note in history."[30]

As the agenda of better law between nations and better development within them stalled at Rio, it was striking how little the summit had to say about human rights and peace as they relate to the environment. The outcome document tipped its hat to recognized international human rights to food, water, health, and development, and conceded that "some countries recognize the rights of nature in the context of the promotion of sustainable development."[31] But it was studiously silent on whether there exists a human right to a safe and healthy environment, or on the links between human rights and sustainability, or on what a rights-based approach to building a green economy would look like. This silence came despite a terse open letter from the UN high commissioner for human rights to member states shortly before the meeting, warning of rights-related flaws in the draft outcome document and pleading that they "fully integrate key human rights considerations."[32] As with rights, so with peace: the assembled governments had nothing to say about violent conflict over natural resources, the environmental toll of war, or how to tap the peacebuilding opportunities inherent in cooperative governance of natural resources.

KEY QUESTIONS

The UN's skewed approach to environmental action leads to three questions at the heart of this book. First, how did we get here? If peace, development, international law, and human rights are the four principled languages of the UN, why is the great debate about the planet's future being conducted in only two of these four tongues? Why has it been possible for the UN to see, think, and act upon the environment as a matter of promoting social progress within nations and building law among nations—but not one of preventing the scourge of war or securing the dignity and worth of people? How did it come to pass that the UN embraced this limited way of seeing, understanding, and addressing environmental challenges?

Finding answers requires a look not only at the bureaucratic-organizational structure of the UN and the political agendas of its member states, but also tracing the history of the environmental conversation that came to be embedded and legitimized within the UN. The conventional way of telling the UN's environmental story starts with the 1972 Stockholm Conference, which put environmental concerns on the global agenda. However, as discussed in chapter 2, the full story has deeper roots, including the process of global decolonization after World War II and the struggle of newly independent states to exert meaningful sovereignty over their natural resources. The story also includes important elements of political entrepreneurship around ideas, with more such opportunities and fewer constraints in the "law" and "development" regions of the UN's bureaucratic-administrative landscape than in the neighborhoods of "peace" and "rights."

Second, what are the consequences of basing UN environmental initiatives on only two of the four pillars in the UN Charter? How does it matter that the UN framework on the environment is so unbalanced in reflecting the charter's aspirations? What gets lost when some tools are used and others are not? Here, the quick version of the answer is that conversations have consequences. It is not simply a semantic distinction to frame the environment as a matter of development but not of peace, or as part of the law of nations but not the rights of people. Quite the contrary: these choices have had profound ramifications. Core issues go unaddressed, important tools remain unused, effectiveness is impeded, opportunities for progress are blocked or missed. The actions that can be taken, or even imagined, depend profoundly on how the problem is understood.

The third question looks forward. If it is true that the UN's narrow environmental framework and its limited success are linked, then what is to be done? How can the UN make more effective progress on environmental challenges, in a way that incorporates the full scope of its mandate? These questions have a newfound urgency in the wake of the disastrous Rio+20 summit, which failed to offer a compelling path forward and exposed the law-and-development approach as increasingly spent. Would it be helpful to add highly contentious domains such as peace and human rights to the already flagging efforts on environment? Can we make progress by adding these elements to the mix, or will that just muddy the waters further?

What are the components of a new strategic vision, and how should the missing mandate domains of peace and human rights be developed and strengthened as part of it?

As subsequent chapters will discuss more thoroughly, the argument for moving the peace- and rights-related dimensions of global environmental governance from the margins to the center of UN activities rests on several foundations. One is the need to break the cycle of vulnerability. *Where the peace- and rights-related elements of environmental protection are ignored, it is much harder for the world's poorest and most marginalized communities to break destructive cycles linking environmental degradation, human insecurity, conflict, and economic marginalization.* For too many of the world's peoples, these factors interact to create downward spirals that repeatedly undermine human security and defeat efforts for human development. The failure to see environmental challenges creatively—as opportunities to enhance human security, reduce vulnerability, and unleash human potential—causes us to miss important opportunities to break this cycle.

Peace is critical to preventing or breaking out of this downward spiral, because conflict undercuts even the best-intentioned efforts for sustainable development. Conflict enhances vulnerability, marginalization, and the risks associated with disasters and extreme events. Conflict also undercuts a nation's capacity to comply with its international environmental commitments and responsibilities, causing local consequences to reverberate globally. Natural resources can be a key element in sustained or recurrent episodes of violent conflict; thus, conflict-sensitive resource management is crucial to breaking the cycle.

Human rights, too, are crucial to breaking the cycle. Rights-based approaches make it possible to secure access to livelihood resources, while protecting those resources from ill-conceived schemes for economic development. Rights are also crucial to fending off dubious approaches to environmental protection, which too often seek to accomplish abstract global aims at great local expense—yielding neither effective environmental protection nor social justice.

A second component of the argument involves the important regulatory and accountability functions of peace- and rights-related approaches. *In the absence of a peace-and-rights approach, it is much easier for powerful actors to pursue destructive private agendas that undercut the common good.* The ability of citizens to press rights-based claims is a critical tool to thwart such activity. This fact is well recognized in local terms, but in a globalized world economy it must also be applied to the global chains of production that snake across national borders, beyond the regulatory reach of individual nation-states. Too often, harmful activities hide in the unregulated space between national laws and global agreements, beyond the reach of either. Despite early optimism that market-based forces such as green product certification could fill the gap, it is increasingly clear that socially responsible shopping is no substitute for strong protections at the source of the problem. Without global recognition of those protections as human rights, there will always be another neighborhood—and another country—onto which the harmful effects can be externalized, exported, and dumped. Conflict is also a central element in this equation, because the lawlessness and impunity surrounding the production of "conflict resources" for global markets is an extreme, and all too common, example of the larger problem.

Using rights to push accountability back upstream in global commodity chains is a challenging political project. It cannot happen without the requisite social forces coming together with a common purpose. Strengthening the presence of the UN's human rights and peace-and-security mandates in the environmental conversation also plays an important function of political coalition-building, in the sense that it allows for important new synergies and partnerships among rights advocates, environmentalists, peace activists, and champions of grassroots development strategies. Centering the quest exclusively on better law between nations and better development within them has blunted the full development of this coalition.

A third component of the argument stresses positive synergies. *Focusing on the environment as a matter of peace and human rights broadens the spectrum of possible proactive measures*—including action that would not even be imagined if the starting point is the UN's narrow environmental discourse of law and development. A peace and confidence-building agenda offers governments a chance to transcend the zero-sum mentality of scarcity around shared resources, realizing powerful gains for all through more effective cooperation (an effect that development agencies like to refer to as "enlarging the pie"). More broadly, it challenges us to identify environmental initiatives that can also be peace-enhancing, vulnerability-reducing, and rights-affirming—thereby replacing the destructive downward spirals flagged earlier with upward-trending positive synergies. It also further reinforces the political element—again, the possibility of powerful synergies across civil society, linking groups engaged in the struggles for peace, human rights, environmental protection, grassroots development, and political empowerment into broader and more effective movements for positive social change.

The fourth and final component of the argument engages the much-abused concept of a "system-wide" UN response. In UN parlance, the term means mobilizing all parts of the UN system to achieve a cross-cutting or overarching goal. The importance of doing so is widely noted in UN circles, and has become a central theme in the debate about how to overcome fragmentation and promote effective reforms.[33] Currently, however, *the lack of emphasis on the peace- and rights-related dimensions of environmental efforts limits the UN to least-common-denominator responses and allows for a cynical game of venue-shifting.* Fragmentation limits a truly system-wide response to tepid initiatives such as the "Greening the Blue" campaign to improve the UN's environmental footprint. Worse, the current state of affairs creates opportunities for governments to play one venue against another, taking up issues only in those arenas where it does them the most political good while avoiding real responsibility. Thus, the United States can fail to acknowledge its substantial responsibility for climate change and shed commitments it made under the UNFCCC—but then laud the very same UNFCCC as the proper venue when trying to keep environmental human rights off the radar of the UN Human Rights Council. Or China can warn the Security Council not to butt into the sensitive negotiations of the UNFCCC process, only to prove itself quite ready to abandon that process for a side deal with the United States at the 2009 Copenhagen climate talks. Until the environment resonates across the full scope of the UN mandate, a truly system-wide response remains impossible—and ducking, dodging, and venue-shifting will remain the norm across the fragmented institutional landscape.

How can the UN's environmental efforts be transformed along the lines suggested by this argument? I will suggest that doing so means making those efforts *rights-based, accountability-oriented, conflict-sensitive,* and *peace-enhancing.* Throughout the book I identify several such activities, including initiatives that have emerged already in various pockets of the UN and deserve to be nurtured. In the concluding chapter, I lay out six specific avenues for change and reform:

- Find an explicit human right to a safe and healthy environment
- Acknowledge an environmental responsibility to protect
- Infuse the law-and-development approach with stronger peace-and-rights practice
- Find a legitimate (and clearly limited) environmental role for the UN Security Council
- Exploit opportunities for environmental peacebuilding
- Reconceive and strengthen what it means for the UN to make a "system-wide" response on environmental problems

Such reforms, while challenging, promise a dual benefit: more effective and lasting environmental protection, as well as better service to the UN's full mandate of peace, development, human rights, and international law.

A FRAMEWORK FOR UNDERSTANDING THE UN

In the nearly seven decades since its inception, the UN has changed in many ways. Membership has nearly quadrupled from the fifty nations meeting in San Francisco in 1945. The Secretary-General's office has grown in size and influence. Many new agencies, funds, and programs have been created. Civil society has found a stronger voice within the organization. Practices not even envisioned when the organization was founded, ranging from peacekeeping missions to multistakeholder dialogues to global issue-area summits, have become part of the UN repertoire. Yet, for all these changes, the UN remains much as it was conceived: an organization of nation-states, with a four-part mandate to create peace and security, strengthen human rights, promote development, and establish a firmer legal basis for cooperation among its sovereign members.

Few serious observers of the UN would argue that it has had resounding success in pursuing these lofty aims. War and insecurity endure; development remains, for a majority of the world's people, a largely theoretical aspiration; human rights are routinely disrespected, unprotected, and unfulfilled; and international law frequently reflects the asymmetries of power in world politics and the stubborn defense of parochial interests, rather than the legitimacy of a consensually rule-governed system. Still, there have been accomplishments. The human rights mandate has yielded a string of important human rights treaties. The mandate on development has spawned a proliferation of UN organs working on issues ranging from resource management to public health to education to technological innovation, as well as conceptual revolutions driven by ideas about human development and sustainability. The mandate to strengthen international law has produced a deeply institutionalized process for negotiating and codifying treaties on everything from universal technical standards to the rights of the disabled. The peace mandate has yielded more than sixty peacekeeping interventions around the world, an increasingly institutionalized system of imposing sanctions on parties in conflict, a string of increasingly ambitious peacebuilding initiatives in the wake of conflict, and the beginnings of a system (in conjunction with the International Criminal Court) to hold at least some perpetrators accountable for war crimes, genocide, and crimes against humanity.

Although the environment is not mentioned in the UN Charter, the issue's emergence and growth as a key part of the organization's agenda is not difficult to explain. The problems are serious; their transnational and global dimensions have become increasingly apparent; people worldwide are increasingly aware and concerned; the responses of governments often must be coordinated to be effective or politically feasible; and activists have mobilized new knowledge and exerted sometimes powerful pressures for change. Nor is it difficult to explain the limits of what the UN does on the environment. The problems are complex; interests are often in conflict; the stakes are high for some very powerful actors; and the potential losers from environmental protection often have the power to preserve the status quo.

But my core purpose is not simply to understand why the UN has engaged environmental issues so extensively, or the extent of its effectiveness. Rather, it is to understand why the UN has taken up and internalized the issue in the particular way that it has, with such strong emphasis on links to development and international law and parallel de-emphasis of peace and human rights. That answer requires understanding more than simply when and why the UN chooses to act. We must explain how it comes to understand and frame action, which actors grow into the operational space that is created when new challenges emerge, and how particular types of responses come to be institutionalized over time. In a sense, then, the question is how an organization learns.

The concept of learning comes with an important caveat when used in bureaucratic-organizational settings: what is "learned" could just as easily be how to expand one's budget, how to defend one's bureaucratic turf, or how to prevent a response that threatens parochial interests. A second caveat gets at the heart of how the UN operates: any such learning takes place unevenly over the organization's complex landscape.

For the UN, that landscape is complex indeed. The UN Charter created an organization with six principal organs (table 1.1). Over time, a complex array of functional entities has sprung up around these core organs, producing the sprawling organizational chart of the contemporary UN system (figure 1.1). An important feature of this landscape is the presence of sixteen specialized agencies of the UN, such as the Food and Agriculture Organization, the World Health Organization, the International Labour Organization, and the UN Educational, Scientific, and Cultural Organization (UNESCO). Specialized agencies are autonomous organizations with a separate charter under international law, and are linked to the UN through explicit international agreements. As discussed below, these entities often enjoy substantial autonomy; a few,

Table 1.1   PRINCIPAL ORGANS OF THE UN

- The **General Assembly**, in which all member states are represented, and which passes resolutions on the basis of one state, one vote. The General Assembly has the power to discuss and make recommendations on any matter within the scope of the UN Charter, with the exception of disputes actively being handled by the Security Council.
- The **Security Council**, which consists of five permanent members bearing the veto and ten member states elected regionally for two-year terms. Through the charter, UN member states confer upon the Council "primary responsibility for the maintenance of international peace and security." The Council may call upon states to resolve disputes or to take actions that support international peace and security, such as the observance of sanctions. It also has power, under Chapter VII of the charter, to use force—although it lacks a standing military force or a standing budget for military operations, and has not operationalized the Military Staff Committee authorized for it by the charter.
- The **Economic and Social Council**, which consists of fifty-four member states, elected from the General Assembly. ECOSOC has the power to report to the General Assembly on a wide range of economic, social, and cultural issues; to make recommendations on the promotion of human rights; and to call international conferences on those topics. It also fields reports from the specialized agencies, funds, programs, and other bureaucratic-administrative organs of the UN.
- The **Trusteeship Council**, tasked under the charter with administering the UN's commitment to the independence of "territories whose peoples have not yet attained a full measure of self-government." These include the so-called trust territories—former colonies that came under the control of the League of Nations, and responsibility for which the UN inherited. The Trusteeship Council suspended operations in 1994 when the last trust territory, Palau, joined the UN.
- The **International Court of Justice**, popularly known as the World Court. The ICJ is the successor body to the Permanent Court of International Justice, and UN member states are automatically accorded membership in it under the UN Charter. The ICJ hears cases only when both parties to a dispute (which must be member states) have previously agreed to be bound by ICJ rulings on that matter. Justices of the ICJ are chosen to represent all of the world's major legal systems. The ICJ also provides advisory opinions under international law for the General Assembly and other UN organs, when requested.
- The **Secretariat**, headed by the UN's chief administrative officer, the Secretary-General, and including "such staff as the organization may require." The SG performs those tasks entrusted to him by the General Assembly and the three UN councils. Under the charter, the Secretariat has a purely international status and responsibilities; member states are precluded from seeking to influence the SG.

Source: Charter of the United Nations.

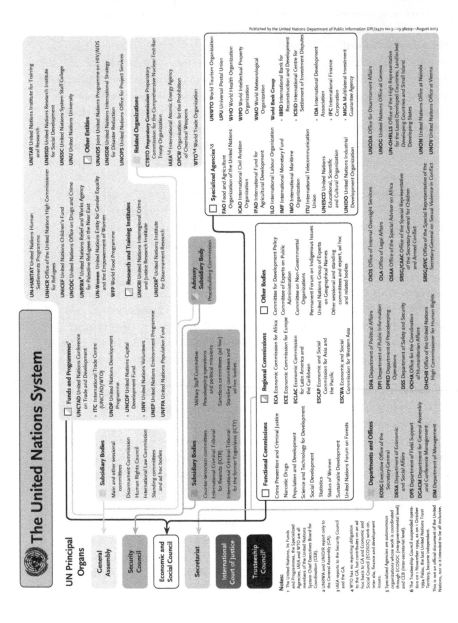

Figure 1.1 The UN system

From the United Nations Department of Public Information © 2013 United Nations. Reprinted with the permission of the United Nations.

prominently including the World Bank and International Monetary Fund, are so autonomous from the reach of the UN as to be affiliated only in a formal/legal, as opposed to operational, sense.

A second major feature of the UN landscape is the large number of organs—including funds, programs, regional commissions, functional commissions, research institutes, offices, and agencies—deployed by ECOSOC. Another key feature consists of the departments and offices that have sprung up within the Secretariat and which report to the Secretary-General, including those entities that oversee peacekeeping operations, provide field support for UN operations worldwide, coordinate humanitarian affairs, support the SG's diplomatic and political undertakings, and administer the UN bureaucracy.

In tackling the question of how the UN has come to understand, internalize, and act upon an environmental mission, we may begin by dismissing a few cartoonish images of what the organization is and why it acts as it does. The first such caricature is that the UN consists of nothing more than the preferences of its member states, and that attention to the UN as an actor in its own right merely distracts from understanding the real stuff of global politics—coercion, bargaining, hegemony, and other forms of political interaction between nations. In this view, the UN's environmental mission can be nothing more or less than what the most powerful member states want. A second, very different caricature portrays the UN as a powerful agent that deliberately and confidently pursues an agenda of establishing world government, sapping nations and localities of important elements of sovereignty in the process. In this view, the environmental agenda is part and parcel of that larger purpose, with would-be global governors finding a green rationale for world government. The first caricature portrays an organization that is simply derivative of more powerful agents, while the second sketches a willful, autonomous, and quite powerful actor.

Although these dichotomous views are often found in media accounts, public discourse, and policy debates, they bear little resemblance to the more complex reality of the UN. Given their persistent inaccuracies, they are probably more useful to explain the interests of their purveyors than the actual developments we see. The world-domination image of the UN can be dismissed quickly. Simply put: world domination is a steep climb for an organization with a total budget smaller than the gross domestic product of Costa Rica, more than half of which consists of voluntary contributions over which a few dozen donor governments retain extensive control. Other inconvenient conditions for global despotism include chronic budget arrears, an institutional design that often seems built deliberately for paralysis, decision-making processes that often retreat into least-common denominator positions of universal consensus, the chronic slowness that accompanies international legal culture and procedures, the dissipating effects of weak performance-accountability mechanisms, a nontrivial amount of corruption that bleeds an already underresourced mission, and the oddly jerry-rigged rules of hiring and promotion that mark the international civil service.[34] Those who fear the tyranny of the black helicopters and the blue helmets would do well to spend more time in the vicinity of the actual organization that is the UN, which at times seems to expend more energy arguing about the design of the helmets or the country from which the helicopters will be procured than about the missions for which they are intended.

The other common image, that the UN is a mere reflection or tool of government interests, is not so quickly dismissed. In this view, UN activity is simply a product of what member states want, with outcomes dictated by the resulting push-and-pull of bargaining, coercion, and the like. It is interesting to note that *which* member states are said to have the power to do the pushing and pulling varies, but typically flags some combination of the United States, the leading economic powers, and the veto-wielding permanent members of the UN Security Council. (A notable exception is found in the debate on the UN in the United States, where one finds a well-established discourse on the organization's anti-American proclivities and the supposed tyranny of an anti-American majority in the General Assembly.)[35]

Applying this state-based explanation of UN behavior to the environmental issue-area provides some important insights. As discussed in chapter 5, for example, the Security Council has been highly selective in its attention to matters involving the conflict dimensions of environment and natural resources. On climate change, it has undertaken only very limited discussion, consisting of brief, prescripted monologues by member states. Yet the Council has been more active in addressing another natural-resource issue: the conflict-fueling effects of high-value natural resources such as diamonds, strategic minerals, and hardwood timber. A map of member-state interests is indispensable as a starting point for explaining the politics of either issue, or the difference in how the Council has taken them up. On climate, countries pushing the issue within the Council tend to be either European democracies, which have strong domestic constituencies with green foreign-policy preferences, or small-island developing countries, whose very existence is threatened by sea-level rise. Arrayed against them are influential member states, including China, Russia, and India, that perceive little advantage in a securitized and interventionist stance on the climate threat. On natural resources and conflict, in contrast, the more active response and the stronger con-sensus within the Council are consistent with the shared interests of key member states in managing civil conflict and stabilizing resource extrac-tion in sub-Saharan Africa.

Similarly, consider the most contentious debate seen in the run-up to the 2012 Rio+20 summit meeting: whether to frame the conference agenda in the more traditional terms of "sustainable development" or under a new rubric of "green economy." Europe, Japan, and the United States have strong interests in shaping the terms of the new political economy of energy, including emerging carbon markets—and very little desire to rehash the sustainability commitments they made (and often failed to honor) at the original Earth Summit, two decades earlier. For the less-developed countries that populate the Group of 77, the interests are very different but equally clear: they fear that shifting the frame to a green economy will make it harder to hold rich nations accountable for funding sustainable-development efforts, while making it easier for a new wave of "green" barriers to trade and investment that would put them at a competi-tive disadvantage and hamper their economic development. Again, a map of state interests is indispensable to understand the resulting politics.

Yet the lens of state interests also misses some important dimensions. How do governments know what is in their interest, especially in a tech-nically complex and often unpredictable issue area such as the environ-ment? Once determined, how are those interests pursued in a domain where the persuasive power of ideas may be as important as the material power of carrots and sticks? What happens when the system is populated not simply by governments, but also by other kinds of actors? And what happens when the whole process has come to be embedded in a particular set of historical, institutional, and discursive frameworks—frameworks that make some actions easier to take, even as others become harder to imagine? To understand the trajectory of the UN's engagement on envi-ronmental issues, we need to take advantage of scholarly insights in three areas: the bureaucratic-organizational autonomy of institutions, the role of ideas, and the path-dependent character of institutionalized processes.

TOWARD A BETTER MODEL: INSTITUTIONS, IDEAS, AND PATH-DEPENDENT HISTORICAL TRAJECTORIES

Institutions and Bureaucratic-Organizational Autonomy

One potential pitfall of a straightforward interest-based explanation is the failure to take seriously the potential for autonomous action by UN organs—the various councils, programs, funds, commissions, committees, expert panels, working groups, and other bodies that carry out myriad day-to-day activities across the UN system. A large body of research has taught us that, under certain circumstances, intergovernmental organizations (IGOs) may have substantial discretion to undertake independent action.

One source of potential autonomy for IGOs lies in the complexity of the bureaucratic-administrative landscape in which they reside and the resulting difficulties that even powerful actors face in controlling them.[36] Even when member states know precisely what they want from an international bureaucracy, they face several nontrivial challenges to making it so. The price of getting an international agreement with which a majority can live may be imprecision in the mandate given to organizations, which in turn may allow space for creative interpretation of that mandate. Moreover, there may be slippage within the "delegation chains" through which member states assign these organizations their tasks, given the challenges of holding them accountable for performing those tasks as expected. Finally, new tasks may sit at the intersection of organizational mandates rather than fitting neatly into the existing UN organizational chart, creating gaps and overlaps that further complicate the exercise of control.

Adding to these difficulties of control, bureaucratic organizations are not powerless in seeking to create space for autonomous action. Bureaucratic entrepreneurs may take it upon themselves to define or redefine the organization's mission, to defend the organization's established turf against encroachment, or to expand into new domains of action. (Sometimes this happens in practice, but it can even be a design feature when a new organization is created, to the extent that bureaucratic operatives in preexisting organizations typically play a key role in the design of new entities. Scholar Tana Johnson has argued that this process of "organizational progeny" has greatly complicated the ability of states to exert control.)[37]

A key determinant of an organization's capacity to maneuver, or to be maneuvered, is the extent to which it can wield *authority*, or the rightful and accepted use of power.[38] A certain measure of authority is granted to international organizations when governments endow them with a charter-based legal mandate for action, or when governments explicitly delegate specific responsibilities to them. Beyond this, organizations may have additional bases for claiming authority: they may hold particular expertise on an issue, or they may make a persuasive claim that they represent a compelling and broadly shared value. These various sources of authority—legal, delegated, expert, or moral—vary substantially over time and across organizations, but they can be substantial.[39]

Organizations may also enhance their influence and create space for more autonomous action by forming effective partnerships with advocacy networks, foundations, or interest groups.[40] In international life, with its thinly articulated system of rules and norms for adjudicating disputes, these partnerships often coalesce around IGOs, which provide a type of political coral reef to which advocacy networks may attach themselves. If subsequent efforts to construct new international rules and norms gain traction, this can give the organization important new allies, resources, and sources of legitimacy.[41] A classic example of this process is the international campaign against land mines in which, as researcher Richard Price explained, "relationships with the UN provided NGOs with a stage for voicing their concerns and a primary point of access to the international political process in the form of international negotiations orchestrated by intergovernmental organizations. Through such venues NGOs have been able to directly connect the local agenda—the sufferings of civilians and the activities of grass-roots activist networks—to the interstate agenda."[42]

As globalization adds to the complex functional roles assigned to IGOs, all of the challenges that governments face in exerting control over their creations may be enhanced.[43] Thus, *one broad class of explanations for the UN's uneven environmental landscape is the possibility that different parts of the UN have had differing amounts of space and capacity for autonomous action.* Perhaps the legal and developmental boxes on the UN's organization chart have been better able to create such space than have their counterparts on the peace and human rights sides of the UN, or simply better able to find and exploit whatever space was available. Perhaps they have been better at slipping the chain of member-state control, or more compellingly authoritative in their expertise, or more cleverly entrepreneurial in their maneuvering, or better positioned to build partnerships with important allies.

Ideas and Discursive Frameworks

If the lens of member-state interests alone cannot account for this *micro* level of bureaucratic entrepreneurialism, organizational autonomy, and social networking, it also misses an equally important *midrange* level of analysis: the ideational and discursive frameworks within which such maneuvering takes place. The UN is not simply a bureaucratic landscape defined by an organizational chart—it is also a landscape of ideas. In their research on the intellectual history of the UN, Richard Jolly, Louis Emmerij, and Thomas Weiss make a strong case for the importance of ideas as a currency of power in the UN system.[44] The authors trace the historical significance of specific concepts—including but not limited to decolonization, basic needs, human development, and sustainability—in catalyzing what the UN does. In tracing and comparing these histories, the authors identify a specific set of mechanisms by which ideas effect change within the UN. These mechanisms include the creation of a standardized description of reality, the establishment of measurable goals, the stimulation of interest in new problems, the destabilization of prevailing orthodoxies, and the definition of specific frameworks for responsive action. In the UN, ideas have consequences.

Importantly, complex concepts such as sustainability or human development do not roam freely as stand-alone ideas. Over time, they become embedded in wider discursive frameworks that give them content, context, and significance. These wider frameworks can be thought of as creating increasingly well-worn paths along which political energies may travel more easily. The field of water policy provides an example, with the concept of "integrated water resource management" evolving from a heretical notion held by a handful of water experts in the 1970s to become, within just a few decades, the only broadly legitimate language with which to launch international policy initiatives on water.[45] Similarly, when scientists discovered the loss of stratospheric ozone, an intense debate emerged over whether the process was physical or chemical in nature. Was declining ozone the result of atmospheric circulatory patterns, culprit chemical emissions, or a combination of the two? As Karen Litfin's history of the ensuing international diplomacy has documented, the "chemical" framework became not only the favored scientific explanation, but also the dominant discourse within which negotiations proceeded—to such an extent that the idea of stabilizing chlorine concentrations in the upper atmosphere evolved from being one means to the end of ozone protection to become the dominant goal of international agreement.[46] Both of these examples suggest that expert networks are one important source for the construction of such interpretive frames.

Social movements are another source. Social scientists have long recognized that one of the most important thing social movements do is to popularize a particular understanding of problems and solutions.[47] Consider the dueling efforts of proabortion and antiabortion advocates to define abortion in the public mind as, respectively, a woman's freedom to control her own body or the taking of an innocent human life. Critics of the World

Bank's environmental and human rights track record succeeded in framing signature Bank projects such as mines, dams, and forest colonization schemes as ecological and social disasters, rather than the pinnacles of development the Bank portrayed.[48]

Because movements seek to prod society toward nonincremental change, they are often challenged not simply to frame an issue but to *reframe* it—to sever the traditional associations an audience makes between the issue and prevailing social values, and to replace that understanding with a dramatically different interpretation. A classic example is the civil rights movement in the United States, which retooled the race issue in the minds of a key potential ally, northern white liberals, by associating civil rights campaigns with American liberalism's core values of equal opportunity, human decency, and fair play.[49] The movement also succeeded in rescripting the moral cast of characters. By deliberately provoking repression from the white-dominated state apparatus of the American South, it fed northern white liberals a steady dose of jarringly reversed images, in which clean-cut, collegiate-looking African American youth were subjected to violence from the tools of the state: fire hoses, police dogs, truncheons.

The environmental organization Greenpeace played a similar reframing role on the issue of whaling. Using handheld video and attention-getting direct actions on the high seas, they reframed the traditional cultural image of heroic, vulnerable sailors battling monstrous whales on a treacherous sea.[50] Greenpeace showed the fragility and vulnerability of whales in the face of the precision brutality of modern whaling fleets. In both of these examples, a key process is *frame alignment*, in which the frame being built around a controversial proposal (racial equality; an end to whaling) is matched to an existing framework of broadly consensual values and social norms (human decency and fair play; prevention of cruelty to innocent living creatures).

Along with expert networks and social movements, IGOs also construct such interpretive frames. When faced with complex new challenges, states will often look to IGOs to play a teaching function: to help governments understand what is true in the world and where their interests lie.[51] More generally, Michael Barnett and Martha Finnemore have shown how IGOs, as bureaucracies that control information and wield knowledge-power, can "fix meaning" about the social world that governments occupy, in ways that "orient action and establish boundaries for acceptable action."[52] Examples include the ability of the International Monetary Fund to define loan conditionality and a healthy economy, the ability of the UN Refugee Agency (UNHCR) to define the meaning of solutions to refugee problems, and the Security Council's determination, through practice, of the meaning of peacekeeping. The fixing of meaning, which relies heavily on the construction of interpretive frames, is a source of power for IGOs—power not simply to regulate or incentivize action, but more fundamentally to "constitute the world" within which such action occurs.[53]

Whether built by expert networks, social movements, bureaucratic-administrative entities, or some combination thereof, interpretive frames can powerfully elevate certain causal understandings, problem definitions, and policy solutions. Tellingly, they can also make other things harder to see. When scientific data first began to show drastic reductions in Antarctic ozone levels, the measurements were assumed to be spurious; they were attributed to measurement error and ignored because they failed to fit the prevailing conceptual framework for understanding polar atmospheric chemistry.[54] Conservation organizations have faced a similar set of frame-related blinders: for decades, they have viewed ecosystems and their living creatures as tied to places, and thus fought for place-based conservation. As climate change prompts the increased mobility of creatures and ecosystems in response to changing conditions, a paradigm shift is beginning to occur—but is made all the more difficult by the hegemony of the prior lens.[55]

In the environmental realm, ideas grounded in interpretive frames guide how governments and other actors make sense of their interests on particular matters such as climate change, the hazardous waste trade, or biodiversity. They also crystallize understandings of what it is effective and appropriate (or ineffective and inappropriate) for UN organizations to do. Thus, when member states argue that it is both *unwise* and *inappropriate* to discuss climate change in the Security Council, and that it should be discussed *instead* in the UN's developmental and legal arenas, what are they really saying? The argument rests on a particular understanding of the nature of the climate problem, as well as a particular presumption of how the UN's mandate domains fit together and where the lines are properly drawn between them.

Of course, governments may make such arguments for purely instrumental reasons: they may simply be seeking to move the climate issue to a more favorable venue for their interests. Governments make arguments for reasons of political strategy or tactical expediency—as well as for reasons related to deeply held values, causal beliefs, a lack of imagination, or simply habit. But whatever the motive, they remain *arguments*—and what gives an argument resonance and persuasive power is its connection to an established interpretive frame that orders, separates, fixes, and stabilizes a particular understanding. In this case, the argument against "climate security" takes advantage of a previously built and deeply embedded framing of the global environment as a matter for sustainable development and international law. The best evidence that such framings matter is the large amount of energy governments of every stripe expend in appealing to such frames to contextualize their positions and win their arguments, whether the audience for such claims consists of other governments, their own domestic citizenry, interest groups, or the international community writ large.

This discussion of ideas and interpretive frames suggests a second broad class of explanations: *the UN's uneven environmental landscape may be a product of the power of certain ideas, the unequal ability of different actors to fix the meaning of environmental problems and solutions, and the staying power of certain interpretive frames.* A key set of questions emerges from this line of reasoning. Which particular ideas have come to the foreground, and why? Which interpretive frames have come to predominate, and why? In Barnett's and Finnemore's terminology, who "fixed" the meaning of the world's environmental to-do list as one of better law between nations and better development within them, and what made it possible for them to do so?[56]

Historical Trajectories and Path-Dependent Change

Combining these two elements—the bureaucratic-organizational conditions for authoritative action and the shaping power of ideas and discursive frameworks—suggests another important possibility: that the two may become mutually reinforcing over time. Effectively framed ideas may create space for bureaucratic entrepreneurs within organizations; well-positioned organizations may have an advantage in pushing their ideas to the center of policy agendas. Over time, the combined effect may be to make some of the metaphorical "paths" discussed previously much easier to travel and much more familiar to the travelers. As will be discussed in chapter 2, the growth and development of important elements of the UN's approach to environmental challenges can be explained in these terms.

Nevertheless, such an explanation begs a few important questions. When, how, and why do such new pathways get started? What correlation of forces is necessary and sufficient to create a new path, or to change the direction of an existing one? It seems unlikely that new ideas and clever framing strategies will be enough, especially in the hands of otherwise relatively weak actors. Nor is it obvious how such projects are sustained in their crucial beginning stages. Who or what provides the energy to maintain the new path, until some combination of interests and inertia establishes it as the favored route of the states that traverse it? Who or what keeps the emerging path clear of brush, so to speak, or fills in eroded portions of the trail? To answer these questions, we must look not just to organizations themselves, but also to strategic opportunities and constraints in the wider landscape where they operate.

Here, Craig Murphy's seminal work on changing historical patterns of international organization since the mid-nineteenth century may be applied usefully to the environmental domain.[57] Murphy views the construction of IGO as part of a longstanding project of liberal internationalism in the industrial age. Most models of international institution building stress the diffusion of values or the ability of actors to overcome barriers to cooperation and realize joint gains. Murphy, however, stresses *social conflict* as the prime motive force for dynamism in global governance. He shows how the expansion of industrial capitalism has repeatedly generated conflict and controversy as economic change creates losers (be they older social orders, workers, or peripheral communities of the hinterlands being newly subjected to industrialization). While the liberal-internationalist project has generally been optimistic about the ability of "progress" to smooth over the pains of adjustment, some liberal internationalists have recognized the need for reform, so as to manage the inevitable conflicts that accompany change. Murphy shows how the work of these liberal internationalists for system reforms provided, over the sweep of more than a century, much of the impetus for creating or strengthening IGOs, and yielding new layers of institutionalized governance in the process.

The result of this episodic flaring of conflict is a sort of punctuated equilibrium in which new systemic reforms are periodically implemented, without abandoning the liberal internationalist vision of the expanding global economic order that underpins the whole enterprise. For Murphy, the process is akin to building a cathedral:

> Building the international institutions of a world order in an industrial age is a bit like building a cathedral in late medieval Europe. While the aims of liberal internationalism provide designers with a single general plan, the way that the rituals of medieval Catholicism demanded structural similarity among all diocesan seats, the final form of the order of the Free World differed as greatly as Salisbury and Chartres. Like most gothic cathedrals, the institutions of each of the successive world orders have been built sporadically over many dozens of years as the interest of the community to be served waxed and

waned and as different sponsors and benefactors were found to realize one or another part of the originally imagined project. As a result, if we look closely at the completed edifices we see a host of mismatched parts.[58]

As the history sketched in chapter 2 will show, the UN response to the challenge of how to live in the natural world can be read in these terms: as the successive agglomeration of component parts, often mismatched, in response to direct environmental challenges to the global economic order. This offers us a third broad class of explanation: *that the law-and-development approach to global environmental governance has been embedded in larger efforts to reform the liberal internationalist project in the face of significant challenges to it.* The end of World War II and the sweeping pace of global decolonization raised a first such challenge, around the question of national sovereignty over natural resources in the context of a resource-hungry world economy. The reformist response to this conflict laid down important legal and normative rules around the sovereign use and control of natural resources, and spawned several bureaucratic-organizational initiatives to help nations—newly sovereign nations, in particular—to manage resources better. The environmental movement then raised a second and equally profound challenge to the still-globalizing industrial order, around questions of pollution and resource depletion—but it did so at a time when the cathedral's foundation, so to speak, had already been established by the prior conflict over resource sovereignty. The reformist response to this second challenge added a layer to the edifice. This layer came to be expressed in the paired architectural forms of sustainable development and international environmental law. Today, the process continues with a third wave of challenges. Climate change and the effort to construct new global political economies of energy, water, and food provide a new stimulus for reform—but do so, again, upon the foundation of the previously built edifice.

PLAN FOR THE REMAINING CHAPTERS

The institutionalized framing of the environment as a matter—and only a matter—of international law and economic development makes it easier to keep questions such as climate change, water deprivation, or human insecurity out of the Security Council or the Human Rights Council. It also makes it harder for UN organs with environmental expertise to move into activities in the peace-and-security or human rights spheres of the UN system, or to partner with entities operating in those spheres. Over time, then, the weak construction of the environment as a matter of peace and human rights has become part and parcel of its strong construction as an issue of law and development.

Promoting better global environmental governance, then, requires us to understand how the construction, reproduction, and institutionalization of particular frames takes place within the UN system—and in particular, how that process becomes both a political resource and an ideational guide for a wide range of actors in and around the UN system. Understanding this process means accounting for member-state interests, to be sure. But it requires attention to three other key factors, as well: bureaucratic-organizational dynamics, which endow different organs with different capacities for autonomous action; ideas and discursive framing, which shape the characterization of environmental issues and how they fit into the UN landscape; and the broad historical trajectories of particular political projects in global governance, which create the political demands to which ideas and institutions respond and which allocate path-dependent opportunities to stay the course or change direction.

Using this framework, chapter 2 recounts how the environment—a word that does not appear in the UN Charter—emerged onto the agenda and came to grow so unevenly across the UN's four-part mandate. The early portion of this history is not particularly well known in environmental circles, because the most popular way of telling the story of the UN and the environment starts with the 1972 Stockholm Conference. This overlooks the long and highly contentious process of decolonization that consumed the UN's first few decades, and which laid down an important body of principles and practices on natural resources, sovereignty, global markets, and the rights of newly independent states. This pre-Stockholm politics strongly conditioned what would follow, and remains important to this day. From these origins, the chapter traces the differential development of environmental activities across the four mandate domains, culminating in the near-hegemony of the law-and-development approach by the time of the 1992 Earth Summit. The discussion also flags missed opportunities and closed doors within the mandate domains on peace and human rights.

Chapter 3 then assesses the record of the law-and-development approach to global environmental governance. The grand strategy the UN has pursued is first assessed in its own terms. Has it achieved its core aims of better environmental law between nations and greener development within them? Why has it been unable to sustain its momentum, as seen in the debacle of the Rio+20 summit meeting? I will argue that, whatever it may count as accomplishments, the strategy faces increasingly severe limits in a globalized world economy, a political system marked by the continued devolution of authority away from sovereign nation-states, and the newly emerging transnational political economies of food, water, and energy. The chapter uses these insights to develop more fully the case for a rights-based and peace-based approach.

Chapters 4 and 5 then turn to look more closely at the underdeveloped parts of the UN's environmental framework: the mandate domains of human rights and peace and security. Here, the emphasis is not simply on how existing framings and trajectories of action have inhibited the UN's ability to "see" environmental challenges in these terms, although this is an important part of the story. The chapters also evaluate whether and how things may be changing or could be changed; they examine some promising new initiatives and ask where entry points for effective action may lie. Chapter 4 does so by looking at the long and tortuous process of determining whether there exists a human right to environmental protection, the emergence of rights-based environmental practices in some parts of the UN, and ongoing rights controversies around clean water and climate change. Chapter 5 does so by examining the evolving debate on "environmental security," the emergent environment-conflict-peacebuilding linkages some UN agencies are starting to make in their work, and the Security Council's engagement on issues of "conflict resources" and the implications of climate change.

Chapter 6 concludes the book with a series of recommendations for moving the UN toward a more balanced, progressive, and comprehensive framework for environmental action. The chapter's goals are to identify ways to nurture some of the most promising activities around environmental rights and environmental peace identified in previous chapters; and to identify opportunities to infuse current practices and the ambiguous agenda laid down at Rio+20 with a stronger peace-and-rights architecture. The recommendations are organized into three strands, identifying opportunities to strengthen and invigorate the UN's environmental activities normatively, institutionally, and programmatically.

On the last day of the disastrous Rio+20 summit, Executive Director Achim Steiner of UNEP made a statement that summed up what had become apparent during the meeting: "We can't legislate sustainable development in the current state of international relations."[59] Steiner's remark tapped the frustration of the moment: the world's governments failed to reconcile how efforts to build a "green economy" fit into the UN's commitment to "sustainable development"; failed to forge a serious consensus on how to reform the UN's environmental organs; and failed to even broach larger questions such as how to reinvigorate flagging treaty regimes or provide adequate funding. Steiner's comment also highlights the challenging context of the current political moment: a global economy vulnerable to financial instability and weak growth; Europe in the throes of budgetary and currency crises; the United States beset by domestic political turbulence and the corrosive effects of an interminable war on terror; and emerging powers able to reshape the world economy, but still struggling to provide food security, clean water, and breathable air for their citizens.

But Steiner's comment may also be read on a deeper level. Is the problem, in fact, one of "legislating sustainable development," as the UN has traditionally framed it? A significant cost of defining the problem this way has been that the UN has limited itself to only a portion of its mandate, and to using only some of the tools at its disposal. To understand why the task is repeatedly framed in these terms, chapter 2 takes up the history of how the UN came to institutionalize its particular approach to environmental challenges—as a matter of better law between nations and better development within them.

CHAPTER 2

Law among Nations, Development within Them

Origins and Growth of the

UN's Environmental Framework

THE UN'S "PRE-ENVIRONMENTAL" ORIGINS

When international delegates finalized the Charter of the United Nations in San Francisco during the North American spring of 1945, they showed no signs of thinking about the natural world. The charter makes no mention of the Earth, ecosystems, pollution, natural resources, or sustainability. The word *environment* had yet to take on its current significance, and the theme was missing from the debate on the new organization's purpose, structure, and rules.

The delegates' silence on the theme should not surprise us. Consider the transportation and communications infrastructure through which they experienced the world around them. Unlike today's jet-setting diplomats, many arrived on trains that plodded across the North American continent. Never having seen a photograph of the planet from space—much less being able to zoom in, out, and around with Google Earth—many of them were seeing the great expanse and variety of the American landscape for the first time.[1] News of the signing of the UN charter also spread slowly. While the story was carried by major newspapers of the day, it became vivid for many people only through cinematic newsreels in the weeks that followed.[2]

The delegates might even be excused for failing to grasp humanity's impressive ability to transform and disrupt the natural world, even in the wake of a war of unprecedented destructive power. The new organization was born in the last moments of the prenuclear era: the charter was signed three weeks before the United States conducted a secret nuclear explosion in the mountains of New Mexico, and six weeks before the bombing of Hiroshima and Nagasaki. Few could have imagined a world in which nuclear weapons would be possessed by several nations, built in the thousands, attached to missiles of intercontinental range, and placed at the heart of the great powers' security doctrines.

Just as they lacked a vision of the planet as a global ecosystem, most of the delegates did not see the new UN as part of a global political system of nation-states. The organization was born not as the universal forum it symbolizes today; it sprang from a political alliance of the victors in World War II. The defeated Axis powers were excluded from membership, and a fierce debate ensued over admitting fascist-leaning Argentina. Indeed, many of the world's peoples were left out of the proceedings entirely, admitted only after the sweeping decolonization of Africa and Asia that yielded over one hundred new countries in a mere two decades. Those hoping to give the new organization a broad decolonization mission ran squarely into Winston Churchill's fulsome refusal to "preside over the liquidation of the British Empire"; on decolonization, the UN Charter confined itself to a specific handful of "trust" territories inherited from the League of Nations.[3] For all of these reasons, it is no surprise that the delegates failed to imagine the world as a tightly coupled social and ecological system, subject to potentially dangerous levels of environmental damage from a global trajectory of increasing resource extraction, production, consumption, and pollution.

Today, of course, the picture is quite different, with environmental concerns a central part of what the UN does. This chapter traces the UN's environmental history—from the organization's origins, to the seminal 1972 Stockholm Conference, to the rise of the "sustainable development" and "global change" paradigms during the 1980s, and culminating in the 1992 Earth Summit, which marked the height of the UN's environmental ambitions. In doing so, the chapter pays particular attention to how environmental and natural resources issues came to be articulated and acted upon across the UN's four mandate domains. Emphasis is placed on the explanatory variables set out in chapter 1: organizational incentives, ideas, and the historical trajectory of global governance.

The chapter divides this history into four periods: the UN's early years, marked by decolonization, membership growth, and struggles over natural resource sovereignty; the era of the Stockholm Conference, which saw the rising salience of global environmental concerns; the 1980s, during which the "law and development" approach to global environmental governance first began to take serious root; and the 1990s, marked by the further consolidation of that approach in the Earth Summit era. Each historical section begins with a short summary of the era's significance. Briefly, the argument runs as follows. In the early years, the resource sovereignty debate blunted the development of environmental linkages on the peace and human rights sides of the UN, while specialized agencies taking a functional approach to development issues began to make the environmental issue their own. The Stockholm era, despite some important innovations, would largely reflect, consolidate, and extend this emergent framework, discourse, and division of labor on all things environmental at the UN. The 1980s saw an expansion of environmental activity across the UN, in a largely dispersed and uncoordinated manner, but added important ideational elements through emergent concepts of "sustainable development" and "global change." By the early 1990s, a "grand strategy" of liberal-internationalist environmentalism had emerged, grounded primarily in international law (read: issue-specific regulatory regimes on transboundary and global-commons issues) and sustainable development (read: greening development practice through national reforms, bolstered by foreign aid and technical assistance). The overall pattern is clear: a combination of ideas, institutional incentives, and the broader trajectory of global governance yielded a largely unquestioned UN approach to the environment, one that rested on only two of the organization's four mandate pillars.

THE DECOLONIZATION YEARS: NATURAL RESOURCES, EMERGENT SOVEREIGNTY, AND THE GLOBAL ECONOMY

Political elites present at the UN's creation may have failed to see the world as a tightly coupled global ecosystem, but they were quite attuned to the role of natural resources in global commerce and state power. Indeed, concerns about the adequacy of natural resource supplies for world commerce predated World War II. In his study of US, Soviet, and British resource policies during this period, Ronnie Lipschutz notes that "raw material problems . . . occupied a good deal of the time and energy of diplomats and decisionmakers during the 1920s and 1930s."[4] Several factors contributed to this growing salience, including instability in international commodity markets, rising economic nationalism, and geopolitical maneuvering over oil fields. Tensions only heightened with the emergence of Germany and Japan as powers that preferred direct control of resources to reliance on global markets.

The issue was of sufficient concern to the Allied powers that it is mentioned in the 1941 Atlantic Charter, which cemented the British-American alliance, seeded the Allied coalition in World War II, and gave birth to the name "United Nations." The Atlantic Charter committed its signatories to "endeavor, with due respect for their existing obligations, to further the enjoyment by all States, great or small, victor or vanquished, of access, on equal terms, to the trade and to the raw materials of the world which are needed for their economic prosperity."[5] After the war, references to the importance of adequate supplies of natural resources found their way into the preamble to the General Agreement on Tariffs and Trade and the articles of agreement for the International Monetary Fund and the World Bank.[6] Lipschutz has documented how the issue of raw material supplies became part of the foreign policy strategies of the leading powers following the war—be it US support for a liberal trading system, British efforts to maintain the empire, or Soviet resource diplomacy in patron-client relationships with emerging Third World states.[7] In 1951, when US president Harry Truman appointed a President's Materials Policy Commission, he asserted that "we cannot allow shortages of materials to jeopardize our national security nor to become a bottleneck to our economic expansion."[8]

These great-power concerns about the international flow of natural resources collided directly with the fears and aspirations of newly independent states. Control of resource supplies had been a central driver of colonialism and a powerful mechanism of imperial domination. Resource commodities were extracted from the colonial hinterlands to feed the demands of the imperial powers for food, energy, and industrial feedstock. The cycle was completed when these resources, now embodied in manufactured products, were sold back to the colonies' captive markets. Michael Manley, twice prime minister of Jamaica and a leader in the Non-Aligned Movement (NAM) during the 1970s and 1980s, described the cycle by tracing the process through which sugar from Jamaica and cocoa from West Africa were extracted, processed, and sold back to the colonies as a European chocolate bar:

> Marry the [Jamaican] sugar and the [West African] cocoa and a chocolate bar is produced. . . . But the story is not yet finished. The confectionary then crosses railways, the Atlantic, and ports to the original people who grew the sugar cane and grew the cocoa bean who now buy that same chocolate bar with all the "value added" and profits made both ways across the Atlantic. There

is a sense in which this story is oversimplified, but it reveals the heart of the economic process that shaped the Third World within which so many of us are trapped.[9]

Even the genesis of the modern environmental movement can be traced to this political economy of resource domination. The challenges colonial powers faced in understanding and controlling the new landscapes and ecosystems they encountered spurred the growth of geographical societies, botanical gardens, and national scientific academies in the eighteenth and nineteenth centuries.[10]

Thus, it was no accident that Gandhi used cotton, salt, and forests as potent symbols in the campaign for India's independence. The growing of cotton in India for milling in Britain, and the destruction of India's household-scale textile industry through tax policies that favored imported British fabrics, was part and parcel of British colonial domination.[11] As with cotton, so with salt: the salt trade in India was notoriously monopolized and heavily taxed by the British, creating widespread dissent that was tapped effectively in Gandhi's famous "salt march" of 1930.[12]

With independence, former colonies on the receiving end of this cycle of resource domination obtained sovereign statehood—but remained saddled with skewed economies built during the colonial era, highly dependent on raw-material exports and the vagaries of global commodity markets. Newly independent states confronted difficult trade-offs between exploiting their existing capacity to export natural resources and agricultural products on the one hand, and promoting economic transformation away from commodity dependence on the other. Different states chose different approaches, and the tensions would repeatedly divide emergent coalitions in the global South such as the NAM and the Group of 77. Despite these divisions, there were common elements to the global economic policies most developing countries sought: greater price stability in notoriously volatile commodity markets, technology transfer and investment to make it possible to tap those markets more effectively, and support for economic diversification to help them capture more of the value added further down the production chain. The final communiqué of the 1955 Bandung Conference, which launched the NAM, called for commodity price stabilization and economic diversification through the processing of raw materials prior to export.[13]

Whether emergent nations sought to exploit their dependence on resource commodity exports, to capture more of the "value added" by processing those resources into finished goods, or to diversify away from the resource sector entirely, one important and broadly shared theme in their emerging global economic agenda was to increase national control over key assets, including natural resources. Several governments nationalized strategic assets previously subject to external control, including the railroads in Korea after World War II (1946), the Suez Canal Company in Egypt under Nasser (1956), and foreign-owned companies in general after the Cuban Revolution (1959). Strategic natural resources, most notably including petroleum, were often targeted in such processes, as in Mexico during the Cárdenas regime (1938) or in Iran under the Mossadegh government (1951).

The Permanent Sovereignty Debate

In this context, the 1950s saw heated debates on the issue of natural resources, economic sovereignty, and international trade within the UN General Assembly.[14] Former colonies joining the UN found common cause with the older but economically underdeveloped countries of Latin America, several of which spent the 1950s in the throes of divisive national debates about control of national petroleum and mining companies. The General Assembly took up the question with a series of resolutions on the rights of developing countries to exploit their resource wealth. In 1952, Resolution 523 affirmed that "under-developed countries have the right to determine freely the use of their natural resources" and Resolution 626 reaffirmed the "right to exploit freely natural wealth and resources."[15] Both resolutions triggered sharp objections from the United States and other Western industrialized countries.[16] The original language proposed for 523, put forward by Poland, affirmed the "full rights" of developing countries. Uruguay's original language for 626, proposed in the wake of Iranian nationalization of the Anglo-American oil company, affirmed the right to nationalize natural wealth. In their final form, both resolutions softened the language of earlier drafts, referring to the needs of international trade and the global economy, but remained highly contentious.

Controversy deepened when the General Assembly took up debate on the draft articles for what would become the major human rights covenants of the 1960s. Western governments strongly opposed a Chilean proposal containing strong language on the absolute rights of sovereignty over natural wealth, tied to the right of peoples to self-determination. Nico Schrijver's detailed account of this debate reports that France refused to "legalize the autarchic practices of certain States which had a virtual monopoly of the raw materials indispensable to the international community" and argued that "some sovereignty would have to be surrendered to international organizations."[17]

Contentious debate on the topic culminated in the creation of the UN Commission on Permanent Sovereignty over Natural Resources (PSNR) in 1958, which was charged with conducting "a full survey of the status of permanent sovereignty over natural wealth and resources as a basic constituent of the right to self-determination."[18] Debate over how to frame a resolution on PSNR remained highly polarizing. Schrijver describes one "breathtaking" vote on a Soviet amendment that would have affirmed "the inalienable right of peoples and nations to the unobstructed execution of nationalization, expropriation and other essential measures aimed at protecting and strengthening their sovereignty over their natural wealth and resources."[19] It failed to pass on a tied vote of thirty to thirty, with thirty-three abstentions. Eventually, the UNGA reached agreement on the 1962 Declaration on Permanent Sovereignty over Natural Resources, which defined sovereignty over resource wealth as a right of "peoples and nations."[20] In their intellectual history of the UN, Richard Jolly and colleagues refer to this resolution as "the economic pendant of the decolonization declaration."[21]

From Permanent Sovereignty to the NIEO

While establishing some robust—and, in the eyes of postcolonial member states, hard-won—legal principles on resource sovereignty, the PSNR debate also set the stage for acrimonious struggle over the question of control of economic activities tied to resource extraction. Rapid change in General Assembly membership during this period only fanned the flames. When the PSNR debate had begun in the early 1950s, the UN consisted of 60 members—the 51 original charter signatories, a few states that did not participate in the San Francisco conference, and a handful of newly independent countries such as Burma, Pakistan, Indonesia, and Israel. By 1966, membership had exploded to include 122 states, with most of the new membership from Africa, the Middle East, Southeast Asia, and Eastern Europe. Few were liberal capitalist democracies, and the working majority in the General Assembly tilted decidedly away from the pro-Western climate of the UN's earliest years. In this context, the debate shifted from legal sovereignty over natural resources to their direct economic control. In 1966 the General Assembly passed Resolution 2158, which, under the rubric of PSNR, recognized

the right of all countries, and in particular of the developing countries, to secure and increase their share in the administration of enterprises which are fully or partly operated by foreign capital and to have a greater share in the advantages and profits derived therefrom on an equitable basis, with due regard to the development needs and objectives of the peoples concerned and to mutually acceptable contract practices, and calls upon the countries from which such capital originates to refrain from any action which would hinder the exercise of that right.[22]

Tensions heightened with a renewed wave of nationalizations in the late 1960s and early 1970s—notably including copper mines in Chile and petroleum resources in Libya and Iraq—and with the growing assertiveness of the Organization of the Petroleum Exporting Countries (OPEC). In 1974, the General Assembly approved Resolution 3281, which reaffirmed PSNR and asserted that the legal basis for compensation when assets were nationalized should be national, rather than international, law.[23]

By the early 1970s, an array of developing-country concerns had begun to coalesce into demands for a "New International Economic Order" (NIEO). The NIEO agenda emphasized the control and pricing of resource commodities in the world economy, the problem of unfettered power of multinationals operating across national boundaries, and inequities in the rules and norms governing (or failing to govern) global trade and investment practices.[24] To a striking extent that has not been recognized in much of the scholarly literature on the origins of global environmental politics, the NIEO emerged directly alongside the birth of the environmental era at the UN:

- In 1968, the General Assembly approved the Swedish proposal for the UN Conference on the Human Environment (UNCHE), to be held in Stockholm; the UN Educational, Scientific, and Cultural Organization (UNESCO) held the Paris Biosphere Conference—and the second meeting of the UN Conference on Trade and Development (UNCTAD) took up the question of managed trade and price supports for a range of natural-resource commodities.
- In 1970, the planning for the Stockholm environmental conference was well underway, the first Earth Day was held—and the NAM, meeting in Lusaka, called for "urgent structural changes in the world economy."[25]
- In 1974, the fledgling UN Environment Programme was getting its operations underway, the danger of chlorofluorocarbons to the stratospheric ozone layer was first reported—and the General Assembly adopted its "Declaration for the Establishment of a New International

Economic Order," formally launching the debate that would dominate global political economy for the rest of the decade.

THE IMPACT ON THE FOUR MANDATE DOMAINS

The acrimonious politics of natural resources during the UN's first two decades played a strong role in structuring the organization's subsequent environmental debate. These effects can be seen in the way that environmental issues first came to be articulated in each of the four UN mandate domains during this period.

International Law: Embedding the Permanent Sovereignty Principle

The content of international law is generally understood to arise from a number of sources. Chief among these are international treaties, the rulings of international tribunals such as the International Court of Justice (ICJ, aka the "World Court"), and customary international law as defined by the enduring practices of states. The legitimacy of international law derives from the fact that it is rooted in the "prior free will" of states, meaning that it has binding power upon them only to the extent that they willingly bind themselves to it by prior acts. Thus, treaty law is binding upon a state when (and only when) the state has ratified an agreement and the agreement has entered into force (which typically requires ratification by a specified minimum number of other state-parties to the accord). Similarly, decisions of international bodies—be it a judicial body such as the International Criminal Court (ICC) or a delegated authority such as the UN Security Council—are binding upon a state when (and only when) the state has previously ratified a legal instrument making it so (the Rome Statute of the ICC in the former instance, the UN Charter in the latter). Customary international law is binding upon states in a somewhat different sense, but still derives from prior free will. Customary law exists when countries have practiced a principle—such as freedom of the seas or the nonrepatriation of refugees into war zones—with sufficient duration and consistency that it can be said to have passed into the realm of custom. It also requires, however, that such practice be rooted in *opinion juris*, or a sense of obligation to follow said custom. Whether a rule of practice has been normalized sufficiently to constitute customary international law thus requires interpretation (for example, through a ruling from the ICJ).

Law's influence, however, is normative as well as juridical. "Soft law"—principled rules that lack the formal juridical status of the "hard" instruments of treaty, case law, and recognized custom—may also shape the behavior of governments. Soft law is found in an assortment of places: UN resolutions, the joint declarations of governments at international conferences, the reasoning of national courts and other deliberative bodies, and the writings of eminent jurists and legal scholars. In some instances, soft law may exert its influence by making its way into hard law—if its norms are incorporated into international treaties, utilized as a basis for the rulings of international tribunals such as the ICJ, or authoritatively recognized as a reflection of customary international law. In other instances, the effects of soft law are political: generating pressures on governments, shaping the actions and demands of social movements, or creating increasingly routine expectations about behavior.[26]

Having been framed and standardized in a series of General Assembly resolutions, PSNR by the early 1970s stood as a recognizable "soft law" principle. At some point thereafter, it crossed the threshold from soft law into customary international law. This, at least, was the authoritative view of the ICJ, as expressed in a 2005 ruling over whether Uganda had engaged in or enabled wartime plunder of natural resources in the Democratic Republic of Congo.[27] Some observers have gone as far as to argue that PSNR rises to the level of *jus cogens*, or a hierarchically peremptory principle of international law.[28] However, the international arbitral tribunal in the case of *Aminoil v. Kuwait* (1982) rejected this *jus cogens* argument.[29] Others have taken a narrower and more contingent view. Perrez, for example, suggests that PSNR constitutes not a new principle but rather a "restatement" of customary international law, to the extent that it recognizes a legal obligation to compensate in the case of nationalization.[30]

While case law from international tribunals can play a key role in clarifying customary international law, such judgments are notoriously slow to appear. In the first seventy years of its existence (through 2014), the ICJ accepted 161 cases for consideration, or just more than two per year, as well as handing down twenty-six advisory opinions to intergovernmental organizations. The ICJ did not affirm the status of PSNR as customary law until 2005, more than forty years after the 1962 General Assembly declaration. Thus, it is primarily through treaty law—hardly rapid or dynamic, but more so than international case law—that PSNR has translated from "soft" to "hard" international law. As Schrijver points out, over time PSNR has been "incorporated in treaty law in various fields, including human rights, State succession, law of the sea, international environmental law, and international energy and investment law."[31]

A look at the data, however, indicates that environmental treaty law did not immediately take up the concept. During the ten-year period between the UNGA's seminal PSNR declaration (December 1962) and the Stockholm Conference (June 1972), seventy-four multilateral environmental agreements were concluded on a wide array of topics, including fisheries, shared river basins, ocean pollution, and nuclear energy.[32] Several of these agreements make general references to the sovereign rights of states. Yet specific invocations of PSNR, or of the 1962 General Assembly declaration as a way to reserve states' rights or qualify environmental obligations, begin to appear in environmental treaties only in the early 1970s. Such language is included in the 1972 *Convention on the Prevention of Marine Pollution by Dumping of Wastes and other Matter*, the 1973 *International Convention for the Prevention of Pollution from Ships*, and the 1976 *Agreement Establishing the South Pacific Regional Environment Program*. The most important translation of PSNR into the environmental realm came with the 1982 *United Nations Convention on the Law of the Sea* (UNCLOS). UNCLOS is often noted for establishing the principle of the oceans' resources as the common heritage of humankind. Yet the convention also extended sovereign territorial waters dramatically, through the creation of two-hundred-mile exclusive economic zones in coastal waters, and Article 56 reaffirmed coastal states' sovereign control over the natural resources therein. In this manner, and also in its emphasis on shared benefits from deep-sea minerals, technology transfer, and other provisions, UNCLOS clearly felt the influence of the rising NIEO agenda of the 1970s.[33]

Development: The Rise of Environmental Agendas in the Specialized Agencies

While legal principles of natural-resource sovereignty occupied the General Assembly during this period, environmental protection, nature conservation, and the more pedestrian aspects of natural-resource management lacked the broad salience or politically charged character of PSNR for most member states. As discussed below, such activities were treated primarily as functional concerns and technical challenges associated with economic development. In the absence of a central institutional home, several of the UN's specialized agencies and other programs took up specific initiatives on pollution, conservation, and natural resource management. Later, as we shall see, when the political salience of environmental challenges became more apparent, collaborative initiatives and crosscutting activities would become more common. But these system-wide concerns took root only after several UN organs had staked their turf around independent bases of activity. Some of them did so in areas that were logical extensions of their expertise and mandate; others were prodded to do so by member-state interests or world events; and some—notably, UNESCO—would use the breadth of their mandate to launch a wide array of activities. Thus, by the time the environmental agenda exploded on the scene in the second half of the 1960s, the UN was already deeply immersed in various environmental activities, albeit in a highly dispersed, primarily technical, and largely uncoordinated manner.

The splintering of activities became inevitable when proposals to create a UN-based organization for nature conservation were blocked after World War II. John McCormick's history of this period documents the divisions among nature advocates across Europe and the United States, which led to the creation of the independent International Union for the Protection of Nature (IUPN) rather than a UN-affiliated entity.[34] Born in the politics of compromise, IUPN was a hybrid body consisting of both governmental and nongovernmental members. Although it would later gain traction as the organization known today as the International Union for Conservation of Nature (IUCN), IUPN proved to be a divided, underfunded, and unwieldy body in its early years.[35]

While failing to create a dedicated organ, the UN did hold a Conference on the Conservation and Utilization of Resources in 1949. Jointly organized by the Food and Agriculture Organization (FAO), the International Labour Organization (ILO), UNESCO, and the World Health Organization (WHO), and matched with a concurrent IUPN event on the protection of nature, the conference included delegates from forty-nine countries and featured a broad agenda that McCormick characterizes as having "remarkable breadth and foresight."[36] But the discussion stressed science over policy, and the conferees neither developed nor endorsed policy recommendations for member states.

By their largely separate actions, the specialized agencies filled the space. Although the constitutional mandate of the Food and Agriculture Organization (FAO) included conservation of natural resources, the organization was much more strongly oriented toward production and marketing of resource commodities than environmental management. Founded in 1945, FAO put most of its initial efforts into addressing postwar food shortages. A timber shortfall in Europe led FAO to organize a conference in 1947 that "stressed the need for a satisfactory distribution of timber supplies and the imperative of identifying and implementing long-term measures to restore forests as a part of European reconstruction."[37] FAO also came to be involved in the development of international conventions. It played a key role in the 1958 *Convention on Fishing and Conservation of the Living Resources of the High Seas*.[38] And FAO played an extensive role in development of the 1968 *African Convention for Conservation of Nature and Natural Resources*, competing with IUCN to define the accord's text.[39]

The constitution of the World Health Organization, which entered into force in 1948, mandated WHO to "promote, in co-operation with other specialized agencies where necessary, the improvement of nutrition, housing, sanitation, recreation, economic or working conditions and other aspects of environmental hygiene."[40] "Environmental sanitation" was one of the focal points for the first World Health Assembly (1948), and WHO established an Expert Committee on Environmental Sanitation that reported periodically through the 1950s.[41] In 1959, the Twelfth World Health Assembly found progress to be too slow and approved a program for improving community water supplies. By 1967, WHO-assisted projects were underway in eighty-three countries.[42] WHO also began partnering with UNICEF on environmental sanitation and rural water supply, with seventy-three joint projects underway by the late 1960s.[43]

By the early 1960s, WHO was starting to move into broader environment-health research, via expert committees on atmospheric pollution, water pollution control, and the environmental determinants of health. The latter paid particular attention to new organic chemical pollutants (which previously had received far less attention than inorganic pollutants and sewage contamination) as well as multiple pathways of exposure and long-term health effects. Over a two-year period beginning in November 1963, WHO convened five scientific groups to examine health effects of organic chemical pollution.[44] WHO also began supporting research on the long-term health effects of pesticides, and in 1967 established the Air Pollution Research Unit of the Medical Research Council, London, to promote research on long-term health effects.[45] By 1972, the year of the Stockholm Conference, WHO was developing a planning guide for national environmental health programs and supporting the development of environmental health professionals and programs at national, provincial, and local levels in several countries. Environmental health had become a recurring theme of the World Health Assembly, with the twenty-fourth assembly (1971) conducting a comprehensive review of the principal problems and making recommendations on water and sanitation, international cooperation on codes of environmental health practices, the development of epidemiologic environmental health surveillance, knowledge dissemination, and personnel training.[46]

The International Maritime Organization (IMO) became extensively involved in promoting treaty-based environmental cooperation in the pre-Stockholm era. The IMO was created by the *Convention on the International Maritime Organization* (negotiated in 1948 but not entering into force until 1958).[47] The convention mandated the organization "to provide machinery for cooperation among Governments in the field of governmental regulation and practices relating to technical matters of all kinds affecting shipping engaged in international trade; to encourage and facilitate the general adoption of the highest practicable standards in matters concerning maritime safety, efficiency of navigation and prevention and control of marine pollution from ships."[48] Although the primary focus of activity in its early years was shipboard safety, high-profile oil spills such as the 1967 Torrey Canyon episode prodded IMO to move on marine pollution. IMO was the key catalyst for international agreements on civil liability and compensation for damage from oil pollution (1969 and 1971) and the 1973 *International Convention for the Prevention of Pollution from Ships* (aka MARPOL Convention).

With a mandate to "contribute to peace and security by promoting collaboration among nations through education, science and culture," the initial engagements of the United Nations Educational, Scientific and Cultural Organization in the realm of environment and natural resources were an outgrowth of its support for activities in the natural sciences. Key developments were UNESCO's link to the International Council of Scientific Unions (ICSU) and its support for the International Geophysical Year (1957–1958). During the 1960s, scientific projects led UNESCO repeatedly into broader initiatives with policy overtones. On conservation, support for the International Biological Program (1962–1972) of the ICSU led to the 1968 Biosphere Conference and UNESCO's "Man and the Biosphere" program, which conducts research on and promotes biosphere reserves.[49] On water resources, a UNESCO research project on arid zones in the 1950s led to the 1965 launch of the International Hydrologic Decade, which aimed to promote the rational use of water resources. On oceans, the organization's marine science programs of the 1950s led it to create the International Oceanographic Commission in 1960 as a focal point for international marine science initiatives.[50]

Like FAO and IMO, UNESCO also forayed into the realm of international treaty negotiations during this period, promulgating the *World Heritage Convention*. UNESCO became involved in cultural preservation in 1959, when it launched a campaign to preserve cultural artifacts threatened by the Aswan High Dam in Egypt.[51] Subsequent efforts at cultural safeguarding developed in parallel to a 1968 IUCN proposal to protect sites of natural heritage. The two initiatives were combined into the *World Heritage Convention*, which was adopted by UNESCO's General Conference in 1972 and entered into force in 1975.

Other agencies and programs that took a technical-functional slice of environmental and natural-resource activities in this period included the World Meteorological Organization (WMO), ILO, and the UN Development Programme (UNDP). Although UNDP would by the 1990s play a key role in fostering the paradigm of "human development" with important sustainability dimensions, it began in this domain primarily through technical projects in natural resource management. By 1966, UNDP's Special Fund sector was supporting some seventy projects in nonagricultural resource development, as well as providing technical assistance on mineral, water, and energy resource development.[52]

Peace: The Missing Domain

In stark contrast to these institutional developments around international law and economic development, the ledger on treating the environment as a peace and security issue has few entries during this period. The Security Council played essentially no role in the emerging environmental debate within the UN during the 1960s and early 1970s. In its silence, the Council was hardly unique; the committee for the Nobel Peace Prize—which would later embrace the environment as a peace issue by honoring Wangari Maathai (2004) and the Intergovernmental Panel on Climate Change and Al Gore (2007)—chose to make no award in 1972, the year of the Stockholm Conference.

One obvious reason for the Security Council's absence from the conversation was its frequent polarization and paralysis during the Cold War. In 1952 the Council passed only two resolutions (one consisting of a single sentence that dissolved the Commission for Conventional Armaments). The structure of the Council, and in particular the veto power held by its five permanent members, also played a role. During the 1972 Stockholm Conference, several governments raised the issue of the vast environmental despoliation of the Vietnam War, keyed by the United States' unprecedented use of explosives, napalm, herbicides, and defoliants. But the American veto meant that the matter would never be addressed by the Security Council.

Importantly, however, the Council also lacked a bureaucratic-entrepreneurial foundation to move into this emergent policy arena. The UN's peace-related activities today extend far beyond the Council, and are institutionalized in the Department of Peacekeeping Operations (DPKO), the Department of Political Affairs (DPA), the Peacebuilding Commission (PBC), the Security Council's ties to the International Criminal Court, and the array of peacebuilding activities of UNDP and other UN organs. The tools of peace have also multiplied over time, to include mediation, sanctions regimes, peacekeeping forces, humanitarian intervention, post-conflict peacebuilding, counterterrorism activities, and international criminal prosecution, among others. Most of this organizational apparatus was not envisioned in the UN Charter, and has grown over time through trial-and-error practice and innovations born of necessity. As discussed in chapter 5, it is primarily in these domains, rather than in the Security Council itself, that environmental peacebuilding initiatives have recently begun to take root.

Beyond these structural and institutional features of the Council, another reason for its absence from the environmental conversation during this period was the state of authoritative knowledge about environment, resources, and conflict. The idea that problems of pollution, conservation, and resource depletion could be linked to matters of international peace and conflict was certainly not unknown in the UN's early years. Books such as Fairfield Osborn's *Our Plundered Planet* and William Vogt's *Road to Survival*, both published in 1948, drew links between environmental issues and conflict, and had some modest success in popularizing concern about the effects of pollution, resource depletion, and population growth.[53] The idea also cropped up occasionally in policy circles. Gifford Pinchot, a former director of the US Forest Service, prodded US president Franklin Roosevelt to support an international organization for nature protection as part of the post–World War II intergovernmental architecture. While ultimately unsuccessful, Pinchot's efforts prompted Roosevelt to write to his secretary of state, Cordell Hull, "Conservation is a basis of permanent peace."[54] Nevertheless, the intellectual connections linking environment, resources, and conflict were still several decades away from being made in a sufficiently authoritative manner (see chapter 5).

Thus, prior to the rise of environmental discourse within the UN in the late 1960s, the Security Council had essentially nothing to say about the issue of resources, environment, peace, and conflict. Yet the historical record shows that connections were there for the making in each of the Council's three main areas of activity during this period: peaceful dispute resolution, conflict intervention, and disarmament. The legacy of the era is primarily one of failure to act on, or even recognize, such connections.

Certainly there were missed opportunities with regard to dispute resolution. The Suez Crisis, which led to the first significant UN peacekeeping operation in 1956, showed the conflict potential around strategic resources.[55] The crisis centered on military intervention by Israel, Britain, and France following Egypt's decision to nationalize the Suez Canal. Notably, Egypt's nationalization was triggered by the withdrawal of US and British funding for the Aswan High Dam on the Nile River. The dam reflected Egypt's strategic priority to control the Nile's water resources and was a centerpiece of Egyptian development planning. Egyptian president Nasser justified the nationalization by suggesting that revenues from the canal would replace the lost funding for the dam. In this context, the admission of Sudan to the UN that same year and the subsequent admission of nations upstream along the Nile River were missed opportunities to address water-related tensions among states in the basin. A 1929 treaty had largely ceded to Egypt the water rights of Britain's upstream colonies along the Nile. Egypt and newly independent Sudan clashed on the water question and the plans for Aswan, to the point that Egypt mobilized troops when Sudan rejected the 1929 accord. Tensions were defused when a military coup brought a more compliant Sudanese regime to power, and the two countries negotiated a 1959 accord defining Sudanese water rights and clearing the way for the dam to be built. By ignoring future water needs of upstream states, the 1959 accord planted the seeds for tension that has only grown with time. That shared rivers could be a source of conflict and instability was clearly recognized during this era, most obviously in the World Bank's initiative throughout the 1950s to bring India and Pakistan into a treaty regime for the Indus River, culminating in the *Indus Waters Treaty* of 1960.

To be sure, addressing the Nile as a challenge of shared resources and a problem of conflict resolution would have required of the Security Council both great foresight and a path around Cold War paralysis. A more glaring failure to make such links is seen in the postindependence crisis of the former Belgian Congo, an episode that went beyond dispute resolution to include military intervention. The Congo Crisis (1960–1965) was a complex affair that, according to one historical account, "had the characteristics of anti-colonial struggle, a secessionist war with the province of Katanga, a United Nations peacekeeping operation, and a Cold War proxy battle between the United States and the Soviet Union."[56] Unlike other peacekeeping operations of the UN's first few decades, which used lightly armed observers as a symbolic deterrent to the resumption of conflict, Congo was an active military operation that bore greater resemblance to the more complex "peacebuilding" initiatives of the post–Cold War era. As such, the crisis eerily presaged episodes of "conflict resources" in which the Security Council has become engaged in recent years (see chapter 5).

Congo had been a Belgian colony, exploited for its natural resource wealth and ruled oppressively even by the standards of colonialism. Growing pressure for independence and mounting political instability triggered an abrupt, chaotic end to Belgian rule in 1960. Rapidly arranged elections yielded a weak central government, with various factions emerging to control key provinces. This in turn led to a complex sequence of events: rebellion, insurgency, and secession in several provinces; intervention by Belgian and UN troops on opposing sides of the conflict; a multipronged civil war between the central state and the rebellious provinces, some of which received external support from Belgium or the Soviet Union; and a military coup supported by the US Central Intelligence Agency.

At the heart of this complex crisis were the separate decisions of the mineral-rich provinces of Katanga and South Kasai to secede from the newly independent nation. The Katanga secession was supported by Belgian commercial interests and backed by Belgian military and mercenary support. The UN sent troops with an ambiguous mandate that would evolve into supporting the central government against the Katanga secession. The military effort went badly; at one point of particular crisis for the UN mission, Secretary- General Dag Hammarskjöld flew to Congo to take personal charge of ceasefire negotiations, only to be killed en route when his plane crashed under suspicious circumstances.

Although analysis at the time of the crisis stressed Cold War rivalries, it has become clear that commercial interests around the control of natural resources were a central element of the conflict. It is now known that US support was covertly tilting toward mineral-rich Katanga well before Soviet support for the central government even entered the scene.[57] Indeed, the conflict bore several of the hallmarks of the problem of "conflict resources" that has increasingly engaged the Security Council in recent years. First, natural-resource wealth was central to the motives for provincial secession (copper and other minerals in Katanga, diamonds in South Kasai). Second, revenues from resource extraction enabled the purchase of arms and hiring of mercenaries, prolonging the violence. Third, the connection of resource-extraction activities to international commodity chains greatly complicated the quest for peace, as rival transnational commercial interests maneuvered for advantage in ways that badly undermined international peacemaking efforts.[58] Fourth, the "resource curse" proved all too evident in the authoritarian Mobutu regime that emerged from the crisis and plundered Congo's resource wealth for more than two decades. Yet the problem was not framed in these terms, and the array of tools used in more recent resource-conflict episodes was not yet in place to support the Council's actions (see chapter 5). When another complex, resource-fueled secessionist struggle emerged in the form of Nigeria's Biafran War (1967–1970), the Council—burned by the Congo debacle, and seemingly preferring a military victory by the central Nigerian state—took essentially no action during the horrific violence that followed.

Nor did the Council make environment-security connections in its third locus of activity during this era, disarmament. The first act of the brand-new General Assembly in 1946 was to create the UN Atomic Energy Commission, and the question of international control of atomic energy dominated the UN agenda in its first few years. But Security Council deliberations on the matter did not broach the question of nuclear accidents or environmental effects. The 1950s debate on atmospheric nuclear fallout did link the issues of environment and security explicitly, eventually yielding the Limited Nuclear Test Ban Treaty (1963). But the Security Council was bypassed in these negotiations in favor of direct superpower bargaining. Soviet dissident Andrei Sakharov gave global environmental issues and their links to disarmament explicit treatment in his 1968 acceptance speech for the Nobel Peace Prize.[59] That same year, the Security Council formally extended its security umbrella to states that agreed to foreswear the development and possession of nuclear weapons—but failed to broach the threats posed by mishandling of nuclear materials, the dumping of nuclear waste, accidental releases to the environment, or inadequate safeguards at nuclear facilities.[60]

Human Rights: Natural Resources as the Right of "Peoples"

If links to the UN mandate on peace were largely missing when it came to natural resources and the environment during this period, the same cannot be said for human rights. The developing-country coalition that drove the resource-sovereignty debate clearly understood it to be a question of human rights. The General Assembly sent the PSNR debate not to its Second Committee, which addresses economic and financial matters, but rather to the Third Committee, which handles human rights issues. The UN Commission on Human Rights also took up the question.

What emerged from these channels, however, was not a "human" rights formulation but rather a strongly nationalized and state-based conception of the rights surrounding natural resources. A critical result of the debate was to affirm natural resources as a right tied specifically to self-determination, and thus to nations rather than individuals or local communities.

As early as 1952, the Chilean government proposed the following language—hotly disputed at the time—for the draft texts that would eventually become the *International Covenant on Civil and Political Rights* (ICCPR) and the *International Covenant on Economic, Social and Cultural Rights* (ICESCR):

> The rights of the peoples to self-determination shall also include permanent sovereignty over their natural wealth and resources. In no case may a people be deprived of its own means of subsistence on the grounds of any rights that may be claimed by other States.[61]

After intense debate, the General Assembly softened this language with references to international cooperation, mutual benefit, and international law—but preserving the formulation of natural resources as a collective right of "peoples" in the specific contest of self-determination. This formulation of permanent resource sovereignty also appeared in the General Assembly's milestone "Declaration on the Granting of Independence to Colonial Peoples and Countries" (1960), which called for immediate action to transfer power to the peoples of all territories that had not yet attained independence.[62] It also appeared in the two foundational treaties of the modern human rights era, the ICESCR and ICCPR. The two covenants, adopted by the General Assembly and opened for state ratification in 1966, contain identical language:

> All peoples may, for their own ends, freely dispose of their natural wealth and resources without prejudice to any obligations arising out of international economic co-operation, based upon the principle of mutual benefit, and international law. In no case may a people be deprived of its own means of subsistence.[63]

With the concept thus embedded in the context of self-determination and nationhood, future resolutions would simply refer to the rights of *countries*.[64] In this way, the framing of natural resource management as a matter of self-determination and the collective sovereign rights of "a people" (read: a member state) was already deeply embedded within the UN, as a matter of both formal international declaration and general political discourse, by the time the 1972 Stockholm Conference elevated the environmental question.

In other words, it was not that a rights-based framework on the natural world had been overlooked, but rather that it had already been built—and channeled quite clearly into a framework of state sovereignty and national self-determination. As discussed in chapter 4, this framing has made it much more difficult to conceive of and act upon the environment as a human right.

THE STOCKHOLM CONFERENCE

As the 1960s progressed, citizen concerns about pollution, resource depletion, and environmental health became widespread across Western Europe and the United States. Fallout from atmospheric nuclear testing, episodes of toxic contamination such as the infamous Minamata case in Japan, and the publication of Rachel Carson's seminal book *Silent Spring* sensitized mass publics across the industrialized world to toxic dangers. Acute air-pollution episodes from weather inversions in London (1962) and New York (1963 and 1966) left scores of people dead. Proposals to build hydroelectric dams on major rivers in the United States, Norway, and elsewhere galvanized opposition and injected a new radicalism into existing conservation organizations. Oil spills off the coasts of England (1967) and Southern California (1969) exposed the unpreparedness of governments for ecological disasters, while popular accounts such as Paul and Anne Ehrlich's *The Population Bomb* and Garrett Hardin's "Tragedy of the Commons" essay in the journal *Science* portrayed a grim future of resource scarcity, social conflict, and environmental decline. In the United States, a nationwide "teach-in" known as Earth Day mobilized several million participants in cities and towns across the nation. *The Ecologist* magazine's 1972 *Blueprint for Survival*, which reached best-seller status in the UK, asserted, "If current trends are allowed to persist, the breakdown of society and the irreversible disruption of the life-support systems on this planet, possibly by the end of the century, certainly within the lifetimes of our children, are inevitable."[65]

Across the industrialized world, some political and economic elites saw in these emerging concerns a significant threat to prevailing practices of economic development, global commerce, and political order. The Club of Rome was founded in 1968 "as an informal association of independent leading personalities from politics, business and science" concerned about the implications of global resource use and pollution for sustaining economic growth and capitalist industrial development.[66] Others saw opportunities: to standardize regulations at the national level, to use "regulatory competition" for corporate or sectoral advantage, and to mobilize subsidies for pollution control. Indeed, much of the activist Left of the 1960s viewed the new environmental agenda with suspicion, fearing that it was intended to blunt the movements against war, poverty, and racial injustice by draining off attention and support.[67]

At the international level, a good portion of the political energy of governments went into blocking specific items on the emerging environmental agenda. As one chronicler of the Stockholm Conference put it:

> Many participating nations had skeletons in their closets that they did not want examined in Stockholm. For example, the United States did not want ecocidal warfare on the agenda; Japan did not want to discuss a ban on whaling; Brazil tried to sabotage resolutions on forest conservation and on environmental responsibilities to neighboring countries (Argentina); and France and China voted against a ban on nuclear testing. National interests were indeed paramount.[68]

Governments also responded, however, by establishing national environmental ministries and imposing or strengthening regulations on toxics, air pollution, and water quality.

So, too, was the UN's environmental agenda widened and elevated considerably over the space of just a few years. The 1961 *Yearbook of the United Nations* made only passing mention of environmental protection in the context of a few specific projects of the specialized agencies.[69] By 1965, the Co-Ordination Committee of the Economic and Social Council (ECOSOC) was concluding that "the time had come when action was required on pollution."[70] By 1968, an entire chapter of the *Yearbook* was devoted to "Problems of the Human Environment."[71] Policy debates began to move from the confines of the specialized agencies to the more politicized ECOSOC and the General Assembly; new issues such as air pollution and toxic chemicals shouldered their way onto the agenda beside more traditional concerns about conservation and natural resource development. This growing sense of political salience was the backdrop when 113 member states gathered in Stockholm in June 1972 for the seminal UN Conference on the Human Environment.

Much like the UN's organizational landscape of this period, the Stockholm Conference reflected the uneven articulation of the environmental issue across the four mandate domains, as sketched previously. The conference was a contentious affair. Most Soviet-bloc nations did not participate, due to a dispute on seating Cold War–divided Germany. Among the nations that did attend, bitter differences on environment and development marked the intergovernmental discussions. Diplomats from across the global South argued that, unlike the industrialized world, poor countries suffered from a "pollution of poverty" rooted in underdevelopment. They rebutted fears about population growth and resource scarcity by pointing to the vast gap in consumption levels between rich and poor nations. And they rejected many of the proffered solutions, arguing that stricter pollution controls and conservation efforts would lock in the global economic inequities at the root of the problem.[72]

Much of the resistance from developing countries was presaged in the Founex Report on Development and Environment, which flagged the unique challenges of developing countries facing a "pollution of poverty" distinct from the agenda-defining environmental concerns of the industrialized world.[73] The report also highlighted the concern that "environmental actions by developed countries may have a profound and manifold impact on the growth and external economic relations of developing countries" through import restrictions, nontariff barriers to trade, the cost of traded goods, and the effects of materials conservation and recycling on demand for primary commodities.[74] In contrast, Founex had nothing to say about peace, and the only allusion to human rights was to reject environmental protectionism as analogous to the "fallacious" rights arguments attacking developing countries on labor conditions.[75]

The environment-development controversies at Stockholm added an overtly political dimension to what had previously been largely technical initiatives dispersed across several UN organs. The combination of dispersion and technical orientation meant that no single entity would be the focal point (a situation that endured until the seating of the Brundtland Commission in 1983). It also meant that there were several UN organs, and their member-state patrons, with a vested interest in preventing the emergence of a focal organization. The predictable result was the creation of the UN Environment Programme (UNEP) as a marginal entity, lacking both the resources and political backing to discipline and herd the larger specialized agencies into coordinated action.

The international legal dimensions of the environmental question were less central than environment-development issues at Stockholm. The conference occurred prior to the modern heyday of international environmental treaty-writing (which, as discussed in the next chapter, was triggered by the globalization of the environmental NGO movement and the growing political salience of "global commons" challenges in the 1980s). There were no specific negotiations for environmental treaty regimes at Stockholm. While the conference clearly broached global themes about pollution, resource use, population growth, and the planetary fate, the idea was not yet in evidence that the solution was to write issue-specific regulatory treaties.

Stockholm did play an important role in framing how that subsequent era of treaty writing would be positioned atop the pillar of the UN's international-law mandate, however. The oft-cited Principle 21 of the Stockholm Declaration articulates a balance between states' rights and obligations:

> States have, in accordance with the Charter of the United Nations and the principles of international law, the sovereign right to exploit their own resources pursuant to their own environmental policies, and the responsibility to ensure that activities within their jurisdiction or control do not cause damage to the environment of other States or of areas beyond the limits of national jurisdiction.[76]

The obligation not to cause harm via transboundary pollution was recognized in international law prior to the formation of the UN (with the Trail Smelter dispute between parties in Canada and the United States serving as a seminal case). More generally, sovereign rights are widely understood to come with an obligation to respect the sovereign rights of others. Thus, the duty not to harm reflects the more general obligation of all states "to protect within their territory the rights of other states."[77]

Many observers have cited Principle 21 as elevating the idea of responsibilities relative to rights. While this may be true, the chief responsibility thus elevated is the obligation to respect the sovereignty of other states by not causing *transboundary* environmental harm. In this sense, Stockholm codified—normatively, if not in hard law—a strict territorialization of environmental problems, in which physically internalized damage is the state's prerogative. This territorialization would become a key underpinning of the UN's "better law between states, better development within them" approach on the environment. Its consequences are twofold: it codifies the subordination of a human rights framework to a states' rights framework, as discussed previously. And as argued in subsequent chapters, it has been of limited usefulness in a world of global commodity chains that snake across borders, and which localize the harm attached to a global logic of production.

This is not to suggest that the concept of environmental human rights was entirely missing at Stockholm. The first principle of the conference's outcome document, the Stockholm Declaration, asserted, "Man has the fundamental right to freedom, equality and adequate conditions of life in an environment of a quality that permits a life of dignity and well-being."[78]

But developing countries had a strong interest in not seeing environmental concerns derail the two-decades-long battle they had just fought over natural resource sovereignty. Many industrial countries, for their part, had no particular desire to find a new array of social and economic rights centered on environmental protection. In this sense, the Stockholm Declaration reflected what would become a common practice in global environmental summitry—leading off with a general pronouncement on the rights of people, only to follow with a more detailed framework that subordinates those rights to an interstate logic of territorially bounded cooperation.

Attempts to link environmental challenges to the UN's peace mandate were also made at Stockholm, but gained little traction. France and China blocked a statement condemning nuclear weapons testing for its environmental effects. The Vietnam War also proved contentious, with the head of the Chinese delegation, Tang Ke, urging the conference to "strongly condemn the United States for their wanton bombings and shellings, use of chemical weapons, massacre of the people, destruction of human lives, annihilation of plants and animals and pollution of the environment." The Swedish prime minister, Olaf Palme, referred to US actions in Vietnam as "an outrage sometimes described as ecocide, which requires urgent international attention." The US response, delivered by then-chairperson of the White House Council on Environmental Quality, Russell Train, argued that the aim to "work together in a spirit of reason and cooperation for international development and environmental protection . . . will not be served by bringing into our deliberations highly charged issues, extraneous to our agenda and impossible of solution in this forum."[79] The civil-society side of the Stockholm Conference also pressed the issue, through both the Environment Forum[80] and a string of unaffiliated panels, debates, lectures, and a youth tent commune outside the city. Speakers at the Forum criticized the official conference proceedings for failing to engage questions related to war and militarism. EPA administrator William Ruckelshaus was challenged aggressively on the war and US foreign policy. When asked how he would report these concerns back to the US president, Ruckelshaus replied, "I shall tell him that I was invited to a very interesting meeting where there were a lot of people who seemed to regard the issues of war and the environment as one and the same."[81] A thousand-strong youth demonstration presented conference Secretary-General Maurice Strong with a call for a ten-year moratorium on the killing of human beings.[82]

Stockholm's Legacy

In hindsight, it can be said that the Stockholm Conference yielded a few significant outcomes. The Stockholm Declaration provided a principled roadmap for subsequent UN activities, stressing sovereign rights and responsibilities and the need to address environmental issues in the context of development and poverty concerns. The UN Environment Programme was created in the meeting's aftermath. The active resistance of developing countries to shibboleths about population bombs and resource doom forced a more intelligent discussion about growth, limits, and the means and ends of economic development. In this sense, Stockholm was a fractious but necessary step in the emergence of the sustainable development movement during the 1980s.

Less obvious but just as important was how Stockholm reflected, consolidated, and extended an already emergent framework, discourse, and division of labor on things environmental at the UN. The Action Plan adopted by the conference reflected the major features of the emerging approach.[83] Its 109 recommendations had a strongly developmental orientation, paying particular attention to issues such as human settlements, food and agriculture, water supply, and the development of national environmental management capabilities. The recommendations also reflected the pattern of bureaucratic-administrative dispersal established in the 1960s, calling on several UN organs to deepen their specialized activity in a largely uncoordinated manner. The recommendations also took a largely technical and managerial approach to international cooperation, framing the challenge as one of exchanging information, developing monitoring programs, and aiding in the construction of national administrative systems. Finally, the Action Plan reflected the prevailing G-77 sensitivities on trade, protectionism, and resource rights. The plan included an admonition that environmental concerns not be used "as a pretext for discriminatory trade policies or for reduced access to markets" and an affirmation that "all countries agree that uniform environmental standards should not be expected to be applied universally by all countries" unless warranted by transboundary effects.[84]

UN activities to this point still lacked the political and conceptual glue provided by the "sustainable development" concept, which would emerge in the 1980s and reach hegemonic status in UN circles by the 1990s. Nevertheless, they clearly presaged the idea of better law between nations and better development within them, which would become the hallmarks of the UN's environmental agenda.

FROM STOCKHOLM TO RIO: THE EMERGING HEGEMONY
OF LAW AND DEVELOPMENT

The UN's environmental activities expanded in the first decade after the seminal Stockholm Conference. But the response remained largely unco-ordinated, dispersed across rival organs, and constrained by the norma-tive commitment to resource sovereignty, particularly among developing countries. By the early 1990s, however, something akin to a "grand strat-egy" of liberal-internationalist environmentalism would emerge, with two principal thrusts: law, which came to mean negotiating broadly multilateral regulatory regimes to manage specific global-commons and transboundary issues; and development, which signified the greening of development practices through national-level policy reforms, bolstered by foreign aid and technical assistance.

As we shall see, this strategic shift would not originate primarily with UN-based actors or organizations. Nevertheless, the UN provided sev-eral key arenas for its development. The law-and-development approach gained traction within the UN for several reasons. It served the interests of some important states and some broad member-state coalitions. It was embraced by a wide swath of environmental advocates, who lobbied both at the member-state level and directly in UN venues. And it gained important underpinnings of scientific and political legitimacy from some powerful new ideas, including the concepts of "global change" and "sus-tainable development," which institutional entrepreneurs could exploit to support a range of initiatives.

In the process, tendencies already well in evidence were deepened: UN organs linked to the UN's mandates on economic development and inter-national law were better positioned to make the environmental issue their own, compared to those on human rights or international peace and secu-rity. Conceptual, discursive, and institutional frameworks that "develop-mentalized" and "legalized" the environment proceeded apace.

In the Wake of Stockholm

The Stockholm Conference led directly to the creation of UNEP, which was given a mandate to coordinate and catalyze UN activities on the issue. UNEP became the first significant UN organ headquartered in a devel-oping country (Kenya), and the new program charted an agenda with a strong environment-and-development orientation.[85] UNEP's small size, vague mandate, remote location, and funding limitations meant, however, that most of the action would remain centered on the larger and more autonomous specialized agencies, which continued to add environmental components to their work on health, education, science, natural resource management, labor, and a host of other development-related activities. The World Health Organization, for example, resolved in the wake of Stockholm to "make a substantial contribution to the coordinated environment program of the UN system by assuming leadership in the health aspects," stressing support for member states on safe water supplies and waste disposal, pollutant monitoring, environmental health standards setting, and promotion and coordination of appropriate research activities.[86]

The legal strand of the emerging law-and-development approach was less clear initially. The Stockholm Conference framed international cooperation in terms of development assistance, information exchange, and capacity building, rather than stressing the negotiation of regulatory treaties. The number of bilateral environmental agreements did grow noticeably in the decade following Stockholm, much as it did following the subsequent 1992 Earth Summit (figure 2.1). This suggests a possible stimulus effect of the global conference on treaty formation. However, growth in agreements must be compared to growth in the number of member states, which increases the number of actors available to sign bilateral agreements. Figure 2.2 shows the growth in bilateral environmental accords per member state, and thus adjusts for the number of available partners. It shows that the number of accords per UN member state grew

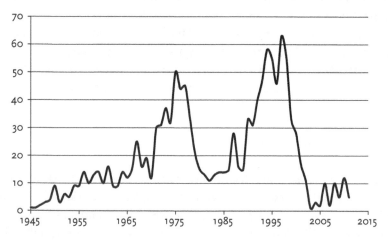

Figure 2.1 Bilateral environmental agreements signed per year, 1945–2011
Note: Excludes amendments and other modifications to existing agreements.
Source: International Environmental Agreements (IEA) Database Project.

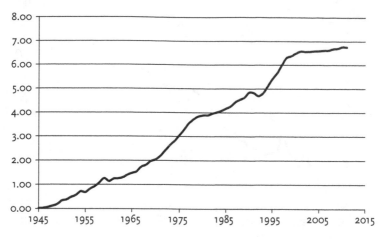

Figure 2.2 Cumulative number of bilateral environmental agreements per member state, 1945–2011
Note: Excludes amendments and other modifications to existing agreements.
Source: International Environmental Agreements (IEA) Database Project.

steadily over time, but that there is no evidence of a Stockholm Conference effect. The same is true if we compare the growing number of agreements to the growing number of dyads, or pairs of states, in the international system. Of course, most pairs of states are unlikely candidates for an environmental accord, as states that are not in geographic proximity with one another are far less likely to negotiate bilateral treaties on most environmental issues. Nevertheless, the number of pairs defines the number of axes along which a bilateral accord could theoretically be reached on any given issue. Figure 2.3, which plots the cumulative number of accords per one hundred dyads, shows that states in this era were filling this available "treaty space" with bilateral agreements at a steady clip—but with no discernible increase in the trajectory of the curve after Stockholm. Bilateral treaty-writing during this period was responding, slowly but steadily, to growing concern about environmental issues, rather than as a particular pulse of agenda-setting keyed by Stockholm.

Multilateral agreements (those with three or more parties), however, follow a different logic. Adding a new member state to the international system does not increase the "treaty space" for a multilateral accord in the same way that it adds new dyadic opportunities for bilateral accords; existing states could have negotiated the same multilateral accord before the new state came along.[87] If anything, multilateral accords become more difficult to negotiate as the number of potential parties grows, given the complicating effects of increasing group size for bargaining dynamics. Thus, an increase in multilateral accords could not be explained away

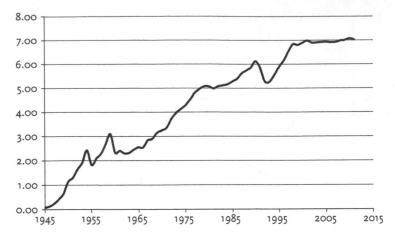

Figure 2.3 Cumulative number of bilateral environmental agreements per 100 member-state dyads, 1945–2011
Note: Excludes amendments and other modifications to existing agreements.
Source: International Environmental Agreements (IEA) Database Project.

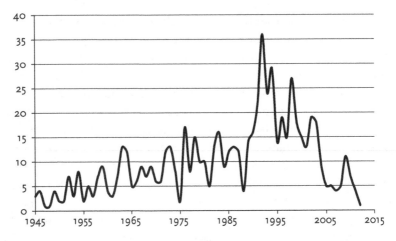

Figure 2.4 Multilateral environmental agreements signed per year, 1945–2011
Note: Excludes amendments and other modifications to existing agreements.
Source: International Environmental Agreements (IEA) Database Project.

simply as the result of growing state numbers. However, the data on multilateral accords do not show a Stockholm effect on the overall pace of multilateral treaty formation. The decade after the conference saw neither an increase in the annual rate of formation of multilateral accords (figure 2.4) nor in the rate of accumulation of multilateral accords per member state (figure 2.5).

Rather, the significance of multilateral accords after Stockholm is in the rise of a particular *type* of agreement—broadly global in focus and

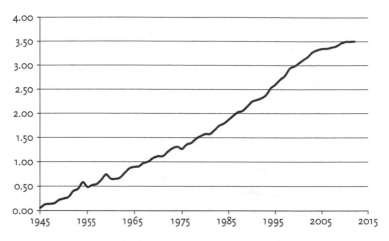

Figure 2.5 Cumulative number of multilateral environmental agreements per member state, 1945–2011
Note: Excludes amendments and other modifications to existing agreements.
Source: International Environmental Agreements (IEA) Database Project.

regulatory intent. Prior to Stockholm, there were some environmental and natural-resource accords with broad, cross-regional membership, primarily related to species conservation and governance of the oceans. Eight such broadly multilateral accords were created in the 1950s (five stemming from the Law of the Sea Conference in 1958) and four more during the 1960s. But the pace accelerated with fifteen new cross-regional or global accords during the 1970s, and another seventeen during the 1980s (Figure 2.6).[88]

These new accords were significant not simply for their more universal membership ambitions but also, in several cases, for placing greater emphasis on restricting and mandating certain behaviors, as opposed to the more traditional practices of articulating conservation aspirations, coordinating state actions, and sharing information. Important post-Stockholm accords of this type include the 1972 *Convention on the Prevention of Marine Pollution by Dumping of Wastes and Other Matter* (also known as the London Convention), the 1973 *Convention on International Trade in Endangered Species of Wild Fauna and Flora* (aka CITES), and the 1973 *International Convention for the Prevention of Pollution from Ships* (aka MARPOL), as well as innovative regional agreements to protect the Baltic Sea (1974), Mediterranean Sea (1976), and Rhine River (1976).

Yet, the emerging law-and-development template for global environmental governance still lacked what might be termed a "grand strategy." According to Steven Bernstein's history of this period, "The set of norms

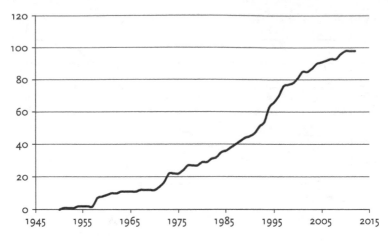

Figure 2.6 Growth of broadly multilateral or "global" environmental accords, by date
Note: Includes multilateral accords that are not limited to a single region or to specific states at a particular level of economic development. Excludes amendments and other modifications to existing agreements.
Source: Compiled by author from information on agreements in the International Environmental Agreements (IEA) Database Project.

produced at Stockholm lacked a unifying theme either to forge consensus between North and South or to capture the imagination of world opinion."[89] There was no unifying conceptual framework, and the enduring tensions around development, resource sovereignty, the NIEO, and historical responsibility for environmental harm continued to inhibit a broad political bargain among UN member states.

Under such circumstances, environmental considerations remained at the margins of relevant political developments. Consider the most ambitious global negotiations in the decade after Stockholm, the UN Conference on the Law of the Sea (UNCLOS). The conference's protracted talks eventually yielded the 1982 *United Nations Convention on the Law of the Sea*, which embraced the notion of the high seas as the "common heritage of mankind," a pre-Stockholm legal concept emerging from the law of war and the uses of outer space. The convention also created a general obligation "to protect and preserve the marine environment."[90] The core impact of UNCLOS, however, was not to create a framework for sustaining the global marine commons but rather to carve up marine resource rights. It did this by extending coastal states' exclusive economic zones far offshore, as well as capturing a share of deep-sea resource rights for states unable to engage in deep-sea fishing or seabed mining.[91] The final accord, which was strongly shaped by the NIEO agenda, was essentially an exercise in mapping permanent sovereignty over natural resources (PSNR) onto emergent possibilities for marine resource exploitation.

Environmental issues remained highly contentious among member states during this period. Controversies flared at the 1982 meeting of UNEP's Governing Council, which also served as the official UN commemoration of Stockholm's tenth anniversary. The council acknowledged progress on environmental awareness and in the development of basic tools in environmental science, law, and administration, but expressed disappointment over sluggish implementation of the Stockholm Action Plan.[92] The meeting also reflected the enduring divisions over the NIEO, and underscored the polarizing perception of different environmental agendas in the global North and global South.[93] Under such circumstances, a coherent political strategy for promoting environmental action remained elusive.

FROM ACCUMULATED PRACTICE TO GRAND STRATEGY

If the decade from Stockholm 1972 to Nairobi 1982 saw the elements of the law-and-development approach accumulate in an uncoordinated and disjointed manner, the next ten years, culminating in the 1992 UNCED summit in Rio de Janeiro, saw them coalesce into liberal internationalism's grand strategy for global environmental governance. Several important developments produced this acceleration. One was the rise of "sustainable development" as a politically powerful and broadly unifying concept, which allowed certain forms of environmental action to flourish without threatening the strategic priorities of powerful economic actors or upsetting the existing UN landscape. A second key development, also on the conceptual front, was the emergence of a new science of "global change," which stressed the planet as an integrated, dynamic ecosystem and called attention to key processes therein that were at risk of disruption from human activities. The embrace of this concept by an important segment of environmentalists, scientists, and other advocates of global environmental governance helped push global treaty negotiations to the top of the international environmental agenda.

The concepts of sustainable development and global change took different paths to UN salience. Sustainable development emerged directly from UN-affiliated activities, and was designed from the start to bridge the North-South political gap exposed at Stockholm. Global change was bred largely in the scientific community and popularized by environmentalists with few direct ties to the UN, but who subsequently took their newfound political agenda of global environmental governance into UN forums, both directly and via member states. Despite these different routes to significance, the combination of sustainable development and global change helped unlock political possibilities for environmental action, particularly when linked to the UN's mandate domains of international law and economic development. The concepts came together at, and were given further momentum by, the 1992 UNCED conference in Rio. UNCED would finish the consolidation of the law-and-development approach as the hegemonic framework for the UN's environmental activity—and arguably constituted its high-water mark in terms of acceptance, acclaim, and political momentum.

The Rise of Sustainable Development

The origin of the concept of sustainable development is usually traced to the World Conservation Strategy (WCS), developed by the mixed-membership[94] international environmental organization IUCN in 1980. Intended as a strategic framework for governments, conservationists, and development practitioners, the WCS was developed at the behest of UNEP, and included input from WWF, FAO, and UNESCO. Its core message was that, for biodiversity conservation efforts to work, economic development must be made ecologically and socially sustainable. This in turn meant that development "must take account of social and ecological factors, as well as economic ones; of the living and non-living resource base; and of the long term as well as the short term advantages and disadvantages of alternative actions."[95] The WCS stressed threats to biodiversity stemming from population growth, prevailing development practices, and poverty, including the "hundreds of millions of rural people in developing countries, including 500 million malnourished and 800 million destitute" who are "compelled to destroy the resources necessary to free them from starvation and poverty."[96] The report called for economic development in poor countries and reduced consumption in affluent societies as ways to reduce pressures on ecosystems. The WCS was also a harbinger of a new emphasis on global framework accords: it stressed the trans-sovereign character of threats to biodiversity, the weakness of existing international agreements, and the need for strong international law as "perhaps the most important form of international action."[97] Following the WCS, the General Assembly in 1982 passed a resolution endorsing the World Charter for Nature and embracing the concept of sustainability.[98]

Although the WCS put the concept of sustainable development into play, the key step in its legitimization was a high-level UN panel, the World Commission on Environment and Development (WCED). In 1983 the General Assembly endorsed a proposal from UNEP's Governing Council calling for such a panel, and tasked the WCED with proposing "long-term environmental strategies for achieving sustainable development to the year 2000 and beyond."[99] Gro Harlem Brundtland, the prime minister of Norway and formerly that country's environmental minister, was appointed chair (leading the body to be known popularly as the Brundtland Commission).

As a diagnosis of global environmental problems and a set of policy recommendations for response, the Brundtland Commission's influential 1987 report, *Our Common Future*, actually broke very little new ground. Several of its key themes—enhancing national capabilities, improving national policy frameworks, and strengthening international cooperation—were reflected in *Only One Earth*, the report commissioned fifteen years earlier for the Stockholm Conference.[100] Nor did the legal principles it advocated break much new ground: the commission focused mostly on the well-established problems of managing transboundary harm from one state to another and of building on customary legal norms of equity, liability, compensation, and nondiscrimination.[101] The report's assessment of the global commons emphasized the well-traveled political ground of the oceans and outer space, and had strikingly little to say about the emerging "global commons" issues of climate, stratospheric ozone, and biodiversity, which would soon dominate the global environmental agenda.

Even the recommendations that pushed the UN policy envelope were not so new. The WCED's calls for greater involvement of scientific groups and civil society in international deliberations, partnerships with industry, the strengthening of UNEP, and greater use of risk-assessment tools, while innovative for their time, were hardly radical notions by the late 1980s. As many observers have noted, the report's advocacy of rapid economic growth in developing countries was a departure from environmental advocacy rooted in the "limits to growth" mentality that pervaded 1970s environmentalism.[102] But this too had a clear UN lineage: the 1972 Stockholm Declaration, the G-77's 1974 Cocoyoc Declaration on Environment and Development, the 1980 World Conservation Strategy, and the 1982 Nairobi Declaration all flagged poverty as a core threat to the environment, to be addressed through economic development and the opening of Northern markets to Southern products.[103]

The Brundtland report's impact came not from these conventional calls for action, but rather from its legitimization and popularization of the politically powerful concept of sustainable development. Although the concept is used in different ways throughout the report, the most frequently cited definition is development that "meets the needs of the present without compromising the ability of future generations to meet their own needs."[104] Thusly defined, the concept was actually not very different from the idea of "eco-development" that had emerged within UNEP in the late 1970s.[105]

Much ink has been spilled debating the concept of sustainability and its relevance to development.[106] Many environmental scientists have criticized the term for its generality, vagueness, and lack of precise specification. Some segments of the environmental movement have viewed it as a failure to come to grips with the consequences of economic growth, expanding consumption, and global capitalism. Some justice advocates and grassroots development groups have challenged its emphasis on equity between generations, suggesting that this obscures already-existing inequities of the current world system. Despite these criticisms, the concept's ability to create a bridge beyond the North-South polarization of Stockholm was a key element in consolidation of the law-and-development approach. The sustainable-development rubric would allow for convergence on certain forms of environmental action, without threatening the strategic priorities of powerful actors in an increasingly neoliberal world economy.

Moreover, the concept thrived not simply by being a vague formulation that offered something for everyone. As Steven Bernstein's evaluation of the history of the concept has shown, it emerged from the convergence of distinct "Northern" and "Southern" trajectories of environment-development thinking, and thus tapped specific interests on both sides of the environment-development divide. The Brundtland Commission's emphasis on the ecological harm of Third World debt and international trade restrictions, combined with its call for renewed economic growth, aligned with the G-77's agenda of global economic reforms. At the same time, the emphasis on domestic policy reforms in the South resonated strongly with liberal-internationalist environmental aims in the North.[107]

A key to finding this space for compromise was reframing (some might say capturing) the environment as fundamentally a development issue. Pratap Chatterjee and Matthias Finger noted,

> The only new element is that development is now looked at from a planetary or global perspective. Instead of stressing the development of a given society or country, the stress is now on the development of the planet as a whole. In that sense, the Brundtland Commission . . . has managed to make the development discourse universal. . . . [T]he commission . . . thinks that the major limits to growth are not natural resources, but the state of technology and social

organization. Output limits are only of interest to the Commission if they risk damaging the resource base.[108]

Similarly, Bernstein notes that "for WCED, the synthesis of environmental and developmental goals suggested that governance of both rests on a common normative foundation, with economic growth at its center. Stockholm merely placed the two sets of interests side by side."[109] This reframing can be seen in the Brundtland Commission's selective attention to global political economy, which emphasized factors inhibiting or distorting growth patterns in the global South (Northern trade protectionism, external debt) while largely overlooking global consumption patterns, the regulatory challenges inherent in economic globalization, or the environmental ramifications of transnational commodity chains and global production platforms.

In theory, a focus on environmental human rights could have served as a corrective balance to this "developmentalization" of the environmental issue, by making the environmental rights of people, both individually and in local communities, a central responsibility of governance. Thus, the dwindling of a rights-based discourse during this period (as discussed below and in chapter 4) is an important development that warrants explanation. As Balakrishnan Rajagopal has documented, the UN was undergoing during this period a parallel process of the "developmentalization" of human rights discourse and action.[110] By the early 1980s, the NIEO quest for global equity via economic redistribution and reform of global trade and investment rules was in retreat. The neoliberalism of Reagan and Thatcher was politically ascendant in the North, and Third World debt was proving to be a crippling form of Northern leverage. At the 1981 Cancun Summit on International Development Issues, the United States and like-minded nations blunted efforts for a broad North-South multilateral economic agreement, rejecting the NIEO-friendly recommendations of the Independent Commission on International Development Issues (aka the Brandt Commission after its chair, former West German chancellor Willie Brandt).

In this increasingly unfavorable context, the G-77 made a strategic shift away from the NIEO's global-bargaining strategy and toward affirming a "right to development," which the General Assembly codified in 1986. As Rajagopal has documented, an important consequence of this shift was to channel much of the human rights dialogue at the UN into the context of North-South struggles over development. This "developmentalization" of human rights only accelerated as the Cold War wound down. With the right to development adhering to states, resource-strapped

Southern governments and the intergovernmental organizations working with them became accountable not for providing economic, social, and cultural rights around natural resources, but rather for the "progressive realization" of development. Struggles for rights to breathable air, drinkable water, and the like thus remained largely captive of business-as-usual development approaches, sprinkled with reforms such as environmental impact assessment and modest funding for positive environmental projects.[111]

The Political Evolution of International Environmental Law

Treaty-based initiatives also underwent significant shifts in this period. As discussed previously, Stockholm had charted an international legal course stressing information sharing, global monitoring, and cooperative efforts to build national capacity. The run-up to the 1992 Earth Summit, in contrast, saw increasing strategic emphasis on a particular type of international accord—global in scope, regulatory in ambition, and issue-specific in focus. Behind the push for this particular type of treaty law was an emerging environmental science of "global change." This new paradigm stressed the idea of the planet as a dynamic, integrated system with tight couplings among oceans, atmosphere, biosphere, and the human activities therein. *One Earth One Future*, a 1990 publication of the US National Academy of Sciences, reflected the core of this new framework:

> The earth's land masses, oceans and atmosphere, and biological communities are increasingly seen by scientists, as well as by the public, as part of a unified system. . . . This new approach to the study of our planet is referred to as earth system science. Its practitioners strive to understand how the world works on a global scale by describing how its parts and their interactions evolved, how they function today, and how they may be expected to function in both the near and distant future. In this light, the earth system is seen as a set of interacting subsystems characterized by processes that vary on spatial scales from millimeters to the circumference of the earth, and on time scales from seconds to billions of years. It has become ever more clear that despite wide separations in distance and time, many processes are connected, and that a change in one component can propagate through the entire system.[112]

The new science of global change focused the environmental agenda on a particular type of "global" problem: the perturbation of major Earth systems, including the global climate; the planet's thinning layer of stratospheric ozone; and key terrestrial biomes such as forests or arid lands. The difference from previous ways of constructing the global environmental problematique is striking, and can be seen by contrasting this new agenda with that of the Brundtland Commission, which worked in the mid-1980s and did not feel the full force of the new science of global change. Their report identified space, Antarctica, and the oceans as the principal global commons, and did not apply that concept to such core agenda items of "global change" science as climate, ozone, biodiversity, or tropical forests.

A prototype global-change issue during this period was the threat to Earth's stratospheric ozone layer, which filters damaging ultraviolet radiation. Scientists identified damage to the ozone layer in the 1970s and by the mid-1980s were increasingly in agreement that the culprit was widespread use of chlorofluorocarbons and other industrial chemicals. A series of international accords wove an increasingly tight regulatory net around the problem, and became a powerful model for advocates of regulatory agreements of global scope.[113] The ozone accords reflected the twin elements of the new global legalism. First, they set in motion a process that scholars have termed "progressive legalization": starting with "soft" cooperation around general principles, then moving to a loose "framework" agreement defining the problem and generalized responsibilities, and culminating in a series of ever-tighter measures fueled by more precise science and broader political consensus.[114] Second, the ozone regime took a narrowly functional, sector-specific definition of the problem to be controlled, targeting a specific family of culprit chemicals rather than industrial pollution, chemical use, or atmospheric contamination more generally. One result of this narrow problem definition was that sector-specific costs of pollution control and the emergence of new technological options became the key parameters shaping the evolution of the regulatory regime.[115]

Global-change science offered a rationale for global-scale regulatory agreements—but science alone was not enough. Political impetus came from the decision of several major environmental groups in the United States and Europe to prioritize the new agenda. Kirkpatrick Sale's history of American environmentalism describes an intensive, if somewhat inchoate, "new international strategy" during these years:

Greenpeace and the National Wildlife Federation, for example, fought for laws to ban international trade in toxic chemicals, Earth Island went to the defense of Central American forests, [Environmental Defense Fund] pushed for an international ban on dumping plastic waste at sea, Greenpeace took an activist position on the International Whaling Commission, newer groups like the Global Greenhouse Network and the Better World Society drew public attention to global warming, the Campaign to End Hunger and LIFE (Love is Feeding Everyone) worked on malnutrition and starvation worldwide, and Conservation International and World Resources Institute studied and initiated environment-protective "debt-for-nature swaps."[116]

Within this hodgepodge of international activity, some of the newer organizations—including Environmental Defense Fund (founded in 1967), Natural Resources Defense Council (1970), and Conservation International (1987)—were quickest to embrace the "global change" agenda. These organizations had a more science-based ethos than older American conservation groups born in the late nineteenth and early twentieth centuries; they also had fewer sunk costs in the traditional domestic environmental agenda. They were joined by other relatively new groups rooted in broader international networks, including World Wildlife Fund (1961), Friends of the Earth (1969), and Greenpeace (1971). There were, of course, ideological divisions within this emerging American brand of international environmentalism, which would be exposed when the movement splintered badly in the mid-1990s over the proposed North American Free Trade Agreement (NAFTA).[117] But the run-up to the 1992 UNCED meeting offered favorable terrain for the new "global change" agenda: a record-breaking heat wave swept across much of the United States in 1988, leading the influential American magazine *Time* to confer its "newsmaker of the year" award upon "The Endangered Earth."

Europe's movement during this period took on a somewhat more politicized shade of green, developing as it did primarily through political parties rather than the American-style nongovernmental organization (NGO).[118] Green parties in Europe saw strong growth in the 1980s, followed by the increasing incorporation or co-optation of their agendas by mainstream parties.[119] Despite this different political trajectory, Europe's green movement underwent a similar globalization of focus. The global dimension of the antitoxics campaign was a natural outgrowth of the Greens' paradigm of Cold War toxification, and climate change and the rain forests readily found their place alongside traditional green themes such as antinuclear advocacy.

Of course, the modern environmental movement in the industrialized world had always relied on planetary imagery to state its case. Photographic images of Earth from space, first taken in 1968, quickly reached iconic status. But the global narrative of 1960s and 1970s environmental activism was mainly one of crowding and scarcity, seen in the titles of several of the era's definitive texts: *Spaceship Earth, The Population Bomb, The Limits to Growth, Only One Earth, The Closing Circle.* The new science of global change offered a different narrative—of sensitive, life-sustaining processes that were easily disrupted by human actions (and for some, perhaps even of symbiosis between living and nonliving matter so tightly coupled as to suggest a living Earth itself).[120] Moreover, while the global symbolism of the earlier era stressed macro trends of population growth and resource depletion, the new focus was on specific, global-scale environmental systems and processes for which some sort of regulatory arrangement of broadly international scope seemed necessary. Thus, Chatterjee and Finger have described the new globalism of the 1980s as part of a move away from a broad eco-political critique of industrial development and toward a new paradigm of "planetary management."[121] In this view, the new science of global change resonated with the more technocratic tendencies of an environmental movement that was by this time increasingly mainstreamed, bureaucratized, and involved in "insider" politics (lobbying in Washington, party politics in Europe). For this wing of environmentalism, international environmental law simply meant applying at the global level the same regulatory tools of environmental management for which environmentalists had been fighting on a national scale.

The impact of global change's science-turned-advocacy can be seen in the data on international environmental treaties presented previously. The number of existing multilateral accords grew fairly steadily from the end of World War II through the late 1980s, but then exploded in the decade from 1989 to 1998 (figure 2.4), with 216 new multilateral conventions and protocols during this period. Within this treaty-writing boom, "global" accords (defined as not limited to a single region or a narrow club of states) saw particularly strong growth (figure 2.6).

UNCED as the High-Water Mark

The 1992 UN Conference on Environment and Development (UNCED), known popularly as the Earth Summit, marked a convergence of these three trends—the "sustainable developmentalization" of the environmental issue, the subsuming of human rights to a statist North-South discourse on development, and the prioritization of global regulatory accords. Held in Rio de Janeiro, UNCED was an unprecedented global gathering; it featured the heads of state for nearly all UN members and a panoply of civil-society organizations that straddled the formal and informal activities.

UNCED produced half-a-dozen major outputs, the form of which clearly reflected the now-consolidated grand strategy of liberal environmentalism. Better law between nations? UNCED finalized high-profile global treaties on climate change and biodiversity, two issues that had risen to the top of the agenda of global-change science and internationalized environmentalism, and narrowly missed on a third, forests (settling for a nonbinding statement of forest principles). Better development within nations? UNCED yielded *Agenda 21*, a 351-page action plan for making development sustainable, with the "means of implementation" stressing national initiatives on awareness, capacity building, and policy reform, supplemented by the traditional development-regime practices of international finance and technology transfer.

While privileging law and development, the products of Rio reflected also a systematic failure to build links to the UN mandates on human rights and international peace and security. The forest principles agreement affirms sovereign rights to convert forests to other uses, while urging conservation, better management, and sustainable forest development and calling for international cost-sharing to make it so. But no reference is made to regulating the cross-border commodity chains that harvest and process timber for the global market, or the impact of "converting" forests on local rights and livelihoods, or the violence and illegality that infuse a substantial portion of the world forest trade.[122] The *Convention on Biological Diversity* recognizes biodiversity conservation as the "common concern of humankind," embraces a paradigm of sustainable use, and calls for transfers of funding and technology to help poor countries comply. But it conceptualizes rights solely in terms of the sovereign rights of states to make use of their national biological resources. Thus, it avoids framing the needs, interests, and concerns of local communities as in any way entailing *rights*, while vesting at the national level all authority for determining access to biological resources. The convention makes equity in sharing the benefits of biodiversity (read: biotechnology) primarily a matter of relations between the "contracting parties" (nation-states), while merely "encouraging" equitable sharing of benefits derived from local and indigenous knowledge about biodiversity.[123] The convention contains a dispute resolution mechanism for disputes among parties to the agreement, but provides no guidance on transnational stakeholder conflicts that involve indigenous communities, transnational corporations, scientific groups, or consumers.

Indeed, Rio marked the culmination of a steady backpedaling from the idea of environmental rights. The 1972 Stockholm Declaration had stated, "Man has the fundamental right to freedom, equality and adequate conditions of life, in an environment of a quality that permits a life of dignity and well-being."[124] Fifteen years later, the Brundtland Commission took a more equivocal position. Among its proposed legal principles was the idea that "all human beings have the fundamental right to an environment adequate for their health and well-being."[125] But the commission largely banished rights-based analysis from its discussion of core issues in the report. UNCED's Rio Declaration stepped back even further from affirming such rights, conceding merely that "human beings are at the center of concerns for sustainable development. They are entitled to a healthy and productive life in harmony with nature."[126] In August 1991, at the third preparatory conference for UNCED in 1991, the G-77 blocked an effort to have UNCED adopt a more expansive "Earth Charter," analogous to the Universal Declaration of Human Rights.[127]

As with rights, so with peace. The Brundtland Commission had devoted a chapter to "peace, security, development and the environment" (stressing environmental change as a source of conflict, and conflict as a threat to sustainable development).[128] But UNCED's *Agenda 21* refers to peace exactly once in its 351 pages (a passing reference to the importance of settling international disputes peacefully).[129] The document contains no recommendations for addressing, or even acknowledging, links between environmental change or natural resource use and conflict, war, violence, or peace. The Rio Declaration did link environmental issues explicitly to international peace and security (table 2.1), including the promising observation that "peace, development and environmental protection are interdependent and indivisible" (Principle 25). The implicit logic of the conference, however, was to treat peace as a natural byproduct of

---

Table 2.1   RIO DECLARATION PRINCIPLES ADDRESSING
PEACE AND SECURITY

Principle 24	"Warfare is inherently destructive of sustainable development. States shall therefore respect international law providing protection for the environment in times of armed conflict and cooperate in its further development, as necessary."
Principle 25	"Peace, development and environmental protection are interdependent and indivisible."
Principle 26	"States shall resolve all their environmental disputes peacefully and by appropriate means in accordance with the Charter of the United Nations."

Source: United Nations Conference on Environment and Development, *Rio Declaration on Environment and Development* (1992).

interstate cooperation. The idea that peace is a public good put at risk by environmental damage was not in evidence; no political energy was expended on institution building for the purpose of resolving environmental or natural-resource conflicts; nor did the idea of building peace through strategically targeted efforts of environmental cooperation enter into the intergovernmental deliberations.

Nothing but Neoliberalism?

Some observers have argued that the Earth Summit simply marked the furtherance of a neoliberally tinged "market environmentalism." Bernstein, focusing on the evolution of governance norms, has argued that Brundtland-style sustainable development is significant primarily as a way station on the road from Stockholm to market environmentalism.[130] Chatterjee and Finger stress UNCED's market-friendly, technocratic embrace of environmental managerialism, which failed to question the core tenets of growth-oriented capitalism.[131] Newell emphasizes the role of UNCED's global accords in structuring market competition, facilitating strategic investments in technology development, and establishing corporate-friendly property rights to nature.[132]

As a description of the general direction global environmentalism has taken in recent decades, these observations ring true. Indeed, the inability to create an effective, legitimate model of global regulation will be discussed in the next chapter as a core flaw in the law-and-development approach, with market-friendly liberal environmentalism an important manifestation of that failure. But to understand the institutionalization of the law-and-development approach at the UN, it is important that UNCED not be read solely in these terms. UNCED played a critical role in completing the process of grounding the UN's environmental efforts overwhelmingly in the mandate pillars of development and international law, and in sealing a broad political bargain in those terms among member states.[133] In doing so, it helped to saddle the UN with a framework that, whatever its merits, cannot effectively engage some of today's most pressing global environmental challenges.

Evidence of this limitation is also seen in the fact that the most salient "market oriented" environmental activity has taken place outside the UN orbit, in settings such as the World Trade Organization, the World Bank Group, and the OECD. This fact underscores the UN's increasing marginalization on environmental issues. To be sure, one reason for this bypassing may be that the UN takes a kinder, gentler approach to law and

development than these other institutions, in an era that is not particularly kind or gentle. The UN embraces a somewhat more human-faced
development paradigm, based on Amartya Sen and "human development"
rather than the more neoliberal variant of, say, the World Bank. And its
commitment to international environmental law pays somewhat more
attention to regulation than to the WTO's emphasis on property rights
and regulatory minimalism. But the larger problem remains, as we shall
see in the next chapter: without bringing to bear its mandates on rights
and peace, the UN is unable to grapple effectively with the most contentious transnational dimensions of global environmental politics.

CONCLUSION: STOCKHOLM TO RIO ... BUT ALSO
SAN FRANCISCO TO STOCKHOLM

Chronicles of the UN's environmental activities usually begin with the 1972
Stockholm Conference. According to the conference's Secretary-General,
Maurice Strong, Stockholm was "the beginning of a 'new journey of hope'
where we put the environment firmly on the global agenda."[134] There is
some truth to this claim: through the mid-1960s, UN activities on pollution or conservation were mostly limited to the specific concerns of a few
specialized agencies such as FAO, WHO, and WMO. This picture changed
quickly as public anxiety about the environment exploded across Western
Europe and the United States, with the Stockholm Conference following
in short order.

Yet to start the story in 1972 is to miss important prior developments
that have shaped how the UN engages environmental issues. Prior to the
UN's environmental era, the new organization and the postwar global
economic order went through far-reaching and fundamental adjustments
related to natural resources. Decolonization forced the UN to wrestle
with contentious questions—at times escalating into white-hot political
controversy—about the meaning of national sovereignty over natural
resources. These early debates, in turn, had important ramifications for
the development of international environmental law and for the blunted
relationship between environmental concerns and the UN's human rights
mandate.

Also prior to Stockholm, several of the UN's specialized agencies and
programs launched projects to promote natural resource management as
part of national economic development strategies. These activities created
a natural platform for subsequent environmental initiatives and a set
of vested organizational interests in framing environmental challenges

in particular ways. In contrast, the organizational apparatus on the peace-and-security side of the UN, and in particular the UN Security Council, failed to act on several opportunities to address linkages between natural resources and the international peace mandate. The same was largely true for the human rights-related apparatus of the UN, which had not yet experienced the bureaucratic-organizational expansion marking today's human rights system, and which remained at the time overwhelmingly state-based.

If organizational incentives tell part of this story, then so do ideas. Powerful ideational concepts of the environment as a set of natural resources for national economic development, and of resource rights as adhering to newly independent nations, channeled the UN's environmental agenda primarily into the law and development domains. Potentially powerful alternative ways of framing the environment as a human right or a peace issue were decades away from obtaining anything close to authoritative status.

Thus, by the time the global environment took center stage at the UN in the 1970s, there was already a deeply embedded script, including some well-established ways of thinking, a legal and policy framework, and an accompanying array of organizational interests and procedures. As a result, the environment slid fairly quickly into the more accommodating mandate domains of national development and international law, while lagging behind in the domains of human rights and peace and security. By the latter 1980s, another surge of environmental concern—culminating in the Brundtland Commission, the sustainability movement, and the 1992 Earth Summit—would, for the most part, follow this path of least resistance across the UN landscape, deepening rather than altering the dominant approach.

With this understanding of the history in hand, chapter 3 now turns to a summary assessment of the successes and failures of the law-and-development approach to global environmental governance. The strategy is first assessed in its own terms: has it achieved its core aims of better environmental law between nations and greener development within them? As my assessment will suggest, it has indeed been difficult to, in the words of UNEP director Achim Steiner, "legislate sustainable development." A second layer of critique will argue that, even where it has taken root, the strategy faces increasingly severe limits in a globalized world political economy. Simply put, better law between states and better development within them, while essential, fails to address an increasingly important swath of the global environmental reality of the twenty-first century.

CHAPTER 3

The Limits of Law and Development and the Case for Peace and Rights

It's not with environmental ministers that you achieve sustainable development.

Ignacy Sachs, *special adviser to the Secretary-General for the UNCHE and UNCED conferences*

LAW AND DEVELOPMENT: ARE WE GETTING THERE?

How well has the UN's law-and-development paradigm of global environmental governance performed? This chapter addresses the question on several levels. It begins by taking the paradigm's definition of the task at face value: To what extent have the efforts of the past few decades produced better environmental law between nations and more sustainable development within them? I will argue that, while several important accomplishments must be acknowledged, the limits of progress and a generalized loss of momentum across the UN system are increasingly apparent. The chapter then develops a broader critique, stressing how the world political-economic system generates environmental problems that sit beyond the reach of the law-and-development paradigm's primary tools. Building on this critique, the chapter develops more fully the argument asserted in chapter 1: that stronger emphasis on the missing mandate elements of peace and human rights offers an important corrective.

Better Environmental Law between Nations?

The global legalism that emerged as a key element of grand strategy in the late 1980s and early 1990s has added several useful international accords to the toolkit of global environmental governance. The planet is better off for having broadly multilateral treaties on the ozone layer, ocean pollution, endangered species, and persistent organic pollutants, to name but a few. While the effectiveness of international environmental law has varied, as discussed below, there are certainly many examples of effective accords. In a summary assessment, researcher Norichika Kanie reminds us that

> describing the difficulty of the endeavor should still not blind us, as analysts, to the fact that amazing accomplishments have been achieved multilaterally over the last 30 years. . . . [H]undreds of MEAs have been adopted. Many of these MEAs have actually been effective at improving the environment by inducing states to change policies in a manner conducive to a cleaner environment. Stratospheric ozone pollution has been reduced. European acid rain is greatly reduced. Oil spills in the oceans are down in number and volume. Considering the pace with which economies have grown in the last 30 years, these should be recognized as considerable accomplishments.[1]

Nonetheless, there is substantial evidence that the international legal side of law and development has met neither its purveyors' expectations nor the planet's needs. In the effort to stitch together a web of global environmental governance, one treaty-strand at a time, three problems stand out. First, adding a sufficient number of strands to the web has proven difficult. As the political climate for environmental diplomacy has steadily worsened, the rate of multilateral accord formation has declined precipitously. Second, it has been difficult to strengthen the individual strands over time; the strategy of progressive legalization, or relying on incremental improvements to initially weak "framework" accords, has often been impossible to execute. Third, and as a result, the strength of many existing strands in the web is questionable; studies of treaty-regime effectiveness draw at best a mixed picture.

Figure 3.1 shows a precipitous drop-off in the number of multilateral environmental agreements reached annually over the past two decades. (Multilateral agreements are those with three or more parties; bilateral accords, which follow a very different political dynamic, are discussed separately, below). Unlike prior global summits in Stockholm (1972) and Rio (1992), the 2002 World Summit on Sustainable Development (WSSD) in Johannesburg yielded no noticeable stimulus for multilateral accords, particularly at the supraregional or global levels. The decade after the 1972 Stockholm Conference (1973–1982) yielded 101 new multilateral accords, and the decade after the 1992 Earth Summit (1993–2002) yielded 193.

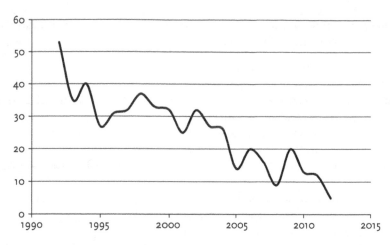

Figure 3.1 Annual multilateral environmental agreements and amendments, 1992–2011
Note: "Agreements" includes new conventions and new protocols to existing conventions; "amendments" includes amendments and modifications to preexisting conventions and protocols.
Source: International Environmental Agreements (IEA) Database Project.

In 1998 alone, 27 new multilateral accords and protocols were reached. These included a pair of accords with broadly global significance (one on prior informed consent on hazardous chemical shipments, the other on citizen access to environmental information, public participation, and justice), as well as regional agreements on topics ranging from environmental preservation in the Alps to water in Central Asia to protecting Caribbean sea turtles.

In contrast, there have been only fourteen such agreements reached in the decade-plus since Johannesburg (table 3.1). Most of these accords simply fill in details on existing treaty regimes; only one, the 2013 *Minamata Convention on Mercury*, combines broad scope, a new issue-area, and significant environmental rulemaking. Perhaps the strongest evidence for a loss of momentum is that there are, as of this writing, no significant, ongoing talks that promise to yield another such accord on a previously unaddressed challenge.

Since the 2002 Johannesburg summit, the regional level has fared somewhat better than the global, with potentially significant accords on nature conservation in Africa; marine environmental protection for the Caspian, Mediterranean, and Black Seas and the western Indian Ocean; sustainable development accords for Central Asia and the Lake Victoria subregion of East Africa; and several new agreements on shared river basins. Some have argued that the regional scale is emerging as a new zone of innovation in global environmental governance.[2] But much of the enthusiasm for the "new regionalism" can be attributed to the profound

Table 3.1 SUPRAREGIONAL OR GLOBAL MULTILATERAL ENVIRONMENTAL
ACCORDS SINCE THE 2002 WORLD SUMMIT ON SUSTAINABLE DEVELOPMENT

2013	Minamata Convention on Mercury
2010	Nagoya-Kuala Lumpur Supplementary Protocol on Liability and Redress
2010	Nagoya Protocol on Access to Genetic Resources and the Fair and Equitable Sharing of Benefits Arising from their Utilization
2009	Agreement on Port State Measures to Prevent, Deter and Eliminate Illegal, Unreported and Unregulated Fishing
2009	2009 International Convention for the Safe and Environmentally Sound Recycling of Ships
2009	Statute for the International Renewable Energy Agency
2007	International Convention on the Removal of Wrecks
2006	International Tropical Timber Agreement
2005	Protocol of Amendments to the Convention on the International Hydrographic Organization
2004	Constitution of the Global Crop Diversity Trust
2004	Agreement for the Establishment of the Global Crop Diversity Trust
2004	International Convention for the Control and Management of Ships' Ballast Water and Sediments
2003	World Health Organization Framework Convention on Tobacco Control
2003	Protocol to Amend the 1992 International Convention on the Establishment of an International Fund for Compensation for Oil Pollution Damage

Note: Excludes regional agreements. Includes new conventions and new protocols to existing conventions; excludes amendments and modifications to preexisting conventions and protocols (unless amendments are embodied in a new protocol).
Source: Compiled from data in International Environmental Agreements (IEA) Database Project.

sense of drift in global environmental diplomacy, and barriers to collective action at the regional scale are far from trivial.[3]

Bilateral diplomacy has fared no better (figure 3.2). The annual rate of bilateral agreement formation showed some growth in the 1990s (a period of dramatic post–Cold War expansion in the number of UN member states). But the annual number of bilateral accords reached has seen a precipitous decline in the last decade, reaching almost zero early in the twenty-first century and limping along at fewer than ten accords per year since then.

Of course, tallying the number of agreements over time is only a crude indicator of the vigor of international environmental diplomacy. In theory, decline could even be a byproduct of success, in that an increasingly robust and comprehensive body of international environmental law might require fewer new accords as it reduced the number of problems to be solved. Indeed, a key element of the "progressive legalization" strategy

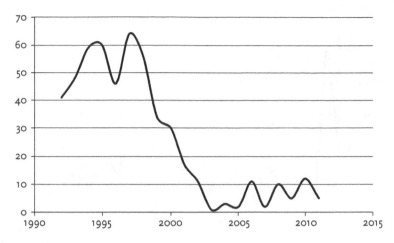

Figure 3.2 Annual bilateral environmental agreements and amendments, 1992–2011
Note: "Agreements" includes new conventions and new protocols to existing conventions; "amendments" includes amendments and modifications to preexisting conventions and protocols.
Source: International Environmental Agreements (IEA) Database Project.

that emerged in the 1990s was to work initially for loose and broadly palatable framework agreements, which could then be tightened in subsequent protocols, amendments, and other modifications. Progressive legalization presumes that agreements will take on some specific aspects of strengthening over time: enhanced *obligation*, in the sense of increasingly binding rules; enhanced *precision*, in the sense of increasingly specific, explicit, and unambiguous rules; and enhanced *delegation*, in the sense of assigning authority to apply and interpret rules.[4]

This was the strategy pursued successfully in the treaty regime on stratospheric ozone; a highly general and noncommittal initial accord (the 1985 *Vienna Convention for the Protection of the Ozone Layer*) was followed by a cascade of increasingly ambitious targets and tightened rules that started with the *Montreal Protocol on Substances that Deplete the Ozone Layer* (1987) and continued with seventeen amendments and adjustments to the protocol between 1990 and 2007. This approach was to some extent replicated in the *UN Framework Convention on Climate Change* (1992), which was followed by the Kyoto Protocol (1997), and in the 1992 *Convention on Biological Diversity* (CBD), which was followed by the *Cartagena Protocol on Biosafety* (2000) and the *Nagoya Protocol on Access to Genetic Resources and the Fair and Equitable Sharing of Benefits Arising from their Utilization* (2010).[5]

In the aggregate, however, the incrementalist strategy has fared poorly in sustaining innovation. As the rate of new agreement formation has declined, so too has the rate of amending and otherwise adjusting existing

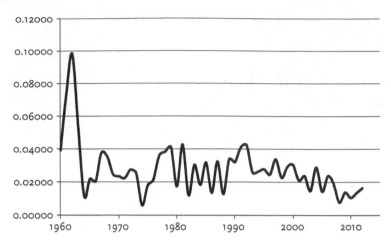

Figure 3.3 Number of amendments annually per existing environmental agreement, 1960–2012
Note: "Agreements" includes new conventions and new protocols to existing conventions; "amendments" includes amendments and modifications to preexisting conventions and protocols.
Source: International Environmental Agreements (IEA) Database Project.

agreements. As a crude measure of the dynamism seen in the existing body of agreements, figure 3.3 shows the "amendment rate" over time for multilateral environmental accords, calculated by dividing the number of new amendments and other adjustments adopted in a given year by the number of existing agreements that were available to be amended. The figure reveals a distinct pattern: the rate at which existing accords were amended increased for the Stockholm-to-Rio period, but has declined steadily in the two decades following the 1992 Earth Summit. During the late 1980s and early 1990s, roughly 4 percent of existing agreements were being amended annually. By 2010, the rate had fallen fourfold, to about 1 percent annually. For a strategy premised on improving effectiveness through progressive legalization, the declining momentum to modify and improve the provisions of existing international accords is a significant problem.

The real question, of course, is how effective the body of international environmental law has been. The declining rate of agreement formation and the decrease in the rate of innovation through amending existing agreements are worrisome, but speak to the effectiveness question only obliquely. Treaties, of course, are only one factor in the complex systems of cause and effect that shape environmental outcomes; their impact is diffi-cult to isolate. Worsening environmental outcomes after an international agreement are not by themselves evidence of a treaty's ineffectiveness; the poor result may be driven by other factors, and the agreement may even have been effective in slowing the rate of worsening outcomes. Given these analytic difficulties, scholars have used multiple measures of effectiveness for environmental regulatory regimes, including the regime's ability to create rules and procedures, its ability to alter the behavior of states and other actors, and the extent to which its explicitly articulated goals were in fact realized.[6]

In a recent review of the large body of research on environmental regime effectiveness, Oran Young found a mixed picture.[7] Several case studies have documented individual instances in which regimes seemed to promote effective responses, in some or all of the senses of "effectiveness" sketched above (rulemaking, behavioral change, and goal realization). Agreements widely regarded as successful include the global accord on stratospheric ozone and several regional accords—particularly in Europe—on marine pollution, shared rivers, and fisheries. Yet it is just as easy to produce a list of failed or ineffectual agreements.[8] Studies assessing effectiveness over a larger set of regimes have found that half or more of the regimes assessed have been ineffective.[9]

One key finding in research into environmental regime effectiveness is that, while the scope and structure of the problem matter, so do the characteristics of the agreement reached.[10] Young identifies several critical variables: the specific design features of the accord, the ability to build a broad coalition around the regime, and a widespread perception of fairness in how the regime allocates the costs of compliance.[11] None of these key variables can be expected to sit still for very long during the lifetime of a problem. Treaty regimes, therefore, will be most effective when they are dynamic institutions that prove willing and able to adapt key design features to changes in the distribution of costs and benefits, in the rise of new polluters or problems, in technology, or in demand for regulation. Again, the flagging rate of innovating by amending is troubling.

Another problem with weaving a web from so many separate, thin, and at least initially weak strands is that it can produce a paralyzing set of coordination tasks. The overlap between separate agreements creates a need for extensive coordination between the regulatory regimes they create. The literature on "institutional interplay" has been relatively optimistic about the ability of separate treaty regimes (such as those for the so-called chemicals conventions of Basel, Stockholm, and Rotterdam) to coordinate at the level of interaction between treaty secretariats or harmonization of global rule systems.[12] The more practical elements of such coordination can be daunting, however, for entities with limited staff and budgets. And at the nation-state level, the sheer number of institutions overtaxes the capacity of states to implement the rules, or even to keep up with the international dialogue conducted via conferences of the parties, expert working groups, thematic clusters, regional implementation meetings, and the like. Indeed, one of the few consensual points in the UN's environmental reform debate has been on the corrosive effects of treaty fatigue.

Efforts to control the international trade in hazardous waste illustrate these web-weaving problems of international environmental law. The key legal instrument on the waste trade is the *Convention on the Control of Transboundary Hazardous Wastes and their Disposal*, signed at Basel, Switzerland, in 1989. The Basel Convention came into being in the wake of some shocking investigative reporting on how rich countries were dumping their waste in poor ones in a largely unregulated manner.[13] The convention regulates the hazardous waste trade from the global North to the global South, using a "prior informed consent" approach. The treaty identifies a list of hazardous materials and requires written prior approval from both the exporting and importing nation when such materials are transferred.

As an accord that is global in scope, issue-specific in focus, and ambitious in its regulatory aspirations, the Basel Convention is a prototype of the emergent legal strategy of global environmentalism in the 1980s and 1990s. The talks aimed from the start for a global accord, and the convention has reached near-global ratification (with 181 parties and only two signatories that have not yet ratified, Haiti and the United States).[14] The convention is also narrowly specific, targeting the waste trade as one specific element of a far larger chemical hazards problem that includes synthesis of toxic materials, their use in agricultural and industrial processes, their embodiment in the products of modern life, their disposal or release at each of these links in the chain, and their ultimate fate in the environment. As the chain of chemical production, consumption, and use snakes across borders in a globalized world economy, so do the risks to workers, consumers, communities, and ecosystems.

Rather than regulating these hazards in "cradle to grave" fashion, the strategy on toxics regulation has been to create several narrower accords. At its core are three separate UN treaties: the 1989 Basel Convention; the *Convention on the Prior Informed Consent Procedure for Certain Hazardous Chemicals and Pesticides in International Trade*, signed at Rotterdam in 1998; and the *Stockholm Convention on Persistent Organic Pollutants*, signed at Stockholm in 2001. The Rotterdam Convention flags chemicals that have been banned in multiple domestic jurisdictions, requires parties to indicate whether they will continue to allow such flagged chemicals to be imported, and obligates parties to recognize and comply with any resulting import bans or restrictions. The Stockholm Convention requires parties to take measures to eliminate the production and use of specified members of a particularly troubling family of chemicals known as persistent organic pollutants (POPs).[15]

The waste-trade problem has been a dynamic one, and the effort to regulate it has been much like squeezing a balloon, with intervention in one area causing the problem to swell in another part of the system. As Jennifer Clapp has described it, "New regulations to stop one form of hazard transfer are soon circumvented either by the opening up of new channels through which hazards can be relocated or through a rewriting of the rules."[16] When domestic regulations on waste raised disposal costs across the industrialized world in the 1970s, the international trade in hazardous wastes flourished. With tightening restrictions on the waste trade beginning in the early 1990s, the use of "recycling" loopholes exploded. More recently, as some countries have begun to observe an outright ban on the North-to-South waste trade, North-to-North and South-to-South trades have flourished. Explosive growth in electronic wastes has added a difficult new challenge to the regulatory task. Lurking behind all of these trends is the problem of illicit waste trafficking, which occurs to an unknown but potentially vast extent.[17]

Basel has struggled to keep pace with this dynamism, in part because the parties have been locked for more than two decades in a contentious debate on whether to replace the "prior informed consent" regulations with an outright ban on the North-to-South waste trade. The ban has been embraced by the European Union and many less developed countries, particularly in Africa, but has been opposed by Australia, Canada, Japan, New Zealand, the United States, and others. The 1994 conference of the parties (COP) adopted the ban, but opponents argued that a change of such magnitude required formal amendment of the accord and separate ratification of any such amendment by the parties. The 1995 COP amended the convention to adopt the ban, but the ban amendment remains short of the required number of national ratifications to enter into force. Paralyzed by this split, Basel has plodded along with its working groups, COPs, and regional centers, while a shifting global economy has given rise to a world of waste not recognized by the original accord. Indeed, most of the world's hazardous waste trade now flows outside of the regime's North-to-South regulatory framework entirely.[18]

Basel also reflects broader problems with a narrowly issue-specific regulatory strategy in a globalized world economy. The Basel, Rotterdam, and Stockholm conventions, which form the heart of global chemicals regulation, fit together poorly in several important ways. Each targets a small and specific subset of the larger problem: Basel focuses on part of the hazardous waste trade, Rotterdam addresses chemicals that have been banned in particular domestic jurisdictions, and Stockholm targets POPs as a particular family of chemicals. Each convention embraces a different regulatory philosophy: Basel uses the prior informed consent of both parties to a transaction to determine whether that transaction is legitimate; Rotterdam allows individual countries the freedom of choice to permit or ban chemicals, but requires them to make a public decision that other parties must respect; and Stockholm obligates parties to take steps to eliminate specific chemicals. Each uses a different means to determine its scope of action: Basel targets a wide array of hazardous substances, but only as waste and only for North-to-South transactions; Stockholm mandates action by all parties, but only for a short list of priority chemicals; and Rotterdam uses the independent actions of individual countries to determine which chemicals are relevant. And the three conventions only partially fill and define the regulatory space. Ancillary to them are a hodgepodge of agreements that engage specific slices of the toxics issue-area, including ocean dumping, nuclear materials, mercury pollution, protection of regional seas, proscriptions on chemical weapons, or the rules of civil liability—replete with gaps, overlaps, redundancies, clashing norms, and contradictory incentives. Efforts to promote greater coordination and "clustering" of such overlapping regimes offer some benefits in terms of information sharing, aligning schedules, and reducing the strain on travel-weary diplomats, but cannot address these larger problems.

Thus, while the Basel accord certainly has value, it also reflects the limited achievements of a strategy of international environmental law that has sought to weave a global fabric from many thin regulatory strands, and then strengthen and adapt those strands over time. Basel also hints at some deeper flaws in the strategy, in terms of how poorly it fits the scale, organization, structure, and dynamism of the global political economy. These deeper challenges are developed later in the chapter, after a parallel performance review of the development side of the law-and-development approach.

More Sustainable Development within Nations?

Assessing the reach, dynamism, and effectiveness of international environmental law is daunting—but it pales in comparison to the task of assessing progress toward sustainable development. This is in part because of the vague and normative character of the concept of sustainability, and in part because of the myriad activities that constitute development practice. Given these challenges, this section will approach the question from multiple directions. The assessment begins by looking at the extent of goal attainment for *Agenda 21*, the sustainable-development blueprint adopted for the 1992 Earth Summit. It then turns to a few specific issue-domains (forests, fresh water, and consumption patterns), and finally, to a few specific places (the small West African nation of Sierra Leone and the American state of California). While this choice of issues and places is to some extent arbitrary, these examples reveal important elements of a broader critique of the law-and-development approach presented later in the chapter, and will also help to illustrate the utility of a peace-and-rights approach.

Perhaps the most comprehensive review of progress on sustainable development is an assessment conducted by the Stakeholder Forum for a Sustainable Future. As part of a project called "Sustainable Development in the 21st Century," done in collaboration with the UN Department of Economic and Social Affairs (UNDESA) and the European Commission's Directorate-General for Environment, the Stakeholder Forum assessed progress in implementing two key outputs of the 1992 Earth Summit: *Agenda 21*, the forty-chapter blueprint for sustainability, and the Rio Declaration on Environment and Development, a consensus political statement of twenty-seven guiding principles. Stakeholder Forum's summary conclusion:

> Humanity has not progressed on the road to sustainability as far as hoped in 1992. We can celebrate some notable successes, in particular the fact that hundreds of millions of people have been lifted from poverty during the last two decades. Yet, many of the global problems we are facing today are more acute or larger in scale than they were in 1992. . . . *The political deal that emerged from the Earth Summit in 1992 has, for various reasons, never been fulfilled.* Neither the expected outcomes—elimination of poverty, reduction in disparities in standard of living, patterns of consumption and production that are compatible with the carrying capacity of ecosystems, sustainable management of renewable resources—nor the agreed means to achieve them, have materialized.[19]

They also concluded that the record on development in the two decades since Rio had been "mixed," that "global environmental problems have become more acute," and that the world is "getting closer to global ecological limits."[20]

To arrive at this conclusion, Stakeholder Forum used a "traffic light" color-coding system to score each of the thirty-nine thematic chapters of *Agenda 21*, indicating the extent of implementation of the chapter's recommendations. As indicated in table 3.2, only five of the thirty-nine areas were scored as having made good or good-to-excellent progress toward attainment: "science for sustainable development," strengthening the role of NGOs, strengthening the role of local authorities, international institutional arrangements, and international legal instruments and mechanisms (the latter justified largely on the strength of the few accords negotiated at the Rio conference, rather than the broader pattern of international environmental law as discussed previously). A few other chapters, on toxics and some elements of stakeholder incorporation, received mixed scores somewhere between limited and good progress. The remaining chapters—including those on freshwater resources, oceans, biodiversity, sustainable agriculture, land use, protection of the atmosphere, human settlements, environmental health, and consumption patterns, among others—received scores reflecting either limited progress ("far from target"), no progress, or regression.[21]

Consider, for example, the challenge of combating deforestation. *Agenda 21* had called for a three-pronged approach of better forest management, better data and information, and strengthened regional and international cooperation and coordination.[22] Stakeholder Forum's assessment of progress noted a modest decline in the estimated global deforestation rate; growing (if still incomplete) recognition of the nontimber value of forests; and a spate of international institutional mechanisms, including several intergovernmental panels in the late 1990s and ECOSOC's resolution in 2000 to create the UN Forum on Forests.[23] They also noted a daunting list of enduring obstacles: failure to address the economic drivers of deforestation, including agricultural pressures; weak national laws and institutions; poorly conceived decentralization processes that delegated responsibilities but not resources; illegal logging; and inadequate international technical and financial aid.[24]

Or consider freshwater. *Agenda 21* defined the problem primarily as a need for "integrated water resources management." It called for an ambitious set of target activities including national action plans; protection of water supplies; development of better data, modeling, and impact assessment; improved allocation mechanisms; strengthened public awareness; development of new and alternative sources; conservation measures; participatory procedures; and enhanced international cooperation at all levels.[25] Stakeholder Forum found progress toward the Millennium Development Goal on drinking water, growing awareness of

Table 3.2 STAKEHOLDER FORUM ASSESSMENT OF PROGRESS ON AGENDA 21

Score	Definition	Agenda 21 chapters receiving that score
Blue	"Excellent progress / fully achieved"	(none)
Mixed green/blue		28. Major Groups—Local Authorities
		38. International Institutional Arrangements
Green	"Good progress / on target"	27. Major Groups—NGOs
		35. Science for Sustainable Development
		39. International Legal Instruments and Mechanisms
Mixed yellow/green		19. Environmentally Sound Management of Toxic Chemicals, including Prevention of Illegal International Traffic in Toxic and Dangerous Products
		23. Major Groups—Preamble
		31. Major Groups—Science & Technology
Yellow	"Limited progress /far from target"	2. International Cooperation to Accelerate Sustainable Development in Developing Countries and Related Domestic Policies
		3. Combating Poverty
		5. Demographic Dynamics and Sustainability
		6. Protecting and Promoting Human Health Conditions
		8. Integrating Environment and Development into Decision-making
		11. Combating Deforestation
		12. Managing Fragile Ecosystems: Combating Desertification and Drought
		13. Managing Fragile Ecosystems: Sustainable Mountain Development
		14. Promoting Sustainable Agriculture and Rural Development
		15. Conservation of Biological Diversity
		16. Environmentally Sound Management of Biotechnology
		17. Protection of the Oceans, All Kinds of Seas, including Enclosed and Semi-enclosed Seas, and Coastal Areas and the Protection, Rational Use and Development of their Living Resources

(continued)

Table 3.2 (CONTINUED)

Score	Definition	Agenda 21 chapters receiving that score
		18. Protection of the Quality and Supply of Freshwater Resources: Application of Integrated Approaches to the Development, Management and Use of Water Resources
		20. Environmentally Sound Management of Hazardous Wastes, Including Prevention of Illegal International Traffic in Hazardous Wastes
		21. Environmentally Sound Management of Solid Wastes and Sewage-related Issues
		22. Safe and Environmentally Sound Management of Radioactive Wastes
		24. Major Groups—Women
		25. Major Groups—Children & Youth
		26. Major Groups—Indigenous Peoples
		30. Major Groups—Business & Industry
		32. Major Groups—Farmers
		33. Financial Resources and Mechanisms
		34. Transfer of Environmentally Sound Technology, Cooperation and Capacity-building
		36. Promoting Education, Public Awareness and Training
		37. National Mechanisms and International Cooperation for Capacity-building in Developing Countries
		40. Information for Decision Making
Mixed red/yellow		10. Integrated Approach to the Planning and Management of Land Resources
		29. Major Groups—Workers & Trade Unions
Red	"No progress or regression"	4. Changing Consumption Patterns
		7. Promoting Sustainable Human Settlement Development
		9. Protection of the Atmosphere

Source: Stakeholder Forum for a Sustainable Future, *Review of Implementation of Agenda 21 and the Rio Principles. Synthesis Report* (January 2012), table 2, pp. 22–39. January 2012.

the implications of climate change, some hopeful technological innovations, and a mixed picture of national-level institutional reforms. Arrayed
against these modest gains were mounting scarcity in several parts of
the world, enduring data limitations, the continuation of business-as-
usual approaches, and the "daunting" challenge of merging the myriad
dimensions of water use into an integrated policy and decision-making
framework.[26]

Despite what were, on balance, pessimistic assessments, Stakeholder
Forum assigned a score of yellow for "limited progress" on both forests
and fresh water. One area scoring red, signifying no progress or regression, was that of changing consumption patterns. *Agenda 21* had stressed
a two-pronged approach of identifying unsustainable patterns of production and consumption and developing national strategies to change
them.[27] Stakeholder Forum's progress report stressed the global growth
in resource use (approximately 50 percent in the past twenty-five years);
the world's growing waste footprint; a failure to extensively decouple
economic growth from material throughput; a resulting "rise in overall
environmental impact of humans on planetary systems"; and the rise of
consumerist culture.[28]

While these sector-specific assessments make for grim reading, the
prospects for and barriers to sustainable development must also be understood in the context of specific places. Consider Sierra Leone, a small West
African nation that gained its independence from British colonial rule in
1961. Sierra Leone is one of the world's poorest countries: more than half
of Sierra Leoneans live below the official poverty line, and the country's
per capita annual income is estimated at $680.[29] Average life expectancy
is forty-five years, and 45 percent of children under five are malnourished.
The country is highly trade-dependent, with trade accounting for between
41 and 70 percent of GDP in 2009–2011. The country's principal exports
are diamonds, aluminum and other metal ores, and unprocessed cocoa
beans; its primary imports, petroleum, manufactured goods, and rice.

Sierra Leone is deeply enmeshed in UN-related development assistance activities. UN agencies with a presence in-country include
UNDP, the UN Population Fund (UNFPA), the Joint UN Programme
on HIV/AIDS, the UN International Children's Fund (UNICEF), the UN
Development Fund for Women, the World Food Programme, the World
Health Organization, and the UN Refugee Agency. In-country work by
these and other international organizations brings with it, in principle,
a set of environmental standards for impact assessment, protecting
natural resources, creating sustainable livelihoods, promoting environmental health, and reinforcing best practices. For example, UNDP's

in-country work has included efforts to promote sustainable land management via legal and budgetary reforms, a "preventive development" project to reduce risks from natural disasters, a pilot initiative on sustainable waste management, and even initiatives on reducing the use of ozone-depleting substances.[30]

Sierra Leone is also a party to many UN-sponsored international treaties, including the *UN Framework Convention on Climate Change*, the CBD, the *UN Convention to Combat Desertification*, the *Stockholm Convention on Persistent Organic Pollutants*, and several others. These treaties can have a strong influence on the shape and scope of environmental activities within the country. The Sierra Leone River estuary has been designated a wetlands area of international importance under the *Convention on Wetlands of International Importance, especially as Waterfowl Habitat* (aka the Ramsar convention), giving protected status to some 295,000 hectares of land. A project has been proposed to reforest degraded lands in the Makeni region, Tonkalili District of Sierra Leone under the auspices of the UNFCC's Clean Development Mechanism.[31] Sierra Leone has developed a National Biodiversity Strategy Action Plan, in the context of its treaty obligations under the CBD, which commits the country to a set of legal, institutional, and management reforms for better biodiversity conservation.[32]

Yet, if sustainable development consists of meeting present needs while also protecting the ecosystems and natural resources essential to future needs, then Sierra Leoneans suffer from conditions of profound unsustainability on both counts. Even as the needs of the current citizenry go unmet, practices related to land use and natural resource extraction are undermining the natural capital on which the well-being of future generations of Sierra Leoneans depends.[33] The Environmental Performance Index (EPI), a 2014 Yale University study that ranked 178 nations on a range of environmental performance indicators, scored Sierra Leone 173rd overall. Among the components of the EPI, the country scored particularly poorly in the areas of health impacts, water and sanitation, air quality, and biodiversity and habitat.[34] Beyond such aggregate metrics, country-specific analysis draws a similar picture. A 2010 UNEP assessment of the state of Sierra Leone's environment found vast problems of water quality and availability, despite adequate water resources; substantial pressures on agricultural land; loss of the country's dwindling forest cover at a rate that clearly outpaced forest regeneration; and threats to biodiversity from agriculture, mining, deforestation, and urban and infrastructural development. The assessment also found crosscutting problems of poor institutional capacity, conflicting mandates, low degrees of transparency and accountability, reliance on unsustainable livelihoods, and poor benefit-sharing.[35]

Obviously, Sierra Leone faces environmental challenges linked to poverty, and in that regard has much in common with neighboring countries. Yet in the aforementioned Yale study, the country's EPI score was well below the average for its comparable income group (the poorest 10 percent of countries studied) and for its geographic group (sub-Saharan Africa). One reason for such profound unsustainability, even compared to its peers, has been conflict. Sierra Leone found itself embroiled in a brutal and widely destabilizing civil war from 1991 to 2002, during which perhaps 70,000 people were killed and some 2.6 million (more than half the population) were uprooted from their homes.[36] According to a UN assessment, "The conditions that led to the war included a repressive predatory state, dependence on mineral rents, the impact of structural adjustment, a large excluded youth population, the availability of small arms after the end of the Cold War, and interference from regional neighbors."[37] The role of natural resources (and diamonds in particular) in the conflict has been widely documented. Sierra Leone's postconflict Truth and Reconciliation Commission warned against a simplistic "blood diamonds" perspective on the war, but noted that diamonds were both one indirect cause of the conflict (through misappropriation of revenues and resulting social disparities) and an important factor in sustaining the conflict (with illicit diamond revenues financing arms, ammunition, and combatants).[38]

According to UNEP's 2010 environmental assessment, the war had several negative consequences for sustainability. The fighting caused extensive damage to water infrastructure and agricultural infrastructure in rural areas, much of which had not been repaired at the time of the assessment, nearly a decade after the conflict's end. As is generally the case, however, the institutional consequences have done more lasting damage to the environment than the direct physical effects of war.[39] The conflict left environmental governance "in shambles," with land degradation, land grabs, and unsustainable resource use the norm in the absence of effective governance structures and given minimal state capacity.[40] A further consequence of weak governance was that unsustainable coping strategies—which for many became necessary when the war profoundly disrupted agricultural livelihoods and forced vast numbers to flee—endured beyond the conflict and were increasingly becoming institutionalized.

Human rights are also implicated in Sierra Leone's sustainability challenges. A constitutional democracy emerged from the civil war, yet the country is scored as only "partly free" by the international human rights organization Freedom House; Amnesty International's annual report, while noting some progress in consolidating democracy, has cited ongoing political, sexual, and gender-based violence.[41] Rights-related challenges are clearly evident in the environmental and natural resource sectors. First, Sierra Leonean citizens struggle to realize the participatory rights affirmed through Principle 10 of the 1992 Rio Declaration, including "appropriate access to information concerning the environment," "the opportunity to participate in decision-making processes," and "effective access to judicial and administrative proceedings."[42] UNEP flagged the low degree of transparency and accountability around natural resource sectors as a leading threat to the peacebuilding process, and stressed the need for strengthened participation and consultation.[43]

The rights problem is substantive as well as procedural: Sierra Leoneans have little protection, in either domestic or international venues, when their internationally recognized human rights to food security, water, or health face environmental threats. Moreover, rights-related concerns are not limited to domestic considerations. They have a strong transnational component as well, in part because the years of conflict have created zones of impunity across Sierra Leone and in neighboring countries, which transnational actors are quick to exploit. Foreign companies are widely reported to be involved in illegal logging, and were implicated in illegal exports and corrupt practices that led to a temporary ban on timber exports in 2008.[44] UNEP reported a high likelihood that foreign fishing boats illegally trawled the coast during the war, and international NGO accounts suggest that such illegal catches continue.[45] While Sierra Leone participates in the Kimberley Process, which certifies diamonds as "conflict-free," smuggling that skirts the process may still account for as much as half of the country's international diamond trade.[46] More generally, Sierra Leone's heavy dependence on the export of natural resource commodities, in some highly competitive sectors for which it is but one of a number of suppliers, leaves it in a position of substantial weakness relative to the transnational commodity chains in which it is embedded.

More than ten thousand kilometers from Sierra Leone, a very different but equally instructive picture of sustainability challenges is seen in California, a state on the west coast of the United States. California's 2013 population of 38 million (about the same as Algeria, Sudan, or Poland) and its territory of some 423,970 km^2 (slightly smaller than Iraq or Sweden) make it a country-sized unit. Certainly, its environmental impact is country-sized: According to a recent assessment by the Global Footprint Network, "If California were a country, it would have the world's 15th largest per capita Ecological Footprint."[47]

California is one of the wealthiest regions on the planet, although substantial pockets of poverty exist in both urban and rural areas; some 15 percent of the state's population lives below the official poverty level. California is endowed with a rich array of natural resources—forests, fisheries, cultivable land, rivers, minerals—that have long been tapped for human use. California has also been, in recent decades, a locus of American environmentalism. The state has implemented cutting-edge environmental legislation on everything from emissions controls to protected areas, and in the process has set ambitious targets, mandated state-of-the-art assessment methods, and created mechanisms for extensive citizen participation. On climate change in particular, the state has forged ahead with action despite the national political paralysis on the issue and the US withdrawal from its Kyoto Protocol commitments.

California projects as "green" in another sense: it helps to bankroll American environmentalism. All the major environmental organizations in the United States have a strong West Coast presence, and draw extensive financial support from affluent pockets of progressivism around the state, notably including Hollywood and the San Francisco Bay Area. The actor Leonardo DiCaprio is a board member of the World Wildlife Fund–US; entertainers Robert Redford and James Taylor, as well as entertainment conglomerates Sony and Disney, hold seats on the board of trustees of the Natural Resources Defense Council.

Yet Californians are also among the world's most voracious consumers of natural resources, yielding one of the world's largest environmental footprints, and the state's image as the epitome of global consumer culture is well deserved. How has the state's green sensibility found a way to coexist with one of the world's highest rates of material throughput? The primary answer is outsourcing: a state that once lived by extracting from its own forests, fields, mines and fisheries now imports the bulk of its food, fuel, wood products, chemicals, and other resource-intensive commodities, while legislating protected status for its remaining pristine areas of forest, mountain, desert, and coastline.[48] As a result, California consumes more than five times the state's available ecological resources, according to the aforementioned footprint assessment.[49]

In international legal terms, Californians are by and large not held accountable for their unsustainable practices. One reason is that the United States has either declined to sign or failed to ratify most of the important global environmental accords of the past few decades. A deeper problem, however, is that those treaties, even if ratified and fully implemented, regulate environmental harm primarily at its source of production. California's dominant position at the consuming end of global commodity chains—for gasoline, mobile phones, cut flowers, bananas, or basketball shoes—means that the environmental consequences of its consumption are mostly found not in California, but upstream in the production chain where raw materials are extracted, materials are processed, and hazardous chemicals are manufactured and used in production. As long as there are places in the world that escape the regulatory net of international environmental law—be it through nonratification, nonimplementation, or noncompliance—California will always have the option of outsourcing its environmental harm with relative impunity.

California's outsourcing has important implications not only for global sustainability but for peace and human rights, as well. Chevron, a globally operating oil company headquartered east of San Francisco, owns one of the state's largest networks of gasoline retail outlets and has major refining operations outside of both San Francisco and Los Angeles. Chevron has been implicated in rights controversies and violent conflict on two continents. The firm has been implicated in environmental destruction and human rights violations in Ecuador, leading to a long-running transnational legal battle by indigenous people to hold the company accountable.[50] Chevron's crude-oil pipeline in Nigeria has been subject to attack by the Movement for the Emancipation of the Niger Delta (MEND).[51] A lawsuit against the company uncovered evidence that Chevron may have been responsible for actions by the Nigerian military that led to the deaths of several anti-Chevron Nigerian protestors.[52] Activists have dubbed the delta the "world capital of oil pollution," and life expectancy is reportedly lower than it was two generations ago.[53] While a comprehensive, independent assessment of Chevron's operations in Nigeria is not available, it is reasonable to infer from a UNEP assessment of the impacts of oil production in Ogoniland, a region of the Niger Delta where another transnational oil giant, Shell, has been particularly active.[54] UNEP found many sites where soil pollution and groundwater contamination exceeded Nigerian law, with attendant damage to ecosystems, fisheries, and agricultural production. The study also determined that control, maintenance, remediation, and decommissioning had failed to meet both industry standards and Nigerian law, creating significant consequences for public health. According to UNEP, "Since average life expectancy in Nigeria is less than 50 years, it is a fair assumption that most members of the current Ogoniland community have lived with chronic oil pollution throughout their lives."[55] Gasoline prices in California do not reflect these real human costs of doing business.

Californians and Nigerians both import fish. Californians do so to exploit their purchasing power in global markets, and to replace production from protected coastal zones at home. For many Nigerians, the decimation of fish stocks by oil production for distant consumers has left them little choice. Similarly, both Californians and Ecuadorians have at time sought legal redress for the environmental damage that comes with oil production. But whereas Californians have had recourse to a strong domestic legal system for environmental protection, Ecuadorians have found a much weaker platform in international human rights law, which has remained largely silent on their environmental rights.

THE DEEPER PROBLEMS: UNREACHABLE SPACES AND CONFLICT TRAPS

The preceding discussion suggests that the grand strategy of liberal environmentalism has struggled in its quest to create better law between nations and better development within them. Some noteworthy gains notwithstanding, it has not been possible to weave a comprehensive fabric of international environmental law, one treaty-strand at a time, or to infuse those strands with a sustained capacity for progressive innovation. Implementation of the sustainable-development vision embodied by *Agenda 21* has also been limited.

In the process of these struggles, we find exposed some deeper problems than simply limited efficacy. The strategy has lacked a clear vision of how to deal with some of the dynamic elements of economic globalization, limiting its reach into the transnational spaces that sit between domestic development and international law. Also, it has failed to recognize the problems of violent conflict, political instability, and failing states as hindrances to its ambitions for legislating and implementing sustainable development. And it has been unable, for these and other reasons, to sustain the political momentum generated in the Stockholm-to-Rio period.

Understanding these deeper problems provides more than just a conceptual critique of the law-and-development approach. It also generates a set of arguments for building upon the UN's mandate domains of international peace and human rights, as steps toward renewing the UN's relevance and efficacy in global environmental governance.

The Globalization Problem: Hiding Places and Unreachable Spaces in Global Production-Consumption Chains

The accelerating pace of economic globalization in recent decades has exposed a seam in the law-and-development approach. Transnationalized systems of production and consumption, organized around globalized supply chains, snake in and out of national borders with a dynamism, complexity, and spatial configuration that confounds existing approaches to regulation through international law and domestic policy. Failure to understand the implications of this global economic trajectory has been the biggest blind spot of the Stockholm-to-Rio era. As my colleagues Jacob Park and Matthias Finger and I put it in a previous critique: "The Rio process underestimated—indeed, ignored—the dynamic trajectory of industrial civilization in the second half of the twentieth century and failed to account for the underlying, reinforcing dynamics of economic growth and technological diffusion that have come to define industrial development on an increasingly global scale."[56] Jennifer Clapp and Eric Helleiner have offered a similar critique that stresses in particular the globalization of financial markets, the integration and growing power of emerging economies, and the volatility of commodity markets as specific elements of structural economic change.[57] The Brundtland Commission and the string of successive global environmental summit meetings barely broached this dynamic of globalization and the attendant challenges of transnational regulation, much less engaged them.

Economic globalization challenges existing approaches to environmental regulation because it is not simply an intensification of transactions across borders, such as international trade, migration, or information flows. These transactions are important byproducts of globalization, but its essence lies in the construction of increasingly globalized platforms of production and equally globalized aspirations for consumption. The result, which has been underway for some decades now, is a world economic system that differs fundamentally from the largely separate "national" economies of the industrial age.[58] In this new economic world, the supply chains that turn ideas, raw materials, and investments into finished products, marketed goods, and waste streams snake in and out of national borders and respond to a global logic of incentives, behavior, and profit. From an environmental point of view, efficiency gains sometimes result from the dizzying shifts in production and consumption patterns. But there is also an enormous cost in the disruptive effects felt by local communities. Moreover, the harmful activities tied to globalized systems of production (e.g., the use of toxic chemicals) and consumption (e.g., waste disposal) will often occur in the unregulated spaces in between national laws and global agreements—neither of which is well suited to bound their transnational, fluid, and frequently shape-shifting character.

Where in the system do we find these unregulated political-economic spaces that law-and-development fails to reach, with either its "carrots" of positive incentives and best practices, or its "sticks" of regulation, taxation and restriction? One such space, obviously, is found in nations with weak state capacity or low willingness to regulate environmental harm. Simply put, there are just too many locations, in too many countries, onto which the harmful environmental effects of production and consumption can be pushed. California will always be able to outsource its supply, and externalize any resulting harm, to *somewhere*. This creates inherent limits to a grand strategy in which internationally specified goals translate into national-level standards, which are then administered and applied locally, at the specific geographic point of production of an environmental "bad."

The outsourcing problem is sometimes described as producing a regulatory "race to the bottom," in which investors have incentives to externalize costs by moving to countries with weaker regulation, and national policymakers have incentives to gut regulations as a way to attract investment.[59] But this framing can obscure other important dimensions of the problem, including the abundant hiding places that are found *inside* of nation-states as well as between them, and the chilling effect that even the possible threat of relocation can have on regulations.[60]

Moreover, the problem is not simply weak regulation in some locations; it also involves the dynamism of transnational production-consumption chains, and in particular the capacity to shift problems to a different link up or down the chain. Thus, another unreachable space is seen in the "balloon squeezing" character of efforts to regulate toxic hazards, as discussed previously in the context of the Basel waste-trade regime. A regulatory patch is applied to one symptom of the problem—often, a symptom that sits at an easier-to-regulate link in the global chain. While this may be useful, it can also create incentives to shift activities upstream or downstream, to a less regulated, more remote, or more opaque segment of the chain. In this manner, new approaches to regulation or new strategies of waste reduction seem to be constantly one step (or more) behind the challenge. The resulting problem is directly analogous to the well-known phenomenon of "transfer pricing," in which multinational companies conduct artificial "billing" between their various subunits, so as to shift profits and losses to the jurisdiction of maximum after-tax profitability.

Thus, the spaces that law-and-development fails to reach may be those stages of the production-consumption chain that are hardest to regulate effectively, or they may be those locales at any given stage that have weaker regulations, less effective implementation, or weaker citizen power. It has been much debated whether externalizing environmental harm in this manner is a deliberate cost-minimizing corporate strategy, or simply the natural workings of a market that adjusts "as if by an invisible hand." Either way, the environmental consequences are acute for those locations that extract natural resources and feed them into the world's supply chains, or those that have become magnet-like repositories for the resulting waste streams, or those that see sustainable livelihoods melt away with outsourcing, or those that have the simple misfortune of being downstream or downwind of something bad.

Some have suggested that market-based processes such as green product certification can fill these regulatory gaps of economic globalization. It is increasingly clear, however, that even when socially responsible shopping or corporate green branding generates improvements, they are no substitute for strong environmental protection at the source of harm.[61] Both international treaties and national sustainable development efforts often lack the capacity to implement such protections or even the political impetus to create them. As discussed below, this incapacity underscores the importance of human rights: without global recognition of environmental protection as a human right, there will always be another neighborhood, another country, or another link in the supply chain onto which those harmful effects can be externalized, exported, and dumped—short-circuiting the quest for greener practices up and down the chain.

The Conflict Problem: Destructive Cycles and Downward Spirals

A second underlying problem with the law-and-development approach is tied to what Paul Collier has labelled "the conflict trap." Collier uses this term to describe the dynamic process by which poverty, poor governance, and violent conflict combine to keep some of the world's poorest people trapped in very difficult circumstances of vulnerability, marginalization, and human insecurity. Simply put, the challenge for which law-and-development has not had an effective answer is this: How can many of the world's countries hope to attain sustainable development or to comply with international environmental agreements if they cannot first achieve a sustained peace? Without peace, there is little hope of mustering the requisite degrees of legitimacy and stability to carry out tasks of environmental governance and socio-ecological transformation.

The conflict problem is a "trap" because, much like the aforementioned challenge of economic globalization, it has dynamic elements. The issue is not simply the destructive consequences of a violent conflict for development (sustainable or otherwise), although these can be devastating. The problem's dynamic elements include (1) the discouragingly high rate of conflict recurrence and recidivism, with the best predictor of violent conflict being a prior episode of violent conflict; (2) the corrosive effects that a high risk of conflict can have on actors' behavior and expectations; and (3) the limited capacity or incentive to manage peacefully the disputes that can trigger conflict.[62]

The cumulative effects of the "conflict trap" cast a shadow across the international system, the scope of which may surprise the casual observer. In the period between the end of World War II and 2011, there were a total of 246 armed conflicts in 153 countries.[63] Paul Steinberg has calculated that, between 1970 and 2010, among countries of the global South or the former Soviet Union, one out of six experienced a full collapse of central governmental authority for at least a year.[64]

Turning to the question of violent conflict and the environment, one way to see the scope of the problem is to look at measures of environmental performance on a country-by-country basis. Attempts to create global indices of national environmental performance are fraught with peril, for obvious reasons: the problems are diverse from country to country, assessing performance is notoriously difficult, and the data are often sketchy. Nevertheless, using the best available assessment data provides an important insight: poor environmental performance, episodes of violent conflict, and human rights violations are tightly coupled.

Table 3.3 lists the forty countries with the poorest performance on the aforementioned EPI. As a quick scan of the table indicates, income level is an important but incomplete predictor of whether a country will be listed as a poor environmental performer. There are some extremely poor countries in the list, to be sure; one-half have a per capita income of less than $2,000 annually. But there are also countries on the list with substantially higher "human development" rankings, as well, including Iraq, Grenada, and Tajikistan. And many of the world's very poorest countries are missing from the list.

Tellingly, violent conflict is widespread in these countries. Thirty-eight of the forty have had one or more episodes of significant violent civil conflict since 1990, according to the conflict database maintained by Uppsala University. Adding human rights status to the equation is also revealing. Only five of the forty countries in table 3.3 are classified as "free" by the human rights organization Freedom House. Eighteen are categorized "not free" and seventeen, "partly free." Strikingly, only one of the forty countries in this table of poor environmental performers, Benin, is listed as both "free" and lacking in violent civil conflict.

War is a risk factor for poor environmental performance, in several ways. Violent conflict does direct harm to ecosystems. In most cases, however,

Country	Environmental Performance Index ranking	Freedom House classification	Human Development Index ranking	Violent conflict since 1990?
Nepal	139	Partly Free	145	Y
Kenya	140	Partly Free	147	Y
Cameroon	141	Not Free	152	Y
Niger	142	Partly Free	187	Y
Tanzania	143	Partly Free	159	Y
Guinea-Bissau	144	Not Free	177	Y
Cambodia	145	Not Free	136	Y
Rwanda	146	Not Free	151	Y
Grenada	147	Free	79	Y
Pakistan	148	Partly Free	146	Y
Iraq	149	Not Free	120	Y
Benin	150	Free	165	N
Ghana	151	Free	138	Y
Solomon Islands	152	Partly Free	157	N
Comoros	153	Partly Free	159	Y
Tajikistan	154	Not Free	133	Y
India	155	Free	135	Y
Chad	156	Not Free	184	Y
Yemen	157	Not Free	154	Y
Mozambique	158	Partly Free	178	Y
Gambia	159	Not Free	172	Y
Angola	160	Not Free	149	Y
Djibouti	161	Not Free	170	Y
Guinea	162	Partly Free	179	Y
Togo	163	Partly Free	166	Y
Myanmar	164	Not Free	150	Y
Mauritania	165	Not Free	161	Y
Madagascar	166	Partly Free	155	Y
Burundi	167	Partly Free	180	Y
Eritrea	168	Not Free	182	Y
Bangladesh	169	Partly Free	142	Y
Dem. Rep. Congo	170	Not Free	186	Y
Sudan	171	Not Free	166	Y
Liberia	172	Partly Free	175	Y
Sierra Leone	173	Partly Free	183	Y

Table 3.3 (CONTINUED)

Country	Environmental Performance Index ranking	Freedom House classification	Human Development Index ranking	Violent conflict since 1990?
Afghanistan	174	Not Free	169	Y
Lesotho	175	Free	162	Y
Haiti	176	Partly Free	168	Y
Mali	177	Partly Free	176	Y
Somalia	178	Not Free	Not ranked	Y

Source: Compiled from Yale Center for Environmental Law and Policy and Center for International Earth Science Information Network, *2014 Environmental Performance Index*, Country Rankings, available at http://epi.yale.edu/epi/country-rankings; Freedom House, *2014 Freedom in the World*, Freedom in the World Country Ratings, available at http://www.freedomhouse.org/report-types/freedom-world#. VAddHvl5Me2; UNDP, *Human Development Report 2014*, table 1: "Human Development Index and Its Components," available at http://hdr.undp.org/en/content/table-1-human-development-index-and-i ts-components; and Uppsala Conflict Data Program, Uppsala University Department of Peace and Conflict Research, available at http://www.ucdp.uu.se/gpdatabase/search.php.

war's more significant impact is to disrupt institutions, governance, and practices that are critical to environmental protection and sustainable resource management.[65] Violent conflict also enhances human vulnerability, social marginalization, and the risks associated with disasters and extreme events. It forces people into unsustainable practices as it displaces them from more sustainable livelihoods. It undercuts a nation's capacity to comply with its international environmental commitments, causing local consequences to reverberate globally. And it can create zones of lawlessness and impunity in which incentives for resource plunder can be great and deterrents, few.

The causal links among poverty, violent conflict, human rights, and environmental performance, are complex, however, and the causal arrow may also run in the opposite direction. It may be, as some scholars have argued, that poor environmental performance is itself a risk factor for war, in the sense that deforestation, soil erosion, water pollution, or other forms of environmental harm can create grievances in society that could result in violent conflict. This claim has been hotly debated (see chapter 5). Conflict scholars have identified high dependence on natural resource commodity exports as a major risk factor for civil war, but this linkage probably has more to do with revenue disputes, incentives for succession to control resource wealth, and the bad governance that commodity-based economies can breed, as opposed to environmental harm per se.[66]

Whether or not natural resources trigger violent conflict, it is clear that their extraction can be a tool for sustaining it; oil, diamonds, timber, precious minerals, and other valuable resource commodities provide whoever controls them with a revenue source for arms, ammunition, and soldiers. Another increasingly apparent link comes in the wake of war: poor management of natural resources and environmental systems can cripple the prospects for peace. Moreover, environmental change may also be a cause of peace, in the sense that strategic efforts to promote environmental cooperation and positive practices may enhance trust, create shared benefits, often conflict identities, or have other "environmental peacebuilding" benefits. If so, then the failure to see environmental challenges creatively—as opportunities to enhance human security and reduce vulnerability—causes us to miss important opportunities to break the cycle. (The evidence for and debates around each of these possible links between environmental causes and conflict effects are discussed in detail in chapter 5.)

Rather than looking for one-directional causality running from environmental change to war or vice versa, it makes more sense to view the problem as a cycle, and the policy challenge as one of reversing the downward spiral caused by the reinforcing effects of violent conflict, human insecurity, poor environmental governance, and increased vulnerability. The aforementioned case of Sierra Leone provides a clear illustration of several of these links. So does the example of California, albeit less directly: the global commodity chains feeding the consumer culture are not incidental to the violence seen in the Ecuadorian Amazon, the Niger Delta, or Sierra Leone. Conflict also reinforces the regulatory problems of globalization, discussed previously: the lawlessness and impunity surrounding the production of "conflict resources" for global markets is an extreme, and all too common, example of the larger global regulatory problem.

THE MISSING MANDATE DOMAINS: THE CASE FOR PEACE AND HUMAN RIGHTS IN GLOBAL ENVIRONMENTAL GOVERNANCE

The case for bringing the UN's mandate domains of peace and human rights squarely into a renewed strategy for global environmental governance, then, rests on the revealed failings of the law-and-development approach. International environmental law lacks an internal driver of sustained innovation, an incentive structure for more effective regulatory performance, and the reactive capacity to keep pace with a dynamic global economy. Sustainable development is frequently derailed by conflict and state fragility, overstates the extent to which governments control the natural world within their borders, and has proved incapable of addressing the significant problem of the externalization of adjustment costs in a global system. How can rights-based and peace-based strategies help?

Clearly, the failure to protect the environment adequately puts at risk a wide range of recognized human rights.[67] Some of the most fundamental conditions for life, well-being, and human security have a direct environmental component: clean drinking water, breathable air, uncontaminated food. Although the pathbreaking 1948 Universal Declaration of Human Rights makes no explicit mention of the environment, few of the rights named therein can have meaning without a healthy environment in which to realize them. Rights that most immediately hinge on environmental quality include "life, liberty, and security of person" (Article 4); the right to property (Article 17); the right to social security (Article 22); and the right to an adequate standard of living (Article 25).[68] Considering the close ties between human-occupied landscapes, natural resource use, and cultural identity, one must also include the right to a nationality (Article 15) and an individual's right to "the economic, social and cultural rights indispensable for his dignity and the free development of his personality" (Article 22). The advocacy organization EarthJustice cites rights to life, health, water, work, culture, information, participation, and shelter—all established rights under international law—as the basis for recognizing the environment as a human right.[69] As chapter 4 will discuss in detail, the UN system has been moving—at a snail's pace—toward recognition of these linkages under human rights law.

The importance of environmental protection for human rights, however, does not by itself mean that rights-based approaches will enhance environmental protection, or that the UN's environmental protection efforts will be stronger if they mobilize the organization's human rights organs and practices. Making that case rests on several additional strands:

Human rights enable substantive environmental claims against governments and intergovernmental organizations

Several decades into the era of global environmental politics, it has become apparent that governments consistently underprovide environmental public goods, both in the domestic sphere and when striking deals in the international realm, unless pressed by social forces.[70] Rights-based environmental claims against the state need not be rooted in *human* rights, of course; effective property rights or rights of access to natural resources can be central to campaigns for environmental protection (or despoliation). However, given the chronic inequities in how property rights are allocated and the important public-goods dimensions of environmental protection, substantive rights to breathable air, clean water, and public health are indispensable tools for prodding governments into action.

Human rights enable access to processes and decisions in regulatory arenas

Along with a substantive right to particular environmental outcomes such as clean water, process-oriented rights play a key procedural role in environmental action. Environmental protection is a widely recognized public function of the modern state. As more and more governments build up established bodies of environmental law and policy, decisions about the environment increasingly occur in the context of technically complex, information-intensive regulatory processes. If such processes are to yield effective decisions in a legitimate and accountable manner, then rights—the right to enjoy equal protection under the law, the right to have access to information, and the right to participate in the processes of government—are fundamental. A large body of evidence shows that environmental protection works best when citizens' procedural rights have real meaning in the corridors of environmental policy, municipal planning, and economic development.[71] This reasoning is codified in Principle 10 of the Rio Declaration on Environment and Development, negotiated by governments at the 1992 Earth Summit:

> Environmental issues are best handled with participation of all concerned citizens, at the relevant level. At the national level, each individual shall have appropriate access to information concerning the environment that is held by public authorities, including information on hazardous materials and activities in their communities, and the opportunity to participate in decision-making processes. States shall facilitate and encourage public awareness and participation by making information widely available. Effective access to judicial and administrative proceedings, including redress and remedy, shall be provided.[72]

Human rights create transnational normative force

Rights-based approaches to environmental protection are important not only for the substantive and procedural claims they allow within a single jurisdiction, but also for the normative force and creative coalitions they enable across jurisdictions. This is a key reason why rights-based approaches limited to the national sphere and encapsulated in sustainable-development initiatives, while important, are not enough. Scholars have found that transnational advocacy campaigns often achieve the greatest resonance when they are able to frame their cause as a threat of bodily harm or as a denial of equal opportunity.[73] In several campaigns in which activists have framed environmental issues this way, what started out as loose and episodic transnational advocacy coalitions have consolidated into strong and effective networks—opposing large dams, fighting rampant deforestation, or exposing pesticide abuse. These networks link environmental despoliation and human rights abuses to the aforementioned themes of bodily harm and opportunity denied. This process of transnational contention has been an important mechanism not only to register environmental grievances, but also to generate new and increasingly institutionalized forms and norms of environmental governance.[74]

Rights-based approaches can be used to link distant nodes in transnational supply chains

A particularly important category of violations of environmentally related human rights occurs when, as Wolfgang Sachs explains, "the resource claims of core states collide with the subsistence rights of the periphery."[75] Much of the environmental burden of the world's oil use, for example, is visited on poor, politically marginalized, and resource-dependent communities in the forests or coastal zones where oil fields are developed, including the Niger Delta, the Andean Amazon, and the Gulf Coast of North America, among many others. Similarly, large dams built to power hydroelectric industrialization, to steer water into irrigation schemes, or to quench thirsty metropolises are typically located in remote areas where people (often, religiously, culturally, or ethnically distinct minority communities) derive their livelihoods and cultural identities from the ecosystems that such projects threaten. The same is true of industrial-scale mining enterprises, agricultural operations, and more recently, biofuel schemes that feed critical raw materials into global commodity chains.

Mechanisms by which individuals or communities may press such rights-based claims are currently thinly developed. As discussed in chapter 4, for example, efforts to press rights claims related to climate change are still largely insipient, and challenge the capacity of existing institutional settings such as regional international human rights tribunals. There are also institution-specific mechanisms such as the World Bank's Inspection Panel, which, despite its imperfect functioning and dependence on the Bank's less-than-ideal internal standards, underscores the potential power of pressing such claims transnationally.[76]

Human rights shine the spotlight on those communities most likely to be marginalized from environmental policy processes

The social enterprise organization Capacity Global identified at least four distinct circumstances in which environmental harm can be understood to constitute a human rights violation:

- When people lack an adequately gclean and healthy environment to enjoy such basic rights as the right to life, health, or food
- When people are denied participatory rights in decision-making processes about the environment or natural resource use
- When environmental impacts are distributed unfairly, forcing some social groups to bear a disproportionate burden of pollution and resource degradation (or, for that matter, of the costs and consequences of environmental protection)
- When some people are denied a fair share of access to the benefits of nature and natural resources[77]

These forms of harm are not distributed equally; often, they are visited with particular force on exactly those communities most likely to be marginalized from both international treaty deliberations and national development planning. Thus, in Europe, the Roma and other distinct minority groups have faced disproportionate environmental burdens.[78] In the United States, race is a statistically significant predictor of who lives closest to hazardous waste facilities.[79] Across the Amazon basin, controversial hydroelectric, mining, and petroleum projects have visited environmental impacts disproportionately on indigenous peoples and other economically marginalized communities.[80] In each of these examples, all of the preceding conditions apply: poor environmental quality undermines a community's health and well-being; the problem can be traced to inadequate voice and representation in decisions about planning, project site selection, resource use, and pollution control; the burdens are highly disproportionate when compared to the society as a whole; and a degraded environment denies people access to other benefits of nature or livelihood resources.

Human rights defend environmental defenders

A fundamental contribution of rights-based approaches is the shield they may provide for environmental advocates who confront power.[81] *Environmentalists under Fire*, a report released jointly by the environmental organization Sierra Club and the human rights organization Amnesty International in 2000, documented ten high-profile cases of environmental advocates suffering human rights abuses for their efforts.[82] The UN Human Rights Council's independent expert on environmental human rights reported in 2013 that he was "troubled by the many reports of failures to protect environmental human rights defenders."[83] Soon thereafter, the advocacy organization Global Witness reported that "between 2002 and 2013, we have been able to verify that 908 citizens were killed protecting rights to their land and environment," and noted that such deaths had increased sharply in the last few years.[84]

To be sure, there are complex questions about who has the power to define whom as an environmentalist. Memorializing Chico Mendes and Ken Saro-Wiwa as "environmentalists"—rather than as, say, a rural union organizer (Mendes) or an ethnic-minority separatist (Saro-Wiwa)—may say as much about the power of media-savvy groups in the North to "brand" complex struggles as it says about the struggles themselves.[85] Nevertheless, high-profile international awards for environmental advocates, such as the Goldman Prize and the Right Livelihood Award, have recognized, empowered, and protected activists who have challenged dams, mining projects, or deforestation schemes at substantial personal risk.

Human rights provide tools to keep environmental protection efforts honest

Along with pollution, resource degradation, and ecosystem disruption, environmental *protection* may also lead to human rights violations—in part because some strands of environmental advocacy have taken their inspiration from a "wilderness model" that presupposes the radical separateness of the human and natural spheres of existence.[86] Nancy Peluso refers to cases in which international environmental initiatives have violated local community rights as instances of "coercing conservation."[87] Anthropologist Mac Chapin has identified several instances in which global conservation organizations have undertaken projects that clash with, or inadequately consult, indigenous communities—in part, he suggests, because of a backlash within these organizations against the community-based conservation schemes that emerged in the late 1980s and early 1990s.[88] Such episodes of coerced conservation typically combine both procedural and substantive rights violations.[89] A classic example is the conflict over the Lacandon Selva in southern Mexico, where land struggles around the Montes Azules Biosphere Reserve pitted poor settlers against state authorities and international environmentalists.[90]

To be sure, there will be instances in which natural-resource rights guarantees for individuals and communities will create challenging trade-offs with environmental protection—for instance, when the legitimate practices of indigenous communities clash with the legitimate concerns of conservationists regarding threatened species. More generally, rights guarantees may create new challenges of environmentally harmful resource use for local consumption. The much larger point, however, is that international environmental initiatives that trample on people's rights or sweep aside their concerns as stakeholders have little chance of succeeding in the long term. The best way to create stronger legitimacy for environmental efforts, and to ensure that they contain the elements of equity required for long-term efficacy, is to apply a human rights lens to the crafting of such efforts, even if it means that some forms of nature protection become less viable.

Thus, both domestically and transnationally, rights-based approaches make several distinct contributions to addressing the specific problems identified in the law-and-development approach. Importantly, these mechanisms are reinforced in *multiple* ways by the UN's endorsement of human rights and rights-based approaches, and the broadly global stamp of approval that such endorsement brings. First, UN backing can create additional pressure for national-level processes to become rights-based. Second, where formally codified rights exist at the national level but are not being realized in practice (a common occurrence, as discussed in chapter 4), UN backing can create resources, information, and training for local civil society to press rights-based claims. Finally, rights affirmation and recognition at the global level can create space for people to press claims upstream and down in transnational commodity chains, by using international forums such as regional human rights bodies or cross-jurisdictional strategies.[91]

As discussed in chapter 4, the barriers to realizing these contributions can be substantial. Nevertheless, rights-based approaches offer important possibilities precisely where the law-and-development model has failed: creating stronger mechanisms of accountability, opening up access to critical arenas of decision-making, injecting essential but unheard voices into the process, securing access to livelihood resources on a more sustainable basis, protecting those resources from ill-conceived schemes for economic development, and fending off dubious approaches to environmental protection.

The Case for Peace and Security

As with human rights, the case for linking environmental protection to the UN's peace mandate rests on several foundations:

Poor natural resource management and environmental degradation are central parts of the conflict trap

As discussed in detail in chapter 5, natural resource disputes are frequently implicated in civil violence and civil war, and the revenues from plundering resources (be it by the state or insurgent groups) can prolong violent conflict by providing revenue streams and a rationale for retaining territorial control. As we shall see, recidivism and conflict recurrence are also more likely in conflicts that involve natural resources, and peacekeeping missions in such cases are significantly longer and more costly. Better natural resource management is, thus, a central element of escaping the conflict trap. The links between environmental degradation and violent conflict are less direct (and, as chapter 5 explains, much debated). But there is no question that environmental degradation enhances human insecurity, increases state fragility, and overtaxes the state's capacity to respond—key elements of the conflict trap.

Violent conflict deepens and extends the globalization problem of unregulated spaces and hiding places

War creates transnational spaces that sit beyond the reach of effective environmental-protection regulations, thus exacerbating one of the core environmental problems of globalization alluded to previously. While it may be an inconvenient truth for Western governments and firms, the processes by which natural-resource wealth may fuel or exacerbate violent conflict are not limited to localized combatants. They also have a strong transnational component, with multinational and neighboring-country firms playing a key role in facilitating resource extraction—often illegally—from war zones, failed states, or the war-torn regions of conflict-affected states.[92] There has been a growing recognition in UN peacebuilding circles that peace, public order, control of rampant lawlessness, and security from "spoilers" are critical underpinnings of the wider economic and social processes necessary for peacebuilding in war-torn societies.[93] Bringing natural resource management under the rule of law is a front-line challenge in the effort to break these links.

Dispute resolution mechanisms are a key missing link in global environmental governance

One of the more subtle but important failings of the law-and-development approach has been its failure to create mechanisms to address and resolve natural-resource and environmental conflicts. As a result, the lack of transnational dispute-resolution procedures is perhaps the single biggest lacuna in the institutional apparatus of global environmental governance.[94] Interstate forums lack the ability to capture the political dynamics and authority relations that surround "stakeholder" controversies such as the construction of large dams, deforestation, overfishing in coastal-zone communities, or the rapid land-use changes implicated in so-called land grabs. Multistakeholder forums represent innovative experiments in global governance, and may generate normative trajectories that become increasingly embedded in society and practice. But a strong impetus from states and intergovernmental organizations is needed to sustain such processes, and in some cases even to get them started.

Linking peace and environment reintroduces a political element that has been sorely lacking from global environmental governance

The claim that environmental diplomacy has become depoliticized may seem strange, when the interest-based barriers thrown up by so many states have been central to the flagging momentum of international environmental protection. But consider the politics around internationally shared river basins. Efforts to produce agreement on the norms that should govern international relations around shared watercourses have not yielded a broad political consensus. Despite a low threshold for entry into force, the UN Watercourses Convention—a highly generalized framework, and one with no binding power at the basin level—required fourteen years to enter into force. Lacking a broader political dimension, efforts to promote international cooperation in shared river basins, when they exist at all, are usually limited to a "development" agenda that struggles to break through the larger zero-sum logic separating upstream and downstream states.[95] The World Bank's Nile Basin Initiative provides a powerful example of the resulting impasse: externally funded development projects and joint technical initiatives have softened some tensions, but fail to engage the larger questions around sharing water and its benefits in the basin. Similar dynamics can be seen around the Mekong, the Indus, and many other rivers.

Highlighting conflict risks and peace opportunities broadens the range of focal points for, and benefits of, environmental cooperation

A focus on the environment as a matter of peace and international security broadens the spectrum of possible proactive measures around which governments can cooperate. As discussed in chapter 5, there are risks to "securitizing" environmental issues, if they reinforce the zero-sum logic of international conflict and enhance the voice of actors and institutions that insist on seeing interstate relations that way. Nevertheless, recognizing peace-and-conflict linkages to the environment can make it possible to bring important actions into focus—confidence-building measures, dispute resolution practices, joint risk management—that are difficult even to envision when the starting point is solely a discourse of law and development. Adding a peace- and confidence-building agenda to environmental cooperation offers governments a chance—if they will take it—to transcend the zero-sum mentality of scarcity around shared resources.

Such cooperative synergies are not limited to governments. Linking peace and environment also offers the possibility of powerful synergies across civil society, uniting groups engaged in quests for peace, human rights, environmental protection, and grassroots development. Just as the human rights emphasis makes people an important political agent for positive change, environmental peacebuilding strategies may allow political empowerment and coalition building necessary to re-energize international environmental diplomacy.

Linking peace and environment enables integrative strategies of environmental peacebuilding

Taken together, the preceding arguments suggest that peace and sustainability must be seen as codependent. On the one hand, environmental initiatives must support peace; resource-management and environmental-protection efforts must become far more conflict-sensitive, to prevent practices that may trigger, sustain, or worsen conflict. Peace initiatives, meanwhile, must also support the environment: conflict-transformation and peacebuilding strategies must become far more sensitive to the environmental and natural-resource dimensions of human insecurity, and should seek to minimize harm to critical ecosystem services and livelihood resources.

However, mutual sensitivity between environmental governance and conflict management, while essential, is not enough. The two aims must also be integrated in a way that transforms the unsustainability-conflict nexus by broadening the spectrum of possible proactive measures. This transformative strategy has come to be known as environmental peacebuilding.[96] In this approach, using environmental challenges creatively—as tools to enhance peace and bolster human security, even as they reinforce sustainability—creates opportunities to break the dismal cycle that links unsustainability, human insecurity, and violence. Carefully designed and implemented environmental initiatives may yield better mutual understanding, build a habit of cooperation across social divisions, and soften conflict identities by creating a stronger sense of people's shared landscape and shared interests in sustainability across that landscape. Finding environmental initiatives that can also be peace-enhancing, vulnerability-reducing, and rights-affirming makes it possible to replace the destructive downward spirals flagged earlier with upward-trending positive synergies.

CONCLUSION: FROM LAW-AND-DEVELOPMENT TO THE FULL FORCE OF THE MANDATE

The paradigm of better law between nations and better development within them fails to recognize some of the key consequences of globalization. States face severe limits of regulatory capacity in a world where complex and dynamic global chains of production and consumption weave in and out of national territory. Some of the most important forms of power in these systems are wielded in the "trans-sovereign" spaces of the global political economy, and by actors other than national governments. As long as relative costs rule, the system has an almost limitless capacity to export the costs of adjustment onto less powerful actors somewhere else. The ability to shift environmental damage onto peripheral communities, remote regions, and the urban underclass is a central mechanism of sustaining the unsustainable.

Advocates of environmental protection have adapted to this new world in a variety of ways, mostly notably by creating voluntary systems of best practices among global corporate actors and tapping the power of consumers through product certification and green purchasing. While observers debate the efficacy of such measures, it has become increasingly clear that they are no substitute for an explicit right to environmental quality at the specific nodes in the global chain where environmental impacts are felt most directly. Such a right at the most vulnerable points in global commodity chains—be it harm from extractive industries far upstream, worker risks in manufacturing and assembly at midstream, or toxic waste disposal and contaminated food far downstream—is a starting point for creating accountability and responsible practice across the entire chain.

A second blind spot of law and development has been violent conflict. The absence of peace has profoundly undermined the ability of people in conflict zones around the world to achieve anything remotely approaching sustainable development, while creating a legal vacuum in broad swaths of territory where resource plunder and environmental exploitation become the norm. Where peace is not secured, sustainable practices cannot take root; where peace is lost, sustainable practices are among its first casualties.[97] Moreover, just as sustainability requires peace, so does peace need sustainability. Peace can be a casualty of the profoundly unsustainable ways that natural resources are managed and critical ecosystems are disrupted. Poor environmental governance, unsustainable extraction, assaulted landscapes, and unwise, inequitable natural resource management can worsen the prospects for peace, trigger conflict, and make it easier to sustain violence.

Moving peace and human rights from the margins to the mainstream of the UN's environmental activities can be seen as an effort to fix these "blind spots" of law and development, as sketched above. It can also be seen in strategic terms, as an attempt to renew political commitment for environmental action. Adding peace and human rights to the mix creates possibilities for tapping a wider set of state interests, building new political coalitions internationally, and enhancing citizen agency both domestically and transnationally. For the UN in particular, an additional goal is to create a more effective platform for the badly needed, often exhorted, but rarely realized goal of a "system-wide" response (a theme discussed in chapter 6).

To be sure, both a large body of research and some common sense should caution us that rights-based frameworks and peacebuilding efforts are not enough. Rights are, at best, only one means to the larger objective of enhancing people's capabilities.[98] To be effective, rights must be actionable rather than theoretical, meaningful rather than minimal, inalienable rather than tradable, and integrated rather than fragmented into separate civil/political and socioeconomic components. Without this, environmental rights can quickly become mere minimum standards—just barely enough, just clean enough, just close enough—that may blunt rather than catalyze pressure for change. Much the same is true of environmental peacebuilding efforts: engaging high-political interests of state, and thus "securitizing" the issue area, is likely to have pernicious consequences if not centered in a robust and broadly legitimate quest to transform conflict into peace.

Can the UN's environmental efforts be transformed along the lines suggested by this argument? Can they be made rights-based, accountability-oriented, conflict-sensitive, and peace-enhancing? Chapters 4 and 5 examine progress to date, as well as barriers along the road, in strengthening the mandate domains of human rights and international peace and security in global environmental governance. Such reforms, while challenging, promise a dual benefit: more effective and lasting environmental protection, as well as better service to the UN's mandate of peace, development, human rights, and international cooperation.

CHAPTER 4

The Dignity and Worth of People in Nature

Strengthening Environmental

Human Rights

INTRODUCTION: THE SILENCE ON ENVIRONMENTAL HUMAN RIGHTS

The UN has for several decades been the world's most important forum for the articulation, codification, and institutionalization of human rights principles.[1] The family of human rights treaties negotiated through the UN has become the central reference point for legal and political debates on human rights across the international system. The UN also plays an important role in the practical defense of human rights. The Office of the High Commissioner for Human Rights (OHCHR) has the power to focus world attention on particularly egregious abuses, and the UN Human Rights Council (UNHRC) performs universal periodic reviews of the human rights situation in each member state. Both bodies also play a role in calling attention to new human rights issues for consideration by member states.

When it comes to human rights, however, the UN has had almost nothing to say about the environment. Existing human rights treaties do not address the environment. A few environmental-rights initiatives emerged from the now-defunct UN Commission on Human Rights (UNCHR) and its successor, UNHRC. But they have crawled through the system at a snail's pace and gravitate toward vague, noncommittal statements. Both environmental protection and human rights are increasingly recognized as pillars of human development, and UN development initiatives have increasingly embraced both rights-based and sustainability-oriented approaches. But little has been done to merge these two foundations by giving environmental human rights specific meaning or recognition. As a result, advocates of environmental protection have found their concerns to have little resonance at the heart of UN human rights work.

This gap is problematic, from both a rights perspective and an environmental perspective. A sound environment is essential to realizing a broad array of established human rights, including but not limited to the rights to life, health, food, water, development, and cultural identity. At the same time, human rights are necessary for a sound environment, because rights allow citizens to obtain information, press claims, participate in decision-making arenas, express disagreement, and protest when necessary. Thus, when the environment is protected, human rights are more likely to flourish; when human rights are protected, the environment is more likely to be sustained. The failure to couple these two potent forces inhibits some powerful synergies.

This chapter examines the evolving relationship between human rights and the environment within the UN system. The discussion traces the enduring barriers to giving environmental human rights real meaning, but also the possibilities emerging within a newly broadened realm of UN human rights practice. The UN human rights apparatus has been undergoing dynamic change over the past few decades, with its center of gravity shifting from a legalistic core of international treaties to a wider, more active, and increasingly institutionalized system of practice. This shift provides important opportunities—as yet, largely untapped—to establish and strengthen environmental human rights. To illustrate both the barriers and the opportunities, the chapter examines recent campaigns on the right to water and on the links between climate change and human rights.

WHY SO LITTLE MOVEMENT ON ENVIRONMENTAL HUMAN RIGHTS?

The UN has experienced great dynamism in the domain of human rights over the past few decades, leading to a widening array of practices. As Julie Mertus has pointed out, "UN human rights practice used to happen where the name plate on the door said 'human rights.' So, human rights were almost entirely contained within a limited set of specific human rights bodies. This is no longer the case."[2]

Among the factors that Mertus identifies behind this shift, three stand out. First is a broader conception of the rights mandate that shades into previously separate organizational domains of development, trade, labor, refugees, security, and humanitarian aid. A second factor is the emergence of new organs, including the Office of the High Commissioner for Human Rights (OHCHR) and the reconfiguration of the old Human Rights Commission (UNCHR) into the new Human Rights Council (UNHRC). Third, there has been a shift in emphasis that moves beyond codification, standards-setting, and monitoring to emphasize implementation and improving states' capacity to comply.

Until recently, this dynamic energy did not translate into growing momentum for environmental human rights. Indeed, as Alan Boyle has pointed out, the developmental trajectory of global environmental governance from the 1972 Stockholm Conference to the 1992 Rio Earth Summit saw not just a lack of progress but an actual step backward for the idea of environmental human rights.[3] The Stockholm Declaration asserted a right: "Man has the fundamental right to freedom, equality and adequate conditions of life, in an environment of a quality that permits a life of dignity and well-being."[4] At Rio twenty years later, member states scaled back that endorsement of a fundamental right, replacing it with the weaker notion of an entitlement, and one linked only indirectly to its natural foundations: "Human beings are at the center of concerns for sustainable development. They are entitled to a healthy and productive life in harmony with nature."[5] UNCHR's independent expert on the environmental human rights question has conceded that the Stockholm Declaration remains, more than four decades later, the closest the UN has come to formulating a human right to a healthy environment.[6]

Or consider *Agenda 21*, the blueprint for sustainability emerging from the 1992 Earth Summit. Across its several hundred pages, *Agenda 21* made no mention of the environment as a human right, and offered only occasional endorsements of various group rights (women's rights, indigenous people's rights, the land rights of the poor) as useful instruments for addressing the environment-development-poverty nexus. A careful reading of *Agenda 21* does reveal several brief references to what would later gain momentum as "rights-based approaches"—including a call for governments to affirm the rights of nongovernmental organizations[7] and qualified support for community right-to-know provisions. But these are marginal and incipient rather than core elements of the blueprint.[8] On hotly contested issues such as biological diversity and marine resource exploitation, *Agenda 21* took care to reaffirm the permanent sovereignty of states over their natural resources.

The failure of the Earth Summit to catalyze rights-based approaches was apparent one year later, in 1993, at the UN-sponsored World Conference on Human Rights held in Vienna. Consistent with the "law and development" model favored at Rio, Vienna affirmed the right to development as the principal means to achieve environmental sustainability.[9] The final report of the conference made only a few passing references to the environment—for example, flagging illicit dumping of toxic waste as a human rights violation—and alluded to the framework established at Rio only when affirming women's rights to "sustainable and equitable development."[10]

Some of the barriers to linking human rights and the environment within the UN system derive from national interests and are not difficult to understand. Powerful states remain wary of the concept or oppose it entirely. The United States, for example, has not ratified the *International Covenant on Economic, Social, and Cultural Rights*; has consistently opposed the discovery or designation of socioeconomic rights by UN bodies; and has preferred to limit any environmental rights discussion to noting the importance of civil and political rights for positive outcomes (environmental and otherwise). More specifically, on problems such as climate change, for which the United States bears a disproportionate historical responsibility, a tighter coupling between environmental change and human rights could have major implications for American obligations; US policy has consistently opposed affirming such a link.[11] Some less-developed countries have also been quite wary of environmental human rights, seeing the concept as a threat to particular strategies of development.

Under these circumstances, debates about rights and responsibilities in global environmental politics frequently play out along interest-based lines. During a 2009 panel discussion of the UNHRC, both the United States and Canada argued that there was no direct connection between climate change and human rights law. In this view, the causal complexity, uncertainties, and global scope of climate change make it difficult to assign strict legal responsibility for causing the problem.[12] Many less-developed countries argued in the same forum that historical responsibility is quite clear and can be seen in a country's legacy of greenhouse gas emissions. This view is consistent with an interest in seeing responsibility attached primarily to the major greenhouse gas emitters, rather than to states that may fail to help their own populations cope with the effects of climate change.

Again, however, interest-based behavior is not a complete explanation for the lack of progress on environmental rights within the UN system.

As discussed in chapter 1, interest-based models fail to account for the frequent uncertainty around interests, the dynamic role of ideas and paradigms, the teaching role of international organizations as to where state interests may reside, or the delegation chains that can give international bureaucracies substantial autonomy. On human rights specifically, simple interest-based models also fail a straightforward empirical test: they cannot explain the great dynamism seen in other domains of human rights advocacy—including the rights of the disabled, the rights of the child, and the rights of indigenous peoples—over the same time period. When the right political conditions, institutional incentives, ideational frameworks, and social catalysts are present, the UN has shown itself quite capable of extending human rights concepts and practices in bold new directions, embracing nonincremental change in ways that strengthen people's rights. Why, then, has this not happened on environmental rights?

The Role of Ideas: Conceptual Complexity, Moral Quandaries, and Strategic Divisions

One barrier to environmental human rights in the UN system has been conceptual. Despite compelling arguments that environmental protection and human rights support and reinforce one another, the debate on environmental human rights is marked by conceptual complexity, legal uncertainty, and ethical quandaries. These features divide advocates, fragment coalitions, and allow opponents to stymie progress in intergovernmental deliberations:

What legal basis?

One conceptual uncertainty involves the precise legal basis for claiming an environmental human right. Is adequate access to natural resource goods and environmental services an express right—that is, a right in and of itself? Or is it simply an enabling condition—a means to realize other rights that are codified in international law? Given the limited references to the environment or natural resources in the "hard" law of human rights treaties, how compelling is the body of customary international law and nonbinding "soft" law with regard to environmental rights? As discussed below, the question of whether there is an express right to environmental quality has plodded through the UN human rights apparatus with no clear resolution, and advocacy groups have been divided on whether it is worth trying to get the UN to "find" an express right.

What type of right?

If some basis exists for the environment as a human right, what type of right is it, exactly? Is it a socioeconomic right, analogous to a right to food or shelter, that requires certain substantive outcomes such as breathable air and drinkable water? Or is it better understood as a civil and political right, realized not in terms of material outcomes but rather through civic procedures such as access to environmental information, participation in environmental deliberations, or the availability of redress when harm occurs? Then again, perhaps the environment is a so-called third-generation human right—transcending the traditional distinction between civil/political rights and socioeconomic rights, and akin to rights of self-determination or cultural heritage.[13] This question entangles environmental human rights in larger controversies, such as the generalized opposition of the United States to extending the codification of socioeconomic rights. It also divides movements, with advocates conceiving of rights in different ways in campaigns for a human right to water, a rights-based approach to climate change, and other efforts.

Whose right is it?

Are environmental rights better understood as attaching to individuals, to communities, or to entire nations? Who or what is the relevant "legal person" under international law, entitled to any such rights? According to a recent review of countries that have codified environmental human rights at the national level, the overwhelming tendency has been to treat it as an individual right.[14] Many environmental conditions and ecosystem services, however, have the character of shared public goods. Again, the case of water is instructive. While UN efforts to promote a human right to water have stressed each individual's right to a safe and adequate supply of water, it can be difficult to secure the ecosystem services on which such supplies depend if rights are individualized. Many indigenous communities have been wary of "payment for ecosystem services" schemes for watershed protection or climate-change mitigation, which, to the extent that they involve individualized and commercialized property-rights mechanisms, can be in tension with indigenous community rights.[15]

What obligations ensue?

Under international law, human rights entail corresponding obligations on states: to respect, to protect, and to fulfill. What sorts of obligations do environmental rights create, and to whom or what do those obligations attach? As Daniel Bodansky has pointed out, international environmental law exists not simply to set out rights and obligations between states, but also to regulate and reverse harmful effects that emanate from the actions of a wide array of private actors.[16] Under those circumstances, what does it mean to perform the classic state responsibilities to respect, protect, and fulfill human rights? Consider the risks to vulnerable populations from extreme weather events, which climate models suggest are becoming more frequent. In a 2009 discussion on climate change in the UNHRC, Canada argued that individual member states bear primary responsibility for climate adaptation and to safeguard their own people through disaster risk reduction. In contrast, several developing countries argued that it is both impractical and unjust to hold national governments primarily responsible for safeguarding people—impractical given prevailing limits on state capacity, and unjust given historical responsibility for the problem.[17]

What consequences?

Does treating the environment as a human right reinforce an excessively human-centered view of the environment—a view that, for many environmentalists, is at the heart of our planetary ecological maladies? Does it go too far in instrumentalizing the environment, valuing it only when it pays benefits for people? Others worry about a different form of instrumentalization, in which human rights are simply a stalking horse for property rights, supplanting broad movements for social justice with a narrowly individualistic and market-friendly approach.[18] Then again, rather than going too far in creating individual entitlements, perhaps environmental human rights do not go far enough. Does the rights-based approach settle for an unjust minimum standard—just enough clean water and breathable air to survive?[19] Wolfgang Sachs has drawn a distinction between *relational* environmental justice, or "proportionate distribution of goods and rights among individuals and groups," and *substantive* environmental justice, or "the minimum goods and rights necessary for a dignified existence."[20] By stressing substantive justice through minimum standards, might environmental human rights too quickly concede, or even lock in, relational injustice? Again, the case of water is instructive: does the human rights approach to water access provide a powerfully transformative strategy, or does it risk locking in a goal of just barely enough water, just clean enough for survival, and just close enough to be hauled home, primarily by young women who should be in school?[21]

The Institutional Dimension

Along with the divisive effects of these conceptual, legal, ethical, and strategic complexities, another barrier to the development of environmental human rights has been institutional. Until recently, the UN approach to protecting human rights has centered on treaties, most of which date to the UN's pre-environmental era. The Charter of the United Nations makes no mention of the natural environment; nor does the UN's most important visionary statement on rights, the 1948 Universal Declaration on Human Rights (UDHR). The environment is not addressed in the two foundational treaties of the modern human rights era, the *International Covenant on Civil and Political Rights* (ICCPR) and *International Covenant on Economic, Social, and Cultural Rights* (ICESCR). All but a few of the most important human rights treaties were negotiated in the period before the 1992 Earth Summit, including not only the ICCPR and the ICESCR (1966) but also accords on racial discrimination (1965), discrimination against women (1979), torture (1984), the rights of the child (1989), and the rights of migrant workers (1990).

The treaty-centered approach to human rights has limited the growth and spread of environment-rights linkages. The core UN human rights organs have lacked, at least until recently, the sort of bureaucratic-entrepreneurial space seen on the "development" wing of the UN, when the specialized agencies grabbed a large slice of the environmental pie in the 1960s (chapter 2). Nor have there been strong incentives across the wider UN system to build environment-rights bridges, given that only a few oblique references to the natural world exist in the core body of human-rights treaty law. As a result, the various environmental-rights coalitions springing up within transnational civil society beginning in the 1980s found more resonance—or, returning to an earlier metaphor, a better coral reef to which to attach themselves—in the development-related spheres of UN activity.

The Historical Trajectory: Stages of Development in Environment-Rights Linkages

When viewing the combination of these considerations around interests, ideas, and institutions historically, the relationship between the environment and human rights in the UN system can be seen to correspond to three distinct stages. First is the period from the formation of the UN to the mid-1960s, when the question of national sovereignty and rights over natural resources took center stage in global governance, as discussed in chapter 2. During this period, the dominant intellectual framework for linking nature and human rights was a postcolonial, nationalistic discourse about the sovereign rights of a "people" to use the natural resource base. Institutionally, the state-centric, treaty-based character of the emerging UN human rights apparatus created little or no space for bureaucratic entrepreneurs or collaboration across the mandate domains. And both ideas and institutions developed in a larger context in which the primary challenge to liberal-internationalist global governance was that of accommodating the rapid influx of developing countries as politically sovereign but economically dependent actors in the world political economy.

The second stage consists of the period from the early 1970s through the 1990s, when "the environment" emerged as a major new global governance challenge to liberal internationalism. Responses within the UN system hewed primarily to the law-and-development approach discussed in chapter 2. Ideationally, sustainable development emerged as the predominant frame. Institutionally, the development-oriented specialized agencies and programs proved to be the most promising coral reef. More broadly, as we have seen, the two-pronged grand strategy of liberal international environmentalism during this period stressed issue-specific international treaties (better law between nations) and a North-South "global bargain" on development reform (better development within nations). This period also witnessed the "developmentalization" of human rights in global governance, as discussed in chapter 2. This process reinforced the tendency to subordinate concerns for individuals and local communities to the larger North-South interstate political-economic narrative. In this context, environmental human rights made little headway in the UN's human rights apparatus, and took up a largely secondary and derivative role in the UN's development-oriented pursuits.

The third stage, and the focus of the rest of this chapter, is the uneven but clearly identifiable rise over the past decade of a more rights-based approach to the environment. During this period, the focus of human rights advocacy has shifted from the negotiation of treaties to the implementation of rights-sensitive programs. A byproduct of this shift has been to create new space for the institutionalization of environment-rights linkages across the UN system. As a result, we are witnessing a still-incipient but more rapid proliferation of rights-based approaches to environmental protection, as well as a growing awareness that environmental conditions are a vital foundation for a wide array of recognized human rights. This growth has occurred even though progress toward member-state acceptance of the environment as an express human right remains, at best, halting and belabored.

THE PLODDING QUEST TO FIND AN EXPLICIT
ENVIRONMENTAL HUMAN RIGHT

Despite the fact that the UN's human-rights apparatus was central to the early debate on permanent sovereignty over natural resources, it was not until the 1990s that the rights system began to engage the question of an individual or local community's right to environmental quality. In 1989, during the run-up to the Rio Earth Summit, a coalition of NGOs called upon the UN Sub-Commission on Prevention of Discrimination and Protection of Minorities—a standing subcommission of UNCHR—to "study the connections between human rights and the environment."[22] This prodding set in motion the appointment in 1990 of one of the subcommission's members, the Algerian diplomat Fatma Zohra Ksentini, as Special Rapporteur on Human Rights and the Environment.

The special rapporteur convened an expert working group that, in 1994, drafted a set of principles on human rights and the environment.[23] The draft principles asserted that "all persons have the right to a secure, healthy and ecologically sound environment," and in that context identified several clusters of rights: freedom from pollution, environmental degradation, and environmentally adverse activities; "protection and preservation of the air, soil, water, sea-ice, flora and fauna, and the essential processes and areas necessary to maintain biological diversity and ecosystems"; safe and healthy working and living conditions; and an equitable share of the benefits of conservation and sustainable resource use. The draft principles also stressed that certain procedural rights related to the environment—including "the right to active, free, and meaningful participation in planning and decision-making activities and processes that may have an impact on the environment and development"—were necessary to the realization of those substantive rights.[24]

In issuing her final report in 1994, the special rapporteur acknowledged that the right to a "healthy and flourishing" environment was an "evolving" one, about which there was no general consensus and for which there were "few specific provisions" in international human rights instruments.[25] The report recommended that several UN human rights treaty bodies, committees, and working groups examine the environmental dimensions of their respective domains, and that the UN as a whole adopt "a set of norms consolidating the right to a satisfactory environment."[26]

Although the subcommission recommended the appointment of a special rapporteur with powers to collect information, investigate, and solicit comments on the draft principles, the full UNHCR declined to do so.[27] Instead, it called for comments on the special rapporteur's report from member states (few of which were forthcoming); requested a report from the Secretary-General (which contained no recommendations); and appointed Ksentini as a special rapporteur with a narrower mandate on the specific issue of toxic wastes. UNHCR received her report in 2001 and issued a resolution in 2004 that condemned the practice of illegally trafficking in and dumping toxic waste, affirming it to be "a serious threat to human rights" and urging governments to take appropriate measures.[28]

One year later, in 2005—that is, more than a decade after the special rapporteur's call to consolidate the matter—the Secretary-General's office reported to UNCHR that there had been "growing recognition of the connection between environmental protection and human rights" at the international, regional, and national levels.[29] Tellingly, only a few concrete examples of UN activity could be identified: the work of the special rapporteur; the health-related provisions of a few multilateral environmental agreements; some general references to the environment in the work of other special rapporteurs; a 2002 general comment of the Committee on Economic, Social and Cultural Rights regarding a human right to water; and a few specific initiatives by FAO and WHO.

Beyond the UN: Moving Forward, but in Piecemeal Fashion

As the concept of environmental human rights was grinding its way through the UN's human rights apparatus, the wider world did not stand still on the question. According to a 2009 review by legal scholar Dinah Shelton, "On the national level, more than 100 constitutions throughout the world guarantee a right to a clean and healthy environment, impose a duty on the state to prevent environmental harm, or mention the protection of the environment or natural resources."[30] The French constitution, for example, was amended in 2005 to add a Charter of the Environment. A list compiled by the environmental NGO EarthJustice in 2007 identified 119 countries with constitutional provisions relating to the environment, including several of the world's most recently written constitutions. The Democratic Republic of Congo's 2003 Draft Constitution of the Transition stated that "all Congolese shall have the right to a healthy environment that is favorable to their development." The new constitution of Afghanistan (2004) provided for a "prosperous life and a sound environment for all those residing in this land." Bhutan's draft constitution of 2005 stated that "the Royal Government shall ... [p]revent pollution and ecological degradation ... (and) [e]nsure a safe and healthy environment."[31]

Regional organizations also filled the void left by UN sluggishness. According to Article 24 of the 1981 African Charter on Human and Peoples' Rights, "All people shall have the right to a general satisfactory environment favorable to their development."[32] A subsequent 2003 protocol affirms the rights of women to "live in a healthy and sustainable environment" and "to fully enjoy their right to sustainable development."[33] The American Convention on Human Rights, in its 1988 additional protocol on economic, social, and cultural rights, states that "everyone shall have the right to live in a healthy environment and to have access to basic public services" and calls upon states parties to "promote the protection, preservation, and improvement of the environment."[34] The 2004 Arab Charter on Human Rights also includes the right to a healthy environment, linking it to adequate living standards, and the Association of Southeast Asian Nations (ASEAN) adopted a similar declaration in 2012.[35] A database compiled by the UNHRC-appointed independent expert on human rights and the environment has identified seventy decisions by regional human rights tribunals on environmental cases since 1985.[36]

Procedural environmental rights also gained traction, most notably in Europe's *Convention on Access to Information, Public Participation and Access to Justice in Environmental Matters*, signed in Aarhus, Denmark, in 1998. Building on Principle 10 of the 1992 Rio Declaration, the Aarhus Convention obligates ratifying states to ensure public rights to information, participation, and justice in environmental decision-making processes.[37] In the wake of Aarhus, the World Resources Institute (WRI), a Washington-based environmental think tank, launched the Access Initiative, a multiyear, multicountry effort to assess progress and barriers in citizen access to these rights. The project found that "generally ... governments have made significant progress in establishing the legal infrastructure of rights and opportunities for 'access.'"[38] A 2006 survey identified sixty-nine countries with freedom-of-information laws, for example. The study also identified limits, however: laws for freedom of information were more widespread than laws on public participation; implementation of relevant codified rights and regulations often had been slow; and, in general, practice lagged behind the development of laws and regulations.

A body of case law has begun to emerge in the wake of these national constitutional rights and regional legal instruments.[39] A 2009 expert meeting organized by UNEP and OHCHR noted "the growing trend in international and regional courts and tribunals to consider human rights issues when adjudicating on environmental disputes." The experts also cautioned, however, that "the law in this area suffered from a lack of coherence."[40] At the international level, much of the case material is generated through complaints submitted to regional and UN treaty bodies, which vary in how they conceive of environmental rights or investigate claims.[41] The African Commission on Human and Peoples' Rights, for example, has a mandate to monitor state compliance; its inter-American counterpart does not. At the national level, Shelton's survey of the field found wide variation in rights, interpretation, and enforcement. Although observing that "the constitutional rights granted are increasingly being enforced by courts," she concluded that "in the absence of a clear international text articulating the links between human rights and the environment, the difficulties facing courts presented human rights claims based on environmental harm are significant."[42] This variation also undermines a potentially decisive legal argument: that environmental rights have obtained the status of customary international law. As the UNHRC's independent expert on the question put it, "While there is no shortage of statements on human rights obligations relating to the environment, the statements do not come together on their own to constitute a coherent set of norms."[43]

From UNCHR to UNHRC

In 2006, a newly formed Human Rights Council (UNHRC) replaced the controversial UNCHR as the UN's central human rights body. Unlike its predecessor, UNHRC selects its members from a vote of the entire General Assembly, limits member states to two consecutive terms, and incorporates new mechanisms for universal periodic review of member states and for the fielding of complaints. UNHRC has also made use of innovative mechanisms: panel discussions, input from a broader group of stakeholders, and research and reporting capabilities of the high commissioner's office. These developments have opened new institutional space for environmental human rights.

Rather than engage the question of an express right to environmental quality, UNHRC initially took a more issue-specific approach (although this is changing, as discussed below). As the council's independent expert on the environmental question, the US law professor John Knox, put it, the focus has been "not on proclaiming a new right to a healthy environment but rather on what might be called 'greening' human rights—that is, examining and highlighting the relationship of existing human rights to the environment."[44] Along those lines, UNHRC reappointed the special rapporteur on toxic wastes; addressed the question of a human right to water, which has received a strong push from advocacy groups and sympathetic governments in recent years; and worked in concert with OHCHR to raise the profile of the human rights implications of global climate change.

FROM FINDING A RIGHT TO PRACTICING IT: THE UN AS A WIDENING FIELD OF HUMAN RIGHTS PRACTICE

As the idea of a human right to environmental quality has plodded through the UN human rights apparatus, a growing recognition of environment-rights linkages has begun to emerge across the wider UN landscape. A key to this development has been the aforementioned broadening of the UN human rights apparatus beyond the treaty regimes. Key elements of this shift include the Office of the High Commissioner, established in 1993; the new and more vigorous UNHRC, established in 2006; and the expanding emphasis on rights-based practices in the specialized agencies and other functional organs.

Institutional diversification has created new opportunities for environment-rights linkages. As a result, a mutually reinforcing relationship has begun to emerge: rights-based pathways to realizing environmental protection and environmental pathways to realizing human rights. Although incipient and uneven, these growing connections can be seen across a widening array of UN practices.

To date, the strong side of environment-rights linkages has been in the development of rights-based initiatives for environmental protection. Such initiatives make rights—including land tenure rights, rights of access to natural resources, informational rights, and participatory rights—central tools in the pursuit of environmental aims. For example, the Environment and Energy Program within UNDP launched a rights-based initiative on "strengthening the rationale for devolving substantive resource rights by improving communication between local and state actors, demonstrating the benefits of community-driven approaches, and increasing the ability of state officials to identify local best practices."[45] UNDP also has an initiative on strengthening community voices in energy and environmental policy processes, which emphasizes building capacity to participate meaningfully in national and international policy forums.[46]

FAO has initiated similar projects in its work on forests and fisheries.[47] In May 2012, The FAO-based Committee on World Food Security[48] adopted the FAO-developed "Voluntary Guidelines on the Responsible Governance of Tenure of Land, Fisheries and Forests in the Context of National Food Security." The guidelines seek to improve and protect access to livelihood resources for poor and vulnerable communities. They call upon governments to implement safeguards "to protect tenure rights of local people from risks that could arise from large-scale land acquisitions, and also to protect human rights, livelihoods, food security and the environment."[49] Despite being less than fully satisfied with their content, activist groups including Via Campesina and FoodFirst recognized the guidelines as progress and called on governments to implement their provisions.[50]

The other side of the potential synergy is to use environmental initiatives as tools to realize human rights. An example, discussed in the next section, is the effort to inject human rights into the largely stalled negotiations on climate change. In this view, the realization and protection of human rights is a central reason to take strong multilateral action on climate. Similarly, some advocates have argued that ecosystem protection is essential for achieving socioeconomic rights such as food security or sustained access to water and sanitation.[51]

In general, however, the embrace of environmental initiatives as tools for human rights remains underdeveloped across the UN system. Consider the environmental underpinnings of the now well-established human rights to health and food. In 2000, the UN Committee on Economic, Social and Cultural Rights (CESCR) released General Comment 14 on the right to health. CESCR is a body of independent experts that advises ECOSOC, which has monitoring duties for the ICESCR. The findings in its general comment reports play an important soft-law role in sharpening and clarifying the content, scope, and determinants of socioeconomic and cultural rights. General Comment 14 identifies environmental conditions as one of the "underlying determinants" of health, and conceives of the right to health as "inclusive" of those determining conditions.[52] Similarly, CESCR's General Comment 12 on food (1999) identifies the right to food as "inseparable from social justice, requiring the adoption of appropriate economic, environmental and social policies, at both the national and international levels, oriented to the eradication of poverty and the fulfillment of all human rights for all."[53]

Yet, for both health and food, the specialized agencies have missed opportunities to incorporate environmental protection as a central element for the realization of these rights. Since the release of General Comment 14, the World Health Organization (WHO) has strengthened its rights-based approach to health. Yet the WHO handbook *Human Rights, Health and Poverty Reduction Strategies* makes only passing mention of environmental rights and health linkages.[54] Similarly, the principal instrument of the Food and Agriculture Organization (FAO) on the right to food, its Voluntary Guidelines, draws no links to rights-based approaches to environmental protection, and merely calls on states to "consider" national policies, legal instruments, and supporting mechanisms on environmental protection as it relates to the right to food.[55]

The outstanding question, of course, is whether rights-based environmental initiatives and environmentally based rights initiatives can combine to create a virtuous cycle in which sustained, mutually reinforcing effects allow the realization of both aims. In the following sections, the examples of water and climate change illustrate the possibilities, as well as the enduring barriers, to realizing this potential.

The Case of Water

There has long been an implicit basis in international law for a human right to water, given that water is fundamental to well-established rights such as life, food, and health.[56] Also, several international human rights agreements make at least passing reference to specific state obligations related to drinking water and sanitation, including the 1979 *Convention on the Elimination of All Forms of Discrimination against Women* (Article 14), the 1985 *Convention on Occupational Health Services of the International Labour Organization* (Article 5), the 1989 *Convention on the Rights of the Child* (Articles 24 and 27), and the 2006 *Convention on the Rights of Persons with Disabilities* (Article 28).[57]

It was not until 28 July 2010, however, that the General Assembly adopted a resolution recognizing "the right to safe and clean drinking water and sanitation as a human right that is essential for the full enjoyment of life and all human rights."[58] While the General Assembly resolution lacks the hard-law status of a ratified treaty, it has become an important symbol of the international community's acceptance of a right to water, and has given impetus to the ongoing shift toward a "rights based" approach to addressing the daunting global problem of water deprivation.

In legal terms, the right to water emerged from a labored journey through the UN's human rights machinery. International attention to the challenge of water poverty first came into focus at the 1977 UN Water Conference held in Mar del Plata, Argentina, which declared that "all peoples, whatever their stage of development and their social and economic conditions, have the right to have access to drinking water in quantities and of a quality equal to their basic needs."[59] The General Assembly marked 1980–1989 as the International Drinking Water Supply and Sanitation Decade; at Rio in 1992, *Agenda 21* endorsed the Mar del Plata statement.[60] A right to water is also referenced in the landmark 1999 General Assembly resolution on the right to development.[61]

Building on this momentum, and taking as its point of departure the 1966 ICESCR, ECOSOC's advisory body CESCR in 2002 produced General Comment 15 on the right to water. The committee found that "water is a limited natural resource and a public good fundamental for life and health. The human right to water is indispensable for leading a life in human dignity. It is a prerequisite for the realization of other human rights."[62] In 2008 UNHRC appointed an independent expert on water, the Portuguese human rights lawyer Catarina de Albequerque, whose findings set the stage for the 2010 UNGA resolution.

While the recognition of a human right to water emerged from this formal-legal process, it also reflects years of sustained advocacy by civil society organizations, trade unions, water experts, and sympathetic governments. Key milestones in the political campaign included the abject failure of the aforementioned International Decade to achieve universal water access, which underscored the need for a rights-based approach; the 1992 Dublin Principles, produced in the run-up to the 1992 Earth Summit, which identified water as a finite, essential resource that must be managed through a participatory approach; and the backlash against the controversial efforts of international financial institutions to privatize water services as a condition of structural-adjustment lending.[63]

Most recently, the movement gained further impetus from the Millennium Development Goals (MDGs), which sought over 2000–2015 to reduce by half the proportion of the world's people who lack adequate drinking water supplies and sanitation. At the time of the 2010 General Assembly declaration of a human right to water, an estimated 900 million people still lacked reliable access to safe drinking water facilities, and a staggering 2.6 billion were without adequate sanitation services.[64] While the global MDG goal on drinking water was reportedly attained as of 2012, progress has been uneven: not all world regions have attained the drinking water goal, some countries have in fact lost ground, and the global target for sanitation was not met by 2015.[65] As these failings became apparent, it further spurred demand to declare a human right to water.

Advocates argue that the rights focus keeps the spotlight on water poverty and deprivation around the world, encourages renewed efforts to meet and surpass the MDG targets, prioritizes basic human needs over other uses of water, and focuses attention on specific national and international obligations to respect, protect, and fulfill the right.[66] Some advocates, including former Soviet premier Mikhail Gorbachev and the NGO Green Cross International, have pushed for an international convention that would give the right to water hard-law status.

The right-to-water movement has taken advantage of the aforementioned broadening field of UN practice on human rights. OHCHR provided an important entry point, partnering with leading NGOs and WHO to produce an important 2003 report that framed the issue for action by the then-existent UNHCR.[67] More recently, the new UNHRC has been more fertile ground for the emergent "rights based" concept than its predecessor. Donor aid for water and sanitation projects has grown in step with the rights-based approach; according to data from Organisation for Economic Co-operation and Development (OECD), bilateral water aid (adjusted for inflation) doubled from 1995 to 2009.[68]

Yet, as water scholar and development expert Lyla Mehta has argued, the critical question is not simply whether people's human rights are acknowledged, but whether their human capabilities are ultimately enhanced.[69] From this perspective, formal recognition of the human right to water and aid programs that seek to expand water supplies for the poor are insufficient. The water deprivation that bedevils too many of the world's people is not an inherent attribute of nature; there are few places in the world where water is so very scarce in an absolute physical sense that wise water use and sensible planning cannot meet basic human needs. Rather, water deprivation and water poverty are in most instances socially constructed products of the political and economic dynamics that surround the resource base.[70]

A human right to water will extend human capabilities only if it can tap the environment/rights synergy in *both* directions. This means, on the one hand, protecting the ecosystems that are essential to sustained access to clean water—a theme that was given no attention in the MDGs, and which is mentioned but not operationalized in the post-2015 Sustainable Development Goals. At the same time, it is also essential to realize the rights to information, participation, and justice enshrined in the Rio

Declaration and the Aarhus Convention, which are essential to protecting the critical ecosystem services that sustain water supplies.

Figure 4.1 illustrates the sort of virtuous cycle that is required. On the right-hand side of the figure, participatory rights enable communities to demand and obtain strengthened protections for watersheds and drinking-water supplies. On the left-hand side of the figure, better protection for watersheds provides the ecological context required for sustained fulfillment of the human right to water. Such protections also illustrate the value of environmental human rights and the benefits of exercising them, reinforcing the positive synergy.

The General Assembly's declaration of a right to water represents real progress, but falls far short of creating the conditions for this virtuous cycle to take root. On the process-rights side of the cycle, the lack of strong "rights content" in the MDGs and follow-on SDGs has been apparent in the water sphere. In its 2002 general comment on the right to water, the ECOSOC advisory body CESCR had noted that "individuals and groups should be given full and equal access to information concerning water, water services and the environment, held by public authorities or third parties"; that "any persons or groups who have been denied their right to water should have access to effective judicial or other appropriate remedies at both national and international levels," and that "national ombudsmen, human rights commissions, and similar institutions should be permitted to address violations of the right."[71] Currently, this is far from the case. In a 2011 survey of governments to assess progress on the water-related MDGs, WHO asked whether citizens "could claim their human right to sanitation and drinking-water in a domestic court."[72]

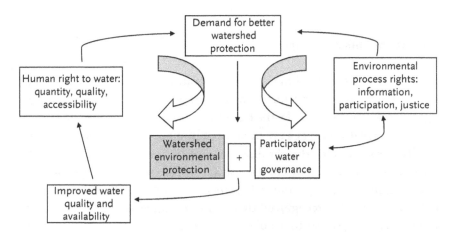

Figure 4.1 Water and rights: building a virtuous cycle

Of the seventy-two governments that responded, less than one in four (22 percent) reported that citizens both had the legal right to do so *and had actually done so* on at least one occasion. Nearly half (46 percent) reported that the ability to claim the right existed in legal terms, but had not been exercised in practice; the remaining one-third reported that no such right existed in the domestic legal system. The survey response filed by the government of the Democratic Republic of Congo stated, "Civil society is not aware of the human right to drinking-water."[73] These numbers show that UN recognition of environmental human rights is important not just to create a right where none exists, but also to empower and stimulate its use, and to strengthen national human rights institutions and practices.[74]

If the foundation for the virtuous cycle is shaky on the process-rights side, it has been almost entirely absent on the ecological side of the UN's construction of a human right to water. CESCR's General Comment 15, which provided the legal rationale for the General Assembly to find a right to water, did not use an environmental basis to infer the right[75] and made only passing reference to the ecosystem services on which water rights ultimately depend. UNHRC's 2010 resolution on a right to water, which accompanied the General Assembly finding, did not include environmental protection responsibilities or actions in the tasks member states are called upon to perform toward realization of the right.[76]

Without strong components of both participatory rights and ecosystem protection, the risk is that the "right" to water will remain limited to "just barely enough"—just enough water to live; just clean enough to meet survival needs; and just close enough to be provisioned through vast investments of household time and effort, particularly by women and girls.

The Case of Climate Change

Despite the reluctance of many member states to view it in those terms, there are several ways in which climate change is fundamentally a human rights issue. Most obviously, the harmful consequences of climate change hamper the realization of a broad range of human rights. A 2009 report by OHCHR provides a forthright discussion of the causal links between the expected effects of climate change and a range of specific rights (life, food, water, health, housing, and self-determination).[77] UNHRC Resolution 7/23 of March 2008 recognized that "climate change poses an immediate and far-reaching threat to people and communities around the world and has implications for the full enjoyment of human rights."[78]

A second key climate-rights link is that those consequences—including changes in water availability, extreme weather events, sea-level rise, loss of snow cover and sea ice, and shifting patterns of agricultural productivity—will disproportionately threaten poor and marginalized communities around the world, even though they have played little or no role in causing the problem. The aforementioned OHCHR report paid particular attention to the impact on vulnerable subgroups, including women, children, and indigenous peoples. For the extreme case of some small-island developing nations, the threat is to the continued existence of a people's very territory. In other words, climate change is not simply a "global" challenge facing all of humanity: it is also a distributive injustice, in which the disproportionate actions of specific actors promise a disproportionate impact on other, equally specific groups of people.

Moreover, human rights are at stake not only in the effects of climate change, but also in the policy responses to it. Proposals emerging from climate diplomacy include controversial measures that seek to sequester carbon by changing land uses. Such measures, grouped under the concept of Reducing Emissions from Deforestation and Forest Degradation in Developing Countries (REDD), are controversial because they may have important ramifications for access to nature and natural resources, particularly for local communities and indigenous peoples in rural areas of less-developed countries.[79] A group of indigenous representatives meeting in Durban, South Africa, in 2011 issued a statement denouncing REDD on several grounds: as a neoliberal commodification of nature, as an unfair targeting of indigenous peoples, as a threat to indigenous communities' self-governance of forest areas, and as "forestland grabbing" that threatened local communities' access to forests, traditional knowledge, and food security.[80] Thus, climate mitigation measures raise important questions about both substantive rights—livelihoods, culture, development, food security—and procedural rights—access to information, decision-making, and redress—in climate diplomacy.[81]

Finally, climate change is a human rights issue because it creates, at least in theory, a human rights obligation to address the problem, despite the unwillingness of most governments to recognize this fact. OHCHR's climate report stressed that international cooperation on climate change is not merely "expedient" but also "a human rights obligation and that its central objective is the realization of human rights."[82] This means that a central purpose of the ongoing global climate negotiations must be to protect climate-threatened rights, a concept that to date has been almost entirely absent from the talks.

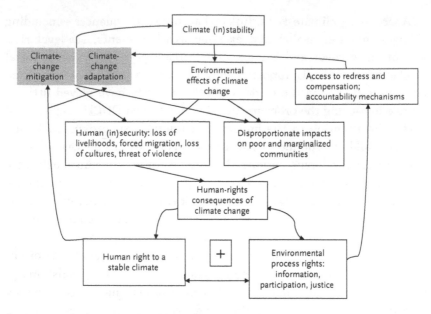

Figure 4.2 Climate and rights: building a virtuous cycle

Figure 4.2 brings together these various linkages between climate change and human rights, in analogous fashion to figure 4.1 on water and rights. Again, the potential exists for a virtuous cycle, in which a combination of the substantive right to a livable climate and procedural environmental rights could strengthen measures on climate mitigation and adaptation, and with the resulting enhancements to "climate security" feeding back on people's ability to realize those rights.

There have been efforts to tap such synergies by framing climate change as a human rights issue within the UN. Small-island developing countries, which stand on the front lines of climate peril given sea-level rise and extreme weather events, have been a leading voice for a rights-based approach. In 2007, the Alliance of Small Island Developing States issued the "Male' Declaration on the Human Dimensions of Global Climate Change," which called for "a detailed study into the effects of climate change on the full enjoyment of human rights" by OHCHR and a UNHRC debate on the subject.[83]

This call led to the aforementioned 2009 OHCHR report, which found that climate change "will potentially have implications for the full range of human rights."[84] It also prompted a 2009 UNHRC panel discussion, which yielded a general consensus that a human rights framework refocused the climate problem in several important ways. According to the panel, climate change (a) calls attention to the "real-life effects" on individuals and communities, (b) highlights threats to the most vulnerable, (c) "empower[s] individuals and communities and [gives] them a voice in decision-making processes, particularly by underlining the importance of the participation of affected communities and the need to take into account the views those affected by policy responses to address the causes and consequences of climate change," and (d) "introduce[s] an accountability framework, holding governments accountable to reducing the vulnerability of their populations to global warming."[85]

Despite these fundamental linkages to human rights, the UN response to climate change provides a clear demonstration of the hegemony the law-and-development approach enjoys on environmental matters. Far from undertaking a truly system-wide response to this broad challenge, the UN has grappled with the issue in a fragmented and mostly ineffectual manner. Worse, as discussed in chapters 5 and 6, this fragmentation has allowed some member states to play a cynical game of venue-shopping, in which they endorse climate action in one setting while blocking it in others.

The dominant feature of the UN's political landscape on climate change is the 1992 *United Nations Framework Convention on Climate Change* (UNFCCC), the existence of which channels the UN's most important climate efforts into the realm of interstate diplomacy. The chief diplomatic challenge in recent years has been to find a formula for climate mitigation that allocates national responsibilities and sets timetables for reducing greenhouse gas emissions. For the developed countries, such a formula was found in the 1997 Kyoto Protocol. But the failure of several states to comply with their commitments, the expiration of Kyoto's first commitment period, and the exclusion of leading emitters from the developing world have been insurmountable hurdles for negotiations of the annual conference of the parties (COP) to the UNFCCC. The 2009 Copenhagen COP almost derailed the UNFCCC process entirely when the United States, China, and a handful of other nations essentially split from the process in an effort to broker a side deal. Subsequent COPs barely broached the issue, expending most of their energy simply getting the "UN process" back on track. The current trend is away from binding targets and timetables, in favor of a very generalized post-Kyoto agreement in which states agree to make self-defined commitments (such as those made by the United States and China in November 2014). As of this writing, it seems likely that the 2015 Paris COP will codify this approach.

If the "law" side of law and development has seen foundering climate diplomacy, the "development" side has focused on a combination of mitigation and adaptation activities. Mitigation has been pursued primarily through the aforementioned REDD initiative on forests and land conversion. As of the end of 2013, UN-REDD had provided support for national-level program development in eighteen countries across the developing world.[86] A wider array of activities has also emerged under the broader rubric of "REDD+" (with the "plus" signifying, in principle, a commitment not only to antideforestation measures but also to conservation efforts, sustainable forest management, and reforestation). Climate adaptation responses include UNDP's various climate-related efforts and the work of the UN Office for Disaster Risk Reduction (UNISDR). Climate-responsive development efforts, however, face significant constraints from the inability of the UNFCCC process to grapple with questions of who bears various responsibilities—to protect people from climate harm, to fund adaptation efforts, or to provide opportunities for redress.

Despite the repeated flaring of rights-related climate issues and controversies, the UN as a whole has had little appetite for addressing climate change in human rights terms. The climate talks have not even acknowledged, much less operationalized, a human rights obligation to act on climate change, despite the recurring efforts of small-island developing states to make it so. This silence endures even when nature serves up a tragically vivid reminder, as when the strongest typhoon ever to make landfall wracked the Philippines just days prior to the 2013 climate talks in Warsaw. Rather, we have seen a recurring pattern in which the UNFCCC process has suppressed, glossed over, or failed to engage effectively the climate-related challenges emerging from rights-related venues.

One example is provided by the rights implications of REDD+. In response to mounting criticism, the 2010 climate COP in Cancún, Mexico, identified a set of general safeguards with which REDD-related activities should comply, and UN-REDD and the World Bank have adopted joint guidelines on stakeholder engagement.[87] However, reports from local activists in Indonesia—a leading focal point for UN-REDD and World Bank REDD-related activities—caused the UN Committee on the Elimination of Racial Discrimination (CERD) to raise human rights concerns with the Indonesian government.[88] The cost of ignoring community-centered, rights-based approaches is clear. According to the World Resources Institute, deforestation rates in community forests with strong legal recognition are dramatically lower than in the forests outside those areas: eleven-fold in the Brazilian Amazon, six-fold in the Peruvian Amazon, and twenty-fold in the Guatemalan Petén.[89] Despite enduring and unresolved rights concerns, the REDD+ train may be leaving the station: The 2013 Warsaw COP adopted the "Warsaw Framework on REDD+," which sets the stage for common standards and institutional procedures, and which garnered funding pledges totaling $280 million from the United States, UK, and Norway.[90]

The question of legal remedies, readily visible through a human rights lens, is another issue the UNFCCC process has failed to address. The Office of the High Commissioner for Human Rights has noted that a human rights approach to climate change "requires access to administrative and judicial remedies in cases of human rights violations."[91] The UNFCCC process has engaged questions of responsibility only in the most general way, through the principle of "common but differentiated responsibility" in the original UNFCCC accord. Discussion of how to deal with loss and damage in particularly vulnerable countries has steered away from the subject of liability.[92]

Another inconvenient question emerging from the rights lens is whether there exists a climate-related "responsibility to protect" and, if so, upon whom that responsibility rests. This topic has been too hot politically for the UNFCCC even to engage. During the 2009 UNHRC panel discussion on climate, "different views were expressed as to whether the main focus of international human rights law in the context of climate change should be on States' national or international obligations."[93] Specifically, several developing countries, including Bangladesh, Pakistan, and the Philippines, argued that human rights violations related to climate change could not simply be attributed to national governments in the countries where such violations occurred, given the broader global dimensions of the issue and the historical responsibility of high-emissions countries. Canada, in contrast, argued "that it was the primary responsibility of States to promote and protect the human rights of individuals under their respective jurisdictions, supported by an international enabling framework."[94]

Rights venues have done more than pose inconvenient questions; they also have begun to generate direct legal challenges in which aggrieved parties seeking findings of responsibility and a right to redress or compensation. The best-known such case involved several individuals affiliated with the Inuit Circumpolar Council, who filed a petition with the Inter-American Commission on Human Rights in 2005 seeking a finding against the United States for the harm climate change has done to Inuit peoples across the Arctic.[95] The Inter-American Commission on Human Rights rejected the petition, saying it contained inadequate information on which to render a determination, and to date has declined to take further action.[96] This case and others have demonstrated some of the steep legal challenges facing such claims, in both domestic and international venues.[97] Yet the paralysis of the UNFCCC process suggests more such challenges are likely, perhaps even from member states themselves. The Pacific island nation of Nauru, when ratifying the Kyoto Protocol to the UNFCCC, declared that ratification "shall in no way constitute a renunciation of any rights under international law concerning State responsibility for the adverse effects of climate change."[98]

THE RENEWED QUEST FOR AN EXPRESS RIGHT

Prodded by growing recognition of the interplay of environmental change and human rights in domains such as climate and water, UNHRC has returned to the broader question of finding a substantive human right to a healthy environment. In 2011 the council requested that OHCHR conduct "a detailed analytical study on the relationship between human rights and the environment." The high commissioner's subsequent report revisited much of the now-established terrain: that environmental quality was important to the realization of a range of recognized human rights, that vulnerable populations feel environmental damage most acutely, and that civil and political rights can improve the effectiveness and legitimacy of environmental policies and practices.[99] Reflecting the broadening field of practice around environment-rights linkages, the report also surveyed national constitutions; regional human rights systems in Africa, the Americas, and Europe; and the activities of the UN human rights treaty bodies (though not of the specialized agencies and UN organs in general).

The high commissioner's report also asserted that fundamental questions remained open, including several of the conceptual issues identified at the start of this chapter: whether there was a need for an explicit human right to a healthy environment, the specific content of any such right, the role and duties of private actors, the extraterritorial reach of environmental rights, how to integrate rights-based approaches into the environmental treaty system, and how to operationalize obligations and monitor results.[100] The high commissioner suggested that the council establish a high-level panel or "special procedure" such as an independent expert or special rapporteur. At its next (2012) session, UNHRC heard Marcos Orellana of the Center for International Environmental Law, on behalf of a broad NGO coalition, call for a special procedure appointment, as well.[101]

Noting the need for clarification on fundamental issues, the HRC appointed an "Independent Expert on the issue of human rights obligations relating to the enjoyment of a safe, clean, healthy and sustainable environment," US legal scholar John Knox. Tellingly, his terms of reference reflected the widening field of practice around environment-rights linkages. They included a directive not only to examine the question of rights obligations related to the environment, but also to document best practices in fulfilling human rights obligations, so as to strengthen environmental policymaking and achieve the water-related Millennium Development Goals. The terms of reference also called for consultation with international organizations, local authorities, and civil society in addition to member states.[102]

The independent expert identified the need for "greater conceptual clarity" as the first priority of his mandate, which seemed to promise further years of study.[103] His subsequent research and reporting, however, have pushed the process forward. Knox's 2013 report to the Council concluded the following:

- That environmental harm threatens the realization of a wide range of existing human rights.
- That states face human-rights obligations related to the environment, and that these obligations emanate from a number of sources, including "(a) United Nations human rights bodies and mechanisms; (b) global human rights treaties; (c) regional human rights systems; and (d) international environmental instruments."[104]
- That, deriving from these sources, member states face both procedural and substantive obligations on the environment. Procedurally, states must assess environmental impacts, make environmental information public, facilitate public participation in decision-making, and provide access to remedies when harm occurs. Substantively, states must "protect against environmental harm that interferes with the enjoyment of human rights," are obliged to adopt legal and institutional frameworks for environmental protection, and must protect human rights from "the extraterritorial environmental effects of actions taken within their territory."[105]

Knox also flagged uncertainties: that the specific obligations facing states depend on the specific human right threatened; that the precise content of the obligation to protect those outside a state's territory "is not always clear"; that some of the sources for his findings are soft-law norms, not all of which have been adopted by all states; and that states "have discretion to strike a balance between environmental protection and other legitimate societal interests" so long as the balance is reasonable and does not infringe rights.[106] UNHRC's response was "to continue its consideration of this matter."[107]

CONCLUSION: CREATING SPACE FOR MUTUALLY REINFORCING PRACTICES

Human rights are not means to an end, but ends in themselves; they are intrinsic to being human. Yet being deprived of a fundamental right also has instrumental consequences, in that it may be an impediment to important outcomes such as acceptable quality of life, realization of human potential, or enjoyment of other rights. Given this instrumental interconnectedness, human rights are generally understood to be, as OHCHR puts it, "indivisible, interrelated and interdependent. The improvement of one right facilitates advancement of the others. Likewise, the deprivation of one right adversely affects the others."[108]

The right to a healthy environment does not enjoy widespread recognition in international law. Rather, it sits at the intersection of a two-way instrumentality. On the one hand, environmental protection has found its footing in human rights because it is a necessary condition to realize fundamental and widely recognized rights. On the other hand, human rights are increasingly understood to be important tools of environmental protection, including rights of local communities to manage their environments, rights of citizens to participate in governmental decision-making processes, and protection of environmental advocates from persecution.

A strong and growing body of evidence demonstrates these linkages in both directions. When UNEP and OHCHR jointly convened a "high level expert meeting" on the future of human rights and the environment, the experts identified three fundamental links between the environment and human rights: environmental quality as a substantive human right in and of itself; procedural rights as a key to effective environmental protection; and environmental protection as a requirement for realization of recognized human rights such as health, food, and water.[109]

As we have seen in this chapter, the first of these linkages, an intrinsic right to environmental quality, has ground its way slowly through the UN's international legal machinery, at times seemingly becoming caught in the gears and stalling the apparatus entirely. Meanwhile, the second and third linkages, taken together, hold out the promise of a mutually reinforcing approach in which environmental protection supports human rights while rights-based practices strengthen environmental protection. This reinforcing approach can be seen emerging across an uneven, still-nascent, but widening array of UN practices.

Perhaps the most important effect of this twinned focus is the creation of a new sensibility in the domain of global environmental governance, with ramifications for both states and citizens. Consider recent developments in the long, slow march of environmental rights through the UN machinery. The current independent expert on the environmental question has reiterated earlier cautions that many issues in the environment-rights nexus need clarification. In a break with established practice, however, he has also cautioned member states that "the lack of a complete understanding as to the content of all environmentally related human rights obligations should not be taken as meaning that no such obligations exist. Indeed, some aspects of the duties are already clear."[110] He has also reminded states that human rights norms "are not frozen in place" and urged governments to note their dynamic evolution, active development, and implementation through forums such as international conferences, special procedures, and regional human rights tribunals.[111] The independent expert's reporting to the UNHRC has also reflected the growing recognition of synergistic practices linking environment and human rights, characterizing as "firmly established" both the harmful impact of environmental degradation on a wide range of established human rights and the important role of human rights in environmental policymaking.[112]

Of course, the ultimate significance of the rights-based approach does not come from formal affirmations of such synergies, or even from the articulation of obligations facing states. It comes, ultimately, from the empowerment of people. According to OHCHR, a human-rights approach to climate change "serves to empower individuals and groups, who should be perceived as active agents of change and not as passive victims."[113]

The stakes in whether people can realize such agency are high. They were expressed powerfully by Raquel Rolnik, UN special rapporteur on housing, in remarks to the UNHRC. Rolnik applied a human rights lens to the climate question by invoking the biblical metaphor of Noah's Ark: "First question: Who is going to build the ark? But [the] second question, which is even more important than the first one: For whom will the ark be accessible?"[114]

CHAPTER 5

Greening the Response to the Scourge of War

Environment, Resources, Conflict, and Peace

I am surprised that the world knows so little about itself. Conservation is a basis of permanent peace.

U.S. president Franklin Roosevelt, in a letter to
Secretary of State Cordell Hull, *October 1944*

To make an uncertain long-term prospect a security threat amounts to an informal amendment of the Charter.

Statement of the government of India during the
UN Security Council's open debate on climate change, *April 2007*

INTRODUCTION: AS WITH RIGHTS, SO WITH PEACE

Environment and peace are inextricably entwined. Environmental challenges and poor natural resource management can threaten peace. Violent conflict undermines even the best efforts to promote sustainability. And better management of natural resources can enhance peace even as it protects the environment. Yet, like human rights, peace historically has been an underdeveloped theme in the UN's environmental work. Just as the UN has been slow to acknowledge and articulate environmental human rights, it has been unwilling to embrace a broad "environmental security" mission to complement its developmental and legal initiatives for sustainability. Again, the barriers include opposing state interests, weak institutional incentives, a challenging bureaucratic terrain, and the disputation of ideas. A more hopeful similarity with the human-rights domain: we are seeing the beginnings of positive synergy between environmental and peacebuilding activities. Conflict-sensitive approaches in the environmental sphere and environmental peacebuilding initiatives in the security sphere are both starting to gain traction.

The chapter begins with a quick sketch of the barriers that have prevented the peace-and-security side of the UN from taking on environmental challenges. The discussion then turns to the emergence of a post–Cold War "environmental security" agenda, driven by a combination of new security challenges, new organizational incentives, and new ideas. The bulk of the chapter assesses various niches within the UN system that have begun, often haltingly, to link peace and the environment. The two most recent Secretaries-General have used their office to highlight environment-peace linkages (albeit selectively, and each in a distinct way). The Security Council has taken action on so-called conflict resources (albeit inconsistently, and with a halfhearted commitment to implementation). The Council also has begun to discuss the implications of climate change for international peace and security (albeit with deep divisions on the appropriateness of doing so). Several functional organs of the UN have begun to incorporate new awareness about environment-conflict-peace linkages into their programs (albeit unsystematically and often facing member-state reluctance). These strands of activity illustrate the potential power of making such connections, as well as the substantial barriers to doing so.

AGAIN, WHY SO LITTLE MOVEMENT?

For most of the UN's history and in most of its actions, peace initiatives have taken little or no account of resource and environmental dimensions, and sustainability efforts have had little to say about human security. There have been occasional calls for transformative approaches, which today can be recognized as pleas for environmental peacebuilding. Examples include Andrei Sakharov's 1968 Nobel acceptance speech, which linked global environmental issues to the disarmament agenda, and the antiwar protesters at the 1972 Stockholm Conference, who sought to end the wastefulness and ecological destructiveness of militarism. Mikhail Gorbachev's 1988 address to the General Assembly warned, "It would be naive to think that the problems plaguing mankind today can be solved with means and methods which were applied or seemed to work in the past."[1] Such calls found little resonance in their day, in either the environmental or security policy communities.

Why failure to connect initiatives for environmental protection to the mandate "to save succeeding generations from the scourge of war"? Again, opposition from powerful states provides an important, if ultimately incomplete, explanation. During the Cold War, both East and West were heavily invested in a nuclear doctrine of mutually assured destruction. That doctrine had dramatic environmental consequences; the scientific-military-industrial complexes on each side left a vast toxic legacy.[2] Committed as the superpowers were to profoundly unsustainable defense postures, to acknowledge environmental roots of insecurity would have struck at the heart of defense strategy, force postures, and the raison d'être of the Cold War security state. Inability to acknowledge the system's unsustainability was seen when the "nuclear winter" hypothesis of the early 1980s, which posited that the consequences of nuclear war would trigger disastrous climatic effects, was met with official responses that ranged from skepticism to derision.[3]

Since the end of the Cold War, defense and foreign policy establishments have grown somewhat more willing to consider the environmental roots of insecurity. The North Atlantic Treaty Organization (NATO) began studying the cross-border environmental impacts of defense activities in the early 1990s under its Science for Peace and Security Program, and joined an Environment and Security Initiative (ENVSEC) that UNDP and UNEP launched with several partners in 2004.[4] The United States has conducted intelligence assessments on climate change and water availability as threats to US national security.[5] Some UN member states have pushed for a stronger Security Council role on environmental issues. Such forays have not led to significant changes in defense doctrine or budgeting among the leading military powers. Nor have governments of the South been particularly receptive to linking environment and security. On the contrary, the G-77 has been quite wary historically of legitimizing international security concerns around how states use their natural resources.

An example of how state interests channel possibilities is the greater willingness of the Security Council to take up the question of conflict resources than the question of climate change (both episodes are discussed in detail later in the chapter). Powerful states have convergent interests in managing resource conflicts in Africa to a much greater extent than they do in "securitizing" a climate problem for which they themselves are primarily responsible, and on which they favor diverging responses.

The Ideational Dimension

Once again, however, state interests tell an incomplete story; ideas must also be considered. As discussed in chapter 1, ideas guide governments as they seek to pursue interests, they teach governments what their interests may be, and they create space for bureaucratic entrepreneurs to promote policy agendas. On environment-peace-conflict linkages, a weak intellectual foundation reinforced the disinclination of states to make such connections during the Cold War era. To many, the idea that an increasingly crowded, polluted, resource-scarce planet would see increased social conflict, including violent conflict, may seem obvious. Yet systematic research and policy advocacy that made such connections persuasively would only emerge with the end of the Cold War. As a result, evidence-based arguments would not begin to gain traction in policy circles until the mid-1990s.

Moreover, the domain remains ideationally contested today. Causal links between environmental degradation and conflict, or between natural resource availability and conflict, are complex. Our understanding remains incomplete, and conventional wisdom has shifted more than once as the knowledge base has deepened. Scholars have documented many cases in which environmental factors or natural resources are linked to violent conflict.[6] However, the causal chain is typically long: economic factors, the performance of state institutions, property rights, and the characteristics of political systems all mediate between an environmental stimulus and a social outcome of violent conflict (or peaceful cooperation). This complexity has made it difficult to substantiate and isolate a direct causal link between environmental changes and violence. More generally, scholarship on conflict tends to infer important causal links from statistical analysis—yet the complexity around environmental variables and the poor state of data thwart our ability to conduct effective statistical tests. Although careful case-study work can tease out such associations, many of the cases in which the environment-conflict link seems most apparent—such as the appalling toll of deforestation in Haiti or the gross inequities in water available to the Palestinian territories—are "overdetermined" for violence, in the sense that violence can be linked to a number of root causes. This makes it difficult to isolate the role of environmental drivers from all the other available causes of conflict.

Another complicating factor in the realm of ideas: what seemed intuitive to an emerging generation of environmental advocates in the 1980s and early 1990s—that growing resource scarcity would beget grievances, which in turn would beget violence—may in fact be incorrect. Many of the concerns about looming violence espoused by environmentalists, policy advocates, the media, or scientists failed to consider a key insight from the scholarly literature on conflict—that grievances are, by themselves, an unreliable predictor of violent conflict. There are several reasons for this: grievance may yield incentives for cooperation that trump incentives for conflict; conflict requires not just the desire to mobilize violence but also the capacity to do so; and effective, legitimate institutions may be able to channel grievances into peaceful forms of dispute resolution or conflict transformation. Thus, while there is research showing that environmental changes may increase violent conflict risks, the causal relationship is more subtle than simply one of growing material scarcity triggering grievance-based violence. Teasing out such subtleties is challenging, and all the more so given the lack of good historical environmental data.

For all of these reasons, while simple bromides about looming environmentally induced conflict may capture the attention of policymakers and the media, such claims have drawn more than a little skepticism in scholarly quarters.[7] As in the human rights arena, ideas have provided raw material for policy entrepreneurs—but their controversial and contested character has legitimized opposition to policy initiatives and undercut the credibility of transformative agendas.

Finally, ideas may also trigger divisions within broad movements for social change. Just as advocates of environmental human rights have met skepticism in some circles that a rights agenda is a stalking horse for neoliberalism, or too narrowly human-centered, so too has the concept of environmental security been challenged on value grounds. Some observers have worried that efforts to "green" security will end up instead militarizing environmental protection.[8] While some environmental organizations have been willing to work with national militaries to secure protected areas and enhance conservation agendas, others have argued that securitization of the issue brings the wrong actors to the table, and that militarization of natural resource management can be a significant part of the problem.[9]

The Institutional Dimension

Ideas matter in context. When new thinking about environmental links to peace and security began to emerge around the end of the Cold War, it found within the UN an institutionally barren terrain. Unlike the law-and-development agendas of this era, which found ready support from institutionalized policy entrepreneurs and turf-expanding agencies, the institutional context for an environmental security agenda was distinctly unfavorable. As discussed in chapter 2, the Security Council was not engaged on environmental matters. And it was not until the 2000s that growth in the scope and complexity of peace operations would pull several functional organs of the UN, including UNDP and UNEP, into peacebuilding activities.

Moreover, the early colonization of the environmental issue by the law and development mandates would have lasting repercussions for policy entrepreneurs seeking to build environment-peace initiatives within the UN. As seen in the Security Council debate on climate change (below), the perception that climate is a "development issue" or a "treaty issue," combined with the more fully formed institutional apparatus in these domains, has made it harder to bring peace considerations to the table.

THE POST–COLD WAR RISE OF AN "ENVIRONMENTAL SECURITY" AGENDA

As discussed in chapter 2, concerns about pollution and resource scarcity as causes of conflict have a long pedigree, stretching back at least to World War II. It was not until the late 1980s and early 1990s, however, that the picture of few institutional incentives, weak intellectual support, and low strategic salience began to change. With the end of the Cold War, a serious call emerged in UN circles for a policy agenda on the links among environment, conflict, and security. Several factors contributed to this shift. The end of the Cold War ushered in a period of both intellectual and institutional fluidity. Ideationally, greater openness to the idea of new, nontraditional security threats allowed policy entrepreneurs to highlight resource scarcity and environmental degradation as one such threat.[10] Institutionally, the Security Council was freed from its Cold War paralysis just as a wave of complex conflicts in the Balkans and sub-Saharan Africa demanded its attention. The result was not only a dramatic upsurge in the frequency of Security Council peacekeeping interventions in the 1990s, but also an increase in the ambitiousness of these interventions, with new concepts of "peacemaking" and "peacebuilding" finding their place alongside the Council's more traditional repertoire.

These shifts set the stage for greater attention to "environmental security" links, in several ways. The Security Council became involved in a string of conflicts in which mismanagement and plunder of natural resources played a central role. The UN's institutional apparatus for peace underwent growth. And a wider array of programs and agencies, including WHO, UNDP, and UNEP, were drawn into the peace-and-conflict sphere.

A second key driver of the emerging environmental security agenda was growing global engagement on environmental issues in general, coinciding with the run-up to the 1992 Earth Summit. An important early statement on environment and security around this time was the Brundtland Commission's report, *Our Common Future*. Although remembered for its endorsement of the sustainable development concept, *Our Common Future* also devoted an entire chapter to "Peace, Security, Development, and the Environment."[11] While stressing that conflicts have multiple causes, the report argued that environmental stress can be "an important part of the web of causality associated with any conflict and can in some cases be catalytic." The report stressed a few mechanisms in particular as key parts of this causal web, including the destabilizing cross-border spillover of environmental refugees, enhanced competition for scarce resources, and competitive pressures on the global commons.

If the Cold War's end and growing attention to global environmental concerns were enabling conditions, a third key factor was scholarship. By the late 1980s, research began to appear that linked violent conflict to scarcity of key renewable resources—forests, soils, croplands, freshwater, fisheries—or to disruption of the critical ecosystem services associated with those resources. Some of this work focused on how environmentally induced scarcity interacted with preexisting social cleavages based on religion, ethnicity, or economic disparity to trigger violent conflict.[12] Other scholars stressed the role of environmental degradation in worsening uneven patterns of regional development and the gap between the traditional and modern segments of economy and society.[13]

The thesis that environmentally induced scarcities stimulated violent conflict was subject to criticism and scholarly debate on a number of fronts. Conceptual frameworks would later shift away from scarcity-induced grievances to explore a wider set of environment-conflict linkages. Nevertheless, the intuitive logic that environmental degradation or resource shortages could trigger violence offered a rhetorically powerful new way to draw programmatic connections between environmental concerns and the peace-and-security sphere of the UN, at a time when that domain was unusually open to change.

Initially, the new environmental security agenda stressed issues of little direct relevance to the Security Council—primarily, calls to reallocate defense budgets to environmental protection and to strengthen international environmental agreements. One issue did catch the early attention of the Council, however: the question of international responses to environmental emergencies. In 1989, twenty-four countries signed the Hague Declaration, which called for new legal principles governing international responses to "vital, urgent, and global" environmental threats.[14] In 1992, Switzerland proposed a "Green Cross" organization for rapid response to environmental disasters, followed by a Swiss-German proposal to the Conference on Security and Cooperation in Europe to create national teams for international response. This upsurge of interest in environmental intervention prodded the Security Council in 1992 to assert its relevance. The Council noted that "the absence of war and military conflicts amongst States does not in itself ensure international peace and security. The non-military sources of instability in the economic, humanitarian and ecological fields may become a threat to peace and security."[15]

Kofi Annan and Human Security

Despite these preliminary forays, it was not until the tenure of Kofi Annan as Secretary-General (1997–2006) that the environment began to enter the mainstream of UN discourse about international security. Annan brought a distinctly public style to the office of the Secretary-General, prodding the UN and its member states toward post–Cold War norms on humanitarian intervention, human rights, the environment, and global poverty.[16] He used his public persona and the power of his office aggressively to that end, making such themes central to his speeches, writings, and public appearances while launching agenda-setting initiatives from the Secretary-General's office.

Environmental initiatives were a substantial, if not particularly successful, part of Annan's agenda. He took high-profile ownership of the agenda for the 2002 Johannesburg World Summit on Sustainable Development and the branding of that event in terms of WEHAB (water, energy, health, agriculture, biodiversity).[17] His quest for a "global compact" based on triangular dialogue among corporate interests, civil society, and UN member states featured corporate environmental responsibility as a central element. Annan was also the first Secretary-General to make climate change a consistent element of his public discourse.

Though he stressed environmental problems as a cause of human insecurity, Annan's environmental initiatives remained comfortably in the mainstream of the UN's law-and-development approach. Nevertheless, he opened doors from the peace-and-security side of the equation. The International Day for Preventing the Exploitation of the Environment in War and Armed Conflict was established in 2001, and the Secretary-General used it as an opportunity to raise themes linking environment, peace, and conflict. More importantly, Annan placed the environment on the list of emerging, unconventional security challenges in a rapidly changing international system. He tried to prod the UN's international security agenda toward several conceptual and institutional shifts: a broadened conception of international security that stressed people's freedom from fear and deprivation alongside more traditional concerns for peace within and between nations; greater attention to a new set of twenty-first-century threats; and enhanced capacity for preventive, anticipatory action.

These themes infused Annan's most important agenda-setting initiative, the Secretary-General's High-Level Panel on Threats, Challenges, and Change. The panel's central thesis was that "the biggest security threats we face now, and in the decades ahead, go far beyond States waging aggressive war."[18] Its 2004 report flagged six clusters of threats for the twenty-first century, ranging from the traditional to the unconventional.[19] One of these, "economic and social threats," identified environmental stresses, along with poverty and infectious diseases, as risk factors for violence:

> Poverty, infectious disease, environmental degradation and war feed one
> another in a deadly cycle. Poverty (as measured by per capita gross domestic
> product (GDP)) is strongly associated with the outbreak of civil war. Such dis-
> eases as malaria and HIV/AIDS continue to cause large numbers of deaths and
> reinforce poverty. Disease and poverty, in turn, are connected to environmen-
> tal degradation; climate change exacerbates the occurrence of such infectious
> disease as malaria and dengue fever. Environmental stress, caused by large
> populations and shortages of land and other natural resources, can contribute
> to civil violence.[20]

Although the High-Level Panel legitimized these connections, it did not address environment-conflict linkages or environmental peacebuilding opportunities directly. Its few specific environmental recommendations fell back upon the law-and-development framework, with calls to develop renewable energy resources, phase out fossil-fuel subsidies, and reinvigorate climate diplomacy. Scandal-induced political weakness during Annan's second term also undercut the report's impact.

Ban Ki-Moon Ups the Stakes

Although Annan's successor, Ban Ki-moon, adopted a far less public style as Secretary-General, he went further to link the environment directly to threats to international peace and security, primarily through high-profile public statements. Such pronouncements increase the legitimacy of making environment-peace linkages within the UN system; statements from the Secretary-General set organizational agendas. But they are an effect of change as well as a cause: they reflect the enhanced ability of policy entrepreneurs to use the Secretary-General's "bully pulpit" and reporting functions to promote favored causes across the UN's complex bureaucratic landscape.

Unlike Annan's focus on human security, broadly defined as people's freedom from fear and deprivation, a common theme in Ban's framing of environment-conflict links was scarcity and resource competition. He gave particular attention to water as a conflict-prone resource:

> As with oil, problems that grow from the scarcity of a vital resource tend to spill over borders. International Alert has identified 46 countries, home to 2.7 billion people, where climate change and water-related crises create a high risk of violent conflict. A further 56 countries, representing another 1.2 billion people, are at high risk of political instability. That's more than half the world.[21]

Similarly, Ban warned the assembled elite at the 2008 World Economic Forum in Davos,

> Our experiences tell us that environmental stress, due to lack of water, may lead to conflict, and would be greater in poor nations. . . . Population growth will make the problem worse. So will climate change. As the global economy grows, so will its thirst. Many more conflicts lie just over the horizon.[22]

Many of Ban's pronouncements on environment and conflict related to his effort to prod action on climate change—which he termed "the right war" in a 2008 essay in the American newsweekly *Time*.[23] His most noteworthy comments on climate and conflict, again emphasizing resource competition, instability, and political crisis, came during a 2011 thematic session on climate change in the Security Council. Ban's unusually strong language drew a stark picture:

> Climate change is real, and it is accelerating in a dangerous manner. It not only exacerbates threats to international peace and security, it is a threat to international peace and security. Extreme weather events continue to grow more frequent and intense, in rich and poor countries alike, not only devastating lives but also infrastructure, institutions and budgets—an unholy brew that can create dangerous security vacuums. . . . Competition between communities

and countries for scarce resources, especially water, is increasing, exacerbating old security dilemmas and creating new ones. Environmental refugees are reshaping the human geography of the planet, a trend that will only increase as deserts advance, forests are felled and sea-levels rise. Mega-crises may well become the new normal.[24]

Ban also used the Secretary-General's reporting function—a more important channel within the bureaucratic-administrative apparatus of the UN than his public speeches—to stress the challenge of managing resource conflicts. His 2009 *Report on Peacebuilding in the Immediate Aftermath of Conflict* noted that "failure to restore State authority, particularly in remote border areas, may create new sources of threat or permit wartime practices of smuggling or illegal trade in natural resources to persist or even expand, undermining State revenue."[25] It also called for "augmenting the existing capacity on the ground and deploying additional international civilian capacity" for the effective management of natural resources.[26] In a hard-fought bureaucratic victory for its proponents, the 2010 version of the report included a statement calling on member states and the UN system "to make questions of natural resource allocation, ownership and access an integral part of peacebuilding strategies."[27] Subsequent reports called on UN entities to pool their expertise on the issue, and to enhance sustainable, transparent management of natural resources in a conflict-sensitive manner.[28] This positioning of the issue coincided with the Security Council's growing engagement with "conflict resources," while also creating somewhat broader space for engaging the environmental dimensions of peacebuilding and conflict prevention, as discussed below.

While finding a risk of conflict in environmental change and resource scarcity, Ban's framing of solutions, like Annan's, relied primarily on a conventional framework of sustainable development. As he noted in the *Time* magazine essay, "The basic building block of peace and security for all peoples is economic and social security, anchored in sustainable development."[29] Similarly, his dire warnings to the Security Council debate on climate change were paired with quite conventional policy appeals for climate law between nations and climate-sensitive development within them.

ENGAGING THE SECURITY COUNCIL

As discussed in subsequent sections of this chapter, these agenda-setting moves by successive Secretaries-General created space for initiatives across the UN system, involving UNDP, UNEP, the Department of Peacekeeping

Operations (DPKO), the Peacebuilding Commission (PBC), and other organs. Inevitably, however, an environmental security agenda also raises the polemical question of the Security Council's role. The Council enjoys extensive powers under the UN Charter, including the authority delegated to it by member states to use military force and other coercive measures to preserve or restore international peace. The Council's rules of operation give permanent membership and veto rights only to the so-called P-5 of China, France, Russia, the United Kingdom, and the United States. This combination of broad powers and institutionalized hierarchy makes the Council a lightning rod for questions of equity, sovereignty, intervention, and the proper scope of global governance. The growing capacity of the P-5 to act in concert after the Cold War, and the concomitant rise of more interventionist doctrines such as the "responsibility to protect," have only enhanced such divisions, even as they create new possibilities for coordinated action.

These broader elements of Security Council politics have been on display as matters related to the environment and natural resources began to crop up on the Council's agenda. The ensuing political fault lines can be seen in two contentious issues: the challenge of how to regulate so-called conflict resources and the question of whether and how climate change threatens international peace and security.

The Security Council and Conflict Resources: The Halting Emergence of a Regulatory Regime

The Security Council's engagement with the question of conflict resources illustrates both opportunities and barriers to addressing conflict-related dimensions of natural resources and the environment. On the one hand, the Council has found the political space to regulate natural resources embroiled in civil violence. It has applied economic sanctions on multiple occasions when resources have been implicated in sustaining violent conflict. It has used expert panels appointed to monitor those sanctions to conduct analytic studies and provide advice on conflict resources; in one instance, the Democratic Republic of Congo (DRC), the Council appointed a panel of experts for that purpose in the absence of a sanctions regime. In a few instances, it has even authorized peacekeeping missions to help implement natural-resource sanctions or otherwise support better resource management in war-torn societies. The approach, however, has been haphazard and case-specific rather than systematic, and has not extended upstream to include conflict-prevention measures. Moreover, to find the political space to act, the Council has had to embed its approach in a larger framework of sustainable development, thereby privileging certain aspects of the problem over others.

Beginning in the 1990s, the Council found itself intervening in a series of civil wars in which natural resources played an important role, including those in Angola, Liberia, Côte d'Ivoire, and Sierra Leone. Through the work of international advocacy groups, local activists, and media, it became clear that illicit exports of valuable natural resources—particularly oil, diamonds, and timber—were providing revenue streams that allowed combatants to sustain the conflict. Indeed, although the claim remains controversial in the scholarly literature, some analysts have argued that such revenue streams had increasingly become the end rather than the means for combatants—that "greed" had outstripped "need" (deprivation) or "creed" (social identity) as the raison d'être for civil war.[30]

Advocacy by nongovernmental organizations (NGOs) and a growing body of documentation played a key role in shaping the Council's thinking on how to engage such conflicts. In 1995, the advocacy organization Global Witness began to document the consequences of illegal exploitation of high-value resources. Global Witness focused initially on timber in Cambodia, drawing a detailed picture of forest plunder as an ugly mix of environmental damage, human rights abuses, corruption, and complicity of international actors. The reports also illustrated the failings of the Cambodian government's ban on timber exports, which was aimed at the Khmer Rouge insurgency and which the Security Council had endorsed.[31] In 1998 Global Witness shifted its attention to Africa, publishing a report on diamonds in Angola, which led in turn to analyses of the global diamond industry and of other commodities such as oil and timber in fueling violent conflict and human rights abuses.[32]

Supporting this advocacy—if not always fully consistent with it—was a growing body of scholarship that pointed to the role of resource abundance as a risk factor for civil conflict. This work, which parted company with earlier studies claiming that resource scarcity was the principal conflict risk, showed the dangers of resource wealth. Research has shown that an abundance of some valuable resource commodities, particularly oil, can increase vulnerability to civil war. Even when resources are not the root cause of the fighting, they sustain violence by providing revenue streams.[33] Summarizing the picture that scholars have drawn, a 2009 UNEP report noted that at least 40 percent of intrastate conflicts in the preceding sixty years involved a natural-resource component, and eighteen violent conflicts since 1990 alone were fueled by natural resources.[34]

Although there is a clear link in the scholarly literature between resource abundance and vulnerability to civil conflict, there is no consensus as to why. Resource wealth may create incentives for insurgency and secession, particularly if the resources are location-specific (as with oil) or easily captured (as with alluvial diamonds). They may trigger subnational disputes about resource control, revenue distribution, or the damages—environmental harm, human rights violations and loss of local livelihoods—associated with large-scale resource extraction. The well-known links between commodity exports and corruption may also play a role. Also, regimes in resource-rich countries may be tempted to pursue unsustainable, debt-burdened development models by borrowing against projected resource revenues. Finally, regimes that live off of excise taxes on natural resources, rather than developing the authority and capacity to tax their citizens, may prove to be brittle, incapable, or illegitimate.[35]

Uncertainty about the specific causal mechanisms notwithstanding, the prominent role of diamonds and timber in the West African civil wars of this period reinforced the popular image of greed as a driver of conflict, with combatants willing to fight for control of "lootable" resources and able to use the lucrative export trade to sustain their ability to fight. This perspective was captured succinctly in the media-popularized notion "blood diamonds."

Facing mounting pressures to address the problem, the Security Council's first step was to impose sanctions on the export of natural resources during civil conflict. Between 1993 and 2005, the Council imposed sanctions on oil, diamond, or timber exports on seven occasions, targeting four African countries (table 5.1). These instances reflected a broader trend of increased Council willingness to use various types of sanctions—trade restrictions, travel restrictions, freezing of assets, and other measures—as conflict-management tools. During the Cold War, the Council established sanctions committees only for white-minority regimes in South Africa and Rhodesia. By 2003, thirteen sanctions committees or equivalent bodies were in place.[36] With the Angola case, the Council imposed sanctions directly on a nonstate actor (the UNITA rebel faction) for the first time.

Along with sanctions, the Council in this period made growing use of expert panels, beginning with the Angola sanctions committee in 1999. The committee documented the ability of UNITA rebels to evade sanctions and export rough diamonds, and named specific countries and actors involved in the illicit trade. This information led to a stakeholder dialogue on cleaning up the diamond trade and a

Table 5.1 SECURITY COUNCIL SANCTIONS ON NATURAL RESOURCE COMMODITIES

1993	Angola	Oil
1997	Sierra Leone	Oil
1998	Angola	Diamonds
2000	Sierra Leone	Diamonds
2001	Liberia	Diamonds
2003	Liberia	Timber
2005	Côte d'Ivoire	Diamonds

Source: compiled by author.

December 2000 General Assembly resolution calling for the certification of rough diamonds as conflict-free. The Security Council endorsed a stakeholder-negotiated certification scheme, the Kimberley Process, in January 2003.[37]

Between 1999 and 2007 six expert panels addressed conflict resources (in the context of sanctions on Angola, Sierra Leone, Afghanistan, Liberia and Côte d'Ivoire, and independent of a sanctions regime in the case of the DRC).[38] A 2006 UN expert workshop on natural resources and conflict in Africa found that such panels had been "crucial in highlighting this issue within the international community," a mechanism Philippe Le Billon has referred to as "naming and shaming" (although, as discussed below, the international response to those named and shamed has often been reluctant and ineffectual).[39]

The work of the DRC panel drew particular attention, as reports in 2001 and 2003 revealed a shocking picture of systematic resource plunder "often carried out in violation of the sovereignty of the Democratic Republic of Congo."[40] The panel found that illicit activities occurred with complicity or active involvement of military forces from neighboring Uganda and Rwanda, as well as local businessmen, foreign companies, and international banks. In addition to documenting short-term looting by foreign armies in occupied zones in 1998 and 1999, the panel identified "systematic and systemic exploitation" of natural resources across the war zone, rooted in preexisting business relationships and transportation networks.[41]

As the Security Council found itself managing a growing number of sanctions regimes on natural resources, it began to authorize selected UN peacekeeping missions to support the sanctions and help governments reassert sovereign control. In 2003, the Council authorized the peacekeeping mission in Liberia (UNMIL) "to assist the transitional government in restoring proper administration of natural resources."[42] In 2004, peacekeepers in Sierra Leone (UNAMSIL) were authorized "to support the Sierra Leone armed forces and police in patrolling the border and diamond-mining areas, including joint operations where appropriate."[43] In both instances, the Council was cautious to respect host-country sovereignty, authorizing peacekeepers only to support the national government's efforts to control conflict resources. Indeed, a 2000 Secretary-General's report explicitly framed natural resources as the sole responsibility of the sovereign state.[44]

As the use of sanctions, expert panels, and peacekeeper mandates increased, the Council found itself under mounting pressure to adopt a more consistent, comprehensive approach. In November 2003, a coalition of humanitarian and conflict-resolution NGOs—including Global Policy Forum, Global Witness, Human Rights Watch, International Peace Academy, and the Save the Children Alliance—called upon the Security Council, member states, and "like-minded delegations" to take several steps: recognize resource plunder as a war crime, end impunity for "well-known persons and companies" involved in illicit activity, and strengthen enforcement of existing resolutions and legal instruments. They also urged the Council to adopt a working definition of conflict resources as "resources that have been traded in a way that drives violent armed conflict and threatens national and regional security" and to "see crisis prevention as central to this initiative, not just peacemaking and post-crisis peace-building, to head off future crises that lurk in every resource-rich country or region."[45] In October 2004, Global Policy Forum, Global Witness, and World Vision reiterated this agenda in a letter to the Secretary-General's High-Level Panel on Threats, Challenges, and Change, urging it to "consider options for a stronger and more systematic UN role in this area."[46]

Calls for a more systematic approach culminated in a Security Council thematic session on conflict resources in June 2007, when Belgium rotated into the monthly position of Council chair. Belgium was drawn into the issue through extensive involvement in the Kimberley Process (the Belgian city of Antwerp being a key node in the global commodity chain for diamonds). Prior to the thematic debate, Belgium circulated a concept paper identifying natural resources as a direct cause of conflict (via disputes over resource control), an indirect cause of conflict (via the combination of resource dependence, weak governance, and poor economic performance), and a means of conflict (via financing of armed groups' activities). The concept paper identified distinct roles for preconflict preventive measures, in-conflict action to prevent the "fueling and perpetuation" of violence, and postconflict action to enhance development and prevent relapse.[47]

The thematic session—which involved the fifteen sitting members of the Security Council and seventeen other UN member states requesting to participate—revealed several points of consensus on the role of natural resources in peace and conflict.[48] These included the conflict potential associated with disputes over natural resource control, revenues, and equity considerations; the risk of conflict attached to overdependence on resource-based development strategies; the dangers of resource trafficking as a means of funding insurgency; and the importance of international support measures and good national governance for stemming illicit trade. The debate also revealed some of the larger fault lines of Security Council politics, including disputes over the Council's role and mandate. The most expansive interpretation of the Council's role on conflict resources was the EU position, which called for coupling sanctions with preventive monitoring initiatives, enhanced transparency and accountability mechanisms at the national level, strengthened international certification schemes along the lines of the Kimberley Process on diamonds, endorsement of the Extractive Industries Transparency Initiative, and funding to transform conflict resources into development assets through postconflict peacekeeping and peacebuilding activities.

In contrast, some member states raised concerns about the Security Council taking up conflict resources as a thematic topic. Brazil asserted that "there is a more relevant, stronger link between natural resources and development, as compared to security"; cautioned against an overly broad reading of the Council's mandate; and warned against encroaching on the sovereign rights of states to exploit their natural resources. India made similar points on development and resource sovereignty, which it described as "immutable," while suggesting that "the international community is arriving through trial and error at a useful approach" on conflict resources. Qatar underscored that natural resources were strictly a development issue, outside the mandate and competence of the Security Council. Proponents of a more comprehensive Council approach responded to sovereignty concerns by stressing that the aim was not domestic interference but, as Belgian foreign minister Karel de Gucht put it, "to reinforce the responsibility of national authorities and avoid that the exploitation of natural resources falls outside state control or is used against it."[49]

An early test of Council resolve after the 2007 debate was the ongoing conflict in the DRC. Spurred by criticism of ineffectual sanctions and expert-panel documentation of continuing problems,[50] the Council began to incorporate some elements of a more systematic approach:

- *Linking natural resources and targeted sanctions*: In December 2008, the Council indicated that individuals and groups involved in the illicit trade in natural resources could be subject to the targeted sanction it had previously authorized in the DRC conflict.[51]
- *Inclusion of external actors*: In 2009, the Council called for the development of guidelines so that "importers, processing industries, and consumers" of mineral resources from the DRC might exercise "due diligence" regarding the importation of conflict-sustaining resources.[52]
- *Peacekeeping mandate*: The original mandate of UN peacekeepers in the DRC (MONUC) did not include a natural-resource component. Reauthorizing the mission in May 2007, the Council urged the DRC government "to strengthen its efforts, with the support of the international community, including specialized international organizations, with a view to effectively extending the State's authority throughout its territory, establishing its control over the exploitation and export of natural resources, and improving the transparency of the management of the revenues from the exploitation of those natural resources."[53] But still it did not authorize a role for MONUC in that process. In 2008, however, MONUC was authorized to use its monitoring and inspection capabilities "to curtail the provision of support to illegal armed groups derived from illicit trade in natural resources."[54] Unlike prior instances in Liberia and Sierra Leone, MONUC was not limited to supporting the government of DRC in this function, although it was tasked to work "in close cooperation" with the government.

Despite the more comprehensive approach, the DRC sanctions regime has been criticized for weak implementation and the failure of member states to take action against clearly identified offenders. Global Witness reported that, more than a year after the Council resolution on targeted sanctions, none of the principal groups enabling the flow of resources out of combatant-controlled areas had been added to the targeted sanctions list.[55]

The Council has remained reluctant to embrace some elements of a more comprehensive approach. It has declined to move from case-by-case consideration to a standing set of tools, such as the seating of a permanent expert panel on resources and conflict. Nor has it responded to the call from Global Witness to "mainstream into the mandate of all peacekeeping missions a monitoring and reporting component related to natural resource exploitation and the cross-border trafficking of weapons."[56] Nor has the Council formally endorsed the work of the Extractive Industries Transparency Initiative (EITI), a multistakeholder initiative that promotes disclosure and verification of natural-resource revenues and payments.[57]

The Council has also been hesitant on the question of conflict prevention as it relates to natural resources. Resolution 1625 (2005), on conflict prevention in Africa, has been widely interpreted as a commitment to a more preventive approach to conflict management. The resolution reaffirmed the Council's "determination to take action against illegal exploitation and trafficking of natural resources and high-value commodities in areas where it contributes to the outbreak, escalation or continuation of armed conflict."[58] A June 2013 thematic session on natural resources and conflict prevention reflected broad consensus on several key points, with only a handful of cautions about permanent sovereignty or undue stretching of the Council's mandate.[59] Yet the Council has been unwilling to adopt an explicit working definition of conflict resources, an important preventive tool,[60] or to endorse vital transparency measures through the EITI or other means.

Despite its preference for episodic, reactive responses and reluctance to develop tools, the Council's evolving practices provide the sketchy outlines of a regulatory regime on conflict resources. The drivers have been a convergence of interests by a broad coalition of states—but also a strong ideational framework, increasing institutional capacity, and the entrepreneurial efforts of both bureaucratic and civil-society actors. In this sense, the case of conflict resources shows the possibility of opening space in the UN system for direct engagement with the peace-and-security dimensions of sustainability.

But the case also shows the enduring pull of the "law and development" framework for environmental governance and resource management. As researcher Michael Beevers has documented in the cases of Sierra Leone and Liberia, the international community's strategy for addressing the role of natural resources in each country's horrific civil war has been to turn "conflict resources" into "peace resources." The means for this have been "securitization," which involves enhanced state control and regulatory capacity, and "marketization," or boosting resource extraction for export-led economic growth.[61] While the strategy has stemmed some of the most egregious practices of natural resource plunder, it has also tended to overlook societally based grievances and inequities around resource use that helped fuel the conflict in the first place.[62]

The Security Council and Climate Change: Bully Pulpit, or Bull in a China Shop?

If the Security Council's forays into conflict resources show its ability to take steps toward addressing natural resources as a peace issue, the issue of climate change exposes the barriers to moving into that new political space. While some governments are anxious to see the Council play a climate role, others prefer that it not even discuss the issue. Some of this fractiousness has come from the rudderless state of climate diplomacy, and much is rooted in wider controversy about the Council's legitimacy and the breadth of its mandate. But the Council debate on climate also demonstrates the strongly institutionalized framing of environment as a development issue and an international legal matter, which can inhibit treating the issue as a threat to peace or a driver of insecurity.

The Council's first foray into climate politics came in April 2007. Britain, which had been sensitized domestically on climate change by the Stern Review,[63] used its turn as Council chair to schedule a one-day thematic session on the topic. The session took place shortly after the Intergovernmental Panel on Climate Change (IPCC) released its Fourth Assessment Report, to broad international attention. The Council session attracted a record fifty-five member-state participants.

Prior to the session, Britain circulated a concept paper offering substantive and institutional rationales for treating climate as a threat to international peace and security.[64] The paper flagged six specific causal links:

- *Border disputes* triggered by physical effects of climate change, including "the possible submergence of entire small island States, dramatically receding coastlines, and the development of new shipping routes"
- *Migration*, with ensuing political and social instability
- Impacts on *energy supplies*, as countries shift sources due to emissions constraints or climate impacts
- Other *resource shortages*, with emphasis on water, agriculture, and fish stocks
- *Societal stress*, with a particular risk of political violence in weaker states facing various forms of inequality
- *Humanitarian crises* in the wake of extreme weather events and longer-term effects such as drought[65]

Britain also justified the topic institutionally, noting the aforementioned Resolution 1625 (2005), which committed the Council to prevent conflict and address its root causes.

Public statements in thematic sessions of the Security Council must be interpreted cautiously. Although the sessions are characterized as debates, country statements are prescripted. Statements may establish a bargaining position, signal a credible commitment, assuage an ally, barter support, reinforce a coalition position, or satisfy domestic political needs. In the British-sponsored climate session, many states used their turn simply to call attention to the climate problem, sketch the outlines of an international response, or tout accomplishments in emissions reductions or energy efficiency.

A few governments, notably Russia and South Africa, objected to the dire characterization of the problem.[66] Most, however, underscored the dangers—some quite dramatically, as when Namibia likened climate change to "low-intensity biological or chemical warfare. ... Indeed, as developing countries, we are facing what I dare to call an unprovoked war being waged on us by developed countries." Similarly, the Pacific island nation of Tuvalu suggested that "the world has moved from a global threat called the cold war to what should now be considered the 'warming war.' Our conflict is not being fought with guns and missiles but with weapons from everyday life—chimney stacks and exhaust pipes. We are confronted with a chemical war of immense proportions."

However, despite near-consensus on the problem's severity, many member states challenged the appropriateness of a Council debate. One strand of objection asserted that the status of climate change as a sustainable development issue precluded considering it a security matter. As the Brazilian representative put it, "My delegation considers that there is a more relevant, stronger link between climate change and development as opposed to security. ... [T]he effects of climatic phenomena per se do not necessarily result in conflicts." Others echoed China's position: "Climate change may have certain security implications, but generally speaking it is in essence an issue of sustainable development." As Bangladesh put it, "Global climate change has the potential to turn out to be a major security concern only if we, through our apathy and inaction, fail to deal with climate change as a sustainable development issue." South Africa's position was blunter: "The issues discussed here are first and foremost of a developmental nature."

Along with development, the constraining influence of the environment-as-law frame was also seen. Several countries argued that the UNFCCC treaty regime provided a sufficient and appropriate mechanism for addressing climate change. The G-77, in a letter to the Council chair objecting to the session, pointed to the UNFCCC as the binding legal instrument and stressed that "no role was envisaged for the Security

Council."[67] China noted the need to "respect existing institutional arrangements," and Venezuela observed that addressing problems "outside the proper bodies for discussion of them could diffuse and complicate international efforts."

To some extent, these arguments reflect instrumental purposes. The G-77 quite naturally prefers the treaty framework; the UNFCCC's Kyoto Protocol created emissions targets and timetables only for industrialized countries, and a treaty-based conference of the parties (COP) is a better political venue for weak states than is the Security Council. Sudan, speaking for the African Group, opposed "attempts to shift matters of interest of all Member States to a body where a few members of the United Nations have been vested with the power to take final decisions." Venue preference also informs the "development, not security" argument: The Economic and Social Council (ECOSOC), which oversees UN development efforts, lacks the Security Council's starker power asymmetries and is more pliable to the G-77's majority in the General Assembly.

But there are larger concerns in play, as well. For many developing countries, a role for the Security Council threatens the commitment across the UN system, more than twenty years in the making, to treat environmental concerns as part of a larger challenge of sustainable development.[68] In this sense, the climate-security debate triggers the same wariness that the proposed "green economy" agenda did at the Rio+20 summit. It raises fears that the industrialized countries hope to slip out of their commitments to promote and fund sustainable development, while imposing new forms of environmental conditionality on resource use.

The climate-security debate also struck a nerve regarding the Council's powers and prerogatives. Several states bristled against an unwarranted expansion of the Council's mandate. Russia argued that the Council "should only deal with the consideration of questions that directly relate to its mandate." Egypt objected that "it is a clear challenge to the general membership of the United Nations to leave the way open for every President of the Security Council to decide a theme for an open debate, even if it lies totally beyond the Council's mandate." The G-77 warned in its letter to the Council chair that "the ever-increasing encroachment by the Security Council on the roles and responsibilities of other principal organs of the United Nations represents a distortion of the principles and purposes of the Charter, infringes on their authority and compromises the rights of the general membership of the United Nations."[69]

Given these concerns, opponents argued that the session should not yield outcomes or be seen to establish precedent. China argued that "the discussions at this meeting should be regarded as an exception giving rise to neither outcome documents nor follow-up actions," and South Africa asserted that the discussion should not "in any way elevate the issue of climate change or the environment to being a Security Council agenda item."

Member states supporting a Security Council role also presented both substantive and institutional arguments. Belgium called for the Council to shift its focus from conflict management to conflict prevention and to move beyond "obsolete" threat assessments. Several small-island nations called for a comprehensive "environmental security" focus, with climate as a permanent agenda item. Most proponents, however, aligned with the more cautious British position, which, while acknowledging that climate is "transforming the way we think about security," framed the problem in traditional security terms as a "threat-multiplier for instability." Most proponents focused on two of the several causal pathways flagged in Britain's concept paper: vulnerability to social dislocation and enhanced international competition for resources.

Institutionally, proponents cautioned against a zero-sum view of the roles of different parts of the UN. The British position was succinct: "This is not either/or." Often, this position was couched as the need for a "system-wide" response on climate. As Japan put it, "involving all relevant organs and bodies of the system" is essential for "system-wide coherence." A few developing countries also endorsed the discussion, arguing that the gravity of the threat superseded legitimate reservations about the Council's mandate. The Republic of Congo noted that "over and above the issue of the competence of the various bodies, we must recognize the seriousness of what is at stake—namely, the need for and the urgency of appropriate responses to a major risk to international peace and security." France offered a similar view, arguing that "institutional squabbling is inappropriate given what is at stake."

Beyond discussing the issue, however, it was not clear what proponents had in mind for a Council role. Most simply noted the value of giving visibility to the issue and endorsed an unspecified role for the Council as part of a "system-wide" UN response. Several pointed to the Council's 2000 debate on the impact of HIV/AIDS on peace and security in Africa, which they said brought important visibility to that question. Given the controversy, there was no consensus Council statement at session's end; the chair simply noted the complexity of the issue and thanked member states for participating.

At this point, the small-island member states shifted the issue to the General Assembly, seeking a resolution to clarify institutional roles and legitimize a system-wide response. In June 2009 the General Assembly, in a compromise brokered by Indonesia, passed a deceptively simple resolution (63/281) with two provisions. It invited "the relevant organs of the United Nations, as appropriate and within their respective mandates, to intensify their efforts in considering and addressing climate change, including its possible security implications." And it requested from the Secretary-General a comprehensive report on the security implications of climate change "based on the views of member states."[70] The resolution also reiterated the division of labor between the Security Council and ECOSOC, and underscored the UNFCCC treaty as the "key instrument" for addressing climate change.[71]

Although the General Assembly debate on the resolution reflected the divisions seen in the Security Council, a new element was more emphatic discussion of the plight of small-island developing states.[72] The Secretary-General then delivered the requested report to the General Assembly in September 2009. Although never mentioning the Security Council, the report repositioned the issue of a Council role in important ways. The Secretary-General narrowed the focus, from the general "threat multiplier" frame to a specific subset of projected climate impacts—those that "already appear highly likely, are large in magnitude, unfold relatively swiftly, have potentially irreversible consequences . . ., impose high costs on human life and well-being, and may require innovative approaches because of their unprecedented nature."[73] Specifically, the report prioritized four specific risks:

- The possibility of large numbers of persons displaced across borders by climate change
- The prospect of "statelessness" of citizens of submerged island nations
- The prospect of the drastic reduction in water availability to hundreds of millions of the world's people as a result of the melting of mountain glaciers and snow pack
- Intensified competition over newly accessible Arctic natural resources and trade routes

The report also sought to legitimize these concerns by combining submitted views of member states with a review of existing scholarship. It identified areas of broad scholarly consensus (e.g., links between climate effects and impacts on vulnerable communities), while acknowledging areas where scholarship was vague as a policy guide (e.g., how coping strategies of local populations may create instability). The report also implied a Council role by introducing a new concept of "threat minimizers." These included not only the standard calls for adaptation, mitigation, and sustainable development, but also tasks well within the Council's mandate and competence: preventive diplomacy, mediation, and peaceful dispute resolution.

Thus, in 2011, when Germany brought the climate issue back for a second thematic session during its monthly Security Council chairmanship, it came armed with a General Assembly resolution that legitimized a Council role as part of a system-wide response, as well as a Secretary-General's report that posed a narrower climate-security agenda plausibly within the Council's purview. This shift appeared, however, against the polarizing backdrop of increasingly unproductive climate talks under the UNFCCC. The climate regime faced increasingly insurmountable difficulties, including a general weakening of country commitments and poor performance of the regime's "flexible" implementation mechanisms. It had become apparent that several key parties would fail to meet their Kyoto Protocol targets for reducing emissions, while the United States during the Bush administration had withdrawn from its Kyoto commitments entirely. Political tensions mounted over how to define a Kyoto successor agreement and, in particular, whether and how the regime should incorporate developing countries. After several years of failure to gain traction on a post-Kyoto framework, the entire process was nearly derailed when China, the United States, India, Brazil, and South Africa struck a side deal at the 2009 COP to the UNFCCC. The 2010 COP, hosted by Mexico, expended great political energy simply to get the UNFCCC multilateral process back on track. The German-sponsored Council debate reflected this atmosphere of urgency and polarization, drawing an unprecedented number (sixty-four) of member-state participants—some anxious to break the logjam on climate action, others fearful of damage to the UNFCCC as the venue for climate diplomacy.

Although the Secretary-General's opening remarks welcomed the session as a step forward, a behind-the-scenes dispute threatened to block it entirely. Opponents of the session, including Russia, China, and India, forced proponents to accept there would be no consensus statement or action items. This prompted Susan Rice, the US ambassador to the UN, to chastise the session's opponents in her remarks:

> In the Council, we have discussed and addressed many emerging security issues, from the links between development and security to HIV/AIDS. Yet, this week we have been unable to reach consensus on even a simple draft presidential statement that climate change has the potential to impact peace and security in the face of the manifest evidence that it does. We have dozens of countries represented in this body and in this very Chamber whose very existence is threatened. They have asked the Council to demonstrate our

understanding that their security is profoundly threatened. Instead, because of the refusal of a few to accept our responsibility, by its silence the Council is saying in effect "tough luck." That is more than disappointing; it is pathetic, short-sighted and, frankly, a dereliction of duty.[74]

France took a similar, if less blunt, position, suggesting that the inability to issue a consensus statement was "not dignified" and dismissing opposition as "bureaucratic concerns."

Beyond the heightened polemics, there were noteworthy differences from the session in 2007. One was the US position, with the Obama administration willing to recognize climate change as a potential threat to peace and security. Second, while a majority of developing countries still aligned themselves with the opposition of the G-77 and the Non-Aligned Movement, a noteworthy handful (including Chile, Colombia, Mexico, and Nigeria) broke ranks and advocated an explicit role for the Security Council. Mexico and several others welcomed the debate for its attention-garnering power and endorsed its appropriateness in light of General Assembly Resolution 63/281 on a system-wide response. There was also substantially more attention to the plight of small-island states in the Pacific. Even India, staunch opponent of a Council role on climate, affirmed the "existential threat" facing those states given "verifiable evidence" that sea levels would rise dramatically by the year 2100.

Still, the session reflected the broad fault lines identified in 2007. Opponents reiterated several prior themes:

- *That the links between climate change and threats to international security are poorly understood and, at best, indirect.* Russia asserted that "the report [of the Secretary-General] refers only to hypothetical impacts of climate change on security and is not able to precisely predict them. It fails to provide empirical data establishing any correlations between these phenomena."
- *That security tools are not the most suitable instruments.* Brazil suggested that "such challenges require political economic, and humanitarian approaches, and not necessarily a security response."
- *That the Security Council lacks the legitimacy of universal-membership organs such as the General Assembly.* China noted that "the Council is not a forum for decision-making with universal representation."
- *That the UNFCCC treaty process, rather than the Council, is the appropriate venue for climate matters.* India argued that "while the Security Council can debate the issue and may recognize the vulnerability and threats induced by climate change, it does not have the wherewithal to address

the situation. ... We therefore have some difficulty in accepting the assertion that the effects of climate change go beyond the mandate of the United Nations Framework Convention on Climate Change."

Proponents of a Council role also stressed prior themes. They continued to call for what Bosnia and Herzegovina termed a "coherent, integrated, and holistic" UN response. They stressed the Council's ability to set the international agenda. And they again failed to shed light on what an ongoing Council role might look like. The concept paper circulated by Germany raised the issue explicitly, flagging for discussion the question of "appropriate mechanisms to periodically bring the security implications of climate change relevant to the work of the Security Council to its attention." The German position stressed integrating climate awareness and action into existing Council operations; it emphasized the risk to "fragile countries" and flagged the consequences of sea-level rise and food insecurity for peacebuilding operations in countries already on the Council's agenda.[75] The Secretary-General, despite unusually strong rhetoric in his opening remarks, advocated specific measures that had nothing to do with the Council: implementation of existing agreements, adoption of stronger mitigation targets, renewed commitment to climate financing, and seizing the opportunity of the then-upcoming Rio+20 meeting. The Pacific island states made the most specific proposal, presented by Nauru's president, Marcus Stephen. They urged the Council to appoint a "special representative" to analyze the security impacts of climate change, and to request "an assessment of the capacity of the United Nations system to respond to such impacts so that vulnerable countries can be assured that it is up to the task." The Council took no action on this proposal.

In the end, despite the drama leading up to the session, a consensus presidential statement was in fact agreed upon. It expressed the Council's concern that "possible adverse effects of climate change may, in the long run, aggravate certain existing threats to international peace and security," and flagging in particular the territorial threat to small-island states due to sea-level rise. The statement included a carefully worded (some would say tortured) phrase on the Council's need to stay informed:

> The Security Council notes that in matters relating to the maintenance of international peace and security under its consideration, conflict analysis and contextual information on, inter alia, possible security implications of climate change is important, when such issues are drivers of conflict, represent a challenge to the implementation of Council mandates or endanger the process of consolidation of peace.[76]

In the past few years, climate change has settled comfortably onto the generic list of "emerging issues" that sit at the margins of the Security Council's activity, alongside such challenges as organized crime, drug trafficking, and HIV/AIDS.[77] Several candidates for Security Council seats in the 2012 election flagged climate change as an issue for the Council to address, including not only OECD members Luxembourg and Australia (which were elected) but also Bhutan and Cambodia (which were not).[78] Yet the polemics around a Council role on climate came to a head in February 2013, when Russia and China blocked outright the effort to hold a third open debate on the issue. The session was conducted instead as an "Arria-formula," or informal, off-the-record gathering of interested Council members outside of Council chambers.[79] Cracks in the G-77 position remained apparent; while the G-77 formally opposed Council consideration of the issue, as it had in the past, the Arria session was cochaired by Pakistan. Ironically, the G-77 statement of opposition was delivered by the ambassador of Fiji, which occupied the rotating G-77 presidency.[80] Three months earlier, in a Council debate on women, peace, and security, Fiji had offered a very different statement, linking climate and security quite directly:

> A discussion on women, peace and security is incomplete without factoring in the security challenges posed by the consequences of climate change. This is so because for exposed countries like Fiji, women and children are among the most affected by natural disasters. The realities of climate change and the consequent proliferation of natural disasters are inescapable challenges for our people and for our land. Aside from the emotional trauma arising from ever-increasing natural disasters, their adverse impacts can be shown to affect food security, access to arable land and increased violence against women.[81]

FROM ENVIRONMENTAL SECURITY TO ENVIRONMENTAL PEACEBUILDING

Below the radar of the Security Council, several operational organs of the UN have begun to engage environment-conflict-peace linkages in their work. The principal catalyst for this growth has been the post–Cold War emergence of complex, multidimensional interventions in zones of recent, active, or potential conflict, under the rubric of "peacebuilding." In 1992, then-Secretary-General Boutros Boutros-Ghali's report *An Agenda for*

Peace conceptualized peacebuilding as action to prevent conflict relapse. In the ensuing two decades, this idea has been institutionalized as the predominant organizing principle for UN actions on international peace and security. According to the UN's Peacebuilding Support Office (PBSO), peacebuilding consists of "a range of measures targeted to reduce the risk of relapsing into conflict by strengthening national capacity at all levels for conflict management, and to lay the foundations for sustainable peace and development. Peacebuilding uses a variety of strategies, processes and activities to sustain peace over the long-term by reducing the risk of relapse into violent conflict."[82]

While in theory such measures could occur prior to, during, or after conflict, peacebuilding in practice has been primarily a postconflict enterprise, typically following in the wake of UN peacekeeping missions. Of sixty-nine peacekeeping operations since 1948, nearly three-fourths (fifty-one missions) have been deployed since 1991.[83] While some of these post–Cold War actions have involved the traditional peacekeeping function of monitoring ceasefires, most have been followed by broader forms of UN engagement with more ambitious peacebuilding components. Surveying the UN's experience in several war-torn countries in the 1990s and 2000s, Roland Paris described peacebuilding as "an enormous experiment in social engineering" with activities "from writing and rewriting national constitutions to drafting criminal laws, organizing and administering elections, tutoring policemen, lawyers, and judges, formulating economic policies, and temporarily taking over the administration of entire territories—all in the hope of establishing the conditions for stable and lasting peace."[84]

The "social engineering" of peacebuilding envisions an expansive list of tasks and a wide array of actors, both inside and outside the UN system, to perform them. Over time, many UN agencies, programs, and other organs have been drawn into peace-related work. Inevitably, peacebuilding engages with environmental considerations: field operatives in war-torn societies seeking solutions on clean water, land reclamation, refugee resettlement, or sustainable livelihoods have recognized they cannot ignore the environmental dimensions of their work. At the same time, the Security Council's growing engagement on conflict resources has pushed questions of sustainable and equitable natural resource management into the peacebuilding discussion at the political level. The impact should not be overstated: For the most part, environmental concerns have been marginal to UN peacebuilding activities, and many barriers seen in the Security Council's experience with conflict resources and climate change are present in these other UN organs and programs. Nevertheless, the rise of peacebuilding has created greater space for policy entrepreneurs seeking to connect environmental and peace activities.

Along with that space, however, comes the UN's highly segmented approach to conflict interventions, which draws sharp conceptual and administrative distinctions among preconflict, in-conflict, and postconflict activities. The need to move beyond this segmentation—to incorporate peacebuilding considerations early on, as part of conflict-management efforts, and to be more sensitive to preventing a new cycle of conflict when doing postconflict programming—has long been recognized across the UN system. Yet the barriers to overcoming segmentation are formidable. Simply put, conflict prevention belongs to the Security Council (even if the Council does little to actually prevent conflict). Conflict management resides primarily with the Council, the Secretariat's Department of Political Affairs (DPA), and the Department of Peacekeeping Operations (DPKO), which has operational responsibility for peacekeeping missions. Postconflict peacebuilding, in contrast, is the task of the entire UN system, and sits at the uneasy intersection of the Security Council, the Peacebuilding Commission, DPA, the UN Development Group (itself a coordinating mechanism for a wide array of UN organs), and important external actors such as the World Bank, European Union (EU), NATO, and various regional organizations. In this complex political terrain, it has been easiest (though hardly easy) for actors seeking to link peace and environment to find entry points in postconflict recovery work. It has been more challenging to do so in conflict-management situations, and almost impossible in the context of conflict prevention.

Postconflict Peacebuilding

UNEP has emerged as one focal point for efforts to highlight the links among environment, resources, conflict, and peacebuilding. UNEP is a small and irregularly funded program that is weakly positioned in the UN system. Its first experience with postconflict environmental assessments came from a series of rapid appraisals conducted in the wake of the 1991 Gulf War. UNEP's entry point for sustained activity in this area came in the late 1990s, when it began to conduct independent postconflict environmental assessments at the request of governments that had experienced the environmental effects of war. Since then, UNEP has undertaken several initiatives to enhance its expertise, build partnerships with other organizations, and educate the wider UN system on the importance of environment and natural resources in the context of peacebuilding.[85]

UNEP was pressed into service in 1999 to evaluate the environmental consequences of the Kosovo conflict (as part of a joint task force with the UN Center for Human Settlements).[86] Neighboring states had feared that the bombing of Serbia had unleashed an environmental catastrophe. Although the task force found this not to be the case, it identified several conflict-related contamination hotspots and documented widespread problems of pollution and hazardous waste that had preconflict origins.[87] The report stressed the need for immediate cleanup and called for the inclusion of environmental aid in humanitarian assistance. Spillover of more than a million refugees to neighboring countries during the conflict drew UNEP into assessments in Albania and Macedonia, focused on toxic hotspots and refugee impacts, as well as cleanup work in Serbia.

Since its work in the Balkans, UNEP has conducted postconflict assessments in nineteen countries and territories, as well as postdisaster assessments in China, Haiti, Indonesia, Japan, Maldives, Myanmar, and Ukraine.[88] Its move into this work area was supported by its executive director, Klaus Töpfer, and led by Pekka Haavisto, previously Minister of the Environment in Finland. UNEP established a Post-Conflict Assessment Unit in 2001, based in Geneva. The unit was later formalized as a Post-Conflict Branch (PCOB) and subsequently merged with UNEP's disaster response operations to form the Post-Conflict and Disaster Management Branch (PCDMB). Some of the branch's assessments have been rapid appraisals, combining site visits with analysis from satellite imagery and historical data. Others have involved more sustained, detailed analyses, yielding essentially a national "state of the environment" report. Still others have been rapid-response appraisals in politically sensitive contexts, such as those performed in the wake of Israel's 2005 withdrawal from Gaza and in the immediate aftermath of the 2006 Israeli incursion into Lebanon. While many of the assessments have been stand-alone exercises, a handful—including early efforts in Serbia and Afghanistan and more recent work in Sudan, Côte d'Ivoire and the DRC—have spawned follow-on projects to strengthen host-country institutions.

UNEP's assessments generally involve consultations with national, regional, and local agency officials; most also rely on input from local civil-society groups and international NGOs. Assessment reports typically provide an environmental history; a geographic overview; a summary of the country's preexisting environmental challenges; analysis of the environmental impacts of conflict; and a survey of the legal, administrative, and bureaucratic context for environmental monitoring, assessment, cleanup, protection, and enforcement. The assessments also make recommendations, ranging from the quite general (as in the Iraq desk study's call for "action to build strong national institutions and capacities for long-term sustainable management of the environment") to the highly specific (addressing individual factories, power stations, waste dumps, water treatment facilities, protected areas, or threatened species).[89]

Given its budget constraints, UNEP has funded postconflict assessment work primarily through case-specific donor commitments. Half-a-dozen European countries funded the first foray in Kosovo, and UNEP's then-director Töepfer stipulated that postconflict activities "should not divert resources from existing [UNEP] programs in other parts of the world."[90] In 2010 disasters and conflicts became one of six core thematic areas for UNEP, with annual support from UNEP's Environment Fund, but most of the support remained irregular and donor-driven. For the 2010–2011 budget biennium, disasters and conflicts were earmarked for only 6 percent of expenditures from UNEP's Environment Fund, substantially less than any of the other thematic priorities.[91] By 2013, the funding share had increased to 12 percent.[92] Despite these limitations, the strong demand from governments for assessments and the usefulness of a rapid-response analytic capacity led to the institutionalization and expansion of disasters-and-conflicts work within UNEP. In 2008, PCDMB established an expert advisory group on Conflict and Peacebuilding.[93]

While postconflict assessment may usefully focus the attention of host governments and donors, a much larger challenge is to "mainstream" environmental considerations into the multidonor process of "postconflict needs assessment" (PCNA). PCNA is an increasingly institutionalized outgrowth of efforts by the UN and World Bank to plan for economic recovery and reconstruction in war-torn societies and allocate resources accordingly. In 2007 the principal organs making up the UN Development Group (UNDG) "endorsed the concept and methodology of PCNA and agreed to use it as a primary entry point" for peacebuilding efforts.[94] Early in its development, PCNA paid little attention to environmental considerations. A 2006 multistakeholder review of several PCNAs conducted from 2000 to 2006 identified problems with incorporating crosscutting issues, including not only the environment but also gender, human rights, and HIV/AIDS. While the importance of environmental protection and good natural resource management would often be noted in general terms, environmental considerations were rarely addressed in detail within the principal thematic "clusters" making up a needs assessment (such as agriculture, shelter, or infrastructure). As a result, the environment factored little at the funding and implementation stages.

The review led to a 2009 UNEP / World Bank guidance note highlighting best practices and needed reforms: assessing not only environmental impacts but also conflict risks and peacebuilding opportunities related to the environment; evaluating national capacities; mobilizing the technical expertise needed for high-quality assessments; treating the environment as a focal point or "cluster" rather than simply a crosscutting issue; and doing all of this earlier in the PCNA process.[95] More recent PCNAs have made some progress in incorporating environmental considerations. According to UNEP, PCNAs conducted early in the 2000s in Iraq and Liberia suffered from the fact that "most cluster leads had little prior experience addressing environmental concerns in their work and it was difficult to integrate environment into their areas of responsibility. While environment was acknowledged as an issue of importance, it failed to have a significant profile when interventions and budgets were crafted."[96] In contrast, in later PCNAs in Somalia and Haiti, "Environment was recognized from the outset as a driver of poverty and conflict. As a result, the issue of environment was given cluster or sub-cluster status, as well as continuing to be treated as a cross-cutting issue. This provided high visibility and political importance to the issue within the PCNA, resulting in more concrete interventions."[97]

Postconflict needs assessment is only one step in a complex process of mobilizing assistance for recovery from conflict. If the first challenge is to raise the profile of resources and environment in the PCNA process, then the second is to carry insights from the PCNA process forward into the broader scope of peacebuilding activities, including legal and administrative reforms, donor funding commitments, and implementation strategies. Here the record has not been impressive. A 2011 assessment of Haiti by Fischer and Levy found that

> Haiti is a fragile state influenced by extreme poverty, a weak government, high natural disaster risk, and severe environmental degradation. . . . Short-term aid interventions in Haiti that focus on natural disaster relief and security have failed to patch these multiple areas of vulnerability and reverse the negative cycles that characterize Haiti's stagnant growth and environmental degradation. The absence of sustained engagement around core development needs undermines environmental stability and sustainable growth, which are critical for conflict prevention.[98]

The authors cited in particular the absence or underfunding of "long-term development and sustained strategic planning." In an effort to help fill such gaps, in 2012 a UNDG working group led by UNEP approved system-wide guidelines on natural resources management in transition settings, intended as a required framework for the UN country teams and missions that conduct PCNAs.[99]

UNEP has launched several initiatives to enhance awareness of environment-conflict-peace linkages under the rubric of Environmental Cooperation for Peacebuilding, supported by the governments of Finland and Sweden and by the European Union. These include a series of analytic reports done jointly with other UN organs as a way to build partnerships, a collaboration with the European Union on land and natural resource conflicts, training modules and materials for field operatives, and a knowledge platform on environmental peacebuilding.[100] Given its accumulated expertise, UNEP has also been drawn into activities and partnerships to promote greater environmental awareness "upstream" in the conflict cycle, in the UN's conflict-management and conflict-prevention efforts.

Conflict Management

A recurring theme in environmental peacebuilding has been the need to address resource and environmental considerations at the earliest stages of conflict management, including in peacekeeping operations, mediation efforts, peace agreements, and the development of disarmament and demobilization strategies. Peacebuilding is path-dependent; some of the earliest actions taken to stop conflict and forge peace may have lasting impact on the trajectory of recovery and development. A study by Mason and colleagues of ninety-four peace agreements reached between 1989 and 2004 found that more than half (fifty-one) made reference to natural resources.[101] Of these, 55 percent (twenty-eight of fifty-one) contained specific guidelines or instructions regarding resource use, management, ownership, or revenue sharing. If a rebel faction is promised the right to harvest forest resources as an incentive for joining a peace accord, or if control of key ministries is divided up among rival parties to the conflict, a long shadow may be cast over future sustainability efforts. So, too, may positive provisions, such as robust and equitable revenue-sharing arrangements.

Another reason for an early focus on resources and environment is the fuzzy boundary between "in-conflict" and "postconflict" situations, with conflict-management and peacebuilding activities typically occurring simultaneously, in close proximity, or in rapid succession. UN peacekeeping missions can have a substantial environmental footprint; their choices when siting base camps, building infrastructure, or accessing local resources can have lasting impacts on local communities. Alternately, they may deploy sustainable technologies and good resource-management practices that could benefit those communities long after conflict abates and the force departs. The same is true for humanitarian assistance in conflict zones: refugee camps often evolve into permanent human settlements, meaning that good or bad decisions about siting, land use, and resource use will endure, as well.

Finally, resources and environment are relevant to conflict management because they are often part of the conflict challenge facing peacekeepers on the ground. As the Security Council has moved haltingly toward regulating conflict resources, it has begun to make natural resource considerations part of the mandate of some peacekeeping missions. Even when ignored by the Council, facts on the ground may thrust resource-related challenges upon peacekeepers. A critical question, then, is the ability of a peacekeeping mission to carry out natural resource-related tasks in ways that support peacebuilding and recovery. Yet peacekeepers and others engaged in conflict management typically have little or no capacity or relevant knowledge of how to do so.[102]

Given peacekeepers' lack of familiarity with these linkages and the understandable wariness of seeing yet another mandate added to an already challenging mission, the environmental impact of peacekeeping itself becomes an important entry point. In the context of the system-wide "Greening the Blue" campaign to reduce the UN's environmental footprint, DPKO and UNEP launched a partnership to lessen the environmental footprint of peacekeeping operations.[103] *Greening the Blue Helmets*, which reported the findings of a two-year assessment of the environmental impacts of peacekeeping operations, found highly variable performance and documented several mission-specific examples of "better practices" that lessen the footprint while enhancing opportunities for mission effectiveness.[104] For example, a typical UN peacekeeping operation uses water at a level of eighty-four liters per person per day—an amount twelve times greater than UNHCR's recommended "survival minimum" standard of seven liters for displaced persons.[105] Water and energy efficiency measures, better waste and wastewater management, careful siting decisions, and renewable technologies can reduce stress on local resources, lessen the logistical challenges of resupply, minimize tensions with host communities, and lower the cost of peacekeeping missions.

There are also wider environmental and resource-related risks and opportunities in conflict management. Effective action—to enforce sanctions regimes, support the work of expert panels on conflict resources, aid government efforts to (re)establish authority, or quell illegal resource exploitation by ex-combatants—may allow better resource management to play a peacebuilding role. Such actions can contribute to the reintegration of ex-combatants, enhance trust, resolve local resource conflicts, reduce gender-based violence, and improve human security. When these functions are not performed, the results are predictable: continued illegality, impunity, and human rights violations around resource extraction.[106]

A particular challenge is the relationship between peacekeeping forces and the national government. In Sierra Leone, the peacekeepers deployed after the 1999 peace accord were initially blocked on sovereignty grounds from addressing the illegal trade in diamonds, allowing elements within the coalition government to exploit illicit production and cross-border trade.[107] Similarly, in DRC, when peacekeepers provided support for the government to reassert its authority over mining sites exploited by rebel groups and militias in the country's eastern region, one consequence was illegal resource exploitation and rights abuses by elements within the national military.[108] Regrettably, there have also been instances of UN peacekeepers actively undermining their mission through illegalities, most famously including sexual abuse of local residents but also including smuggling and other illicit activities.[109]

The Missing Link: Conflict Prevention

Conflict prevention is clearly the missing link in the greening of peace efforts. A 2008 review by the conflict-transformation NGO Swisspeace identified thirty-one entities on the UN's organizational chart that were engaged in some form of activity relevant to environmental conflict prevention.[110] The current barriers to more effective preventive work are substantial, however; they include the UN's segmented approach to conflict, polemics about organizational roles and mandates, and the lack of early warning and information systems that would support preventive measures and proactive interventions.

UNDP's conflict prevention work includes natural-resource management. For example, in 2010 UNDP facilitated a workshop on managing resource conflicts in Fiji, in response to a governmental request following a regional workshop on conflict resolution.[111] In partnership with Canadian and Dutch development-assistance organs, UNDP's Energy and Environment focal point conducted a multiyear project on reducing resource conflicts in northern Sudan, with particular attention to tensions between pastoralists and farmers.[112] UNDP highlights its work supporting the management of local resource disputes in Kyrgyzstan as an example of cost-effective conflict prevention,[113] and has flagged local conflict over land and natural resources as a key element of the "changing nature of conflict" to which it must respond.[114]

UNEP has also begun to engage in environmental conflict-prevention activities, within the limited scope allowed by its mandate. In partnership with five other UN bodies and the EU, UNEP has developed an initiative on anticipating and managing natural-resource conflicts.[115] The goal is to "help national stakeholders, as well as UN and EU staff in conflict-affected countries, to better understand and prevent tensions over environmental issues and the management of natural resources."[116] The first phase developed training materials on conflicts around land, extractive industries, and renewable resources; the second phase is carrying out pilot-testing in East Timor, Guinea, Liberia, and Peru. UNEP also participates in the multiorganization ENVSEC, along with UNDP, the UN Economic Commission for Europe (UNECE), and non-UN partners such as NATO and the Organization for Security and Co-operation in Europe (OSCE). Focused on Europe and Central Asia, ENVSEC promotes conflict risk reduction through environmental confidence-building measures, primarily through environmental assessment and capacity-building efforts with local partners.

One barrier to better environmental conflict prevention is the politicized debate across the UN on conflict prevention in general. Initiatives that some member states view as proactive and preventive may be seen by others as inappropriately interventionist or a violation of national sovereignty over natural resources. Some member states remain quite wary of seeing UN organs stretch the boundaries of their mandate to include conflict prevention. UNEP, for example, has been constrained by some of the same political concerns seen in the Security Council debates on climate change. A 1999 UNEP proposal to establish a "green helmets" team for deployment on conflict-related environmental damage raised sovereignty concerns and led to General Assembly Resolution 53/242 (1999), which "reaffirms that, in accordance with its mandate, the United Nations Environment Programme should not become involved in conflict identification, prevention or resolution."[117] Nevertheless, in 2001, UNEP's Governing Council authorized UNEP to engage in "studies on the concept of security and the environment," and in 2005 the GC endorsed its postconflict environmental assessment work[118] Yet, when UNEP partnered with the PBSO to hold a lessons-learned panel discussion on natural resources, environment, and peacebuilding later that year, the governments of Cuba, Egypt, and Russia proposed to halt the proceedings because they considered the topic to be irrelevant to the Peacebuilding Commission. (The panel proceeded when several African member states noted the importance of the issue to the work of the PBC.)[119] The issue came to a head when ECOSOC reviewed UNEP's strategic framework later that year; Russia, Brazil, and Cuba proposed to strike language on conflict prevention, peacebuilding, or environmental security. The enduring sensitivities reappeared at the 2011 meeting of UNEP's Governing Council. Switzerland submitted a "draft decision" for consideration by the council on strengthening environmental capacity in humanitarian responses to crisis. The government of Indonesia requested "the addition of text to ensure national sovereignty and territorial integrity," and the governments of Brazil and Cuba successfully pushed to delete a paragraph that called for the inclusion of postcrisis recovery, reconstruction, and peacebuilding in emergency environmental response, due to "security sensitivities."[120]

A logical focal point for transcending the UN's highly segmented approach to conflict is the UN Peacebuilding Commission (PBC). The PBC, created as part of the broader UN reforms of 2005, is a body of thirty-one member-states with a mandate to support peace efforts in countries emerging from conflict. Its work is supported by the Peacebuilding Support Office and the Secretary-General's Peacebuilding Fund. The commission currently has six countries on its agenda: Burundi, Central African Republic, Guinea, Guinea-Bissau, Liberia, and Sierra Leone. In theory, the PBC is well positioned to identify vulnerable countries, to coordinate actions across many actors involved in peacebuilding, and to transcend "the illusion of sequencing" by providing greater continuity from conflict management to peacebuilding. UNEP seconded a staff member to PBSO in 2008.

In practice, the PBC has struggled to play a useful role in the countries on its agenda. A 2010 review of the PBC's first five years of operation found that, despite some progress in focusing international attention and facilitating more inclusive political dialogue, the PBC had struggled to improve the coherence of planning for postconflict peacebuilding, to involve national stakeholders in the planning process, or to mobilize adequate resources.[121] In a review of PBC activities on natural resources in Sierra Leone and the Central African Republic (CAR), Lehtonen finds a similar pattern.[122] In Sierra Leone—one of the first countries on the PBC agenda, and one in which the links between natural resources and conflict are well documented—weak commitments in the initial PBC-facilitated cooperation framework among major stakeholders yielded weak follow-on in the review process. Moreover, the framework was treated as an add-on rather than a central tool by the UN mission on the ground.

In CAR, given the country's extreme poverty and the pervasive weakness of economic and political institutions, the PBC's strategic framework stressed the rule of law, the security sector, and regional economic development. Among the framework's fourteen priority actions is a specific call to "ensure sound management of natural resources within a protected environment, and guarantee equitable redistribution of their revenues."[123] CAR adopted a new mining code and was accepted into (and later suspended from) the EITI.[124] But the global financial crisis suppressed investment in mining and demand for minerals, hurting the strategy for sector reform. The country also adopted a regulatory framework that calls for a portion of natural-resource revenues to be returned to local communities, but Lehtonen reports that the mechanism has not functioned in practice.[125] CAR joined the Kimberley Process monitoring the diamond trade in 2003. A military coup that year drove most international diamond producers from the country, and a 2011 report from International Crisis Group documented the sector's poor governance, the impoverishment of artisanal miners, and widespread corruption and criminal activity.[126] CAR was suspended from the Kimberley Process in 2013.

A 2009 UNEP assessment found that natural resources were not at that time financing conflict in CAR, but that the risks were significant if preventive action were not taken to promote more "sustainable, equitable and transparent" resource governance.[127] The PBC's 2011 review of progress, however, merely noted improved natural resource management as a future challenge; its only specific recommendation was that the PBC "could consider supporting" the EU's voluntary partnership initiative on forest law enforcement and the timber trade.[128] With the opportunity for preventive action missed, natural-resource plunder subsequently became a significant element in the recent resurgent violence in CAR.[129]

One casualty of the mandate battles and the segmented approach to conflict is early warning—that is, the ability to match, in a timely and coherent manner, information on environmental and resource-use trends to information on conflict vulnerabilities, so that needs may be prioritized and preventive strategies applied. In 1999, UNEP's Governing Council made environmental assessment and early warning one of seven programmatic priority areas.[130] However, UNEP's Division of Early Warning and Assessment (DEWA) has emphasized emergent global issues and broader trend assessment, rather than the type of locally grounded and contextualized assessment necessary for conflict early warning.[131] An analysis of environmental-conflict early warning by Columbia University researchers identified several barriers to effectiveness, including data inadequacies, a lack of methodological development, and few institutional incentives to carry out high-quality assessments.[132]

CONCLUSION: LATE, SLOW, AND CONSTRAINED

Compared to the other ways that the environment is discussed and acted upon across the UN, the conversation about the environment as an issue of international peace and security has been late in getting started. As that conversation has slowly developed, it has been constrained by the wariness of some member states, and subordinated to the notion that the environment belongs instead in the mandate areas of development and international law. This pattern is seen at all levels, from the Security Council's forays into climate change and conflict resources to the programmatic activities of the UN's functional organs.

It is clear that member-state resistance to the idea of "environmental security" goes well beyond a reflexive defense of national sovereignty (although sovereignty concerns clearly inform the positions taken by Russia, China, India, Brazil, Egypt, Cuba, and others). One widely expressed concern, on both conflict resources and climate change, is opposition to an inappropriate expansion of the Security Council's mandate and its encroachment into "development" issues more properly addressed by other UN organs. Never too far below the surface are worries that "security" concerns are a means for the world's rich countries to circumvent existing sustainable-development commitments or justify green protectionism. In other words, the weak construction of the environment as a matter of international peace and security is part and parcel of its strong construction as a matter of sustainable development.

In addition to this overarching constraint, the UN's highly segmented approach to the "conflict cycle" has fragmented environmental peacebuilding initiatives. Postconflict peacebuilding is clearly the zone of broadest consensus, and thus the largest space in which to work. Engagement with resource and environmental issues as part of conflict management is growing, given the pragmatic needs of peacekeeping missions—but it also strikes a nerve in the wider debate about the Security Council's mandate and representativeness. Preconflict, preventive strategies that tap the confidence-building potential of environmental cooperation offer the greatest potential to enhance human security and reduce conflict vulnerabilities—but have gained the least traction to date.

Another constraint has been conceptual. Particularly at the high political levels of the Secretary-General's activities and the Security Council's discussions, environment-conflict linkages are often framed as a problem of scarcity-induced violence, whether it be through growing competition among nations over scarce resources, or the vulnerability of weak states to social dislocation and political violence in the face of scarce livelihood resources. This scarcity-centered, zero-sum approach was a major theme of some of the early eco-conflict research literature. But more recent scholarly work has downplayed this link in favor of models that see conflict vulnerabilities rooted in poor management, distributional inequities, problems of governance, and the destabilizing effects of global markets, rather than in physical scarcity per se. While this newer way of viewing the problem is beginning to translate into programmatic initiatives at the functional level, the higher-order political discourse has been slower to adjust.

Despite these limitations, the UN finds itself increasingly wrestling with the peace-and-conflict dimensions of environmental issues, including the consequences of conflict for sustainable development, the conflict risks around natural-resource extraction, and the peacebuilding potential of better environmental governance and resource management. As discussed in the following chapter, doing so more effectively will require a political compromise around sovereignty concerns. It will also require initiatives that cut across the artificial gaps in conflict-cycle programming. Most of all, it will require a shift away from geopolitical frameworks of scarcity, in favor of human security-centered frameworks that emphasize people's vulnerabilities and capacities.

CHAPTER 6

A Stronger Foundation for Global Environmental Governance

We have become collateral damage to the narrow definition of sustainable development.

President Beretitenti Anote Tong of Kiribati, *addressing the 2012 UN Conference on Sustainable Development*

THE CURRENT IMPASSE

The planet's environmental predicament challenges us to adapt our most fundamental values—justice, peace, freedom, progress, sovereignty, accountability—to new realities, even as we work to preserve their core meaning. Despite its many limitations, the UN has shown a greater ability to develop, disseminate, and legitimize new thinking than any other intergovernmental organization. In tracing the intellectual history of the UN, Jolly, Emmerij, and Weiss note that "the UN has frequently been more ready than other international institutions to develop positions at variance with those of the major powers and to put its finger on issues not yet on the formal agenda."[1] They offer powerful examples: human development, gender equality, human rights, human security, and sustainability.

Such potent ideals come closest to realizing their noble ambitions when they are able to bring to bear the full mandate of the UN. Ideas resonate most strongly not when they promote social progress, or the dignity and worth of the human person, or world peace, or the rule of law among nations, but when they create opportunities to champion all of these ideals in an integrated manner. The synergies we have seen sweep across the UN in the past few decades linking human development, human rights, and gender equity as mutually reinforcing goals provide a telling example.

To date, the UN has missed the opportunity to bring the full force of its mandate to bear on the world's environmental challenges. Environmental considerations have been peripheral to the UN's human rights activity and its work for peace, just as peace and human rights have been the weak links in the UN's environmental efforts. As a result, mutually reinforcing gains go unrealized ... or fall victim to the grindingly slow pace of the UN's policy machinery ... or are shunted aside in favor of the more comfortable frameworks of national development and international law.

The most recent global environmental summit, Rio+20, illustrated this disconnect. The event and its outcomes have been subjected to a range of interpretations. As Steven Bernstein has noted, expectations for the summit were low going in: the "green economy" concept offered by UNEP and others as an organizing principle met heavy contestation, and the event came at a moment of flagging efficacy in multilateralism more generally.[2] In perhaps the most optimistic assessment of what was achieved, Maria Ivanova has argued that the conference offered "subtle, yet significant" impacts, including its promise to upgrade UNEP and its affirmation of the "evolving global norm for participation."[3] Some observers have placed hope in the decision to launch a UN system-wide set of Sustainable Development Goals (SDGs) to succeed the Millennium Development Goals (MDGs).[4] Karen Morrow has argued that the achievement of any outcome document under such difficult circumstances represented at least the avoidance of defeat.[5] More critical interpretations have pointed to the event's lack of vision, its inability to move beyond archaic G-77 versus developed-country polarization, or its failure to embrace serious institutional reform.[6] Critics have also argued that the conferees placed too much[7] or too little[8] faith in market-based solutions.

Clearly, my view of what was accomplished at Rio+20 sits at the weak end of the spectrum. Yet, regardless of which interpretations stand the test of time, when historians pore over the meeting's history they will find few hints that that the governments meeting in Rio were even aware of connections linking environment and human rights or environment and peace. Three months prior to the summit, the United Nations High Commissioner for Human Rights, Navi Pillay, wrote an open letter to member states expressing her alarm at the lack of attention to human rights in the conference preparations, and warning that "the urgency of the matter has become apparent."[9] The Rio outcome document, *The Future We Want*, made a passing reference to well-established human rights (food, health, development, work, education) and the newly recognized right to water. But no explicit environmental links were drawn to any of these rights; nor was any mention made of a human right to a healthy environment. On peace, the meeting's silence was even louder. Among the roughly five hundred officially registered "side events" at the conference, a grand total of four adopted topics making some type of environment/peace/conflict connection.[10] The outcome document, *The Future We Want*, noted "the importance of freedom, peace and security" on page 1, but without drawing any environmental connections, and then never returned to the theme.

FINDING THE WAY FORWARD

We have arrived, thus, at the juncture of two separate roads: one a well-paved two-lane highway, the other a less-defined dirt track. Looking backward on the paved road, we see its ambitious design, its few turns, and the signposts it has provided for the UN's law-and-development caravan of global environmental governance. The road has allowed the caravan to progress to this point, but its disrepair is also evident. Turning to look back on the dirt track, we see a short but interesting stretch used by emerging initiatives within the UN system that link progress on environment to human rights or to peace and security in ways that can be mutually reinforcing. Its passageway is not nearly as well marked, the need to keep clearing away undergrowth in order to move forward is apparent, and there are many tempting side trails that lead back to the more conventional paved road of law and development.

As we turn from the past and set our gaze toward a hazy future, we see that neither road is demarcated in a final sense; indeed, our challenge is to mark a route across the landscape. Looking ahead, we see some rough terrain of political disagreement, and a landscape littered with many barriers to bringing the full force of the UN mandate to bear on environmental challenges. Those barriers are rooted, as always, in member-state resistance and entrenched interests—but also in weak or skewed institutional incentives, ideational contestation, and the already-constructed frameworks that have made "the environment" a matter of law and development, but not of peace and human rights.

Here it is helpful to return to the key variables I have used to explain how that landscape was built: institutions, ideas, and path-dependent historical trajectories. Just as these variables have helped us understand how "global environment" came to mean "law and development" at the UN, so may they help us think about how to navigate the road ahead. The micro-level of bureaucratic-organizational analysis ("institutions") helps us understand the possibilities for action across the uneven organizational landscape of the UN, while the meso-level of ideational frameworks ("ideas") shows how ideas, in context, can constrain or enable such action. The macro-level of historical trajectories and path-dependent change shows how historical cycles of such activity are linked together, and how prior developments make possible new forms of action, while simultaneously shaping the paths along which reformist energies will most likely—though not inevitably—flow.

Bearing these insights in mind, what follows is an attempt to flag several areas in which it may be possible to make tangible progress on environment/rights and environment/peace synergies. While some of the measures may seem small in the face of the planet's dire challenges, they should not be read as an argument for a narrowly incremental strategy. Rather, the goal is to fan out across the landscape and identify possible focal points from which cascades of change might be launched and build momentum. After all, the law-and-development approach itself was not the product of any masterful grand strategy. Rather, it grew out of the cumulative effects of a range of initiatives, choices, institutional developments, and political commitments. Some of these were strategic, some reflexive and habitual, and some accidental byproducts of other purposes—but together, they tapped into the existing political and institutional zeitgeist to create what we have today. The same is likely to be true of peace-based and rights-based approaches.

Nor is what follows an effort to offer an alternate "grand strategy" that should supplant law-and-development. Replacing one-half of the UN's mandate with the other half is unlikely to do much good. Returning to Craig Murphy's analogy from chapter 1, if the historical layers of institutionalized global governance are akin to the episodic construction of a cathedral, then recognizing what the building still requires does not mean tearing down what has been built already.

This view shares much in common with the argument of Kelly Levin and colleagues about the importance of "progressive incrementalism" in the face of "super wicked problems" such as global climate change.[11] Such problems share four characteristics: "time is running out; those who cause the problem also seek to provide a solution; the central authority needed to address it is weak or non-existent; and policy responses discount the future irrationally."[12] Under such circumstances, the authors recommend responses with three characteristics: interventions should launch a "sticky" path of progressive and cumulative, even if initially incremental, change; they should entrench support over time; and they should progressively expand their range of coverage. Launching such a trajectory of renewed environmental vigor across the UN system will require action along three distinct but related dimensions: the normative, the organizational, and the programmatic.

NORMATIVE RENEWAL: EMBRACE A HUMAN RIGHT TO THE ENVIRONMENT AND ACKNOWLEDGE AN ENVIRONMENTAL RESPONSIBILITY TO PROTECT

Respect, Protect, and Fulfill the Human Right to a Healthy Environment

Chapter 4 reached two important conclusions. First, the struggle for an express right to a safe, healthy environment has ground slowly through the UN's human rights machinery, for a combination of interest-based, institutional, and ideational reasons. Second, there are strong synergies to be tapped between human rights practice and environmental protection: a quality environment strengthens a range of human rights, while the exercise of rights creates accountability for protecting the environment. Recent activities of the Human Rights Council's independent expert on the environmental rights question reflect both findings. His reporting to UNHRC has reiterated earlier cautions that many issues in the environment-rights nexus need clarification, which seems to promise further years of study. Yet the same reporting has validated the importance and legitimacy of the links, characterizing both the harmful impact of environmental degradation on established human rights and the role of human rights in environmental policymaking as "firmly established."[13]

The quest for an express right remains important; witness the energizing effects of the General Assembly's finding a human right to water for "rights-based approaches" to the MDGs on drinking water and sanitation. Still, tapping rights-environment synergies in practice provides immediate opportunities to deepen the human rights dimension of global environmental governance. The best strategic opportunities are those issues where the rights-environment coupling is most obvious and immediate, and the rights in question are best established in international law. In other words: food security, toxic exposure, clean water and sanitation, and livelihoods or ways of life tied directly to the health of forests and fisheries. The importance of keeping these issues on the post-2015 development agenda makes the implementation of the SDGs a key battleground (as discussed in the section on programmatic renewal, below).

Another key to realizing environment-rights synergies is to hold governments accountable for obligations that are already clear. In a break with established practice, the Human Rights Council's independent expert has cautioned member states that "the lack of a complete under-standing as to the content of all environmentally related human rights obligations should not be taken as meaning that no such obligations exist. Indeed, some aspects of the duties are already clear."[14] OHCHR's ten-point list of recommendations for building human rights into the Rio+20 deliberations (table 6.1) provides a useful checklist in the quest for accountability. Although largely ignored by governments at Rio, the list underscores three clusters of essential practices that follow logically

Table 6.1 OHCHR'S TEN POINTS FOR INCORPORATING
HUMAN RIGHTS AT RIO+20

1. Commit to ensuring full coherence between efforts to advance the green economy, on the one hand, and the solemn human rights obligations of States on the other.
2. Recognize that all policies and measures adopted to advance sustainable development must be firmly grounded in, and respectful of, all internationally agreed human rights and fundamental freedoms, including the right to development.
3. Resolve to work to advance a human rights-based approach to the green economy, based on the principles of free, active and meaningful participation, accountability (including mechanisms at the national and international levels), non-discrimination, empower-ment, and the rule of law in green economy efforts.
4. Hold that all actors, in both the public and private sectors, should exercise due dili-gence, including through the use of human rights (as well as environmental) impact assessments.
5. Call for particular care to be taken to prevent and remedy any negative impacts on the human rights of vulnerable and marginalized groups, including indigenous peoples, minorities, migrants, persons living in poverty, persons living under repression and occupation, older persons, persons with disabilities, and children.
6. Allow for the full engagement of indigenous peoples in green economy policies, respect for their human rights, and their free, prior and informed consent in matters affecting their traditional lands.
7. Assure the empowerment of women, the protection of their human rights, and their meaningful participation in decision making.
8. Pursue a model of economic growth that is socially and environmentally sustainable, just and equitable, and respectful of all human rights.
9. Use human rights language and give explicit attention to protecting the human rights to food, to water and sanitation, to health, to housing, to education, and to participation in public affairs, in the context of a green economy.
10. Reaffirm the principles of the Rio Declaration, including liability for perpetrators, com-pensation for victims, and legal development to ensure extra-territorial accountability.

Source: Office of the High Commissioner for Human Rights, "OHCHR's 10 Points for Human Rights at Rio+20." Available at http://www.ohchr.org/EN/NewsEvents/Rio20/Pages/Backgroundinformation. aspx

from the discussion in chapter 4: (1) strengthening participatory rights at all levels, particularly for historically disenfranchised or suppressed voices; (2) requiring that development initiatives (green or otherwise) be scrutinized through human rights impact assessment; and (3) extending the domain of accountability beyond the state, to encompass the private sector and other actors—and thereby not only respecting and fulfilling rights, but also protecting them.

Acknowledge an Environmental Responsibility to Protect

Rights logically imply responsibilities. Thus, one key function of rights-based approaches is to create a basis for accountability: defining the responsibilities that correspond to human rights, identifying the parties to whom such responsibilities attach, and highlighting the (in)effectiveness with which those responsibilities are carried out, often through "naming and shaming" techniques.

Traditionally, human rights responsibilities have attached primarily to nation-states, given the grounding of codified human rights in treaty law. With problems such as climate change and disaster risk, however, the limited capacity of many states to actually protect and fulfill the rights of their citizens raises questions about the moral and legal responsibilities of the international system, as well. The question on which the UN has most famously grappled with the balance between domestic and systemic responsibility is how to protect people from organized violence. The result is the still-evolving doctrine of a "responsibility to protect" (R2P). R2P is an emerging norm spelled out in a 2005 General Assembly resolution, which states that *both* sovereign states *and* the international community have a responsibility to prevent genocide, war crimes, ethnic cleansing, and crimes against humanity.[15] While affirming that governments bear primary responsibility for protecting their citizens from these acts, R2P also calls the international community to action when the government in question is unable or unwilling to do so. In this sense, it identifies a globally shared, human dimension to security.

Although the General Assembly defined R2P, the norm's enforcement arm is clearly the Security Council. The Council has now referenced R2P in more than two dozen resolutions—some on specific conflicts, others on crosscutting issues such as the role of policing in peacekeeping, conflict prevention, and the small-arms trade.[16] For many member states, however, the question of when and how to invoke R2P raises concerns about sovereignty, interventionism, and the larger political issues surrounding the Council's makeup and procedures.[17] Thus, the Council has treaded lightly in invoking the idea, usually references a particular state's primary responsibility to protect its people. In a few instances, however, the Council has underscored the international community's responsibility, as well.[18]

An attempt to adapt R2P in an environmental direction, centered on responsibilities to aid people affected by natural disaster, revealed these underlying tensions. When Cyclone Nargis hit Myanmar (Burma) in 2008, the government initially banned international aid operations for several days, which led France to propose that the Security Council invoke R2P. The Council declined to do so, and soon thereafter the Secretary-General affirmed that

> the responsibility to protect applies, until Member States decide otherwise, only to the four specified crimes and violations: genocide, war crimes, ethnic cleansing and crimes against humanity. To try to extend it to cover other calamities, such as HIV/AIDS, climate change or the response to natural disasters, would undermine the 2005 consensus and stretch the concept beyond recognition or operational utility.[19]

The International Law Commission (a body of legal experts elected by the General Assembly), which took up the question of "protection of persons in the event of disasters" after the Southeast Asian tsunami (2004) and Hurricane Katrina (2005), has endorsed the Secretary-General's interpretation of the limits of R2P's applicability. In submitting comments to the ILC's special rapporteur on this question, member states reproduced the debate on sovereignty, intervention, and human security noted previously, as well as concern about the danger of a coercive "responsibility to cooperate." The draft articles put forward thus far by the ILC have been cautious to strike "the proper balance between the need to protect the persons affected by disasters and the respect for the principles of State sovereignty and non-interference."[20]

This slowly unfolding debate on natural disasters is preparing the ground for the inevitable debate on a climate-related responsibility to protect. As climate change drives rising sea levels and increases the supply and severity of extreme weather, pressures will only intensify on the UN system to resolve the ambiguity around this intersection of legal and moral questions. No member state has yet tabled the idea of a "climate R2P" in either the Security Council thematic discussions on climate or in the global climate talks. However, as discussed in chapter 4, the debate on national and international responsibilities for protection has already been joined, with developed countries stressing primary responsibility of governments in countries where the impacts are felt, while developing countries point to their own limited capabilities and the historical responsibility of developed countries for the bulk of greenhouse-gas emissions. Calls to negotiate a treaty on climate refugees have also put the issue in play.[21]

To link environmental responsibilities directly to the norm of R2P would probably destroy the fragile consensus the concept enjoys around organized violence against people. Such a move is also infeasible politically, as long as the concerns many member states hold about the Security Council's unrepresentativeness remain unresolved. A better approach is to articulate the responsibility in ways that reflect the specific structure of the problems of climate change and disaster risk. As a concept born in the context of overt violence against targeted groups of people, R2P constructs the international community as a bystander with a moral obligation to react when a state fails in its duties. On both climate and disasters, this construct fits poorly, for several reasons. There is no lack of early warning in this area; regions of the greatest vulnerability are already identified.[22] Moreover, research shows that preimpact poverty reduction is the most important intervention for communities vulnerable to climate suffering or disaster risk.[23] Another difference is in the moral boundaries of responsibility: the Security Council includes the member states chiefly responsible for directly causing the effects, as the leading emitters of greenhouse gases. Thus, we must speak of layered responsibilities: a state's responsibility to protect, the international community's responsibility not to neglect, and the leading emitters' responsibility for the effects. A climate responsibility to protect cannot be separated from a responsibility to prevent through proactive measures of both mitigation and adaptation. Interestingly, the debate around classic R2P appears to be moving in the same direction, as in the Security Council's recent, explicit linking of the small-arms trade to the international community's responsibilities under R2P.[24]

Addressing the plight of small-island states in the face of sea-level rise could provide a soft path forward in firming up the parameters of an environmental responsibility for protection. The problem is a foreseeable one, allowing for proactive measures. Military means are not appropriate, minimizing the legitimate concerns within the G-77 about interventionism and coercion. Any failure of state responsibility in this case is clearly related to incapacity rather than a lack of will, again curbing the tensions around interventionism. Indeed, the states most affected by the problem, the Small-Island Developing States, have been the most vocal in calling for international action.

ORGANIZATIONAL RENEWAL: REDEFINE "SYSTEM-WIDE" RESPONSES AND FIND A WORKABLE ROLE FOR THE SECURITY COUNCIL

Redefine a "System-Wide" Response to Environmental Challenges

Much ink has been spilled on the question of UN environmental reform—most of it captive of law-and-development thinking. When we shift the goal and ask how to reorganize so that the full force of the mandate may be brought to bear, the issue is not simply one of changing UNEP or linking entities involved in environment-development work, but rather of changing the conduits to all for a truly system-wide response—something that is decidedly not occurring today.

The concept of system-wide response is routinely invoked at the UN. A quick Google search at the time of this writing found it used there in the context of drylands management, gender equity, disaster response, poverty eradication, HIV/AIDS, the war in Syria, climate change, infectious diseases, and the problem of violence against those who work with the UN in conflict settings. The power of acting in a coordinated, system-wide fashion was underscored by the Secretary-General's High-Level Panel on System-Wide Coherence, which Kofi Annan tasked with assessing the UN's coordination problems in development initiatives. The panel's report, *Delivering as One*, concluded that

> a more united system would be a stronger, more responsive and effective United Nations. A system reconfigured to optimally use its assets and expertise in support of country needs and demands would strengthen the voice and action of the United Nations in development, humanitarian assistance and the environment. A repositioned United Nations—delivering as one—would be much more than the sum of its parts.[25]

The panel's proposed reforms were largely administrative. To be sure, there are major administrative challenges to systemic action, including poor fit among administrative procedures of different agencies, competition for scarce funds, and donor-driven pressures to show unrealistically rapid results. But there are also substantive and political problems with the current notion of what constitutes a "system-wide" response. Given the current channeling of the environmental problem into only two of the four mandate domains, and with little interaction between those two, efforts to act across the UN system generate a potpourri of narrow responses. At best, each organ takes its small slice of the issue-pie and gets to work—largely in isolation, and acting without the benefit of insights and opportunities that exist in the other mandate domains.

Consider the MDGs on water and sanitation, which sought to reduce by half the proportion of the world's population lacking access to this vital resource by 2015. Although the goals came to be viewed primarily as aspirational targets, the MDGs were in an important sense not goals at all; they were based on extrapolated trends in development progress rather than bold new ambitions.[26] They were also developed hurriedly and with little consultation, as a desperate move to renew the rapidly fading momentum of the 2000 Millennium Summit. Emerging from this context, the MDGs on water and sanitation failed to incorporate powerful insights from other parts of the UN—about the power of rights-based efforts on water access, the destructive impacts of conflict-prone water development models, and the key role of freshwater ecosystems in sustaining clean water supplies. As one of the MDG architects, Jan Vandemoortele, pointed out, "It would be utopian to believe that one set of macroeconomic, sectoral and institutional reforms can foster human development in each and every country. This would lead to policy myopia and to an artificial separation between development and politics." Yet, cut off from ideas about water available in other parts of the UN landscape, this is exactly what the laudable MDG goal of improving water access ended up doing.

Worse than just missing such synergies, the uneven landscape of UN environmental efforts has raised to an art form the practice of taking contradictory positions in different parts of the UN. The result can be a cynical game of "whose mandate?" that stalls progress by exploiting divisions. Consider the performance of the United States and China across the UN system on the issue of climate change. The US withdrew from its climate-mitigation commitments under the *Kyoto Protocol to the United Nations Framework Convention on Climate Change* (UNFCCC). Yet the United States has resisted discussing climate change in human rights forums, arguing that the UNFCCC is the appropriate venue for discussing human-rights impacts. Then, in 2011, the US representative excoriated the Security Council when some of its members proved reluctant to discuss climate change in that venue rather than UNFCCC.[27]

The United States is hardly alone in playing one venue against another for short-term political gain. China explicitly warned the Security Council that meddling on climate could harm the sensitive UNFCCC negotiations on a post-Kyoto framework. Yet China also proved quite ready to abandon the UNFCCC process for a side deal with the United States and a handful of other countries at the 2009 Copenhagen climate COP. Until the environment resonates across the full scope of the UN mandate, the dodging and shape-shifting seen in these examples will remain the norm across a fragmented institutional landscape.

The shift toward umbrella entities such as UN-Water and UN-Energy is an acknowledgment of the problem of insufficient exchange of information and ideas. Coordination efforts such as those around postconflict needs assessments (chapter 5) also recognize the institutional fragmentation problem. Neither of these responses speaks to the core *political* problem, however—the need for member states to work across the UN, rather than hide in compartmentalized segments of it. A recent assessment of some of the recent coordinating entities launched in the energy, water, and environmental spheres found that their effectiveness will require sharper mandates, better links to political-institutional processes, and stronger ties to wider non-UN networks. The study's authors also warned that "the very feasibility of [coordinating] bodies, their low financial and political cost in terms of upsetting the existing power structures, may also imply a low ability to rapidly steer the international community toward sustainable governance. ... This is especially the case when sustainable development actually calls for restructuring the way we produce, distribute, trade, and consume, rather than for incremental change."[28] Certainly, this passage could describe the history and prospects of UNEP, even with its new universal-membership governing council.

Agree on a Legitimate Role for the Security Council—and Equip the Council to Play It

Clearly, one challenge of system-wide response is to forge a broader consensus on an appropriate role for the Security Council—one that is legitimate, wise, and useful. Currently, dissensus reigns, and for reasons that go beyond short-term member-state interests. On the one hand, the idea that environmental challenges are irrelevant to the Council's mandate does not bear scrutiny in a world where natural resources are so profoundly implicated in the problem of civil war; where the world's many international river basins face severe challenges of water quality, availability, and climate impacts;[29] and where sea-level rise and extreme weather represent an "existential threat" for several UN member states. Nor can the Council's responsibility for the system problem be ignored: its current positioning on climate has made it a prime venue for political maneuvering, marked by divisive jurisdictional arguments and showy statements that need not be backed by action.

On the other hand, member states objecting to a stronger role for the Council have made several good points that environmental advocates would do well to heed. There are real reasons to ask whether the Council can actually be helpful; there is cause to worry about the securitization of problems that will require much stronger international cooperation; and there is a strong case to be made for limiting the role of a body built on stark power asymmetries, a culture of secrecy, and unequal rules of procedure. Any possible Council role faces hard questions: Can it be effective? Can it do so while remaining within the available political space? Can it work in concert with other essential parts of the UN?

The Council's experience with building a de facto regulatory regime around "conflict resources" (chapter 5) indicates that a useful, recurring, and appropriately bounded role can be crafted. Despite the problems of weak implementation and selective enforcement discussed in chapter 5, the Council's use of sanctions and peacekeeping mandates around conflict resources has been helpful in some cases, and as a result has gained broader legitimacy.

A possible starting point for the Council, both to gain experience and to build political legitimacy through responsible action, would be to address how climate change and other environmental trends intersect with core activities that lie unambiguously within its mandate—and in particular, with ongoing peacekeeping and peacebuilding operations in fragile and war-torn states. Germany stressed this theme in chairing the Council's thematic session on climate in 2011, arguing that climate change "presents a particular challenge to fragile countries" and stressing the ramifications for postconflict or failing states already on the Council's agenda.[30]

Accounting for the effects of climate impacts in such cases, however, requires both information and analytic capacity that, at present, the Council does not possess. The consensus statement from the 2011 thematic session took a small step to boost such capacity, requesting that the Secretary-General include "contextual information" on the possible security implications of climate change in his reporting to the Council. The usefulness of such periodic reporting remains unclear, however, given the case-specific character of any such effects. Moreover, the challenge is not simply to provide information, but to use it effectively. Here the Council's experience with natural resources and conflict is again instructive. Use of case-specific expert panels on "conflict resources" has made it possible to tailor peacekeeping mandates and sanctions regimes (even if the Council has not always had the will or consensus to back up such measures).

It may be that such capacity building is best done off the radar of the Council itself. The partnership between the Department of Peacekeeping

Operations and UNEP provides an interesting example: while this work focused initially on reducing the environmental footprint of peacekeeping operations, it also sought to build on this foundation by examining how good natural resource management relates to the larger objectives of peacekeeping and peacebuilding.[31] UNEP also produced an assessment of long-term climate trends across the Sahel that may offer a model.[32] This work, done in conjunction with several other UN organs and with the cooperation of governments across the region, identified linkages among climate variability, migration patterns, and communal conflict. The Council gained a useful picture of the problem, directly related to its current concerns and activities across the region.

Beyond embracing the environmental dimensions of ongoing operations, is there a more overtly political role for the Council? A common assumption among proponents is that the Council can focus international attention and raise the political pressure for action. Indeed, the Secretary-General, in remarks to the Council during its 2011 climate discussion, referred to this ability as the Council's "unique responsibility." During the two thematic sessions on climate, several member states cited the Council's open debate on HIV/AIDS in 2000 as precedent.

Whether the Council actually has such power remains unclear, however, as a more careful look at the supposed HIV/AIDS precedent reveals. The session was intended to raise the political profile of the disease and to add "security" to the list of reasons for combating it. There is some evidence that security considerations may have helped prompt the United States to increase international funding on AIDS during the presidency of George W. Bush. The prompt seems to have come, however, from the US intelligence community rather than the Security Council.[33] There is also evidence that "security" has been less useful than other ways of framing the AIDS problem in mobilizing international efforts.[34] Seeing plausible links to national security may prod governments to action. The question is whether raising global "security" stakes in general terms, without a clear path through the political negotiations to follow, has any prospect of altering political blockage. There may also be costs to the strategy, if the effect of promoting a security framework is for countries to redirect scarce resources away from mitigation efforts, or to privilege zero-sum "security" responses over international cooperation.

A much more targeted and impactful way to use the Council's agenda-setting power would be for the five permanent members to coordinate their voice on climate, speaking as both the arbiters of Council action and the leading greenhouse-gas emitters. As Nigeria noted in the Council's 2011 thematic session, "Seated around the table are those who could encourage developed countries to implement their commitments to reducing emissions and supporting developing countries with the requisite technological and financial assistance to address climate change effectively." Costa Rica urged the P-5 to "make a clear political commitment to reducing greenhouse gases."

A list of the world's leading emitters of greenhouse gases (table 6.2) includes the P-5 and the four leading aspirants to permanent seats on an expanded Security Council (India, Japan, Brazil, and Germany). Together, these nine member states account for two-thirds of global emissions.[35] It may be difficult to envision even symbolic "threat minimizing action" on climate involving joint efforts by Russia, China, and the United States in the current political moment. The US-China climate deal of November 2014 was studiously silent on any conflict-sensitive or peacebuilding rationale for action, much less any actual measures in those directions. But to do so would prod the climate talks in a way that general invocations on international security can never do. And it would illustrate powerfully how to redefine a "system-wide" response—shifting emphasis away from how UN organs coordinate their separate actions and divide their turf, and toward the need for member states to work across those organs in an integrated, coherent way.

One way to prod such commitments may be to leverage the aspirations of emerging powers to gain permanent seats on an expanded and reformed Council. Aspirants to the Council should be challenged to demonstrate constructive leadership by explaining how they see the Council's

Table 6.2 LEADING GREENHOUSE-GAS EMITTERS AMONG SECURITY COUNCIL PERMANENT MEMBERS AND ASPIRANTS

Country	Security Council status	CO_2 equivalent emissions, 2010 (million metric tons)	CO_2 equivalent emissions, 2010 (global rank)
China	Permanent member	9,632	1
United States	Permanent member	6,548	2
India	Aspirant	2,505	3
Russia	Permanent member	2,242	4
Japan	Aspirant	1,280	5
Brazil	Aspirant	1,049	6
Germany	Aspirant	888	7
UK	Permanent member	585	11
France	Permanent member	502	14

Note: Excludes climate effects of land-use changes and forestry.
Source: The Shift Project Data Portal, www.tsp-data-portal.org.

role adapting to new international security challenges such as climate change. Calling the P-5 to action should be flagged as an important part of demonstrating leadership.

A more ambitious role for the Council would be to anticipate, identify, and prevent emergent resource-related or environmentally driven conflicts, as some have suggested may loom ahead for water scarcity or food insecurity. The Secretary-General's 2009 report on climate and security noted that "the international community must anticipate and prepare itself to address a number of largely unprecedented challenges posed by climate change for which the existing mechanisms may prove inadequate," including large numbers of displaced people, statelessness of submerged island nations, drastic reductions in water availability, and enhanced competition for resources.[36] In the 2011 climate debate, US ambassador Susan Rice compared the task facing the Council to the extensive adjustments it made in adapting traditional peacekeeping tools to the complex peacebuilding challenges of the post–Cold War era. She called for improved early warning systems, better information with which to anticipate and prevent resource-driven conflicts, and preventive diplomacy to manage potential disputes.[37]

There is precedent for the Council to at least think in these terms: a June 2013 special session on natural resources, chaired by the United Kingdom, focused explicitly on the preventive dimension. The discussion stressed transparency in resource revenues and financing, better social and environmental impact assessment, and conflict resolution processes as the key needs for conflict prevention.[38] More generally, efforts to promote a more preventive approach to conflict have gained some momentum in the Council through Resolutions 1325 (2000) and 1625 (2005), the 2005 World Summit outcomes, the strengthened budget and analytic capacity of the Department of Political Affairs, General Assembly Resolution 65/283 (2011), the Secretary-General's reporting on preventive diplomacy, and a 2011 Security Council thematic session on conflict prevention. The Secretary-General has pointed to cases such as South Sudan's independence referendum, Guinea's political transition, electoral violence in Kenya, and tensions between Rwanda and the Democratic Republic of Congo as examples of the UN's ability to play a conflict-prevention role.[39] The concept remains controversial, however, given its vagueness and its possible associations with the preventive use of force. A proposal to give the Peacebuilding Commission a preventive mandate was quashed when that body was created, for this reason.[40]

Conflict prevention and early warning remain imperfect arts,[41] and the idea of integrating climate sensitivity into conflict early warning systems encounters several practical difficulties. On the climate side, the challenge is to understand how nonlinear, often unpredictable, and place-specific effects matter for conflict with enough precision to make useful assessments. Research on water and conflict shows that, while there appear to be links between water availability and violence, the problem is far more complex than simply one of water scarcity triggering tensions. It has more to do with the capacity of institutions to adapt, the character of state responses, and the role of unpredictable, extreme events.[42] The broad message emanating from climate-adaptation and disaster-reduction work is similar: risks to human security emanate not simply from hazards, but rather from the particular mix of vulnerabilities and capacities that human communities bring to bear in the face of hazards.[43] Much work lies ahead in reconciling this approach, which stresses a combination of broad risk factors and site-specific conditions, with the crisis-oriented, interventionist, and victim-protecting logic that underpins the conflict early-warning systems currently tapped by the Council.

In the long run, the Council's ability to play any role effectively and legitimately will be tied to progress on the wider question of Security Council reform. This means finding a pathway through thorny questions about the Council's size, composition, and procedures. It also means reforming the closed, secretive, and imperious behavior that has marked too much of the Council's activity. Again, in this context, a central part of the reform debate should be to hear what aspirants to a permanent seat, or proponents of any particular type of reform, think about the Council's role in global environmental governance and their willingness to commit to specific leadership actions.

PROGRAMMATIC RENEWAL: REINVIGORATE LAW-AND-DEVELOPMENT AND EXPLOIT ENVIRONMENTAL PEACEBUILDING OPPORTUNITIES

Infuse Law-and-Development Efforts with Peace-and-Rights Practice

Clearly, my purpose is not to supplant one half of the UN mandate with the other. A peace-and-rights approach would, by itself, be no more effective than the law-and-development framework has been; worse, it would cede some of the latter's important accomplishments. An important goal, then, is to reinvigorate law-and-development practice by infusing it with stronger peace-and-rights content.

With regard to international environmental law, a multipronged approach is needed. One element would be to negotiate environmental treaty-regimes on topics particularly germane to the peace-and-rights dimensions of environmental protection, as in the case of proposals for a treaty on climate refugees, or a strengthened legal instrument on environmental protection in times of war.[44] A second element would be to strengthen and expand international law regarding peoples' procedural environmental rights, as currently embodied in the Aarhus Convention and Principle 10 of the 1992 Rio Declaration (see chapter 4). This could be done by extending the Aarhus accord from Europe to the global level or, more likely, by negotiating analogous regional accords (as is occurring in Latin America under the auspices of the UN Economic Commission for Latin America).[45] Procedural rights can also be strengthened by building more explicit environmental content into the ongoing codification of "good governance" practices, such as the Open Governance Initiative and the UN principles on Business and Human Rights drafted by the Secretary-General's special representative, John Ruggie.[46]

The larger challenge, however, is infusing existing treaty-regimes with stronger peace-and-rights content. One example of such a need is the international law of shared river basins. The 1997 UN Convention on the Non-navigational Uses of Internationally Shared Watercourses, which entered into force in 2014, endorses principles to incorporate when negotiating accords in specific river basins: universal participation by riparian states, information sharing, prior notification, equitable use, avoidance of significant harm, and environmental protection. However, the Watercourses Convention lacks a sufficient grounding in human rights, does not recognize the recently acknowledged human right to water, and fails to endorse rights-based approaches to integrated water resource management. The convention's conflict-sensitive content is also lacking. It contains some guidance on how riparian states should resolve disputes, but remains silent on the primary triggers of violence around water: poorly conceived infrastructure development, unjust or coercive water management practices, and water-related rights violations that occur in the context of land appropriation and uncertain tenure.[47]

Climate change is a second domain in which peace-and-rights content is sorely needed, as evidenced by the controversies around REDD (chapter 4) and the increasing encroachment of the Security Council (chapter 5). The twenty-seven special experts who hold an issue-specific mandate with the Human Rights Council filed a joint appeal to governments meeting in Lima for the 2014 climate COP, urging them to recognize the adverse impacts of climate change on human rights; to adopt "urgent and ambitious" response measures; to ensure that any actions they take on climate are consistent with their existing human rights obligations;

to incorporate specific commitments to protect, promote, and fulfill human rights into the climate agreement anticipated for December 2015 in Paris; and to develop a specific work program toward these ends.[48] The COP apparently did not get the memo—it declined to revisit the "rights" framework for REDD+, dodged a proposed statement on loss and damage, and blocked a proposal from the Philippines for human rights language in the outcome statement.[49] The need for enhanced conflict sensitivity is also becoming apparent; as climate-adaptation efforts gain emphasis in the UNFCCC process, their conflict potential must be not just recognized, but evaluated through peace-and-conflict impact assessment (PCIA) and addressed through conflict-sensitive policy design and informed consent mechanisms.[50]

The challenge of infusing sustainable development with peace-and-rights content is similarly broad. The MDGs had nothing to say about challenges to peace, and "almost entirely neglected to substantively incorporate a human rights-based approach to development."[51] Indeed, the exercise of setting universal development goals is in substantial tension with a rights-based approach, given the top-down character of the goal-setting process and its tendency to see people as objects to be developed rather than subjects in their own development. Nevertheless, the goal-setting process has become the chief framework for UN sustainable development efforts, and affords opportunities for bringing peace and human rights more squarely into the picture.

The UN's process for agreeing upon SDGs, the development goals for the post-2015 period, was initially highly fragmented, with rival activities emanating from the Secretary-General's office and Rio+20 preparations.[52] At Rio+20, governments agreed to fuse the strands, and the General Assembly then appointed an Open Working Group (OWG) of thirty member states which developed a draft set of seventeen goals. As of this writing, both the goals and the indicators and targets accompanying them are still the subject of intense intergovernmental negotiations leading up to the Fall 2015 session of the General Assembly.

Environmentally, the draft SDGs present a mixed picture. Without question, the environmental elements of the goals are more ambitious and detailed than those of the MDGs (which were limited to biodiversity loss, drinking water and sanitation, conditions for slum dwellers, and a general exhortation to "integrate the principles of sustainable development" at the national level). The SDGs include rhetorical commitments to sustainable food production, resilient agricultural practices, reduction in death and illness from pollutant exposure, reduced water pollution and increased wastewater treatment, protection of ecosystems, increased renewable energy and energy efficiency, protection of natural heritage, reduction in fossil fuel subsidies, action on climate change, protection of the oceans, and protection of terrestrial ecosystems.[53] Most, however, do not yet embrace specific targets, and those that do are often wildly optimistic ("by 2020, achieve the environmentally sound management of chemicals and all wastes throughout their life cycle") or hopelessly vague ("by 2030, achieve the sustainable management and efficient use of natural resources").[54]

During its deliberations, the OWG included both human rights and peace and security as discussion themes. In its open discussion on peace and security, several governments expressed doubts about the appropriateness of setting peace goals or even discussing those issues in the context of the SDGs. The only connection to environmental issues in the discussion was a reference by Finland to the Sustainable Development Solutions Network report's theme of "respecting planetary boundaries."[55] Similarly, only a few governments offered environmental points in the human-rights discussion (although the designated representative for "NGOs" flagged the Aarhus/Rio Declaration triumvirate of access to information, participation, and justice).[56] When the OWG fielded written submissions from governments, few of the suggestions on peace and human rights addressed environmental matters.[57]

Nor were the connections made in the "expert voice" of the Sustainable Development Solutions Network (SDSN), which reported to the Secretary-General on the eve of Rio+20.[58] One of the many tensions at Rio+20 was the appropriate balance between "expert" and "political" voices in framing the SDGs—yet the two voices were equally silent on rights-based approaches to environmental protection, or participatory rights of access to decision-making and redress, or natural resources' conflict potential, or environmental peacebuilding. Among the "priority challenges" identified by SDSN, the challenge to "achieve development within planetary boundaries" noted the poor quality of national accounting systems as measures of progress—but not the need of citizens to have access to the information in those accounts. The challenge to "curb human-induced climate change and ensure clean energy for all" stressed decarbonization—but skirted any reference to climate justice or rights-based approaches to contentious land-use decisions. The challenge to "secure ecosystem services and biodiversity, and ensure good management of water and other natural resources" emphasized sound science, policy harmonization, and full-cost pricing—but was silent on the importance of public participation around any of those instruments.[59] Only in the discussion of sustainable management of extractive industries were themes of transparency, public participation, and accountability included. SDSN called peace "the most important public good" for development—but made no mention of environmental conflict resolution or conflict-sensitive development.[60]

The resulting goals produced by the OWG reflect this shared silence of governments and experts. Among the many environmental aims that crop up throughout the text, only those in Goal 5, on gender equality and the empowerment of women and girls, take a clearly rights-based approach (calling for reforms "to give women equal rights to economic resources" including landownership and natural resources).[61] Goal 12, on sustainable production and consumption patterns, includes a call to "ensure that people everywhere have the relevant information and awareness" for sustainable development—but it does not identify information as a right, and it ignores the other key elements of the Rio Declaration / Aarhus Convention framework, rights to participation and rights to redress.[62] The SDGs' environmental silence on peace and conflict is even greater: Goal 16, on the creation of peaceful and inclusive societies, contains no environmental content.

Without infusing the SDG process with a significantly more rights-based approach, the entire enterprise will lack meaningful accountability mechanisms for reaching the targets that have been created. It will also lack the participatory inputs needed to actually protect ecosystems, enhance food security, and reduce toxic exposures. Because the MDGs were framed in terms of reducing rather than eliminating social ills, many countries made progress on the goals by improving outcomes for less impoverished and less marginalized groups—improving national indicators while leaving voiceless and rights-deprived communities behind.[63] The more ambitious SDGs will not have the luxury of cherry-picking the beneficiaries of progress.

One important entry point, then, is the idea of social accountability, which my colleague Jonathan Fox has defined as "an evolving umbrella category that includes: citizen monitoring and oversight of public and/ or private sector performance, user-centered public information access/ dissemination systems, public complaint and grievance redress mechanisms, as well as citizen participation in actual resource allocation decision-making, such as participatory budgeting."[64] Fox's meta-analysis of the research on links between accountability and performance shows that, by itself, access to information—what Ann Florini dubbed "regulation by revelation"[65]—is not a reliably sufficient condition for social accountability. Researcher Aarti Gupta makes a similar point about transnational efforts in global environmental governance, noting that information-transparency efforts assume that good process yields good decision-making and that information is inherently an empowering resource.[66]

More promising are what Fox terms "multi-pronged strategies that encourage enabling environments for collective action and bolster state capacity to actually respond to citizen voice."[67] Such strategies require "pro-accountability" coalitions that cut across the state-society divide, and which seek to create not only "voice" but also "teeth" in the form of capable state responses. If this analysis is correct, then SDG endorsement of access to information is merely a starting point. Such strategies require the full set of access rights written into the Rio Declaration and the Aarhus Convention: access not only to information, but also to participation and to justice through redress and remedy. The full suite of rights is necessary for both coalition-building and state capacity-building: in the former instance, to fend off the barriers to (and reprisal against) public advocacy inevitably erected by anti-accountability forces; and in the latter, to generate meaningful demand for better state performance and empower the position of "reformists" within the state.[68]

Nor will such outcomes be attained if the SDG process remains silent on the conflict potential of natural resources and the need for environmental dispute resolution and conflict-sensitive resource development. A recent analysis of natural resources, conflict, and peacebuilding in the Central African Republic, prepared by the US-based Friends Committee on National Legislation, underscored that country's downward spiral of poor governance, human insecurity, migration, escalating conflicts over resources, and development failure.[69] The report identified three critical interventions to break the cycle and create a foundation for sustainable development: establishing transparent and accountable systems for managing high-value natural resources, to end the practice of funding violence through mining and poaching; promoting resource-related dispute resolution and establishing land and resource rights, in order to "jumpstart economic recovery" and stabilize resource-related livelihoods; and integrating sustainable natural resource management into recovery efforts, so as to minimize collateral damage from international humanitarian interventions and create a more cooperative foundation for recovery.[70]

Resource conflict in the DRC, as discussed in chapter 5, also shows the tight coupling among conflict transformation, rights-based approaches, and development. US financial-regulation legislation (the 2010 Dodd-Frank Act), which requires reporting regarding the conflict status of selected minerals extracted in several sub-Saharan countries, has begun to have a significant impact on transnational corporate practices around conflict minerals.[71] According to an assessment by the Enough Project, armed groups were significantly less present around tin, tantalum, and tungsten mines in the eastern DRC; minerals not passing through the conflict-free certification program sold for 30–60 percent less; and 40 percent of global smelters for the regulated minerals had passed third-party conflict-free certification tests.[72] Dodd-Frank has also been criticized for its impact on workers and local mining economies—impacts that have resulted in part from the failure to implement effective certification of "clean" mining activities in a timely manner, causing some companies to shift to other sources.[73] This experience underscores several key themes of this book: the shifting of production in response to regulatory interventions, a core problem of globalization; the importance of transnational regulatory intervention; and the harm that can occur when local communities lack voice and rights in someone else's process of "safeguarding" their development.

Finally, peace-and-rights content in SDG implementation should also involve peace-plus-rights, or identifying points of synergy. One such point is found in "Do no harm" approaches to contentious projects that risk both rights violations and conflict: extractive industries, large-scale infrastructure projects, and significant changes in land use or resource access. For example, the Mining Working Group at the UN, an NGO coalition on extractive industries, identifies "Do no harm" as the first principle for applying a rights-based "litmus test" on extractives (along with principles of eradicating root causes of poverty, recognizing people as rights-holders, and sustainability). The group recommends specific assessment steps to gauge whether an extractive activity violates human rights, damages vital ecosystems, discriminates by leaving disadvantaged or marginalized groups particularly vulnerable, or risks armed conflict.[74]

Another peace/rights synergy involves mobility—people displaced by environmental harm, people who choose to migrate as a result of environmental factors, and people whose livelihoods are organized around nomadic practices such as herding. Legally and institutionally, the UN system operates around a set of distinctions that, however useful they may have been historically, have little meaning in complex, real-world situations of environmental mobility: victims versus migrants, border-crossing refugees versus internally displaced people, and political victims versus those needing humanitarian assistance. Institutionally, the understanding of people as victims who travel is completely severed from that of people as migrants—despite a clear body of research identifying close ties between the two, and pointing to the need for practical and integrated forms of action that sit beyond the fragmented UN framework for providing assistance.[75] The MDG and SDG processes have tended to frame solutions territorially, thus failing to manage conflicts, recognize rights, or respond to needs related to mobility.

One hopeful sign: as the SDGs were formulated, input from the UN bureaucracy provided a stronger, clearer endorsement of peace-and-rights strategies than either the expert-based or member-state input sketched above. The report of the UN System Task Team on the Post-2015 UN Development Agenda noted explicitly the MDGs' failure to adequately address issues related to human rights, peace, and security, as well as associated concerns such as violence against women, social exclusion, inequality, and the rule of law.[76] Their report identified resource-related conflicts as a key determinant of "conflict, hunger, insecurity, and violence"; flagged human rights as one of three "fundamental principles" (along with equality and sustainability); and identified peace and security as one of the four "core dimensions" within which specific post-2015 goals and targets should be defined (along with inclusive social development, environmental sustainability, and inclusive economic development).[77]

Exploit Opportunities for Environmental Peacebuilding

Anticipating and managing resource and environmental conflicts is a key element of conflict-sensitive development. But a focus solely on conflict potential risks reinforcing a zero-sum logic, in which member states seek to insulate themselves from change, rather than working jointly to manage change and steer it in positive directions. "Securitization" of environmental problems may inhibit opportunities for cooperation.[78]

One response to such concerns has been an emerging strategy that is sometimes referred to as environmental peacemaking or environmental peacebuilding. Such approaches seek to tap collaborative opportunities around the environment and natural resources, in order to transform conflict and establish robust, positive forms of peace that embody more than just the absence of violence.[79] According to one leading organizational practitioner, the NGO EcoPeace / Friends of the Earth Middle East, the process of conflict transformation through environmental initiatives may involve several mechanisms:

> Environmental cooperation is part of a long-time solution to conflict. It offers sustainable solutions for the future. It contributes to the improvement of living conditions, such as for instance the supply of water, and it fosters the building of confidence and trust among adverse societies. Environmental issues and the mutual ecological dependence across territorial borders facilitate and

encourage cooperation, cooperation that often is a first step toward the initiation of an ongoing dialogue, which would be difficult to mediate through political channels. As shared management of environmental resources develops and parties to a conflict are integrated in cooperative negotiation processes political tensions can be overcome and due to the establishment of mutual trust a creation of a common regional identity and the idea of mutual rights and expectations are likely to emerge.[80]

In previous work I have conceptualized environmental peacebuilding as a process that seeks to work through several mechanisms: exploiting interdependencies to find mutual benefits, lengthening the "shadow of the future" in decision-making, generating cooperative knowledge about environmental problems, fostering societally based linkages across various types of boundaries, and softening conflict identities by fostering new solidarities around shared ecosystems and shared approaches to environmental problems.[81]

In its emphasis on conflict transformation, environmental peacebuilding is distinct from the more familiar and often depoliticized practice of implementing "positive" environmental projects such as environmental restoration or the designation of protected areas. As a UNEP review of African peacebuilding efforts around natural resources explained, "Tree planting alone does not promote peace, but resolving issues of land tenure for contested forestry, establishing participatory forest committees and supporting revenue sharing from forest livelihoods contribute to peace, and tree planting would be an appropriate component of such projects."[82] Such opportunities should be sought on many scales: localized co-management of common-property resources and ecosystems; national policy frameworks that incorporate multistakeholder dialogue as a central feature of decision-making and dispute resolution on contentious issues such as land tenure; regionalized approaches to the management of shared watersheds, protected areas, migratory routes, and coastal resources, including better information exchange, impact assessment, joint monitoring, and collaborative planning; and regional or global mechanisms that promote best practices for transparent, equitable, and sustainable resource development.

Much of the work involved in environmental peacebuilding takes place locally, and is closely related to the aforementioned need to infuse sustainable development practice with peace-and-rights content. Here, an important challenge is to move beyond the "postconflict" peacebuilding efforts discussed in chapter 5 to engage the full conflict cycle through conflict-prevention and conflict-management strategies. UNEP's post-conflict environmental assessment of Cote D'Ivoire identifies elements of good resource governance that provide a template for a "life cycle" approach to building peace: developing a vision for sustainability, strengthening institutional and legal frameworks, enhancing state capacity, creating mechanisms to ensure transparency and accountability, involving the public in decision-making, and sharing benefits equitably.[83]

Another key element of environmental peacebuilding is gender. Women's environmental circumstances are often characterized by vulnerability, which stems from gendered land-tenure systems, inheritance practices, and inequitable distributions of economic power at the household and community level. Yet gendered divisions of labor frequently place women in key provisioning roles, particularly around communal and "common property" resources. For example, women play a key role in the household and community provisioning of water resources (even as marketized systems of irrigation or water service provisioning tend to attract and fall under the control of men). A recent assessment conducted jointly by UN Women, UNEP, the UN Peacebuilding Support Office, and UNDP found important peacebuilding potential in women's gatekeeper status, particularly as gender roles shift in the fluid settings of conflict and postconflict economic adaptations. Specifically identified entry points include enhancing women's political participation in peace negotiations, resource decision-making, and environmental governance; strengthening protection and security for women around resource provisioning; and taking rights-based approaches to economic revitalization.[84]

While a localized focus is essential, it is also insufficient. As discussed in chapter 3, local communities often find themselves embedded in larger systems of production, consumption, and resource governance that can disrupt local efforts to manage resources and ecosystems cooperatively and peacefully. Thus, a key complement of localized peacebuilding efforts and conflict-sensitive sustainable development initiatives is a more coherent international regulatory framework for steering natural resource development into equitable, peace-enhancing outcomes.

Such a framework has not been created either by current donor practices or by emerging sets of voluntary standards and "best practices." Regarding donor activities, a 2013 assessment by Chatham House noted, "The overall donor approach to natural resource governance in the developing world has often been disjointed and selective."[85] Problems include a confusion between means (e.g., transparency) and ends (e.g., better governance, equity, accountability); an excessively short-term focus; and narrowly selective emphasis on a few aspects of complex resource

Table 6.3 INTERNATIONAL INITIATIVE ON "GOOD GOVERNANCE"
OF NATURAL RESOURCES

Initiative	Organization(s)
Africa Mining Vision	African Union
Extractive Industries Transparency Initiative	Multistakeholder
G8 2013 summit outcome on transparency and global reporting standards for extractive industries	Group of Eight
Global Compact	UN
ICGLR Regional Initiative against the Illegal Exploitation of Natural Resources	International Conference on the Great Lakes Region
OECD Due Diligence Guidance for Responsible Supply Chains of Minerals from Conflict-Affected and High-Risk Areas	Organisation for Economic Co-operation and Development
Publish What You Pay	Civil-society network
Resolution on Good Governance in the Extractive and Forestry Industries	International Organization of la Francophonie
UN Guiding Principles on Business and Human Rights (Ruggie Principles)	UN
UN-EU Partnership on Natural Resources and Conflict Prevention	European Union and UN
Voluntary Principles on Security and Human Rights	Multistakeholder

Source: Compiled by author.

governance systems, within which donors tend to "cherry-pick the disparate, unconnected elements they want to fund."[86]

Nor have soft law and voluntary transnational initiatives (table 6.3) filled the gap. The proliferation of such efforts reflects the many stakeholders, the border-crossing characteristics of resource commodity chains, and the numerous sectors plagued by corruption, impunity, environmental harm, and conflict. But it also reflects the UN's failure to play an authoritative role that melds international law, sustainable development, and conflict transformation. Bringing coherence to this realm would improve effectiveness and reduce transaction costs. It should also speak to important concerns within the G-77: that creating an automatic, presumptive link between natural resources and violent conflict undercuts resource sovereignty; that concerns about "conflict resources" might be used to justify undue interference in the domestic affairs of sovereign states; and that resource-producing countries cannot address the problem roots that lie beyond their territory.[87]

My critique of the law-and-development approach to global environmental governance has stressed its ineffectiveness, its poor fit with the world's environmental problems, and its failure to mobilize the full set of tools available to the UN. There is also, however, a deeper problem. The flagging momentum for creating international environmental law, the thinning of environmental content in sustainable development efforts, the profound sense of drift and discord seen at Rio+20—all are symptoms of a movement that has run out of steam. What, then, of political renewal?

My views on these questions began to form in the wake of the disappointing 2002 Johannesburg summit. (Before there was a "Rio minus 20," there was "Rio minus 10.") In a previous book, Jacob Park, Matthias Finger, and I argued that there were deeper flaws in what we dubbed "the Rio model" than simply its poor execution of the tasks it had set for itself.[88] We argued that the task itself was misconceived, and that the tools for its execution were poorly matched to the underlying problem. We argued that the Rio model failed to account for the dynamic pattern of industrial development in the world economy, aka "globalization"; that it took a heavily territorialized, sovereignty-bound view of environmental problems; and that it miscast states as capable, willing, and authoritative agents of environmental regulation. If this assessment is correct, then political renewal for global environmental governance will require a far broader movement for change.

The UN itself will not be the source for such a movement. However, mobilizing the powerful ideals embedded in its mandate—strengthening people's human rights in, around, with, and through nature, and securing for them a more peaceful and less vulnerable footing in the human and natural worlds—can surely help to build it.

Throughout this book, I have invoked several metaphors—tools, pillars, landscapes, pathways—to argue that the UN's approach to global environmental governance must embody the full scope of the organization's mandate. Perhaps the most apt metaphor, however, is provided by the story of a sculpture. For his last public commission, the renowned Italian Renaissance sculptor Pietro Tacca took up the challenge of making an enormous bronze equestrian statue of Philip IV of Spain. The project took several years to complete, arriving in Madrid in 1640. At the time, the statue was something of a technical marvel, able to support the weight of the rearing bronze horse on just the two hind legs (with some discreet help from the horse's tail in Tacca's clever design).[89] A technical marvel, but also a political one: the work provided "a superb image of political propaganda" in its heroic presentation of a weak and diffident ruler who was unable to manage the ruinous Thirty Years' War or the growing crisis of Spanish governance.[90]

Tacca's sculpture provides an apt metaphor for the UN's environmental work. Like his horse, the two stronger legs of the UN's approach, sustainable development and international environmental law, must support the entire structure of global environmental governance. To be sure, that work has been a technical feat: it is no small task to get initiatives in international environmental law and sustainable development to stand upright, and such accomplishments are not to be dismissed. But the propagandistic element of the work is also evident, in its increasingly empty claim that better law between nations and better development within them will be enough to provide "the future we want" for the planet and its people. A final similarity with Tacca's sculpture: the UN approach has become frozen in a heroic pose, epitomized by the ambitions of the 1992 Earth Summit and the now-ritualized processes of global summitry, conferences of the parties, and the pronouncement of goals for sustainable development.

The problem is larger, more immediate, and of a sort that the UN's institutionalized approach to environmental challenges cannot address adequately. At this moment of political impasse, drift, and failed imagination, we need more than just fine-tuning of the prevailing legal and developmental strategies. For the horse to start moving—at a steady gait, and along the path to real progress—it needs above all else the use of all four of its legs.

NOTES

CHAPTER 1

1. F. Biermann, K. Abbott, S. Andresen, et al., "Navigating the Anthropocene: Improving Earth System Governance," *Science* 335, no. 6074 (March 2012): 1306–1307.
2. Robert B. Jackson, Stephen R. Carpenter, Clifford N. Dahm, Diane M. McKnight, Robert J. Naiman, Sandra L. Postel, and Steven W. Running, "Water in a Changing World," *Ecological Applications* 11, no. 4 (August 2001): 1027–1045.
3. Intergovernmental Panel on Climate Change, *Climate Change 2014 Synthesis Report: Summary for Policy Makers* (Geneva: IPCC, 2014), 16.
4. United Nations Environment Programme, *Global Environmental Outlook 5* (Nairobi: UNEP, 2012), 46.
5. I am grateful to Peter Gleick for this observation.
6. United Nations Environment Programme, *Global Environmental Outlook 4* (Nairobi: UNEP, 2007), 92.
7. P. Kumar, ed., *The Economics of Ecosystems and Biodiversity: Ecological and Economic Foundations* (Washington, DC: Earthscan, 2010).
8. UNEP, *Global Environmental Outlook 5*, 66.
9. On the UN's conceptual contributions on environment and natural resources, see Nico Schrijver, *Development without Destruction: The UN and Global Resource Management* (Bloomington: Indiana University Press, 2010).
10. World Commission on Environment and Development, *Our Common Future* (New York: Oxford University Press, 1987).
11. High-Level Panel on Threats, Challenges, and Change, *A More Secure World: Report of the Secretary-General's High-Level Panel on Threats, Challenges and Change* (New York: United Nations, 2004).
12. See, for example, Rob Edwards, "World Summit Teeters on Brink of Failure," *New Scientist* 30 (August 2002), available at http://www.newscientist.com/article/dn2744-world-summit-teeters-on-brink-of-failure.html, viewed 13 May 2013.
13. One exception to this is water supply and sanitation, which adopted firm targets and timetables for increasing access—but which contain no specifically environmental provisions regarding the protection of water supplies or ecosystem services. See chapter 4.
14. United Nations General Assembly, *Report of the Open Working Group of the General Assembly on Sustainable Development Goals*, Goal 14.2, p. 20, and Goal 12.2, p. 19. UN Document A/68/970, 12 August 2014. The final text for the SDGs was still being negotiated as this book went to press.

15. UN Environment Programme, *United Nations Environment Programme Annual Report 2013* (Nairobi: UNEP, 2014), 50; American University, *American University Budget, Fiscal Years 2012 and 2013*. Report from the president adopted by the Board of Trustees, 25 February 2011.

16. UNEP, *Annual Report 2013*, 50.

17. Secretary-General's High-Level Panel on UN System-Wide Coherence in the Areas of Development, Humanitarian Assistance, and the Environment, *Delivering as One: Report of the Secretary General's High-Level Panel* (New York: UN, 2006), 29.

18. See Informal Consultative Process on the Institutional Framework for the United Nations' Environmental Activities, Co-Chairs' Options Paper, 14 June 2007.

19. Informal Consultative Process, *Co-Chairs' Options Paper*, 6–7.

20. Frank Biermann and Steffen Bauer, eds., *A World Environment Organization* (Surrey: Ashgate, 2005). See also Peter Newell, "New Environmental Architectures and the Search for Effectiveness," *Global Environmental Politics* 1, no. 1 (February 2001): 35–44.

21. The Rio+20 outcome statement called for UNEP's Governing Council to have universal membership among UN member states, which has been implemented. It also made nonspecific promises of funding improvements for UNEP, and committed to general aims of consolidation, coordination, stakeholder participation, a better science-policy interface, information dissemination, and capacity building. See *The Future We Want*, outcome document of the UN Conference on Sustainable Development, Rio de Janeiro, 19 June 2012. Available at http://www.un.org/en/sustainablefuture/index.shtml, viewed 14 July 2012.

22. See Global Policy Forum, "UN Reform." Available at https://www.globalpolicy.org/un-reform.html, viewed 1 December 2014. See also Ralph Wilde, ed., *United Nations Reform through Practice*. Report of the International Law Association Study Group on United Nations Reform, December 2011.

23. WCED, *Our Common Future*.

24. On "wicked problems," see Horst W. J. Rittel and Melvin M. Webber, "Dilemmas in a General Theory of Planning," *Policy Sciences* 4, no. 2 (1973): 155–169. On "super wicked" problems, a theme to which I return in chapter 6, see Kelly Levin, Benjamin Cashore, Steven Bernstein, and Graeme Auld, "Overcoming the Tragedy of Super Wicked Problems: Constraining Our Future Selves to Ameliorate Global Climate Change," *Policy Sciences* 45, no. 2 (2012): 123–152.

25. UN home page, available at www.un.org, viewed 10 June 2009.

26. The third central council created by the UN Charter, the Trusteeship Council, suspended its operations in 1994 with the independence of Palau as the last remaining UN trust territory.

27. "Security Council Holds First-Ever Debate on Impact of Climate Change on Peace, Security, Hearing over 50 Speakers." UN Department of Public Information, press release, 17 April 2007.

28. United Nations General Assembly, *Annual Report of the United Nations High Commissioner for Human Rights and Reports of the Office of the High Commissioner and the Secretary-General. Report of the Office of the United Nations High Commissioner for Human Rights on the Relationship between Climate Change and Human Rights*. UN Doc. A/HRC/10/6115, January 2009.

29. Thalif Deen, "RIO+20: Promised Green Economy Was a Fake, Say Activists." Inter Press Service News Agency, 22 June 22 2012. Available at http://www.ipsnews.net/2012/06/rio20-promised-green-economy-was-a-fake-say-activists/, viewed 1 December 2014.

30. Kumi Naidoo via @kuminaidoo, 9:06 AM, 19 June 2012. Available at https://twit-ter.com/kuminaidoo/status/215113320632561664, viewed 1 December 2014.
31. *The Future We Want*, paragraph 39, p. 6.
32. Open letter of Navanethem Pillay, High Commissioner for Human Rights, to UN member-states, 30 March 2012.
33. See United Nations, *Delivering as One: Report of the Secretary-General's High-Level Panel on UN System-Wide Coherence in the Areas of Development, Humanitarian Assistance, and the Environment*, 9 November 2006.
34. On these problems and the larger debate over UN reform, see Global Policy Forum, "UN Reform."
35. See Mark Malloch Brown, "Power and Super-power: Global Leadership in the Twenty-First Century." Speech to the Century Foundation and Center for American Progress—Security and Peace Initiative, New York, 6 June 2006. Available at http://www.un.org/News/Press/docs/2006/dsgsm287.doc.htm, viewed December 20, 2011.
36. Among the many works on the theme of autonomy in IGOs, see Darren G. Hawkins, David A. Lake, Daniel L. Nielson, and Michael J. Tierney, eds., *Delegation and Agency in International Organizations* (Cambridge: Cambridge University Press, 2006); Michael Barnett and Martha Finnemore, *Rules for the World: International Organizations in Global Politics* (Ithaca, NY: Cornell University Press, 2004); Frank Biermann and Bernd Siebenhüner, *Managers of Global Change: The Influence of International Environmental Bureaucracies* (Cambridge, MA: MIT Press, 2009).
37. Tana Johnson, *Organizational Progeny: Why Governments Are Losing Control over the Proliferating Structures of Global Governance* (New York: Oxford University Press, 2014).
38. On the concept of authority in international relations, see Ian Hurd, "Legitimacy and Authority in International Politics," *International Organization* 53, no. 2 (March 1999): 379–408.
39. Barnett and Finnemore, *Rules for the World*.
40. Margaret Keck and Kathryn Sikkink, *Activists beyond Borders: Advocacy Networks in International Politics* (Ithaca, NY: Cornell University Press, 1998).
41. Martha Finnemore and Kathryn Sikkink, "International Norm Dynamics and Political Change," *International Organization* 52, no. 4 (Autumn 1998): 887–917; Thomas Weiss and Leon Gordenker, eds., *NGOs, the UN, and Global Governance* (Boulder, CO: Lynne Rienner, 1996).
42. Richard Price, "Reversing the Gun Sights: Transnational Civil Society Targets Land Mines," *International Organization* 52, no. 3 (Summer 1998): 613–644; quoted 623–624. See also Ken Rutherford, "The Evolving Arms Control Agenda: Implications of the Role of NGOs in Banning Antipersonnel Land-mines," *World Politics* 53, no. 1 (October 2000): 74–114.
43. Biermann and Siebenhüner, *Managers of Global Change*.
44. Richard Jolly, Louis Emmerij, and Thomas G. Weiss, *UN Ideas that Changed the World* (Bloomington: Indiana University Press, 2009). See also Jolly, Emmerij, and Weiss, *The Power of UN Ideas: Lessons from the First 60 Years* (New York: UN Intellectual History Project, May 2005).
45. Ken Conca, "Growth and Fragmentation in Expert Networks: The Elusive Quest for Integrated Water Resources Management," in Peter Dauvergne, ed., *Handbook of Global Environmental Politics* (Cheltenham, UK: Edward Elgar, 2005).
46. Karen T. Litfin, *Ozone Discourses* (New York: Columbia University Press, 1994).

47. On the concept of framing, see Robert D. Benford and David A. Snow, "Framing Processes and Social Movements: An Overview and Assessment," *Annual Review of Sociology* 26 (August 2000): 611–639. See also David A. Snow and Robert D. Benford, "Ideology, Frame Resonance, and Participant Mobilization," in Bert Klandermans, Hanspeter Kriesi, and Sidney Tarrow, eds., *International Social Movement Research* (Greenwich, CT: JAI Press, 1988); Dennis Chong and James N. Druckman, "Framing Theory," *Annual Review of Political Science* 10 (June 2007): 103–126.

48. Bruce Rich, *Mortgaging the Earth: The World Bank, Environmental Impoverishment, and the Crisis of Development* (Boston: Beacon Press, 1994); Paul Nelson, *The World Bank and Non-governmental Organizations: The Limits of Apolitical Development* (New York: St. Martin's, 1995).

49. Doug McAdam, *Political Process and the Development of Black Insurgency, 1930–1970* (Chicago: University of Chicago Press, 1999).

50. Paul Wapner, *Environmental Activism and World Civic Politics* (Albany: SUNY Press, 1996); Paul Wapner, "Politics beyond the State: Environmental Activism and World Civic Politics," *World Politics* 47, no. 3 (April 1995): 311–340.

51. Martha Finnemore, *National Interest in International Society* (Ithaca, NY: Cornell University Press, 1996); Ernst B. Haas, *When Knowledge Is Power: Three Models of Change in International Organizations* (Berkeley: University of California Press, 1990); Frank Biermann, Bernd Siebenhüner and Anna Schreyögg, eds., *International Organizations in Global Environmental Governance* (New York: Routledge, 2009).

52. Barnett and Finnemore, *Rules for the World*, 32.

53. Barnett and Finnemore, *Rules for the World*, 31. In addition to fixing meaning, the authors suggest that IGOs also exercise this constitutive power through the use of classification schemes, which assign phenomena to categories (such as "refugees" or "civil war") and through the broad diffusion of behavioral norms (which the authors see IGOs undertaking with great zeal as "the missionaries of our time" (33)).

54. Susan J. Buck, *The Global Commons: An Introduction* (Washington, DC: Island Press, 2012), 123.

55. See, for example, Miguel B Araújo, Diogo Alagador, Mar Cabeza, David Nogués-Bravo, and Wilfried Thuiller, "Climate Change Threatens European Conservation Areas," *Ecology Letters* 14, no. 5 (May 2011): 484–492.

56. Barnet and Finnemore, *Rules for the World*, 32.

57. Craig N. Murphy, *International Organization and Industrial Change: Global Governance since 1850* (Cambridge: Polity Press, 1994).

58. Murphy, *International Organization and Industrial Change*, 33.

59. Fred Pearce, "Beyond Rio's Disappointment, Finding a Path to the Future," *Environment 360*, 28 June 2012. Available at http://e360.yale.edu/feature/beyond_rios_disappointment_finding_a_path_to_the_future/2547/, viewed 6 June 2013.

CHAPTER 2

1. Jean Krasno, "The Founding of the United Nations: International Cooperation as an Evolutionary Process," Academic Council of the United Nations System, Occasional Paper no. 1, 2001.

2. See, for example, "Charter Signed for World Peace / Great Conference of United Nations at San Francisco Closes in Triumph." Available at http://www.

itnsource.com/shotlist//FoxMovietone/1945/06/28/X28064501/, viewed 15 December 2008.

3. Krasno, "Founding of the United Nations," 17. Original source: Yale-UN Oral History Interview with Alger Hiss, 13 February 1990, 1–2.

4. Ronnie D. Lipschutz, *When Nations Clash: Raw Materials, Ideology and Foreign Policy* (New York: Ballinger, 1989), 74.

5. The Atlantic Charter, joint declaration of the governments of the United States and the United Kingdom, 14 August 1941. Available at http://usinfo.org/docs/democracy/53.htm, viewed 16 June 2011.

6. Nico Schrijver, "Natural Resource Management and Sustainable Development," in Thomas G. Weiss and Sam Daws, eds., *The Oxford Handbook of the United Nations* (New York: Oxford University Press, 2007), 594.

7. Lipschutz, *When Nations Clash*.

8. President Harry S. Truman, Letter to William S. Paley on the Creation of the President's Materials Policy Commission, 22 January 1951. Available at http://www.presidency.ucsb.edu/ws/index.php?pid=13876#axzz1Q7Uh251p, viewed 23 June 2011.

9. Michael Manley, *The Poverty of Nations: Reflections on Underdevelopment and the World Economy* (London: Pluto Press, 1991), 14–15.

10. Richard H. Grove, *Green Imperialism: Colonial Expansion, Tropical Island Edens and the Origins of Environmentalism, 1600–1860* (Cambridge: Cambridge University Press, 1995).

11. See, for example, Sandip Hazareesingh, "Cotton, Climate and Colonialism in Dharwar, Western India, 1840–1880," *Journal of Historical Geography* 38, no. 1 (January 2012): 1–17.

12. Dennis Dalton, ed., *Mahatma Gandhi: Selected Political Writings* (Cambridge, MA: Hackett, 1996).

13. Final Communiqué of the Asian-African Conference of Bandung, 24 April 1955. Available at http://www.bandungspirit.org/IMG/pdf/Final_Communique_Bandung_1955.pdf, viewed 20 December 2011.

14. In tracing developments within the UN, and in particular the General Assembly, this section owes a substantial debt to the work of Nico Schrivjer. See in particular Schrijver, *Development without Destruction: The UN and Global Resource Management* (Bloomington: Indiana University Press, 2010) and Schrijver, "Natural Resource Management."

15. UN General Assembly Resolution 523, 12 January 1952; UN General Assembly Resolution 626, 21 December 1952.

16. Schrijver, *Development without Destruction*.

17. Schrijver, "Natural Resource Management," 596.

18. UN General Assembly Resolution 1314, 12 December 1958.

19. Schrijver, *Development without Destruction*, 42.

20. UN General Assembly Resolution 1803, 14 December 1962.

21. Richard Jolly, Luis Emmerij, and Thomas G. Weiss, *The Power of UN Ideas: Lessons from the First 60 Years* (New York: United Nations Intellectual History Project, 2005), 24–25.

22. UN General Assembly Resolution 2158, 25 November 1966.

23. Whereas Resolution 1803 on permanent sovereignty had stressed that nationalization required "appropriate compensation in accordance with the rules in force in the State taking such measures in the exercise of its sovereignty and in accordance with international law," Resolution 3281 asserted that "each State

has the right ... to nationalize" and that compensation should be determined according to the laws and tribunals of the nationalizing state, unless all parties involved agreed to other means. See UN General Assembly Resolution 1803, 14 December 1962 and UN General Assembly Resolution 3281, 12 December 1974.

24. Craig Murphy, *Emergence of the NIEO Ideology* (Boulder, CO: Westview Press, 1994).

25. Non-Aligned Movement, The Declaration of the 3rd Summit of the Heads of State or Government of the Member Countries of the Non-Aligned Movement, Issued on 8–10 September 1970, paragraph 13. In Institute of Foreign Affairs, *Summit Declarations of Non-Aligned Movement (1961–2009)* (Tripureshwor, Kathmandu: IFA, 2011), 33.

26. Harold Hongju Koh, "Why Do Nations Obey International Law?" *Yale Law Journal* 106 (1997): 2599–2659.

27. In finding PSNR to be customary international law, the court noted General Assembly Resolutions 1803 (1962), 3201 (1974), and 3281 (1974). The court also ruled that Uganda was not in violation in this instance, noting that "there is nothing in these General Assembly resolutions which suggests that they are applicable to the specific situation of looting, pillage and exploitation of certain natural resources by members of the army of a State militarily intervening in another State" (251–252). The court did, however, find a violation of *jus in bello* (the law of war), concluding that "Uganda violated its duty of vigilance by not taking adequate measures to ensure that its military forces did not engage in the looting, plundering and exploitation of the DRC's natural resources" (252) and that Uganda also failed in its responsibilities as an occupying power of a portion of DRC territory. See International Court of Justice, *Reports of Judgments, Advisory Opinions and Orders: Case Concerning Armed Activities on the Territory of the Congo (Democratic Republic of the Congo v. Uganda), Judgment of 19 December 2005*.

28. See Dinah Shelton, "Normative Hierarchy in International Law," *American Journal of International Law* 100, no. 2 (April 2006): 291–323, esp. 302–303. Moreover, as Perrez points out, status as *jus cogens* does not say anything about the specific content of the principle, including its limitations. Franz Xaver Perrez, "The Relationship between 'Permanent Sovereignty' and the Obligation Not to Cause Transboundary Environmental Damage," *Environmental Law* 26, no. 4 (1996): 1207–1249.

29. Shelton, "Normative Hierarchy," 303 n. 73.

30. For the same reason, Perrez rejects the notion of customary status for the "stronger" formulation of PSNR tied to the NIEO movement and asserting unfettered rights of nationalize, in contrast to the weaker formulation in the 1962 General Assembly declaration. See Perrez, "Relationship between Permanent Sovereignty."

31. Nico J. Schrijver, "Natural Resources, Permanent Sovereignty Over," *Max Planck Encyclopedia of Public International Law*, 7. Available at www.mpepil.com, viewed 24 June 2011.

32. Data from Ronald B. Mitchell, *International Environmental Agreements Database Project (Version 2010.3)*. Available at http://iea.uoregon.edu/, viewed 9 August 2011. The data set also includes fourteen amendments to prior accords during this period.

33. John Gamble, Jr., "The Third United Nations Conference on the Law of the Sea and the New International Economic Order," *Loyola of Los Angeles International and Comparative Law Review* 6 (1983): 65–80.

34. John McCormick, *Reclaiming Paradise: The Global Environmental Movement* (Bloomington: Indiana University Press, 1989), chapter 2.

35. Founded in 1948, IUPN changed its name in 1956 to the International Union for the Conservation of Nature and Natural Resources (IUCN). In 1990 it shifted to the name World Conservation Union, while preserving the acronym IUCN, before adopting the current name, International Union for Conservation of Nature, in 2008.

36. McCormick, *Reclaiming Paradise*, 37.

37. Schrijver, "Natural Resource Management," 594.

38. Patricia Birnie and Alan Boyle, *International Law and the Environment*, 2nd ed. (Oxford: Oxford University Press, 2002), 59.

39. McCormick, *Reclaiming Paradise*, 45–46.

40. Constitution of the World Health Organization, chapter 2, article 2, paragraph (i).

41. See, for example, World Health Organization, *Air Pollution: Fifth Report of the Expert Committee on Environmental Sanitation* (Geneva: WHO, 1958). WHO Technical Report Series, No. 157, 1958.

42. World Health Organization, *The Second Ten Years of the World Health Organization: 1958–1967* (Geneva: WHO, 1968), 255.

43. World Health Organization, *The Third Ten Years of the World Health Organization: 1968–1977* (Geneva: WHO, 2008), 256.

44. World Health Organization, *Research into Environmental Pollution: Report of Five Scientific Groups* (Geneva: WHO, 1968). WHO Technical Report Series, no. 406.

45. WHO, *The Third Ten Years*, 262–263.

46. World Health Organization, *Health Hazards of the Human Environment* (Geneva: WHO, 1972), 11.

47. Until 1982 the organization was known as the Inter-Governmental Maritime Consultative Organization.

48. International Maritime Organization, "History of the IMO." Available at http://www.imo.org/About/HistoryOfIMO/Pages/Default.aspx, viewed 28 December 2011.

49. UNESCO, "The Biosphere Conference 25 Years Later." Available at http://unesdoc.unesco.org/images/0014/001471/147152eo.pdf, viewed 28 December 2011.

50. UNESCO, "Timeline of IOC." Available at http://portal.unesco.org/science/en/ev.php-URL_ID=8463&URL_DO=DO_TOPIC&URL_SECTION=201.htm, viewed 28 December 2011.

51. UNESCO, "The World Heritage Convention." Available at http://whc.unesco.org/en/convention/, viewed 28 December 2011.

52. On UNDP in this era, see Craig Murphy, *The UN Development Programme: A Better Way?* (Cambridge: Cambridge University Press, 2006).

53. McCormick, *Reclaiming Paradise*, 29–31.

54. Edgar B. Nixon, ed., *Franklin D. Roosevelt and Conservation 1911–1945*, vol. 2 (New York: Franklin D. Roosevelt Library, 1957), 599, as cited in McCormick, *Reclaiming Paradise*, 25.

55. Prior to Suez, the UN had deployed observers to monitor activities on the Greek border (1947), Dutch troop withdrawals in Indonesia (1947), and the Arab-Israeli ceasefire (1948).

56. CongoForum, "History." Available at http://www.congoforum.be/en/congodetail.asp?subitem=21&id=147996&Congofiche=selected, viewed 4 August 2011.

57. David N. Gibbs, "Review: Misrepresenting the Congo Crisis," *African Affairs* 95, no. 380 (July 1996): 453–459.

58. David N. Gibbs, "Dag Hammarskjöld, the United Nations, and the Congo Crisis of 1960–1: A Reinterpretation," *Journal of Modern African Studies* 31, no. 1 (March 1993): 163–174.

59. Andrei Sakharov, acceptance speech read by Elena Bonner Sakharova, Oslo, 10 December 10 1975. Available at http://www.nobelprize.org/nobel_prizes/peace/laureates/1975/sakharov-acceptance.html, viewed 1 August 2011.

60. UN Security Council Resolution 255, 19 June 1968.

61. As quoted in Schrijver, "Natural Resource Management," 595.

62. UN General Assembly Resolution 1514, 14 December 1960.

63. *International Covenant on Civil and Political Rights*, part I, article 1, paragraph 2; *International Covenant on Economic, Social and Cultural Rights*, part I, article 1, paragraph 2.

64. See, for example, UN General Assembly Resolution 2158, 25 November 1966.

65. Kirkpatrick Sale, *The Green Revolution: The American Environmental Movement 1962–1992* (New York: Hill and Wang, 1993), 29.

66. Club of Rome, "About the Club of Rome." Available at http://www.clubofrome.org/?p=324, viewed 10 November 2014.

67. See, for example, Katherine Barkley and Steve Weissman, "The Eco-Establishment," in Editors of Ramparts, eds., *Eco-Catastrophe* (New York: Harper and Row, 1970), 15–24.

68. Norman J. Faramelli, "Toying with the Environment and the Poor: A Report on the Stockholm Environmental Conference," *Boston College Environmental Affairs Law Review* 2, no. 3 (1972): 469–486.

69. United Nations, *Yearbook of the United Nations*. Searchable database available at http://unyearbook.un.org/, viewed 16 June 2011.

70. United Nations, *Yearbook of the United Nations 1965*, part 1, section 2, chapter 6, "Questions Relating to Science and Technology," 359.

71. United Nations, *Yearbook of the United Nations*. Searchable database available at http://unyearbook.un.org/, viewed 16 June 2011.

72. See. for example. João Augusto de Araujo Castro, "Environment and Development: The Case of the Developing Countries," in Ken Conca and Geoffrey D. Dabelko, eds., *Green Planet Blues*, 5th ed. (Boulder, CO: Westview Press, 2014).

73. *The Founex Report on Development and Environment*. Adopted by the Founex Conference, 4–12 June 1971, Founex, Switzerland.

74. *Founex Report*, sections 1.11 and 1.12.

75. *Founex Report*, section 4.4.

76. United Nations Conference on the Human Environment, Declaration of the United Nations Conference on the Human Environment, Principle 21. Adopted 16 June 1972, Stockholm, Sweden.

77. Perrez, "The Relationship between Permanent Sovereignty." Perrez also argues that PSNR is a strictly economic doctrine that does not exempt states from more general obligations under international law.

78. Declaration of the United Nations Conference on the Human Environment, Principle 1.

79. "Special Report: What Happened at Stockholm," *Bulletin of the Atomic Scientists* 28, no. 7 (September 1972): 23.

80. The Environment Forum was sponsored by the conference but intended for unofficial debate and discussion.

81. "Special Report," 28.

82. "Special Report," 29.

83. UN Conference on the Human Environment, *Action Plan for the Human Environment*. Available at http://www.unep.org/Documents.Multilingual/Default.asp?DocumentID=97&ArticleID=1504&l=en, viewed 24 June 2013.

84. *Action Plan for the Human Environment*, Recommendation 103, paragraphs (a) and (e).

85. UNEP's initial priority areas were (1) human settlements, human health, habitat, and well-being; (2) land, water, and desertification; (3) trade, economics, technology, and technology transfer; (4) oceans; (5) conservation of nature, wildlife, and genetic resources; and (6) energy, as well as functional tasks related to capacity building in environmental management and technical assistance. See UN Environment Programme, *Report of the Governing Council on the Work of its Second Session*, 11–22 March 1974.

86. World Health Organization Resolution WHA26.58, May 1973, in World Health Organization, *Handbook of Resolutions and Decisions of the World Health Assembly and the Executive Board*, vol. 2: *1973–1984* (Geneva: WHO, 1985), 110–111.

87. This would not be the case if an entire region were decolonized at the same time, leading to several new member states and creating new possibilities for regional multilateral cooperation, as, for example, in the agreements on the Aral Sea signed by the newly independent central Asian republics of the former Soviet Union.

88. These figures include agreements and protocols to agreements, but exclude amendments and other revisions to existing agreements and protocols.

89. Steven Bernstein, *The Compromise of Liberal Environmentalism* (New York: Columbia University Press, 2001).

90. See preamble and part XII, "Protection and Preservation of the Marine Environment," of *United Nations Convention on the Law of the Sea*, adopted by the Third United Nations Conference on the Law of the Sea, 10 December 1982, Montego Bay, Jamaica. The UNCLOS talks occurred as part of the Third UN Conference on the Law of the Sea, which the General Assembly authorized in 1973. They followed prior UNCLOS rounds that established agreement in principle but failed to address the scope and extent of offshore territorial and deep-sea resource rights. See Schrijver, "Natural Resource Management," 598–600.

91. UNEP Governing Council, Nairobi Declaration on the State of Worldwide Environment, 19 May 1982. UN Document UNEP/GC.10/INF.5. Available at http://www.un-documents.net/nair-dec.htm, viewed 23 June 2013.

92. UNEP Governing Council, Nairobi Declaration.

93. The Nairobi Declaration stated, "A comprehensive and regionally integrated approach emphasizes this interrelationship can lead to environmentally sound and sustainable socio-economic development."

94. The IUCN's members and affiliates include states, individual government agencies, national and international NGOs, and scientific bodies.

95. International Union for the Conservation of Nature and Natural Resources, *World Conservation Strategy: Living Resource Conservation for Sustainable Development* (Gland, Switzerland: IUCN, 1980), section 1, paragraph 3.

96. *World Conservation Strategy*, executive summary.

97. *World Conservation Strategy*, section 15, paragraph 3.

98. The World Charter for Nature states, "Ecosystems and organisms, as well as the land, marine and atmospheric resources that are utilized by man, shall be managed to achieve and maintain optimum sustainable productivity, but not in such a way as to endanger the integrity of those other ecosystems or species with which they coexist." UN General Assembly Resolution 37/7, 28 October 1982, section 1, paragraph 4.

99. UN General Assembly Resolution 38/161, 19 December 1983.
100. Barbara Ward and Rene Dubos, *Only One Earth: The Care and Maintenance of a Small Planet* (London: Penguin, 1972); Pratap Chatterjee and Matthias Finger, *The Earth Brokers: Power, Politics and World Development* (New York: Routledge, 1994).
101. World Commission on Environment and Development, *Our Common Future* (New York: Oxford University Press, 1987). Annex 1, "Summary of Proposed Legal Principles for Environmental Protection and Sustainable Development Adopted by the WCED Experts Group on Environmental Law," 348–351.
102. Larry Lohmann, "Whose Common Future?" *Ecologist* 20, no. 3 (May–June 1990): 82–84; Chatterjee and Finger, *The Earth Brokers*.
103. Bernstein, *Compromise of Liberal Environmentalism*; The Ecologist, *Whose Common Future? Reclaiming the Commons* (Philadelphia, PA: New Society Publishers, 1993); Chatterjee and Finger, *The Earth Brokers*.
104. World Commission on Environment and Development, *Our Common Future*, 43.
105. On eco-development, see Bernstein, *Compromise of Liberal Environmentalism*, 56–58.
106. For a discussion of the range of approaches to the concept of sustainable development, see Sharachchandra M. Lélé, "Sustainable Development: A Critical Review," *World Development* 19, no. 6 (June 1991): 607–621; Timothy Doyle, "Sustainable Development and Agenda 21: The Secular Bible of Global Free Markets and Pluralist Democracy," *Third World Quarterly* 19, no. 4 (1998): 771–786; Bill Hopwood, Mary Mellor, and Geoff O'Brien, "Sustainable Development: Mapping Different Approaches," *Sustainable Development* 13, no. 1 (February 2005): 38–52; Michael Redclift, "Sustainable Development (1987–2005): An Oxymoron Comes of Age," *Sustainable Development* 13, no. 4 (October 2005): 212–227.
107. Bernstein, *Compromise of Liberal Environmentalism*, chapter 2.
108. Chatterjee and Finger, *The Earth Brokers*, 27–28.
109. Bernstein, *Compromise of Liberal Environmentalism*, 67.
110. Balakrishnan Rajagopal, *International Law from Below: Development, Social Movements, and Third World Resistance* (Cambridge: Cambridge University Press, 2003).
111. Balakrishnan Rajagopal, "Human Rights and Development: Legal and Policy Issues with Special Reference to Dams," contributing paper, World Commission on Dams, no date. Prepared for *Thematic Review* 5, no. 4: "Regulation, Compliance and Implementation Options." See also Rajagopal, *International Law from Below*.
112. Cheryl Simon Silver with Ruth F. DeFries for the National Academies of Science, *One Earth, One Future: Our Changing Global Environment* (Washington, DC: National Academy Press, 1990).
113. For a range of views on the evolution of science and politics in the ozone regime, see Karen Litfin, *Ozone Discourses* (New York: Columbia University Press, 1994); Richard Benedick, *Ozone Diplomacy*, 2nd ed. (Cambridge, MA: Harvard University Press, 1998); Edward A. Parson, *Protecting the Ozone Layer* (New York: Oxford University Press, 2003).
114. On progressive legalization, see the special edition of *International Organization* 54, no. 3 (Summer 2000).
115. On functionalism in international environmental law, see Ken Conca, *Governing Water: Contentious Transnational Politics and Global Institution Building* (Cambridge, MA: MIT Press, 2006).

116. Sale, *The Green Revolution*, 85. On the internationalization of American environmentalism during this period, see also Mark Dowie, *Losing Ground* (Cambridge, MA: MIT Press, 1995), chapter 5.

117. John J. Audley, *Green Politics and Global Trade: NAFTA and the Future of Environmental Politics* (Washington, DC: Georgetown University Press, 1997).

118. Miranda A. Schreurs, *Environmental Politics in Japan, Germany, and the United States* (Cambridge: Cambridge University Press, 2002).

119. On European Green parties, see Dick Richardson and Chris Rootes, eds., *The Green Challenge: The Development of Green Parties in Europe* (London: Routledge, 1995); see also the special edition of *Environmental Politics* 11, no. 1 (2002).

120. On the latter, see Lynn Margulis, *The Symbiotic Planet: A New Look at Evolution* (New York: Basic Books, 1999).

121. Chatterjee and Finger, *The Earth Brokers*, 69–71. See also Frederick H. Buttel, Ann P. Hawkins, and Alison G. Power, "From Limits to Growth to Global Change: Constraints and Contradictions in the Evolution of Environmental Science and Ideology," *Global Environmental Change* 1, no. 1 (December 1990): 57–66.

122. On these dimensions of the global political economy of forests, see in particular the reports of the international NGO Global Witness, available at www. globalwitness.org.

123. Convention on Biological Diversity, *Convention on Biological Diversity*, adopted at the United Nations Conference on Environment and Development, 5 June 1992, Rio de Janeiro, Brazil, article 8, paragraph j.

124. Declaration of the United Nations Conference on the Human Environment, Principle 1.

125. World Commission on Environment and Development, *Our Common Future*, annex 1, 348.

126. United Nations Conference on Environment and Development, Rio Declaration on Environment and Development, adopted 14 June 1992, Rio de Janeiro, Brazil, Principle 1.

127. The charter, which calls for "a sustainable global society founded on respect for nature, universal human rights, economic justice, and a culture of peace," evolved instead as a civil society initiative, finalized in 2000 and open for endorsement by an individual or institution. "The Earth Charter," adopted by the Earth Charter Commission, Paris, France, March 2000. Available at http:// www.earthcharterinaction.org, viewed 26 June 2013.

128. World Commission on Environment and Development, *Our Common Future*, chapter 11.

129. United Nations Department of Economic and Social Affairs, Division for Sustainable Development, *Agenda 21*, chapter 39, section D, paragraph 39.10, 1992. Available at http://www.un.org/esa/dsd/agenda21/, viewed 26 December 2011.

130. Bernstein, *Compromise of Liberal Environmentalism*, chapter 2.

131. Chatterjee and Finger, *The Earth Brokers*, especially chapters 7 and 8.

132. Peter Newell, *Globalization and the Environment: Capitalism, Ecology and Power* (New York: Polity Press, 2012).

133. Adil Najam, "Developing Countries and Global Environmental Governance: From Contestation to Participation to Engagement," *International Environmental Agreements* 5, no. 3 (September 2005): 303–321.

134. Maurice Strong, "Message from Maurice Strong," in United Nations Environment Programme, *Multilateral Environmental Agreement Negotiator's Handbook* (Joensuu, Finland: University of Joensuu Department of Law, 2007), v.

CHAPTER 3

1. Norichika Kanie, "Governance with Multilateral Environmental Agreements: A Healthy or Ill-Equipped Fragmentation?" in Lydia Swart and Estelle Siegal Perry, eds., *Global Environmental Governance: Perspectives on the Current Debate* (New York: Center for UN Reform Education, 2007).
2. See the August 2012 special edition of *Global Environmental Politics*.
3. Ken Conca, "The Rise of the Regional in Global Environmental Politics," *Global Environmental Politics* 12, no. 3 (August 2012): 127–133.
4. On the component elements of legalization, see Kenneth W. Abbott, Robert O. Keohane, Andrew Moravcsik, Anne-Marie Slaughter, and Duncan Snidal, "The Concept of Legalization," *International Organization* 54, no. 3 (Summer 2000): 401–419.
5. This sort of dynamism appears to be less common in bilateral environmental treaties. The International Environmental Agreements Database lists more than 1,300 bilateral environmental agreements since 1945, but has identified only eighty amendments and modifications.
6. On environmental regime effectiveness, see Carsten Helm and Detlef Sprinz, "Measuring the Effectiveness of International Environmental Regimes," *Journal of Conflict Resolution* 45, no. 5 (2000): 630–652; Edward L. Miles, Steinar Andresen, Elaine M. Carlin, Jon Birger Skjærseth, Arild Underdal, and Jørgen Wettestad, *International Regime Effectiveness: Confronting Theory with Evidence* (Cambridge, MA: MIT Press, 2002); Jon Hovi, Detlef Sprinz, and Arild Underdal, "The Oslo-Potsdam Solution to Measuring Regime Effectiveness: Critique, Response, and the Road Ahead," *Global Environmental Politics* 3, no. 3 (2003):74–96; Arild Underdal and Oran R. Young, eds., *Regime Consequences* (Dordrecht: Kluwer, 2004); Helmut Breitmeier, Arild Underdal, and Oran R. Young, "The Effectiveness of International Environmental Regimes: Comparing and Contrasting Findings from Quantitative Research," *International Studies Review* 13, no. 4 (2011): 579–605; Olav S. Stokke, *Disaggregating International Regimes: A New Approach to Evaluation and Comparison* (Cambridge, MA: MIT Press, 2012).
7. Oran R. Young, "Effectiveness of International Environmental Regimes: Existing Knowledge, Cutting-Edge Themes, and Research Strategies," *Proceedings of the National Academy of Sciences* 108, no. 50 (December 13, 2011): 19853–19860.
8. Ken Conca, *Governing Water: Contentious Transnational Politics and Global Institution Building* (Cambridge, MA: MIT Press, 2006).
9. Miles et al., *International Regime Effectiveness*; Helmut Breitmeier, Oran R. Young, and Michael Zürn, *Analyzing International Regimes: From Case Study to Database* (Cambridge, MA: MIT Press, 2006).
10. Ronald B. Mitchell, "Problem Structure, Institutional Design, and the Relative Effectiveness of International Environmental Agreements," *Global Environmental Politics* 6, no. 3 (August 2006): 72–89; and Ronald B. Mitchell, "Regime Design Matters: Intentional Oil Pollution and Treaty Compliance," *International Organization* 48, no. 3 (Summer 1994): 425–458.
11. Young, "Effectiveness of International Environmental Regimes."
12. Young finds from his review of the literature that such interplay is "just as likely to produce positive or even synergistic results as it is to lead to interference between or among regimes." Young, "Effectiveness of International Environmental Regimes," 19856. See also Sikina Jinnah, *Post-treaty Politics: Secretariat Influence in Global Environmental Governance* (Cambridge, MA: MIT Press, 2014).

13. See, for example, Center for Investigative Reporting, *Global Dumping Ground: The International Traffic in Hazardous Waste* (Washington, DC: Seven Locks Press, 1990).

14. Basel Convention Secretariat, "Parties to the Basel Convention." Available at http://www.basel.int/Countries/StatusofRatifications/PartiesSignatories, viewed 14 November 2014.

15. POPs are long-lived and toxic organic chemicals, including pesticides, industrial chemicals, and chemical byproducts, which accumulate in fatty tissue and increase in concentrations at higher levels of food chains.

16. Jennifer Clapp, *Toxic Exports: The Transfer of Hazardous Wastes from Rich to Poor Countries* (Ithaca, NY: Cornell University Press, 2001), 150.

17. UN Environment Programme, "UNEP and INTERPOL Assess Impacts of Environmental Crime on Security and Development." Press release, 6 November 2013.

18. See, for example, "Indonesian-Swiss Country-Led Initiative on an Informal Process to Improve the Effectiveness of the Basel Convention." Presentation at the GEN Mission Briefing on the COP 10 of the Basel Convention, 14 September 2011, Geneva.

19. UN Department of Economic and Social Affairs, *Back to Our Common Future: Sustainable Development in the 21st Century Project. Summary for Policy Makers* (New York: UNDESA, 2012), iii, emphasis in original.

20. UNDESA, *Back to Our Common Future*, 1–2.

21. Stakeholder Forum for a Sustainable Future, *Review of Implementation of Agenda 21 and the Rio Principles: Synthesis Report*, January 2012, 22–39, table 2.

22. United Nations Department of Economic and Social Affairs, Division for Sustainable Development, *Agenda 21*, section 3, chapter 11, 1992. Available at http://www.un.org/esa/dsd/agenda21/, viewed 26 December 2011.

23. See UN Department of Economic and Social Affairs, *Review of Implementation of Agenda 21* (New York: United Nations, 2012), chapter 11. Study prepared by the Stakeholder Forum for a Sustainable Future.

24. UNDESA, *Review of Implementation*, chapter 11.

25. *Agenda 21*, chapter 18.

26. UNDESA, *Review of Implementation*, chapter 18.

27. *Agenda 21*, chapter 4.

28. UNDESA, *Review of Implementation*, chapter 4.

29. Statistics in this paragraph are taken from the World Bank data portal. Available at http://data.worldbank.org/, viewed 14 November 2014.

30. See UNDP Sierra Leone, "Recovery for Development." Available at http://www.sl.undp.org/development.htm, viewed 30 August 2010.

31. See the UNFCCC project design document form. Available at http://www.cdm-bazaar.net/UserManagement/FileStorage/EY8IS135ZRGK7O96LAVT0XFD NUW2H4, viewed 30 August 2010.

32. Government of Sierra Leone, *Biodiversity: Strategic Action Plan*, 2003. Available at http://www.cbd.int/countries/profile/default.shtml?country=sl#nbsap, viewed 2 January 2014.

33. UN Environment Programme, *Sierra Leone: Environment, Conflict and Peacebuilding Assessment. Technical Report* (Geneva: UNEP, February 2010).

34. Yale Center for Environmental Law and Policy and Center for International Earth Science Information Network, *Environmental Performance Index 2014*, "Country Profile: Sierra Leone." Available at http://epi.yale.edu/epi/country-profile/sierra-leone, viewed 14 November 2014.

35. UNEP, *Sierra Leone*, executive summary.
36. UN Development Programme, "Human Security: Evaluation of UNDP Assistance to Conflict-Affected Countries. Case Study Sierra Leone," 4. UNDP Evaluation Office, 2006.
37. UNDP, "Human Security."
38. Sierra Leone Truth and Reconciliation Commission, *Witness to Truth: Final Report of the Truth and Reconciliation Commission*, October 2004.
39. Ken Conca and Jennifer Wallace, "Environment and Peacebuilding in War-Torn Societies: Lessons from the UN Environment Programme's Experience with Postconflict Assessment," *Global Governance* 15, no. 4 (October–December 2009): 485–504.
40. UNEP, *Sierra Leone*, 2.
41. Freedom House, "2014 Freedom in the World." Available at https://freedomhouse. org/report-types/freedom-world#.VGo39sntoYQ, viewed 17 November 2014; Amnesty International, "Sierra Leone," in *Amnesty International Report 2013: The State of the World's Human Rights* (London: Amnesty International, 2013). Available at http://www.amnesty.org/en/region/sierra-leone/report-2013, viewed 17 November 2014.
42. United Nations Conference on Environment and Development, Rio Declaration on Environment and Development. Adopted 14 June 1992, Rio de Janeiro, Brazil.
43. UNEP, *Sierra Leone*, chapter 7.
44. As cited in UNEP, *Sierra Leone*, 26 n. 57.
45. UNEP, *Sierra Leone*, 28–29, citing data from the Environmental Justice Foundation.
46. UNEP, *Sierra Leone*, 41; see also E. Harsh, "Conflict Resources: From 'Curse' to Blessing," *Africa Renewal* 20, no. 4 (2007): 17.
47. Global Footprint Network, "Highlights of California's First Ecological Footprint Report." Available at http://www.footprintnetwork.org/en/index.php/newsletter/det/ca, viewed 30 December 2013.
48. See "State of Denial," a special report published in the *Sacramento Bee*, 27 April 2003. Available at http://www.sacbee.com/static/live/news/projects/denial/text.html, viewed 2 January 2014.
49. "State of Denial."
50. See Counterspill, "Ecuador vs. Chevron-Texaco: A Brief History." Available at http://www.counterspill.org/article/ecuador-vs-chevron-texaco-brief-history, viewed 2 January 2014.
51. "Chevron Oil Pipeline Attacked in Nigeria." Reuters (US edition), 8 January 2010. Available at www.reuters.com/article/idUSN0826052520100108, viewed 2 January 2014.
52. While not ruling on the facts of the case, a preliminary ruling in the lawsuit indicated that the plaintiffs had presented enough evidence for the suit to proceed to trial. See "Chevron Can Be Sued for Attacks on Nigerians, U.S. Judge Rules," *San Francisco Chronicle*, 15 August 2007. The suit was later dropped without explanation by the plaintiffs.
53. See Nnimmo Bassey, Emem Okon, Laura Livoti, and Marc Evans, *The True Cost of Chevron: Alternative Annual Report*, May 2011. Excerpted at http://justiceinnigerianow.org/about-chevron, viewed 2 January 2014.
54. UN Environment Programme, *Environmental Assessment of Ogoniland* (Geneva: UNEP, 2011).

55. UNEP, *Environmental Assessment of Ogoniland*, 10.
56. Jacob Park, Ken Conca, and Matthias Finger, "The Death of Rio Environmentalism," in Jacob Park, Ken Conca, and Matthias Finger, eds., *The Crisis of Global Environmental Governance: Toward a New Political Economy of Sustainability* (New York: Routledge, 2009), 6.
57. Jennifer Clapp and Eric Helleiner, "International Political Economy and the Environment: Back to Basics?" *International Affairs* 88, no. 3 (May 2012): 485–501.
58. Ken Conca, "Consumption and Environment in a Global Economy," *Global Environmental Politics* 1, no. 3 (Summer 2001): 53–71.
59. Jaime de Melo, Jean-Marie Grether and Nicole Mathys, "Identifying the Worldwide Pollution Haven Effect," *Vox*, 23 December 2010. Available at http://voxeu.org/index.php?q=node/5961, viewed 6 January 2014.
60. Judith M. Dean, Mary E. Lovely, and Hua Wang, "Are Foreign Investors Attracted to Weak Environmental Regulations? Evaluating the Evidence from China," *Journal of Development Economics* 90, no. 1 (2009): 1–13; Lyuba Zarsky. "Stuck in the Mud? Nation-States, Globalization and Environment," in Ken Conca and Geoffrey D. Dabelko, eds., *Green Planet Blues: Environmental Politics from Stockholm to Johannesburg*, 3rd ed. (Boulder, CO: Westview Press, 2004), 82–93.
61. See, for example, Ralph E. Horne, "Limits to Labels: The Role of Eco-labels in the Assessment of Product Sustainability and Routes to Sustainable Consumption," *International Journal of Consumer Studies* 33, no. 2 (March 2009): 175–182; Jennifer Jacquet, John Hocevar, Sherman Lai, Patricia Majluf, Nathan Pelletier, Tony Pitcher, Enric Sala, Rashid Sumaila, and Daniel Pauly, "Conserving Wild Fish in a Sea of Market-Based Efforts," *Oryx* 44, no. 1 (January 2010): 45–56; Juliane Franze and Andreas Ciroth, "A Comparison of Cut Roses from Ecuador and the Netherlands," *International Journal of Life Cycle Assessment* 16, no. 4 (May 2011): 366–379; Laura T. Raynolds, "Fair Trade Flowers: Global Certification, Environmental Sustainability, and Labor Standards," *Rural Sociology* 77, no. 4 (December 2012): 493–519.
62. Paul Collier, *The Bottom Billion: Why the Poorest Countries Are Failing and What Can Be Done about It* (Oxford: Oxford University Press, 2007).
63. Lotta Themnér and Peter Wallensteen, "Armed Conflicts, 1946–2011," *Journal of Peace Research* 49, no. 4 (July 2012): 565–575, cited in Paul Steinberg, *Who Rules the Earth?* (New York: Oxford University Press, 2014).
64. Steinberg, *Who Rules the Earth?*
65. Conca and Wallace, "Environment and Peacebuilding."
66. Michael Ross, *The Oil Curse* (Princeton, NJ: Princeton University Press, 2012); Ken Conca, "Complex Landscapes and Oil Curse Research," *Global Environmental Politics* 13, no. 3 (August 2013): 131–137.
67. Ken Conca, "Environmental Human Rights: Greening 'the Dignity and Worth of the Human Person,'" in Peter Dauvergne, ed., *Handbook of Global Environmental Politics* (Cheltenham, UK: Edward Elgar, 2012).
68. United Nations General Assembly, The Universal Declaration of Human Rights. Resolution A/RES/217(III) A, adopted 10 December 1948.
69. See EarthJustice, *Environmental Rights Report 2008* (Oakland, CA: EarthJustice, 2008). Available at http://www.earthjustice.org/library/reports/2008-environ-mental-rights-report. pdf, viewed 21 June 2010.
70. On the debate over greening the modern state, see John Barry and Robyn Eckersley, eds., *The State and the Global Ecological Crisis* (Cambridge, MA: MIT Press, 2005).

71. World Resources Institute, *Closing the Gap: Information, Participation, and Justice in Decision-Making for the Environment* (Washington, DC: WRI, 2002).
72. United Nations General Assembly, *Report of the United Nations Conference on Environment and Development (Rio de Janeiro, 3–14 June 1992)*. UN Document A/CONF.151/26. Vol. 4. 28 September 1992.
73. Margaret E. Keck and Kathryn Sikkink, *Activists beyond Borders: Advocacy Networks in International Politics* (Ithaca, NY: Cornell University Press, 1998).
74. Conca, *Governing Water*.
75. Wolfgang Sachs, *Environment and Human Rights* (Berlin: Wuppertal Institute for Climate, Environment, Energy, 2009). Wuppertal Paper no. 137. Available at http://www.uibk.ac.at/peacestudies/downloads/peacelibrary/environment.pdf, viewed 1 September 2010.
76. Dana Clark, Jonathan Fox, and Kay Treakle, eds. *Demanding Accountability: Civil-Society Claims and the World Bank Inspection Panel* (Lanham, MD: Rowman & Littlefield, 2003).
77. These four dimensions are adapted from Capacity Global, "Environmental Justice: A Snapshot," 2009. Available at http://www.capacity.org.uk/downloads/snapshot_for_ej.pdf, viewed 13 July 2010. Capacity Global has subsequently been renamed the Living Space Project; see http://www.livingspaceproject.com.
78. Krista Harper, Tamara Steger, and Richard Filcak, "Environmental Justice and Roma Communities in Central and Eastern Europe," *Environmental Policy and Governance* 19, no. 4 (2009): 251–268.
79. Robert D. Bullard, Paul Mohai, Robin Saha, and Beverly Wright, *Toxic Wastes and Race at 20: 1987–2007*. Report prepared for the United Church of Christ Justice and Witness Ministries, 2007.
80. See for example Amazon Watch, "The Right to Decide," Amazon Watch Briefing Paper, February 2011. Available at http://amazonwatch.org/assets/files/fpic-the-right-to-decide.pdf, viewed 24 May 2011.
81. Folabi K. Olagbaju and Stephen Mills, "Defending Environmental Defenders," *Human Rights Dialogue* 2, no. 11 (2004): 32–33, 37.
82. Amnesty International and Sierra Club, *Environmentalists under Fire: Ten Urgent Cases of Human Rights Abuses* (London: Amnesty International, 2000).
83. UN General Assembly, Human Rights Council, *Report of the Independent Expert on the Issue of Human Rights Obligations Relating to the Enjoyment of a Safe, Clean, Healthy and Sustainable Environment, John H. Knox*, paragraph 83, p. 22. Twenty-Third Session, Agenda item 3, 30 December 2013. UN Document A/HRC/25/53.
84. Global Witness, *Deadly Environment* (London: Global Witness, 2014), 4.
85. Clifford Bob, *The Marketing of Rebellion* (Cambridge: Cambridge University Press, 2005).
86. The material in this section draws upon Ken Conca, "Environmental Governance after Johannesburg: From Stalled Legalization to Environmental Human Rights?" *Journal of International Law and International Relations* 1, nos. 1–2 (2005): 121–138.
87. Nancy Peluso, "Coercing Conservation," in Ronnie D. Lipschutz and Ken Conca, eds., *The State and Social Power in Global Environmental Politics* (New York: Columbia University Press, 1993).
88. Mac Chapin, "A Challenge to Conservationists," *World Watch* 17, no. 6 (November–December 2004): 17–31.
89. Joanne Bauer, "Commentary on 'The Conflict between Rights and Environmentalism'," *Human Rights Dialogue* 2, no. 11 (2004): 19 and 36.

90. Bill Weinberg, "Mexico: Lacandon Selva Conflict Grows," *NACLA Report on the Americas* 36, no. 6 (May–June 2003): 26–47.
91. Andrew Gage and Michael Byers, *Payback Time? What the Internationalization of Climate Litigation Could Mean for Canadian Oil and Gas Companies* (Ottawa: Canadian Center for Policy Alternatives, October 2014).
92. On this theme, see the series of reports by the nongovernmental organization Global Witness, available at www.globalwitness.org.
93. See, for example, UN General Assembly and UN Security Council, *Report of the Secretary-General on Peacebuilding in the Immediate Aftermath of Conflict*. UN Document A/63/881–S/2009/304, 11 June 2009.
94. Conca, *Governing Water*, 384–385.
95. For an elaboration of this argument, see Benjamin Pohl, Alexander Carius, Ken Conca, Geoffrey D. Dableko, Annika Kramer, David Michel, Susanne Schmeier, Ashok Swain, and Aaron Wolf, *The Rise of Hydro-diplomacy: Strengthening Foreign Policy for Transboundary Waters* (Berlin: Adelphi Research and Federal Foreign Office, 2014).
96. See Ken Conca and Geoffrey D. Dabelko, eds., *Environmental Peacemaking* (Washington, DC: Woodrow Wilson Center Press; Baltimore: Johns Hopkins University Press, 2002).
97. Conca and Wallace, "Environment and Peacebuilding."
98. Amartya Sen, *Development as Freedom* (New York: Oxford University Press, 1999).

CHAPTER 4

1. Some of the arguments presented in this chapter appeared in earlier form in Ken Conca, "Environmental Human Rights: Greening 'the Dignity and Worth of the Human Person,'" in Peter Dauvergne, ed., *Handbook of Global Environmental Politics*, 2nd ed. (Cheltenham, UK: Edward Elgar, 2012).
2. Julie A. Mertus, *The United Nations and Human Rights* (London: Routledge, 2005), 3–4.
3. Alan Boyle, "Human Rights or Environmental Rights? A Reassessment," *Fordham Environmental Law Review* 18, no. 3 (2007): 471–511.
4. United Nations Conference on the Human Environment, Declaration of the United Nations Conference on the Human Environment, Principle 1. Adopted 16 June 1972, Stockholm.
5. United Nations Conference on Environment and Development, Rio Declaration on Environment and Development, Principle 1. Adopted 14 June 1992, Rio de Janeiro, Brazil.
6. UN General Assembly, Human Rights Council, *Report of the Independent Expert on the Issue of Human Rights Obligations Relating to the Enjoyment of a Safe, Clean, Healthy and Sustainable Environment, John H. Knox*, 6. Twenty-Second Session, Agenda item 3. UN Document A/HRC/22/43, 24 December 2012.
7. United Nations Department of Economic and Social Affairs, Division for Sustainable Development, *Agenda 21*, section 3, chapter 27, paragraphs 27.10 and 27.13, 1992. Available at http://www.un.org/esa/dsd/agenda21/, viewed December 26, 2011.
8. UNDESA, *Agenda 21*, section 2, chapter 19, paragraph 19.8.
9. United Nations General Assembly, *Report of the World Conference on Human Rights*, paragraph 11. UN Document A/CONF.157/24 (Part I), 13 October 1993.
10. UN General Assembly, *Report of World Conference*, paragraph 36.

11. See, for example, "Observations by the United States of America on the Relationship between Climate Change and Human Rights," comments submitted by the Government of the United States to the Office of the High Commissioner for Human Rights, no date.

12. See United Nations Office of the High Commissioner on Human Rights, *Human Rights Council Panel Discussion on the Relationship between Climate Change and Human Rights: Summary of Discussions*, 15 June 2009, paragraph 58, p. 10.

13. Karel Vasak, "Human Rights: A Thirty-Year Struggle," *UNESCO Courier* 30, no. 11 (1977): 29–32.

14. Dutch Section of the International Commission of Jurists, *2011 OHCHR Study Human Rights and Environment: Stakeholder Input by the Dutch Section of the International Commission of Jurists (NJCM)*, June 2011, 30.

15. See "We Reject Redd+ in All Its Versions," an April 2013 letter to the Governor of California (USA), Jerry Brown, from activists in Chiapas, Mexico, regarding provisions in California's Global Warming Solutions Act. Available at http://www.redd-monitor.org/2013/04/30/we-reject-redd-in-all-its-versions-letter-from-chiapas-mexico-opposing-redd-in-californias-global-warming-solutions-act-ab-32/, viewed 20 May 2013.

16. Daniel M. Bodansky, *The Art and Craft of International Environmental Law* (Cambridge, MA: Harvard University Press, 2009).

17. See OHCHR, *Human Rights Council Panel Discussion*.

18. Balakrishnan Rajagopal, *International Law from Below* (Cambridge: Cambridge University Press, 2003).

19. Jeffery Atik, "Commentary on 'The Relationship between Environmental Rights and Environmental Injustice,'" *Human Rights Dialogue* 2, no. 11 (2004): 26–27, 37.

20. Sachs also defines a third or "procedural" form of environmental justice: "the allocation of advantages and disadvantages that are fair to everyone involved;" See Sachs, *Environment and Human Rights*, 2. On the differences between environmental rights and environmental justice, see also Atik, "Commentary."

21. Ken Conca, *Governing Water: Contentious Transnational Politics and Global Institution Building* (Cambridge, MA: MIT Press, 2006).

22. EarthJustice, *Environmental Rights Report: Human Rights and the Environment* (Oakland, CA: EarthJustice, 2005), 2.

23. UN Sub-Commission on the Prevention of Discrimination and Protection of Minorities, Declaration of Principles on Human Rights and the Environment, 1994. Available at http://www.environmentandhumanrights.org/resources/Draft%20Decl%20of%20Ppls%20on%20HR%20&%20the%20Env.pdf, viewed 2 June 2010.

24. UN Sub-Commission on the Prevention of Discrimination and Protection of Minorities, Declaration of Principles, preamble.

25. United Nations Commission on Human Rights, Sub-commission on Prevention of Discrimination and Protection of Minorities, *Review of Further Developments in Fields with which the Sub-commission Has Been Concerned. Human Rights and The Environment*. UN Document E/CN.4/Sub.2/1994/9 6 July 1004, paragraphs 5 and 34.

26. UNCHR, *Review of Further Developments*, paragraph 261.

27. My account of these recommendations and subsequent developments is based on EarthJustice, *Environmental Rights Report*, 1–5.

28. UN Commission on Human Rights, Resolution 2004/17, 16 April 2004, 2.

29. United Nations Commission on Human Rights, *Human Rights and the Environment as Part of Sustainable Development: Report of the Secretary-General*, 2. UN Document E/CN.4/2005/96, 19 January 2005.

30. Dinah Shelton, "Human Rights and Environment: Past, Present and Future Linkages and the Value of a Declaration." Paper presented at the High Level Expert Meeting on the New Future of Human Rights and Environment: Moving the Global Agenda Forward, Nairobi, 30 November–1 December 2009.

31. See EarthJustice, *Environmental Rights Report 2007* (Oakland, CA: EarthJustice), 126–147.

32. African Charter on Human and Peoples' Rights. Adopted June 1981, Nairobi, Kenya.

33. UN General Assembly, Human Rights Council, *Report of Independent Expert*, 2012.

34. Additional Protocol to the American Convention on Human Rights in the Area of Economic, Social and Cultural Rights, article 11. Adopted 17 November 1988, San Salvador, El Salvador.

35. UN General Assembly, Human Rights Council, *Report of Independent Expert*, 2012, 5.

36. The database includes decisions from the African Commission, European Court, Inter-American Commission, and Inter-American Court. Available at http://ieenvironment.org/regional-decisions/, viewed 23 December 2013.

37. Principle 10 states that "environmental issues are best handled with participation of all concerned citizens, at the relevant level. At the national level, each individual shall have appropriate access to information concerning the environment that is held by public authorities, including information on hazardous materials and activities in their communities, and the opportunity to participate in decision-making processes. States shall facilitate and encourage public awareness and participation by making information widely available. Effective access to judicial and administrative proceedings, including redress and remedy, shall be provided." UNCED, Rio Declaration on Environment and Development, Principle 10.

38. Joseph Foti with Lalanath de Silva, Heather McGray, Linda Shaffer, Jonathan Talbot, and Jacob Werksman, *Voice and Choice: Opening the Door to Environmental Democracy* (Washington, DC: World Resources Institute, 2008), x.

39. For an extensive overview, see Shelton, "Human Rights and Environment."

40. United Nations Environment Programme, "The New Future of Human Rights and Environment: Moving the Global Agenda Forward—High Level Experts Meeting." Available at http://www.unep.org/environmentalgovernance/Events/HumanRightsandEnvironment/HighLevelExpertsMeeting/tabid/2661/language/en-US/Default.aspx, viewed 26 May 2011.

41. Shelton, "Human Rights and Environment," 7.

42. Shelton, "Human Rights and Environment," 27 and 28.

43. UN General Assembly, Human Rights Council, *Report of Independent Expert*, 2012, 13.

44. UN General Assembly, Human Rights Council, *Report of Independent Expert*, 2012, 6–7.

45. United Nations Development Programme, "Promoting Rights and Access to Finance." Available at http://www.undp.org/localdevelopment/topic-promoting-rights-and-access-to-finance.shtml, viewed 25 May 2011.

46. United Nations Development Programme, "Strengthening Community Voices in Policy Processes." Available at http://www.undp.org/localdevelopment/topic-community-voices-in-policy-processes.shtml, viewed 25 May 2011.

47. See for example A. Ramadhani, "Promoting Good Forest Governance for Sustainable Livelihood Improvement: A Tanzanian Example," *Unasylva* 234–235, no. 61 (2010): 54–59.

48. Membership in CFS is open to member states of FAO, the International Fund for Agricultural Development, or the World Food Programme, as well as UN member states.

49. Food and Agriculture Organization, "Countries Adopt Global Guidelines on Tenure of Land, Forests, Fisheries." Press release, 11 May 2012, available at http://www.fao.org/news/story/en/item/142587/icode/, viewed 26 May 2013.

50. See the statement of Ángel Strapazzón, of Movimiento Campesino Indígena–Vía Campesina Argentina, in Food and Agriculture Organization, "Countries Adopt Global Guidelines." See also FoodFirst Information and Action Network, "FAO Tenure Guidelines a Modest Step, Governments Must Commit to Implementation," 15 May 2012, available at http://humanrightshouse.org/Articles/18029.html, viewed 26 May 2013.

51. See, for example, World Wildlife Fund, "Conserving Freshwater Ecosystem Services," available at http://wwf.panda.org/what_we_do/how_we_work/conservation/freshwater/water_development/, viewed 20 May 2013; World Conservation Union, "Food Security: Making the Ecosystem Connections," available at http://www.iucn.org/about/work/programmes/water/?12988/Food-Security-making-the-ecosystem-connections, viewed 20 May 2013.

52. United Nations Committee on Economic, Social and Cultural Rights, *Substantive Issues Arising in the Implementation of the International Covenant on Economic, Social and Cultural Rights: General Comment No. 14.* UN Document E/C.12/2000/4, 11 August 2000.

53. United Nations Committee on Economic, Social and Cultural Rights, *Substantive Issues Arising in the Implementation of the International Covenant on Economic, Social and Cultural Rights: General Comment 12.* UN Document E/C.12/1999/5, 12 May 1999.

54. World Health Organization, *Human Rights, Health and Poverty Reduction Strategies.* Health and Human Rights Publications Series, issue 5, 2008.

55. Food and Agriculture Organization of the United Nations, *Voluntary Guidelines to Support the Progressive Realization of the Right to Adequate Food in the Context of National Food Security* (Rome: FAO, 2005), 19.

56. Peter H. Gleick, "The Human Right to Water," *Water Policy* 1, no. 5 (1998): 487–503.

57. Office of the High Commissioner for Human Rights, UN Habitat, and World Health Organization, "The Right to Water." Fact Sheet No. 35. Geneva: UNHCR, August 2010.

58. UN General Assembly, Resolution 64/292, 108th plenary meeting, 28 July 2010.

59. Report of the United Nations Water Conference, Mar del Plata, March 14–25, 1977, UN Document E.77.II.A.12 (1977), quoted in World Bank, *The Human Right to Water: Legal and Policy Dimensions* (Washington, DC: World Bank, 2004), 8.

60. World Bank, *Human Right to Water*, 9–10.

61. UN General Assembly Resolution 54/175 of 17 December 1999.

62. See United Nations Committee on Economic, Social and Cultural Rights, *Substantive Issues Arising in the Implementation of the International Covenant on Economic, Social and Cultural Rights: General Comment No. 15 (2002): The Right to Water,* UN Document E/C.12/2002/11, 20 January 2003.

63. On the interplay of privatization and rights-based movements, see Conca, *Governing Water*, chapter 7.

64. World Health Organization and UN-Water, *GLAAS 2010: UN-Water Global Annual Assessment of Sanitation and Drinking-Water* (Geneva: World Health Organization, 2010).
65. WHO and UN-Water, *GLAAS 2010*; World Health Organization and United Nations Children's Fund, *Progress on Sanitation and Drinking-Water: 2010 Update* (Geneva: World Health Organization, 2010).
66. See Peter H. Gleick, "The Human Right to Water." Oakland, CA: Pacific Institute, 2007. Available at http://www.pacinst.org/reports/human_right_may_07.pdf, viewed 30 December 2011.
67. Office of the High Commissioner for Human Rights, World Health Organization, Center on Housing Rights and Evictions, Center for Economic and Social Rights, and WaterAid, *The Right to Water* (Geneva: WHO, 2003).
68. OECD, "Financing Water and Sanitation in Developing Countries: The Contribution of External Aid," available at http://webnet.oecd.org/dcdgraphs/water/, viewed 25 November 2013.
69. Lyla Mehta, "Water and Human Development: Capabilities, Entitlements and Power." Human Development Report Office, Occasional Paper 2006/9, UNDP, 2006. Available at http://hdr.undp.org/en/reports/global/hdr2006/papers/Mehta_L_rev.pdf, viewed 30 December 2011.
70. Lyla Mehta, ed., *The Limits to Scarcity: Contesting the Politics of Allocation* (New York: Routledge, 2010).
71. UNCESCR, *General Comment No. 15*, paragraphs 48 and 55.
72. World Health Organization and UN Water, *GLAAS Report 2012: UN-Water Global Analysis and Assessment of Sanitation and Drinking Water* (Geneva: WHO, 2012), 45.
73. WHO and UN Water, *GLAAS Report 2012*, 45.
74. On the improved operationalization of national human rights institutions, see C. Raj Kumar, "National Human Rights Institutions (NHRIs) and Economic, Social and Cultural Rights: Toward the Institutionalization and Developmentalization of Human Rights," *Human Rights Quarterly* 28, no. 3 (August 2006): 755–779.
75. Salman M. A. Salman and Siobhán McInerney-Lankford, *The Human Right to Water: Legal and Policy Dimensions* (Washington, DC: World Bank, 2004). A report of the World Bank's Law, Justice and Development Series.
76. UN General Assembly, Human Rights Council, Fifteenth Session, Agenda item 3. *Promotion and Protection of All Human Rights, Civil, Political, Economic, Social and Cultural rights, Including the Right to Development. 15/ . . . Human Rights and Access to Safe Drinking Water and Sanitation.* UN Document A/HRC/15/L.14.
77. United Nations General Assembly, *Report of the Office of the United Nations High Commissioner for Human Rights on the Relationship between Climate Change and Human Rights.* UN Document A/HRC/10/61, 15 January 2009.
78. United Nations Human Rights Council, *Human Rights and Climate Change.* UN Document A/HRC/7/L.21/Rev.1, 26 March 2008.
79. See J. Campese, T. C. H. Sunderland, T. Greiber, and G. Oviedo, eds., *Rights-Based Approaches: Exploring Issues and Opportunities for Conservation* (Bogor, Indonesia: Center for International Forestry Research and International Union for Conservation of Nature, 2009); Chris van Dam, "Indigenous Territories and REDD in Latin America: Threat or Opportunity?" *Forests* 2 (2011): 394–414.
80. Declaration of Members of the Indigenous Peoples' Biocultural Climate Change Assessment (IPCCA) Initiative, Durban, South Africa, 26 November 2011.

Available at www.redd-monitor.org/2011/11/28/redd-threatens-the-survival-of-indigenous-peoples-new-statement-from-indigenous-peoples-rejects-redd/, viewed 26 November 2013.

81. See Timo Koivurova, Sébastien Duyck, and Leena Heinämäki, "Climate Change and Human Rights," in Erkki J. Hollo, Kati Kulovesi, and Michael Mehling, eds., *Climate Change and the Law* (Dordrecht: Springer, 2013), 287–325. Ius Gentium: Comparative Perspectives on Law and Justice, volume 21.

82. UNGA, *Relationship between Climate Change.*

83. "Male' Declaration on the Human Dimensions of Global Climate Change," adopted at Male', Republic of Maldives, 14 November 2007. On the politics behind the declaration, see John H. Knox, "Linking Human Rights and Climate Change at the United Nations," *Harvard Environmental Law Review* 33 (2009): 477–498.

84. UNGA, *Relationship between Climate Change*, paragraph 20, p. 8.

85. OHCHR, *Human Rights Council Panel Discussion*, paragraph 55, p. 10.

86. Un-REDD Programme, *Fifth Consolidated Annual Progress Report of the UN REDD Programme Fund*, UN-REDD Programme Twelfth Policy Board Meeting, 7–9 July 2014, Lima, Peru.

87. Forest Carbon Partnership Facility and UN-REDD Programme, "Guidelines on Stakeholder Engagement in REDD+ Readiness with a Focus on the Participation of Indigenous Peoples and Other Forest-Dependent Communities," 20 April 2012.

88. CERD wrote three letters to the Indonesian government between 2009 and 2011; see Chris Lang, "Discriminatory Forestry Regulations and REDD Projects in Indonesia." Posted to redd-monitor.org, 24 February 2012. Available at http://www.redd-monitor.org/2012/02/24/discriminatory-forestry-regulations-and-redd-projects-in-indonesia/.

89. World Resources Institute, "Infographic: Securing Rights, Combating Climate Change." Available at http://www.wri.org/resources/data-visualizations/infographic-securing-rights-combating-climate-change, viewed 15 January 2015.

90. "UN Climate Change Conference in Warsaw Keeps Governments on a Track towards 2015 Climate Agreement." Press release, United Nations Climate Change Secretariat, 23 November 2013.

91. United Nations General Assembly, Human Rights Council, *Annual Report of the United Nations High Commissioner for Human Rights and Reports of the Office of the High Commissioner and the Secretary-General. Report of the Office of the High Commissioner for Human Rights on the Relationship between Climate Change and Human Rights.* UN Document A/HRC/10/61, 15 January 2009, paragraph 83, 27.

92. Koivurova, Duyck, and Heinämäki, "Climate Change."

93. OHCHR, *Human Rights Council Panel Discussion*, paragraph 68, p. 11.

94. OHCHR, *Human Rights Council Panel Discussion*, paragraphs 72–75, p. 12. Legal expert John Knox (who would later be appointed the HRC's independent expert on environmental human rights) sought to bridge this divide by noting that developed countries bore more responsibility than developing countries, but that all states must do more and that "no State should point to another State's failure to take steps to comply with its human rights obligations as an excuse for its own failure to meet its own human rights obligations" (14).

95. *Petition to the Inter American Commission on Human Rights Seeking Relief from Violations Resulting from Global Warming Caused by Acts and Omissions of the United States*, 7 December 2005. Available at www.inuitcircumpolar.com/files/uploads/icc-files/FINALPetitionICC.pdf, viewed 25 November 2013.

96. A 2008 resolution of the Organization of American States directed IACHR "to contribute, within its capacities, to the efforts to determine the possible existence of a link between adverse effects of climate change and the full enjoyment of human rights." See Organization of American States, "Human Rights and Climate Change in the Americas," AG/RES. 2429 (XXXVIII-O/08), adopted at the Fourth Plenary Session, 3 June 2008.

97. Luciano Butti, "The Tortuous Road to Liability: A Critical Survey on Climate Change Litigation in Europe and North America," *Sustainable Development Law & Policy* 11, no. 2 (2011): 32–36, 82–84.

98. See United Nations Framework Convention on Climate Change, "Declarations and Reservations by Parties—Kyoto Protocol: Nauru," available at http://unfccc.int/kyoto_protocol/status_of_ratification/items/5424.php, cited in Koivurova, Duyck, and Heinämäki, "Climate Change."

99. UN Human Rights Council, *Analytical Study on the Relationship between Human Rights and the Environment: Report of the United Nations High Commissioner for Human Rights.* UN Document A/HRC/19/34, 16 December 2011.

100. Human Rights Council, *Analytical Study*, paragraph 78, p. 16.

101. Dr. Marcos Orellana, Center for International Environmental Law, "Statement to the UN Human Rights Council," Nineteenth Session, 1 March 2012, 1.

102. UN Human Rights Council, Decision 19/10, "Human Rights and the Environment." Fifty-Third Meeting, 22 March 2012.

103. UN General Assembly, Human Rights Council, *Report of Independent Expert*, 2012, 1. Among the issues said to need clarification are "the relationship between human rights obligations and best practices; the connections between substantive and procedural rights and duties; vulnerable groups and non-discrimination; human rights obligations relating to transboundary and global environmental harm; the application of human rights norms to non-State actors; and the relationship between a right to a healthy environment and other human rights" (paragraph 36, p. 12).

104. UN General Assembly, Human Rights Council, *Report of the Independent Expert on the Issue of Human Rights Obligations Relating to the Enjoyment of a Safe, Clean, Healthy and Sustainable Environment, John H. Knox,* paragraph 9, p. 4. Twenty-Third Session, Agenda item 3, 30 December 2013. UN Document A/HRC/25/53.

105. UN General Assembly, Human Rights Council, *Report of Independent Expert*, 2013, paragraph 44, p. 12 and paragraph 64, p. 17.

106. UN General Assembly, Human Rights Council, *Report of Independent Expert*, 2013, paragraph 63, p. 17 and paragraph 80, p. 21.

107. United Nations General Assembly, Human Rights Council, Twenty-Fifth Session, Agenda item 3. "Human Rights and the Environment." UN Document A/HRC/25/L.31, 24 March 2014.

108. Office of the High Commissioner for Human Rights, "What Are Human Rights?" Available at http://www.ohchr.org/EN/Issues/Pages/WhatareHumanRights.aspx, viewed 29 December 2011.

109. UN Environment Programme and UN Office of the High Commissioner for Human Rights, "High Level Expert Meeting on the New Future of Human Rights and Environment: Moving the Global Agenda Forward." Available at http://www.unep.org/environmentalgovernance/Events/HumanRightsandEnvironment/tabid/2046/language/en-US/Default.aspx, viewed 25 May 2011.

110. UN General Assembly, Human Rights Council, *Report of Independent Expert*, 2012, paragraph 60, p. 18.
111. UN General Assembly, Human Rights Council, *Report of Independent Expert*, 2012, paragraph 62, p. 19.
112. UN General Assembly, Human Rights Council, *Report of Independent Expert*, 2012, paragraph 34, p. 12. See also UN General Assembly, Human Rights Council, *Report of Independent Expert*, 2013.
113. UNGA/HRC, *Report of the OHCHR on the Relationship between Climate Change and Human Rights*, paragraph 94, p. 30.
114. Raquel Rolnik, Comments to the UN Human Rights Council, Eleventh Session, Panel on Human Rights and Climate Change. Geneva, 15 June 2009. Webcast available at http://www.un.org/webcast/unhrc/archive.asp?go=090615, viewed 25 May 2011.

CHAPTER 5

1. Address by Mikhail Gorbachev, Forty-Third Session of the United Nations General Assembly, 7 December 1988.
2. Russell J. Dalton, ed., *Critical Masses: Citizens, Nuclear Weapons Production, and Environmental Destruction in the United States and Russia* (Cambridge, MA: MIT Press, 1999).
3. R. P. Turco, O. B. Toon, T. P. Ackerman, J. B. Pollack, and Carl Sagan, "Nuclear Winter: Global Consequences of Multiple Nuclear Explosions," *Science* 222, no. 4630 (23 December 1983): 1283–92.
4. See North Atlantic Treaty Organization, "Topic: Environmental Security," available at http://www.nato.int/cps/en/natolive/topics_49216.htm, viewed 26 July 2012.
5. US House of Representatives, Permanent Select Committee on Intelligence and Select Committee on Energy Independence and Global Warming, *National Intelligence Assessment on the National Security Implications of Global Climate Change to 2030*, 25 June 2008; Office of the Director of National Intelligence, *Global Water Security. Intelligence Community Assessment ICA 2012-08*, 2 February 2012.
6. Martin identifies at least forty documented cases in the literature. See Adrian Martin, "Environmental Conflict between Refugee and Host Communities," *Journal of Peace Research* 42, no. 3 (2005): 329–346.
7. For a range of critiques, see Marc A. Levy, "Is the Environment a Security Issue?" *International Security* 20, no. 2 (Fall 1995): 35–62; Nils Petter Gleditsch, "Armed Conflict and the Environment," in Paul F. Diehl and Nils Petter Gleditsch, eds., *Environmental Conflict* (Boulder, CO: Westview Press, 2001; Nancy Lee Peluso and Michael Watts, eds., *Violent Environments* (Ithaca, NY: Cornell University Press, 2001).
8. Ken Conca, "In the Name of Sustainability: Peace Studies and Environmental Discourse," *Peace and Change* 19, no. 2 (April 1994): 91–113; Elizabeth Hartmann, "Strategic Scarcity: The Origins and Impact of Environmental Conflict Ideas," PhD diss., London School of Economics, 2002; Matthew A. Schnurr and Larry Swatuk, eds., *Natural Resources and Social Conflict: Towards Critical Environmental Security* (London: Palgrave Macmillan, 2012).
9. Nancy Peluso, "Coercing Conservation," in Ronnie D. Lipschutz and Ken Conca, eds., *The State and Social Power in Global Environmental Politics*

(New York: Columbia University Press, 1993); Mac Chapin, "A Challenge to Conservationists," *World Watch* 17, no. 6 (November–December 2004): 17–31.

10. Jessica Tuchman Mathews, "Redefining Security," *Foreign Affairs* 68, no. 2 (Spring 1989): 162–177.

11. World Commission on Environment and Development, *Our Common Future* (New York: Oxford University Press, 1987), chapter 11.

12. See Thomas F. Homer-Dixon, "Environmental Scarcities and Violent Conflict: Evidence from Cases," *International Security* 19, no. 1 (Summer 1994): 5–40.

13. See Günther Bächler and Kurt R. Spillmann, eds., *Environmental Degradation as a Cause of War* (Zurich: Rüegger, 1996).

14. Linda A. Malone, "Green Helmets: A Conceptual Framework for Security Council Authority in Environmental Emergencies," William & Mary Law School, Faculty Publications, Paper 599, 1996, 519.

15. Malone, "Green Helmets," 520. Original source: Paul C. Szasz, "Restructuring the International Organizational Framework," in Edith B. Weiss, ed., *Environmental Change and International Law* (Tokyo: United Nations University Press, 1992), 360.

16. See Jean Krasno, "Former Secretary-General Kofi Annan: International Law and the Bully Pulpit in Norm Creation," paper presented at the Annual Meeting of the International Studies Association, Montreal, March 2011.

17. See United Nations, "Both Rich and Poor Have Clear Interest in Protecting Environment, Secretary-General Says," Press Release SG/SM/8239 ENV/DEV/637, 14 May 2002.

18. High-Level Panel on Threats, Challenges, and Change, *A More Secure World: Report of the Secretary-General's High-Level Panel on Threats, Challenges and Change* (New York: United Nations, 2004), 9.

19. The six were interstate conflict; internal conflict, including civil war, genocide, and other large-scale atrocities; nuclear, radiological, chemical, and biological weapons; terrorism; transnational organized crime; and economic and social threats, including environmental degradation, poverty, and infectious diseases.

20. High-Level Panel, *A More Secure World*, 15.

21. Ban Ki-moon, "The First Wave in a Tide of Change." Available at http://www.un.org/works/sub3.asp?lang=en&id=124, viewed 1 March 2011. See also UN News Center, "Ban Ki-moon Warns That Water Shortages Are Increasingly Driving Conflicts," 6 February 2008. Available at http://www.un.org/apps/news/story.asp?NewsID=25527&Cr=water&Cr1, viewed 1 March 2011.

22. UN News Center, "At World Economic Forum, Ban Ki-moon Pledges Action on Water Resources," January 2008. Available at http://www.un.org/apps/news/story.asp?NewsID=25398&Cr=davos&Cr1=#, viewed 1 March 2011.

23. Ban Ki-moon, "The Right War," *Time*, April 17, 2008. See also UN News Center, "Ban Ki-moon calls on new generation to take better care of Planet Earth than his own," 1 March 2007. Available at http://www.un.org/apps/news/story.asp?NewsID=21720&Cr=global&Cr1=warming, viewed 1 March 2011.

24. Remarks of Secretary-General Ban Ki-moon to the UN Security Council, 6587th Meeting, 20 July 2011, UN Document S/PV.6587, 2.

25. UN General Assembly and UN Security Council, *Report of the Secretary-General on Peacebuilding in the Immediate Aftermath of Conflict*, paragraph 8. UN Document A/63/881-S/2009/304, 11 June 2009.

26. UNGA/UNSC, *Peacebuilding in Immediate Aftermath*, paragraph 60.

27. UN General Assembly and UN Security Council, *Report of the Secretary-General on Peacebuilding in the Immediate Aftermath of Conflict*, paragraph 44. UN Document A/64/866-S/2010/386, 16 July 2010.

28. UN General Assembly and UN Security Council, *Peacebuilding in the Aftermath of Conflict, Report of the Secretary-General*, paragraph 16. UN Document A/67/499-S/2012/746, 8 October 2012; UN General Assembly and UN Security Council, *Peacebuilding in the Aftermath of Conflict. Report of the Secretary-General*, paragraph 49. UN Document A/69/399-S/2014/694, 23 September 2014.

29. Moon, "The Right War."

30. Paul Collier and Nicholas Sambanis, eds., *Understanding Civil War: Evidence and Analysis*, vol. 1: *Africa* (Washington, DC: World Bank, 2005).

31. Global Witness, *Lessons UNlearned: How the UN and Member States Must Do More to End Natural Resource-Fuelled Conflicts* (London: Global Witness, January 2010), 10.

32. See the series of reports available at www.globalwitness.org/.

33. Michael Ross, *The Oil Curse: How Petroleum Wealth Shapes the Development of Nations* (Princeton, NJ: Princeton University Press, 2012).

34. UN Environment Programme, *From Conflict to Peacebuilding: The Role of Natural Resources and the Environment* (Nairobi: UNEP, 2009). Available at http://www.unep.org/pdf/pcdmb_policy_01.pdf, viewed 1 June 2010.

35. Ross, *The Oil Curse*; Michael Ross, "A Closer Look at Oil, Diamonds, and Civil War," *Annual Review of Political Science* 9 (2006): 265–300.

36. For a complete list of UNSC sanctions committees, see http://www.un.org/en/sc/repertoire/subsidiary_organs/sanctions_and_other_committees.shtml.

37. UNGA Resolution A/RES/55/56, adopted 1 December 2000; UNSC Resolution 1459, adopted 28 January 2003.

38. Philippe Le Billon, "Natural Resources, Armed Conflicts, and the UN Security Council." Paper presented at the Seminar on Natural Resources and Armed Conflicts, UN headquarters, New York, 21 May 2007.

39. UN Office of the Special Adviser on Africa, "Conference Report, UN Expert Group Meeting on Natural Resources and Conflict in Africa: Transforming a Peace Liability into a Peace Asset." Cairo, 17–19 June 2006; Le Billon, "Natural Resources," 2.

40. *Report of the Panel of Experts on the Illegal Exploitation of Natural Resources and Other Forms of Wealth of the Democratic Republic of the Congo*, 2001, paragraph 6.

41. *Report of the Panel of Experts*, paragraphs 46–70.

42. UN Security Council Resolution 1509, 19 September 2003.

43. UN Security Council Resolution 1562, 17 September 2004.

44. UN Security Council, "Third Report of the Secretary-General on the United Nations Mission in Sierra Leone," UN Doc. S/2000/186, 7 March 2000. Quoted in Global Witness, *Lessons UNlearned*, 24.

45. Global Policy Forum, "NGO Proposals on Natural Resources and Conflict." Available at http://www.globalpolicy.org/component/content/article/198/40111.html, viewed 10 February 2011.

46. Global Policy Forum, "NGO Letter to the UN Secretary General's High-Level Panel on Threats, Challenges and Change, October 11, 2004." Available at http://www.globalpolicy.org/security/natres/generaldebate/2004/1011highlevel.htm, viewed 10 February 2011.

47. UN Security Council, "Letter Dated 6 June 2007 from the Permanent Representative of Belgium to the United Nations to the Secretary-General." UN Document S/2007/334, 6 June 2007.

48. The following section draws upon the statements transcribed in UN Documents S/PV.5705 and S/PV.5705 (resumption 1), 25 June 2007.

49. Gerard Aziakou, "UN Spotlights Link between Natural Resources and Conflict," *Agence France Presse*, 25 June 2007.

50. The 2007 interim report of the Group of Experts on the DRC found that "the current situation cannot be viewed solely through the lens of the activities of structured armed groups but incorporates a wider and more complex problem involving State actors, criminality, corruption and other illicit armed activity. The Group's consultations with a broad range of stakeholders suggest that these problems are best addressed by promoting law-abiding industries and responsible Government oversight." See UN Security Council, *Letter dated 25 January 2007 from the Chairman of the Security Council Committee established pursuant to resolution 1533 (2004) concerning the Democratic Republic of the Congo addressed to the President of the Security Council*, paragraph 17, p. 6. UN Document S/2007/40, 31 January 2007.

51. UNSC Resolution 1856, 22 December 2008; Global Witness, *Lessons UNlearned*, 15.

52. UNSC Resolution 1896, 30 November 2009.

53. UNSC Resolution 1756, 15 May 2007.

54. UNSC Resolution 1856, 22 December 2008.

55. Global Witness, *Lessons UNlearned*, 15. See also Global Witness, *Coming Clean: How Supply Chain Controls Can Stop Congo's Minerals Trade Fueling Conflict* (London: Global Witness, May 2012).

56. Global Witness, "Global Witness Open Letter to the UN Security Council, Regarding Conflict Resources and Peacekeeping in Liberia and the Democratic Republic of Congo," 18 March 2005. Available at http://www.globalpolicy.org/component/content/article/198/40117.html, viewed 10 February 2011.

57. Security Council Resolution 1854 of 19 December 2008, on the situation in Liberia, takes note of the EITI, as did the statement of the UNSC president on the occasion of the June 2007 thematic debate on conflict resources. See United Nations Security Council, "Statement by the President of the Security Council," 25 June 2007. UN Document S/PRST/2007/22.

58. UNSC Resolution 1625, 14 September 2005.

59. UN Security Council, *Maintenance of International Peace and Security: Conflict Prevention and Natural Resources*, 19 June 2013. UN Documents S/PV.6982 and S/PV.6982 (resumption 1).

60. Global Witness proposed a definition of conflict resources as "natural resources whose systematic exploitation and trade in a context of conflict contribute to, benefit from or result in the commission of serious violations of human rights, violations of international humanitarian law or violations amounting to crimes under international law." See Global Witness, "Definition of Conflict Resources." Available at http://www.globalpolicy.org/component/content/article/198/40124.html, viewed 10 February 2011.

61. Michael D. Beevers, "Sustaining Peace? Environmental and Natural Resource Governance in Liberia and Sierra Leone." PhD diss., Department of Government and Politics, University of Maryland, 2011.

62. UN Environment Programme, *Sierra Leone Environment, Conflict and Peacebuilding Assessment: Technical Report* (Geneva: UNEP, 2010).

63. The Stern Review was a pathbreaking effort to assess the long-term economic implications of climate change; it estimated that the projected benefits of aggressive and early action to mitigate the effects of climate change would substantially

outweigh the costs. Nicholas Stern, *The Economics of Climate Change: The Stern Review* (Cambridge: Cambridge University Press, 2007).

64. See UN Security Council, *Letter Dated 5 April 2007 from the Permanent Representative of the United Kingdom of Great Britain and Northern Ireland to the United Nations Addressed to the President of the Security Council*, annex. UN Document S/2007/186, 5 April 2007.

65. UNSC, *Letter Dated 5 April 2007.*

66. Russia made an appeal "to avoid panicking and overdramatizing the situation," while South Africa asserted that the effects of climate change "do not as yet directly threaten international peace and security." UN Security Council, 5663rd meeting, New York, 17 April 2007. Unless otherwise noted, all quotes from and observations on country statements during the 2007 thematic session are based on the session transcription, available as UN Documents S/PV.5663 and S/PV.5663 (resumption 1).

67. UN Security Council, *Letter Dated 16 April 2007 from the Permanent Representative of Pakistan to the United Nations Addressed to the Security Council.* UN Document S/2007/211, 16 April 2007. The Non-Aligned Movement offered similar objections; see UN Security Council, *Letter Dated 12 April 2007 from the Chargé d'affaires a.i. of the Permanent Mission of Cuba to the United Nations Addressed to the President of the Security Council*, UN document S/2007/203, 12 April 2007.

68. Adil Najam, "Developing Countries and Global Environmental Governance: From Contestation to Participation to Engagement," *International Environmental Agreements: Politics, Law and Economics* 5, no. 3 (2005): 303–321.

69. *Letter Dated 16 April 2007 from the Permanent Representative of Pakistan.*

70. UN General Assembly, Resolution 63/281, 11 June 2009, 2.

71. UN General Assembly, Resolution 63/281, 11 June 2009, 1.

72. UN General Assembly, Sixty-Third Session, Eighty-Fifth Plenary Meeting, Wednesday, 3 June 2009. UN Document A/63/PV.85.

73. UN General Assembly, *Climate Change and Its Possible Security Implications: Report of the Secretary-General.* Sixty-Fourth Session, 11 September 2009, 5. UN Document A/64/350.

74. UN Security Council, 6587th meeting, New York, 20 July 2011. UN Document S/PV.6587, 7. Unless otherwise noted, all quotes from the 2011 thematic session are taken from the event transcript, available in UN Documents S/PV.6587 and S/PV.6587 (resumption 1).

75. UN Security Council, *Letter Dated 1 July 2011 from the Permanent Representative of Germany to the United Nations Addressed to the Secretary-General.* UN Document S/2011/408, 5 July 2011.

76. Permanent Mission of Germany to the United Nations, Security Council Presidential Statement, July 20, 2011.

77. See, for example, the Council's November 2011 open debate on emerging threats.

78. Security Council Report, "Special Research Report: Security Council Elections 2012." Available at http://www.securitycouncilreport.org/atf/cf/%7B65BFCF9B-6D27-4E9C-8CD3-CF6E4FF96FF9%7D/special_research_report_elections_2012.pdf, viewed 30 May 2013.

79. An Arria Formula Meeting allows interested Security Council members to receive briefings and discuss issues in an informal manner, outside of the council's chambers.

80. See "Statement on Behalf of the Group of 77 and China by Ambassador Peter Thomson, Permanent Representative of Fiji to the United Nations and Chairman of The Group of 77, at the Arria-Formula Meeting on the Security Dimensions of Climate Change," New York, 15 February 2013.

81. See Permanent Mission of Fiji to the United Nations, "Statement at the UN Security Council Debate on Women, Peace and Security (UNSCR 1325)," New York, 29 November 2012. Available at http://www.fijiprun.org/node/22, viewed 30 May 2013.

82. United Nations Peacebuilding Support Office, "Peacebuilding FAQ," available at http://www.un.org/en/peacebuilding/pbso/faq.shtml#q1, viewed 2 April 2015.

83. United Nations, "List of Peacekeeping Operations 1948–2013," available at http://www.un.org/en/peacekeeping/documents/operationslist.pdf, viewed 20 November 2014.

84. Roland Paris, *At War's End: Building Peace after Civil Conflict* (Cambridge: Cambridge University Press, 2004), 3.

85. The author has been a member of UNEP's Expert Advisory Group on Conflict and Peacebuilding since 2008. On the Expert Advisory Group, see http://post-conflict.unep.ch/publications/EAG.pdf

86. UN Environment Programme and United Nations Centre for Human Settlements, *The Kosovo Conflict: Consequences for the Environment and Human Settlements* (Geneva: UNEP and UNCHS, 1999).

87. UNEP and UNCHS, *The Kosovo Conflict.*

88. UN Environment Programme, "Disasters and Conflicts." Available at http://www.unep.org/disastersandconflicts/, viewed 20 November 2014. See also Ken Conca and Jennifer Wallace, "Environment and Peacebuilding in War-Torn Societies: Lessons from the UN Environment Programme's Experience with Postconflict Assessment," *Global Governance* 15, no. 4 (October–December 2009): 485–504.

89. United Nations Environment Programme, *Desk Study on the Environment in Iraq* (Geneva: UNEP, 2003), 87; United Nations Environment Programme, *Desk Study in the Occupied Palestinian Territories* (Geneva: UNEP, 2003), 127.

90. UNEP and UNCHS, *The Kosovo Conflict*, 5.

91. See UNEP, *UNEP Programme Performance Report for the 2010–2011 Biennium*, 4.

92. Calculated from data in UN Environment Programme, *United Nations Environment Programme Annual Report 2013* (Nairobi: UNEP, 2014).

93. The author is a member of this body.

94. See UN Development Group, "Thirty-Sixth Meeting of the United Nations Development Group Thursday, 19 April 2007: Summary of Conclusions." Available at http://pcna.undg.org/index.php?option=com_docman&Itemid=15, viewed 7 August 2012.

95. UNEP, "Integrating Environment in Postconflict Needs Assessments." UNEP Guidance Note, March 2009.

96. UNEP, "Integrating Environment," 9.

97. UNEP, "Integrating Environment."

98. Alex Fischer and Marc A. Levy, "Designing Environmental Restoration Programs in Politically Fragile States: Lessons from Haiti," in Carl Bruch, Mikiyasu Nakayama, and Ilona Coyle, *Harnessing Natural Resources for Peacebuilding: Lessons from U.S. and Japanese Assistance* (Washington, DC: Environmental Law Institute, 2011).

99. UNDG, "Natural Resource Management in Transition Settings," UNDG-ECHA Guidance Note, January 2013.

100. See UNEP, "Environmental Cooperation for Peacebuilding." Available at http://www.unep.org/disastersandconflicts/Introduction/ECP/tabid/105948/Default.aspx, viewed 23 December 2013.

101. Damiano A. Sguaitamatti, Simon J. A. Mason, and Pilar Ramirez Gröbli, "Stepping Stones to Peace? Natural Resource Provisions in Peace Agreements," in Carl Bruch, Carroll Muffett, and Sandra S. Nichols, eds., *Governance, Natural Resources, and Post-conflict Peacebuilding* (New York: Routledge, 2015).

102. UNEP has partnered with the UN Institute for Training and Research (UNITAR) and the International Institute for Sustainable Development (IISD) to develop training materials on environment, natural resources, and peace-keeping operations. See, for example, the introductory module to the online course Natural Resources Management in Post-conflict Countries. Available at http://stream.unitar.org/ptp/StartCourse/player.html, viewed 9 August 2012. The course is part of UNITAR's Peacekeeping Training Program for civilian, military, and police personnel deployed in peace operations.

103. United Nations, "Greening the Blue," available at http://www.greeningtheblue.org/, viewed 9 August 2012.

104. United Nations Environment Programme, *Greening the Blue Helmets: Environ-ment, Natural Resources, and UN Peacekeeping Operations* (Nairobi: UNEP, 2012).

105. UNEP, *Greening the Blue Helmets*, 24.

106. UNEP, *Greening the Blue Helmets*; Global Witness, *Lessons UNlearned*.

107. UNEP, *Greening the Blue Helmets*, 45.

108. UNEP, *Greening the Blue Helmets*, 50.

109. "UN peacekeepers 'Traded Gold and Guns with Congolese rebels,'" *Guardian*, 28 April 2008. Available at http://www.theguardian.com/world/2008/apr/28/congo.unitednations, viewed 1 December 2014.

110. Swisspeace, Center for Security Studies, and Swiss Federal Institute of Technology Zurich, *Linking Environment and Conflict Prevention: The Role of the United Nations* (Zurich: Center for Security Studies; Bern: Swisspeace, 2008).

111. Fiji Government, Strategic Framework for Change Coordinating Office, "PM's Office Partners with UNDP in Finding Solutions to Resource Based Conflicts." Available at http://www.sfcco.gov.fj/index.php?option=com_content&view=article&id=34:pms-office-partners-with-undp-in-finding-solutions-to-resource-based-conflicts&catid=32:header-stories&Itemid=68, viewed 12 August 2012.

112. UNDP Sudan, "Reduction of Resource Based Conflicts among Pastoralists and Farmers." Available at http://www.sd.undp.org/projects/cp3.htm, viewed 12 August 2012.

113. United Nations Development Programme, "Conflict Prevention," available at http://www.undp.org/content/undp/en/home/ourwork/crisispreventionandrecovery/focus_areas/conflictprevention.html, viewed 2 April 2015.

114. United Nations Development Programme, *The Changing Nature of Conflict: Priorities for UNDP Response* (New York: UNDP, 2013), 1.

115. UNEP's UN partners on the initiative are UNDP, DPA, PBSO, the UN Human Settlements Programme, and the Department of Economic and Social Affairs.

116. See UNEP, "UN-EU Partnership on Natural Resources, Conflict and Peace-building." Available at http://www.unep.org/dnc/Introduction/Environmental CooperationforPeacebuilding/OtherECPActivities/UNEUPartnership/tabid/54648/Default.aspx, viewed 10 August 2012.

117. UN General Assembly Resolution 53/242, 10 August 1999, 4.

118. Swisspeace, Center for Security Studies, and Swiss Federal Institute of Technology Zurich, *Linking Environment and Conflict Prevention*, 61–62.

119. Personal communication with Dr. Richard Matthew, 3 April 2015. See also the web page of the UN Peacebuilding Commission's Working Group on Lessons Learned. Available at http://www.un.org/en/peacebuilding/doc_lessons-learned.shtml, viewed 7 August 2012.

120. International Institute for Sustainable Development, "Summary of the 26th Session of the UN Environment Programme Governing Council/Global Ministerial Environment Forum: 21–24 February 2011," *Earth Negotiations Bulletin* 16, no. 89 (28 February 2011).

121. See UN General Assembly and UN Security Council, *Identical Letters Dated 19 July 2010 from the Permanent Representatives of Ireland, Mexico and South Africa to the United Nations Addressed to the President of the General Assembly and the President of the Security Council.* UN Document A/64/868–S/2010/393, 21 July 2010.

122. Matti Lehtonen, "Peacebuilding through Natural Resource Management: The UN Peacebuilding Commission's First Five Years," in Carl Bruch, Carroll Muffett, and Sandra S. Nichols, eds., *Governance, Natural Resources, and Post-conflict Peacebuilding* (New York: Routledge, 2015).

123. Peacebuilding Commission, "Strategic Framework for Peacebuilding in the Central African Republic 2009-2001," 27. UN Document PBC/3/CAF/7, 9 June 2009.

124. CAR applied to join the EITI in 2008 and was accepted as EITI-compliant in 2011. See EITI, "Central African Republic." Available at http://eiti.org/CentralAfricanRepublic, viewed 7 August 2012.

125. Lehtonen, "Peacebuilding through Natural Resource Management."

126. International Crisis Group, "Dangerous Little Stones: Diamonds in the Central African Republic." ICG Africa Report No. 167, 16 December 2010.

127. United Nations Environment Programme, "UNEP Mission Report: Risks and Opportunities from Natural Resources and the Environment for Peacebuilding in the Central African Republic." Draft report, August 2009.

128. Peacebuilding Commission, "Conclusions and Recommendations of the Second Biannual Review of the Strategic Framework for Peacebuilding in the Central African Republic," 4 and 11. UN Document PBC/5/CAF/3, 18 November 2011.

129. Kasper Agger, *Behind the Headlines: Drivers of Violence in the Central African Republic* (Washington, DC: Enough Project, 2014); Friends Committee on National Legislation, *Central African Republic Crisis: Managing Natural Resources for Peace* (Washington, DC: FCNL, 2014).

130. International Institute for Sustainable Development, "The Twentieth Session of the Governing Council of the United Nations Environment' Program," *Earth Negotiations Bulletin* 16, no. 6 (8 February 1999).

131. Heinz Krummenacher, "Economic and Environmental Early Warning for Confidence Building and Conflict Prevention." Discussion paper, OSCE-Chairmanship Workshop on Economic and Environmental Activities as Confidence-Building Measures, Vienna, 30 May 2011.

132. Marc A. Levy and Patrick Philippe Meier, "Early Warning and Assessment of Environment, Conflict, and Cooperation," in United Nations Environment Programme, *Understanding Environmental Conflict and Cooperation* (Nairobi: UNEP; Washington, DC: Woodrow Wilson Center, 2004), 38–47.

CHAPTER 6

1. Richard Jolly, Louis Emmerij, and Thomas G. Weiss, *The Power of UN: Ideas: Lessons from the First 60 Years* (New York: United Nations Intellectual History Project, 2005), 4.
2. Steven Bernstein, "Rio+20: Sustainable Development in a Time of Multilateral Decline," *Global Environmental Politics* 13, no. 4 (November 2013): 12–21.
3. Maria Ivanova, "The Contested Legacy of Rio+20," *Global Environmental Politics* 13, no. 4 (November 2013): 2 and 7.
4. Jürgen Maier, "18 Months after Rio+20—Did the Conference Have any Impact at All?" *Future of Food: Journal on Food, Agriculture and Society* 1, no. 2 (Winter 2013): 119–121; see also Ivanova, "Contested Legacy."
5. Karen Morrow, "Rio+20: A Critique," *Journal of Human Rights and the Environment* 4, no. 1. (2013): 1–5.
6. Bernstein, "Rio+20"; Mark Halle, "Life after Rio: A Commentary," International Institute for Sustainable Development, June 2012.
7. Sam Adelman, "Rio+20: Sustainable Injustice in a Time of Crises," *Journal of Human Rights and the Environment* 4, no. 1. (2013): 6–31.
8. Kenneth W. Abbott, "Engaging the Public and the Private in Global Sustainability Governance," *International Affairs* 88, no. 3 (May 2012): 543–564.
9. Open letter of Navanethem Pillay, UN High Commissioner for Human Rights, to UN member-states, 30 March 2012.
10. The four were a session on conflict in the extractives sector, organized by Centro de Derechos Humanos y Ambiente; one on sustainability in postconflict countries, by the Government of Lebanon; and a pair of sessions on disarmament and food-related conflict, respectively, by International Peace Bureau. Compiled from UN Conference on Sustainable Development, "Side Events at Rio." Available at http://www.uncsd2012.org/meetings_sidevents.html, viewed 28 January 2014.
11. Kelly Levin, Benjamin Cashore, Steven Bernstein, and Graeme Auld, "Overcoming the Tragedy of Super Wicked Problems: Constraining Our Future Selves to Ameliorate Global Climate Change," *Policy Sciences* 45, no. 2 (2012): 123–152.
12. Levin et al., "Overcoming the Tragedy," 123.
13. UN General Assembly, Human Rights Council, *Report of the Independent Expert on the Issue of Human Rights Obligations Relating to the Enjoyment of a Safe, Clean, Healthy and Sustainable Environment, John H. Knox*, paragraph 34, p. 12. Twenty-Second Session, Agenda item 3. UN Document A/HRC/22/43, 24 December 2012.
14. UNGA/HRC, *Report of Independent Expert*, 2012, paragraph 60, p. 18.
15. UN General Assembly, Resolution 60/1, 24 October 2005.
16. See Global Centre for the Responsibility to Protect, "UN Security Council Resolutions Referencing R2P." Available at http://www.globalr2p.org/resources/335, viewed February 10, 2014.
17. Jayshree Bajoria, "The Dilemma of Humanitarian Intervention." Council on Foreign Relations background report, updated 24 March 2011. Available at http://www.cfr.org/human-rights/dilemma-humanitarian-intervention/p16524, viewed 22 July 2012. Natalie Oman, "The Responsibility to Prevent: A Remit for Interventionism?" *Canadian Journal of Law and Jurisprudence* 22, no. 2 (2009): 335–380.

18. The Council has done so by flagging paragraph 139 of the 2005 World Summit Outcomes Document, which identifies the responsibility of the international community (paragraph 138 speaks to the responsibilities of individual states for their citizens). See S/Res/1706 of 31 August 2006 on Sudan and S/Res/2117 of 26 September 2013 on small arms and light weapons.

19. UN General Assembly, *Integrated and Coordinated Implementation of and Follow-up to the Outcomes of the Major United Nations Conferences and Summits in the Economic, Social and Related Fields. Follow-up to the Outcome of the Millennium Summit. Implementing the Responsibility to Protect. Report of the Secretary-General*, paragraph 10(b). UN Document A/63/677, 12 January 2009.

20. International Law Commission, *Fifth Report on the Protection of Persons in the Event of Disasters*, 6. UN Document A/CN.4/652, 9 April 2012.

21. Frank Biermann and Ingrid Boas, "Protecting Climate Refugees: The Case for a Global Protocol," *Environment* 50, no. 6 (2008): 8–16; David Hodgkinson, Tess Burton, Heather Anderson, and Lucy Young, "'The Hour When the Ship Comes In': A Convention for Persons Displaced by Climate Change," *Monash University Law Review* 36, no. 1 (2010): 69–120.

22. See CARE International, *Humanitarian Implications of Climate Change: Mapping Emerging Trends and Risk Hotspots*, 2nd ed. (Geneva: CARE, November 2009).

23. Asunción Lera St. Clair, "Global Poverty and Climate Change: Towards the Responsibility to Protect," in Karen O'Brien, Asunción Lera St. Clair, and Berit Kristoffersen, eds., *Climate Change, Ethics and Human Security* (Cambridge: Cambridge University Press, 2010); Jon Barnett, *Climate Change and Small Island States* (London: Earthscan, 2010).

24. UN Security Council, Resolution 2117, 26 September 2013.

25. United Nations General Assembly, "Letter Dated 9 November 2006 from the Co-Chairs of the High-Level Panel on United Nations System-Wide Coherence in the Areas of Development, Humanitarian Assistance and the Environment Addressed to the Secretary-General." UN Document A/61/583, November 20, 2006.

26. Jan Vandemoortele, "The MDG Story: Intention Denied," *Development and Change* 42, no. 1 (January 2011): 1–21; Jan Vandemoortele, "Advancing the UN Development Agenda Post-2015: Some Practical Suggestions." Report submitted to the UN Task Force regarding the post-2015 framework for development, January 2012.

27. UN Security Council, 6587th meeting, New York, 20 July 2011. UN Document S/PV.6587, 7.

28. S. Schubert and J. Gupta, "Comparing Global Coordination Mechanisms on Energy, Environment, and Water," *Ecology and Society* 18, no. 2 (2013): 22.

29. Shlomi Dinar, David Katz, Lucia De Stefano, and Brian Blankespoor, "Climate Change, Conflict, and Cooperation: Global Analysis of the Resilience of International River Treaties to Increased Water Variability." World Bank Policy Research Paper 6916, June 2014.

30. UN Security Council, *Letter Dated 1 July 2011 from the Permanent Representative of Germany to the United Nations Addressed to the Secretary-General*, 5 July 2011, 2. UN Document S/2011/408.

31. UN Environment Programme, *Greening the Blue Helmets: Environment, Natural Resources, and UN Peacekeeping Operations* (Nairobi: UNEP, 2012).

32. UN Environment Programme, *Livelihood Security: Climate Change, Migration and Conflict in the Sahel* (Nairobi: UNEP, 2011).
33. See National Intelligence Council, *The Global Infectious Disease Threat and Its Implications for the United States*, January 2000; Gwyn Prins, "AIDS and Global Security," *International Affairs* 80, no. 5 (2004): 931–952.
34. Simon Rushton, "Framing AIDS: Securitization, Development-ization, Rights-ization," *Global Health Governance* 4, no. 1 (2010): 1–17; Colin McInnes, "HIV/AIDS and Security," *International Affairs* 82, no. 2 (2006): 315–326.
35. This analysis masks important complexities, such as the role of land-use changes and deforestation in climate change. It also fails to present emissions data in per capita terms, which would denote responsibility more equitably.
36. UN General Assembly, *Climate Change and Its Possible Security Implications: Report of the Secretary-General*. Sixty-Fourth Session, 11 September 2009, 28. UN Document A/64/350.
37. Remarks of US Ambassador Susan Rice to the UN Security Council, 6587th meeting, New York, 20 July 2011. UN Document S/PV.6587, 7.
38. UN Security Council, *Maintenance of International Peace and Security: Conflict Prevention and Natural Resources*. UN Documents S/PV.6982 and S/PV.6982 (resumption 1).
39. UN Security Council, *Preventive Diplomacy: Delivering Results. Report of the Secretary-General*. UN Document S/2011/552, 26 August 2011.
40. Rama Mani, "Peaceful Settlement of Disputes and Conflict Prevention," in Thomas G. Weiss and Sam Daws, *The Oxford Handbook on the United Nations* (Oxford: Oxford University Press, 2007).
41. Development Co-operation Directorate, *Preventing Violence, War and State Collapse: The Future of Conflict Early Warning and Response* (Paris: OECD, 2009).
42. Ken Conca, "Decoupling Water and Violent Conflict," *Issues in Science and Technology* 29, no. 1 (Fall 2012): 39–48.
43. United Nations International Strategy for Disaster Reduction, *Global Assessment Report on Disaster Risk Reduction* (Geneva: UNISDR, 2011). See also IPCC, "Human Security."
44. On climate refugees, see Biermann and Boas, "Protecting Climate Refugees"; and Hodgkinson et al., "Hour When Ship Comes." On environmental protection in times of war, see UN Environment Programme, *Protecting the Environment during Armed Conflict: An Inventory and Analysis of International Law* (Nairobi: UNEP, 2009).
45. See Economic Commission for Latin America and the Caribbean, "Countries of the Region Approve Launching Negotiation of a Common Agreement on Rights of Access in Environmental Matters." Press release, 6 November 2014. Available at http://www.cepal.org/en/pressreleases/countries-region-approve-launching-negotiation-common-agreement-rights-access, viewed 20 November 2014.
46. See Carole Excelle and Consuela Fernandez, "Open Government Partnership: It's Time for Deeper Engagement with the Environment Sector." Blog post, World Resources Institute, 21 November 2013. Available at http://www.wri.org/blog/open-government-partnership-it%E2%80%99s-time-deeper-engagement-envi-ronment-sector, viewed 14 February 2014. See also Human Rights Council, *Report of the Special Representative of the Secretary-General on the Issue of Human Rights and Transnational Corporations and Other Business Enterprises, John Ruggie. Guiding Principles on Business and Human Rights: Implementing the United Nations*

"Protect, Respect and Remedy" Framework. UN Document A/HRC/17/31, 21 March 2011.

47. Conca, "Decoupling Water." See also Lyla Mehta, Gert Jan Veldwisch, and Jennifer Franco, "Introduction to the Special Issue: Water Grabbing? Focus on the (Re)Appropriation of Finite Water Resources," *Water Alternatives* 5, no. 2 (June 2012): 193–207.

48. United Nations Office of the High Commissioner for Human Rights, "A New Climate Change Agreement Must Include Human Rights Protections for All. An Open Letter from Special Procedures Mandate-Holders of the Human Rights Council to the State Parties to the UN Framework Convention on Climate Change on the Occasion of the Meeting of the Ad Hoc Working Group on the Durban Platform for Enhanced Action in Bonn (20–25 October 2014)," 17 October 2014.

49. On Lima, see International Institute for Sustainable Development, "Summary of the Lima Climate Change Conference: 1–14 December 2014," *Earth Negotiations Bulletin* 12, no. 619 (16 December 2014).

50. Dennis Tänzler, Alexander Carius, and Achim Maas, "The Need for Conflict-Sensitive Adaptation," in Geoffrey D. Dabelko, Lauren Herzer, Schuyler Null, Meaghan Parker, and Russell Sticklor, eds., *Backdraft: The Conflict Potential of Climate Change Adaptation and Mitigation* (Washington, DC: Woodrow Wilson International Center for Scholars, 2013). On PCIA, see Peacebuilding Centre, *Peace and Conflict Impact Assessment Handbook*, version 4 (Ottawa: Peacebuilding Centre, 2013).

51. Ellen Dorsey, Mayra Gómez, Bret Thiele, and Paul Nelson, "Falling Short of Our Goals: Transforming the Millennium Development Goals into Millennium Development Rights," *Netherlands Quarterly of Human Rights* 28, no. 4 (2010): 516–522.

52. Prior to the Rio+20 fusion, the Secretary-General had established a UN System Task Team on the Post-2015 UN Development Agenda, consisting of various UN programs, specialized agencies, and other organs; appointed a High-Level Panel of Eminent Persons on the Post-2015 Development Agenda, cochaired by the presidents of Indonesia and Liberia and the prime minister of the United Kingdom; and launched the Sustainable Development Solutions Network, directed by Nobel laureate Jeffery Sachs, to provide scientific and technical advice.

53. United Nations General Assembly, *Report of the Open Working Group of the General Assembly on Sustainable Development Goals*, Goal 14.2, p. 20, and Goal 12.2, p. 19. UN Document A/68/970, 12 August 2014.

54. UNGA, *Report of Open Working Group*, Goals 12.4 and 12.2, p. 19.

55. International Institute for Sustainable Development, "Summary of the Eighth Session of the UN General Assembly Open Working Group on Sustainable Development Goals: 3–7 February 2014," *Earth Negotiations Bulletin* 32, no. 8, 10 February 2014, 11–15.

56. International Institute for Sustainable Development, "Summary of the Sixth Session of the UN General Assembly Open Working Group on Sustainable Development Goals: 9–13 December 2013," *Earth Negotiations Bulletin* 32, no. 6, 16 December 2013, 10–14.

57. Open Working Group on Sustainable Development Goals, "Compilation of Goals and Targets Suggestions from OWG-10 in Response to Co-chairs' Focus Area Document dated 19 March, 2014." 19 April 2014.

58. Sustainable Development Solutions Network, *An Action Agenda for Sustainable Development: Report for the UN Secretary-General*, revised version 23 October 2013.

59. SDSN, *Action Agenda*, 21.
60. SDSN, *Action Agenda*, 15.
61. UNGA, *Report of Open Working Group*, Goal 5, Target a, p. 14.
62. UNGA, *Report of Open Working Group*, Goal 12.8, p. 19.
63. Dorset et al., "Falling Short."
64. Jonathan Fox, "Social Accountability: What Does the Evidence Really Say?" Global Partnership for Social Accountability, GPSA Working Paper No. 1, September 2014, 7.
65. Ann Florini, "The End of Secrecy," *Foreign Policy* 111 (Summer 1998): 50–63.
66. Aarti Gupta, "Transparency under Scrutiny: Information Disclosure in Global Environmental Governance," *Global Environmental Politics* 8, no. 2 (May 2008): 1–8. See also Aarti Gupta and Michael Mason, eds., *Transparency in Global Environmental Governance: Critical Perspectives* (Cambridge, MA: MIT Press, 2014).
67. Fox, "Social Accountability," 5.
68. Fox refers to strategies that rely on both public accountability from below and reform from inside/above as "sandwich strategies." See Fox, "Social Accountability," 33.
69. Friends Committee on National Legislation, *Central African Republic Crisis: Managing Natural Resources for Peace* (Washington, DC: FCNL, November 2014).
70. FCNL, *Central African Republic Crisis*, 13.
71. Under the rules adopted by the US Securities and Exchange Commission for implementing section 1502 of Dodd-Frank, companies that source gold, tantalum, tin, or tungsten from ten sub-Saharan countries must attempt to determine whether the mineral is conflict-free and comply with related disclosure reporting requirements.
72. Fidel Bafilemba, Timo Mueller, and Sasha Lezhnev, *The Impact of Dodd-Frank and Conflict Minerals Reforms on Eastern Congo's Conflict* (Washington, DC: Enough Project, June 2014).
73. "How a Well-Intentioned U.S. Law Left Congolese Miners Jobless," *Washington Post*, 30 November 2014, A-1; Holly Dranginis and Sasha Lezhnev, "Nine Things You Need to Know about Conflict Minerals." Blog post to ThinkProgress, 4 December 2014. Available at http://thinkprogress.org/economy/2014/12/04/3599824/conflict-minerals-enough/, viewed 11 December 2014.
74. Mining Working Group at the UN, "A Rights-Based Approach to Resource Extraction in the Pursuit of Sustainable Development." Advocacy brief, no date. Available at http://miningwg.com/resources-2/mwg-advocacy-brief/, viewed 1 December 2014.
75. W. N. Adger, J. M. Pulhin, J. Barnett, G. D. Dabelko, G. K. Hovelsrud, M. Levy, Ú. Oswald Spring, and C. H. Vogel, "2014: Human Security," in *Climate Change 2014: Impacts, Adaptation, and Vulnerability. Part A: Global and Sectoral Aspects. Contribution of Working Group II to the Fifth Assessment Report of the Intergovernmental Panel on Climate Change* (Cambridge: Cambridge University Press, 2014), 755–791.
76. UN System Task Team on the Post-2015 UN Development Agenda, *Realizing the Future We Want for All: Report to the Secretary-General* (New York: United Nations, June 2012), paragraph 19, p. 7.
77. UN System Task Team on the Post-2015 UN Development Agenda, *Realizing the Future*, summary, i–ii.

78. On securitization, see Barry Buzan, Ole Wæver, and Jaap de Wilde, *Security: A New Framework for Analysis* (Boulder, CO: Lynne Rienner, 1998); Michael C. Williams, "Words, Images, Enemies: Securitization and International Politics," *International Studies Quarterly* 47, no. 4 (2003): 511–531; Rita Floyd, *Security and the Environment: Securitization Theory and US Environmental Security Policy* (Cambridge: Cambridge University Press, 2010).
79. Ken Conca and Geoffrey D. Dabelko, eds., *Environmental Peacemaking* (Washington, DC: Woodrow Wilson Center Press; Baltimore: Johns Hopkins University Press, 2002); Ken Conca, "Environmental Cooperation and International Peace," in Paul F. Diehl and Nils Petter Gleditsch, eds., *Environmental Conflict* (Boulder, CO: Westview Press, 2000).
80. EcoPeace / Friends of the Earth Middle East, *Environmental Peacebuilding Theory and Practice: A Case Study of the Good Water Neighbors Project and In Depth Analysis of the Wadi Fukin / Tzur Hadassah Communities*, January 2008, 6. The authors cite as the source for this idea Alexander Carius, *Environmental Peacebuilding: Environmental Cooperation as an Instrument of Crisis Prevention and Peacebuilding: Conditions for Success and Constraints* (Berlin: Adelphi, 2006).
81. Conca, "Environmental Cooperation."
82. United Nations Environment Programme, *Governance for Peace over Natural Resources: A Review of Transitions in Environmental Governance across Africa as a Resource for Peacebuilding and Environmental Management in Sudan* (Nairobi: UNEP, 2013).
83. United Nations Environment Programme, *Post-conflict Environmental Assessment: Côte d'Ivoire* (Nairobi: UNEP, forthcoming).
84. United Nations Environment Programme, United Nations Entity for Gender Equality and the Empowerment of Women, United Nations Peacebuilding Support Office and United Nations Development Programme, *Women and Natural Resources: Unlocking the Peacebuilding Potential* (Nairobi: UNEP, 2013). The author served as a peer reviewer for this report.
85. Oli Brown, "Encouraging Peacebuilding through Better Natural Resources Management," 5. Chatham House policy briefing, December 2013.
86. Brown, "Encouraging Peacebuilding," 5–6.
87. See, for example, the comments of Argentina, Bolivia, Brazil, and Uganda in UN Security Council, *Maintenance of International Peace and Security. Conflict Prevention and Natural Resources*, 19 June 2013. UN Documents S/PV.6982 and S/PV.6982 (resumption 1).
88. Jacob Park, Ken Conca, and Matthias Finger, eds., *The Crisis of Global Environmental Governance: Towards a New Political Economy of Sustainability* (London: Routledge, 2008).
89. "In Tacca's sculpture, atop a fountain composition that forms the centerpiece of the façade of the Royal Palace, the horse rears, and the entire weight of the sculpture balances on the two rear legs—and, discreetly, its tail—a feat that had never been attempted in a figure on a heroic scale." Wikipedia entry for "Equestrian Statue." Available at http://en.wikipedia.org/wiki/Equestrian_statue, viewed 1 February 2010.
90. "Web Gallery of Art: Tacca, Pietro." Available at http://www.wga.hu/frames-e.html?/html/t/tacca/philip4.html, viewed 1 February 2010.

BIBLIOGRAPHY

Abbott, Kenneth W. "Engaging the Public and the Private in Global Sustainability Governance." *International Affairs* 88, no. 3 (May 2012): 543–564.

Abbott, Kenneth W., Robert O. Keohane, Andrew Moravcsik, Anne-Marie Slaughter, and Duncan Snidal. "The Concept of Legalization." *International Organization* 54, no. 3 (Summer 2000): 401–419.

Adger, W. N., J. M. Pulhin, J. Barnett, G. D. Dabelko, G. K. Hovelsrud, M. Levy, Ú. Oswald Spring, and C. H. Vogel. "2014: Human Security." In *Climate Change 2014: Impacts, Adaptation, and Vulnerability. Part A: Global and Sectoral Aspects. Contribution of Working Group II to the Fifth Assessment Report of the Intergovernmental Panel on Climate Change*, 755–791. Cambridge: Cambridge University Press, 2014.

Additional Protocol to the American Convention on Human Rights in the Area of Economic, Social and Cultural Rights. Adopted 17 November 1988, San Salvador, El Salvador.

Adelman, Sam. "Rio+20: Sustainable Injustice in a Time of Crises." *Journal of Human Rights and the Environment* 4, no. 1 (2013): 6–31.

African Charter on Human and Peoples' Rights. Adopted June 1981, Nairobi, Kenya.

Amazon Watch. "The Right to Decide." Amazon Watch Briefing Paper, February 2011. Available at http://amazonwatch.org/assets/files/fpic-the-right-to-decide. pdf, viewed 24 May 2011.

American University. *American University Budget, Fiscal Years 2012 and 2013*. Report from the President adopted by the Board of Trustees, February 25, 2011.

Amnesty International. "Sierra Leone." In *Amnesty International Report 2013: The State of the World's Human Rights*. London: Amnesty International, 2013. Available at http://www.amnesty.org/en/region/sierra-leone/report-2013, viewed 17 November 2014.

Amnesty International and Sierra Club. *Environmentalists under Fire: Ten Urgent Cases of Human Rights Abuses*. London: Amnesty International, 2000.

Araújo, Miguel B., Diogo Alagador, Mar Cabeza, David Nogués-Bravo, and Wilfried Thuiller. "Climate Change Threatens European Conservation Areas." *Ecology Letters* 14, no. 5 (May 2011): 484–492.

Atik, Jeffery. "Commentary on 'The Relationship between Environmental Rights and Environmental Injustice.'" *Human Rights Dialogue* 2, no. 11 (2004): 26–27.

Atlantic Charter. Joint declaration of the governments of the United States and the United Kingdom, 14 August, 1941. Available at http://usinfo.org/docs/democracy/53.htm, viewed 16 June 2011.

Audley, John J. *Green Politics and Global Trade: NAFTA and the Future of Environmental Politics*. Washington, DC: Georgetown University Press, 1997.

Aziakou, Gerard. "UN Spotlights Link between Natural Resources and Conflict." Agence France Presse, 25 June 2007.

Bächler, Günther, and Kurt R. Spillmann, eds. *Environmental Degradation as a Cause of War*. Zurich: Rüegger, 1996.

Bafilemba, Fidel, Timo Mueller, and Sasha Lezhnev. *The Impact of Dodd-Frank and Conflict Minerals Reforms on Eastern Congo's Conflict*. Washington, DC: Enough Project, June 2014.

Bajoria, Jayshree. "The Dilemma of Humanitarian Intervention." Council on Foreign Relations background report, updated 24 March 2011. Available at http://www.cfr.org/human-rights/dilemma-humanitarian-intervention/p16524, viewed 22 July 2012.

Ban Ki-moon. "The First Wave in a Tide of Change." Available at http://www.un.org/works/sub3.asp?lang=en&id=124, viewed 1 March 2011.

Ban Ki-moon. "The Right War." *Time*, 17 April 2008.

Barkley, Katherine, and Steve Weissman. "The Eco-Establishment." In Editors of Ramparts, eds., *Eco-Catastrophe*, 15–24. New York: Harper and Row, 1970.

Barnett, Jon. *Climate Change and Small Island States*. London: Earthscan, 2010.

Barnett, Michael, and Martha Finnemore. *Rules for the World: International Organizations in Global Politics*. Ithaca, NY: Cornell University Press, 2004.

Barry, John, and Robyn Eckersley, eds. *The State and the Global Ecological Crisis*. Cambridge, MA: MIT Press, 2005.

Basel Convention Secretariat. "Parties to the Basel Convention." Available at http://www.basel.int/Countries/StatusofRatifications/PartiesSignatories, viewed 14 November 2014.

Bassey, Nnimmo, Emem Okon, Laura Livoti, and Marc Evans. *The True Cost of Chevron Alternative Annual Report*. May 2011. Excerpted at http://justiceinnigerianow.org/about-chevron, viewed 2 January 2014.

Bauer, Joanne. "Commentary on 'The Conflict between Rights and Environmentalism.'" *Human Rights Dialogue* 2, no. 11 (2004): 19 and 36.

Beevers, Michael D. "Sustaining Peace? Environmental and Natural Resource Governance in Liberia and Sierra Leone." PhD diss., Department of Government and Politics, University of Maryland, 2011.

Benedick, Richard. *Ozone Diplomacy*. 2nd ed. Cambridge, MA: Harvard University Press, 1998.

Benford, Robert D., and David A. Snow. "Framing Processes and Social Movements: An Overview and Assessment." *Annual Review of Sociology* 26 (August 2000): 611–639.

Bernstein, Steven. *The Compromise of Liberal Environmentalism*. New York: Columbia University Press, 2001.

Bernstein, Steven. "Rio+20: Sustainable Development in a Time of Multilateral Decline." *Global Environmental Politics* 13, no. 4 (November 2013): 12–21.

Biermann, F., K. Abbott, S. Andresen, et al. "Navigating the Anthropocene: Improving Earth System Governance." *Science* 335, no. 6074 (March 2012): 1306–1307.

Biermann, Frank, and Steffen Bauer, eds. *A World Environment Organization*. Surrey: Ashgate, 2005.

Biermann, Frank, and Ingrid Boas. "Protecting Climate Refugees: The Case for a Global Protocol." *Environment* 50, no. 6 (2008): 8–16.

Biermann, Frank, and Bernd Siebenhüner. *Managers of Global Change: The Influence of International Environmental Bureaucracies*. Cambridge, MA: MIT Press, 2009.

Biermann, Frank, Bernd Siebenhüner, and Anna Schreyögg, eds. *International Organizations in Global Environmental Governance*. New York: Routledge, 2009.

Birnie, Patricia, and Alan Boyle. *International Law and the Environment*. 2nd ed. Oxford: Oxford University Press, 2002.

Bob, Clifford. *The Marketing of Rebellion*. Cambridge: Cambridge University Press, 2005.

Bodansky, Daniel M. *The Art and Craft of International Environmental Law*. Cambridge, MA: Harvard University Press, 2009.

Boyle, Alan. "Human Rights or Environmental Rights? A Reassessment." *Fordham Environmental Law Review* 18, no. 3 (2007): 471–511.

Breitmeier, Helmut, Arild Underdal, and Oran R. Young. "The Effectiveness of International Environmental Regimes: Comparing and Contrasting Findings from Quantitative Research." *International Studies Review* 13, no. 4 (2011): 579–605.

Breitmeier, Helmut, Oran R. Young, and Michael Zürn. *Analyzing International Regimes: From Case Study to Database*. Cambridge, MA: MIT Press, 2006.

Brown, Mark Malloch. "Power and Super-power: Global Leadership in the Twenty-First Century." Speech to the Century Foundation and Center for American Progress—Security and Peace Initiative, New York, 6 June 2006. Available at http://www.un.org/News/Press/docs/2006/dsgsm287.doc.htm, viewed 20 December 2011.

Brown, Oli. "Encouraging Peacebuilding through Better Natural Resources Management." Chatham House policy briefing, December 2013.

Buck, Susan J. *The Global Commons: An Introduction*. Washington, DC: Island Press, 2012.

Bullard, Robert D., Paul Mohai, Robin Saha, and Beverly Wright. *Toxic Wastes and Race at 20: 1987–2007*. Report prepared for the United Church of Christ Justice and Witness Ministries, 2007.

Buttel, Frederick H., Ann P. Hawkins, and Alison G. Power. "From Limits to Growth to Global Change: Constraints and Contradictions in the Evolution of Environmental Science and Ideology." *Global Environmental Change* 1, no. 1 (December 1990): 57–66.

Butti, Luciano. "The Tortuous Road to Liability: A Critical Survey on Climate Change Litigation in Europe and North America." *Sustainable Development Law and Policy* 11, no. 2 (2011): 32–36, 82–84.

Buzan, Barry, Ole Wæver, and Jaap de Wilde. *Security: A New Framework for Analysis*. Boulder, CO: Lynne Rienner, 1998.

Campese, J., T. C. H. Sunderland, T. Greiber, and G. Oviedo, eds. *Rights-Based Approaches: Exploring Issues and Opportunities for Conservation*. Bogor, Indonesia: Center for International Forestry Research and International Union for Conservation of Nature, 2009.

Capacity Global. "Environmental Justice: A Snapshot." 2009. Available at http://www.capacity.org.uk/downloads/snapshot_for_ej.pdf, viewed 13 July 2010.

CARE International. *Humanitarian Implications of Climate Change: Mapping Emerging Trends and Risk Hotspots*. 2nd ed. Geneva: CARE, November 2009.

Carius, Alexander. *Environmental Peacebuilding: Environmental Cooperation as an Instrument of Crisis Prevention and Peacebuilding: Conditions for Success and Constraints*. Berlin: Adelphi, 2006.

Castro, João Augusto de Araujo. "Environment and Development: The Case of the Developing Countries." In Ken Conca and Geoffrey D. Dabelko, eds., *Green Planet Blues*. 5th ed. Boulder, CO: Westview Press, 2014.

Center for Investigative Reporting. *Global Dumping Ground: The International Traffic in Hazardous Waste*. Washington, DC: Seven Locks Press, 1990.

Chapin, Mac. "A Challenge to Conservationists." *World Watch* 17, no. 6 (November–December 2004): 17–31.

Charter of the United Nations. Signed at the United Nations Conference on International Organization, 26 June 1945, San Francisco.

"Charter Signed for World Peace/Great Conference of United Nations at San Francisco Closes in Triumph." Available at http://www.itnsource.com/shotlist//FoxMovietone/1945/06/28/X28064501/, viewed 15 December 2008.

Chatterjee, Pratap, and Matthias Finger. *The Earth Brokers: Power, Politics and World Development*. New York: Routledge, 1994.

"Chevron Can Be Sued for Attacks on Nigerians, U.S. Judge Rules." *San Francisco Chronicle*, 15 August 2007.

"Chevron Oil Pipeline Attacked in Nigeria." Reuters (US edition), 8 January 2010. Available at www.reuters.com/article/idUSN0826052520100108, viewed 2 January 2014.

Chong, Dennis, and James N. Druckman. "Framing Theory." *Annual Review of Political Science* 10 (June 2007): 103–126.

Clapp, Jennifer. *Toxic Exports: The Transfer of Hazardous Wastes from Rich to Poor Countries*. Ithaca, NY: Cornell University Press, 2001.

Clapp, Jennifer, and Eric Helleiner. "International Political Economy and the Environment: Back to Basics?" *International Affairs* 88, no. 3 (May 2012): 485–501.

Clark, Dana, Jonathan Fox, and Kay Treakle, eds. *Demanding Accountability: Civil-Society Claims and the World Bank Inspection Panel*. Lanham, MD: Rowman & Littlefield, 2003.

Club of Rome. "About the Club of Rome." Available at http://www.clubofrome.org/?p=324, viewed 10 November 2014.

Collier, Paul. *The Bottom Billion: Why the Poorest Countries Are Failing and What Can Be Done about It*. Oxford: Oxford University Press, 2007.

Collier, Paul, and Nicholas Sambanis, eds. *Understanding Civil War: Evidence and Analysis*. Vol. 1: *Africa*. Washington, DC: World Bank, 2005.

Conca, Ken. "Complex Landscapes and Oil Curse Research." *Global Environmental Politics* 13, no. 3 (August 2013): 131–137.

Conca, Ken. "Consumption and Environment in a Global Economy." *Global Environmental Politics* 1, no. 3 (Summer 2001): 53–71.

Conca, Ken. "Decoupling Water and Violent Conflict." *Issues in Science and Technology* 29, no. 1 (Fall 2012): 39–48.

Conca, Ken. "Environmental Cooperation and International Peace." In Paul F. Diehl and Nils Petter Gleditsch, eds., *Environmental Conflict*. Boulder, CO: Westview Press, 2000.

Conca, Ken. "Environmental Governance after Johannesburg: From Stalled Legalization to Environmental Human Rights?" *Journal of International Law and International Relations* 1, nos. 1–2 (2005): 121–138.

Conca, Ken. "Environmental Human Rights: Greening 'the Dignity and Worth of the Human Person.'" In Peter Dauvergne, ed., *Handbook of Global Environmental Politics*. 2nd ed. Cheltenham, UK: Edward Elgar, 2012.

Conca, Ken. *Governing Water: Contentious Transnational Politics and Global Institution Building.* Cambridge, MA: MIT Press, 2006.

Conca, Ken. "Growth and Fragmentation in Expert Networks: The Elusive Quest for Integrated Water Resources Management." In Peter Dauvergne, ed., *Handbook of Global Environmental Politics.* Cheltenham, UK: Edward Elgar, 2005.

Conca, Ken. "In the Name of Sustainability: Peace Studies and Environmental Discourse." *Peace and Change* 19, no. 2 (April 1994): 91–113.

Conca, Ken. "The Rise of the Regional in Global Environmental Politics." *Global Environmental Politics* 12, no. 3 (August 2012): 127–133.

Conca, Ken, and Geoffrey D. Dabelko, eds. *Environmental Peacemaking.* Washington, DC: Woodrow Wilson Center Press; Baltimore: Johns Hopkins University Press, 2002.

Conca, Ken, and Jennifer Wallace. "Environment and Peacebuilding in War-Torn Societies: Lessons from the UN Environment Programme's Experience with Postconflict Assessment." *Global Governance* 15, no. 4 (October–December 2009): 485–504.

CongoForum. "History." Available at http://www.congoforum.be/en/congodetail.asp?subitem=21&id=147996&Congofiche=selected, viewed 4 August 2011.

Constitution of the World Health Organization. Adopted by the International Health Conference, New York, 22 July 1946.

Convention on Biological Diversity. Adopted at the United Nations Conference on Environment and Development, 5 June 1992, Rio de Janeiro, Brazil.

Counterspill. "Ecuador vs. Chevron-Texaco: A Brief History." Available at http://www.counterspill.org/article/ecuador-vs-chevron-texaco-brief-history, viewed 2 January 2014.

Dalton, Dennis, ed. *Mahatma Gandhi: Selected Political Writings.* Cambridge, MA: Hackett, 1996.

Dalton, Russell J., ed. *Critical Masses: Citizens, Nuclear Weapons Production, and Environmental Destruction in the United States and Russia.* Cambridge, MA: MIT Press, 1999.

de Melo, Jaime, Jean-Marie Grether, and Nicole Mathys. "Identifying the Worldwide Pollution Haven Effect." *Vox,* 23 December 2010. Available at http://voxeu.org/index.php?q=node/5961, viewed 6 January 2014.

Dean, Judith M., Mary E. Lovely, and Hua Wang. "Are Foreign Investors Attracted to Weak Environmental Regulations? Evaluating the Evidence from China." *Journal of Development Economics* 90, no. 1 (2009): 1–13.

Declaration of Members of the Indigenous Peoples' Biocultural Climate Change Assessment (IPCCA) Initiative, Durban, South Africa, 26 November 2011. Available at www.redd-monitor.org/2011/11/28/redd-threatens-the-survival-of-indigenous-peoples-new-statement-from-indigenous-peoples-rejects-redd/, viewed 26 November 2013.

Deen, Thalif. "RIO+20: Promised Green Economy Was a Fake, Say Activists." Inter Press Service News Agency, 22 June 2012. Available at http://www.ipsnews.net/2012/06/rio20-promised-green-economy-was-a-fake-say-activists/, viewed 1 December 2014.

Development Co-operation Directorate. *Preventing Violence, War and State Collapse: The Future of Conflict Early Warning and Response.* Paris: OECD, 2009.

Dinar, Shlomi, David Katz, Lucia De Stefano, and Brian Blankespoor. "Climate Change, Conflict, and Cooperation: Global Analysis of the Resilience of

International River Treaties to Increased Water Variability." World Bank Policy Research Paper 6916, June 2014.

Dorsey, Ellen, Mayra Gómez, Bret Thiele, and Paul Nelson. "Falling Short of Our Goals: Transforming the Millennium Development Goals into Millennium Development Rights." *Netherlands Quarterly of Human Rights* 28, no. 4 (2010): 516–522.

Dowie, Mark. *Losing Ground.* Cambridge, MA: MIT Press, 1995.

Doyle, Timothy. "Sustainable Development and Agenda 21: The Secular Bible of Global Free Markets and Pluralist Democracy." *Third World Quarterly* 19, no. 4 (1998): 771–786.

Dranginis, Holly, and Sasha Lezhnev. "Nine Things You Need to Know about Conflict Minerals." Blog post to ThinkProgress, 4 December 2014. Available at http://thinkprogress.org/economy/2014/12/04/3599824/conflict-minerals-enough/, viewed 11 December 2014.

Dutch Section of the International Commission of Jurists. *2011 OHCHR Study: Human Rights and the Environment.* Stakeholder input by the Dutch Section of the International Commission of Jurists, June 2011.

"The Earth Charter." Adopted by the Earth Charter Commission, Paris France, March 2000. Available at http://www.earthcharterinaction.org, viewed 26 June 2013.

EarthJustice. *Environmental Rights Report* 2007. Oakland, CA: EarthJustice, 2007.

EarthJustice. *Environmental Rights Report* 2008. Oakland, CA: EarthJustice, 2008.

EarthJustice. *Environmental Rights Report: Human Rights and the Environment.* Oakland, CA: EarthJustice, 2005.

Ecologist, The *Whose Common Future? Reclaiming the Commons.* British Columbia: New Society Publishers, 1993.

Economic Commission for Latin America and the Caribbean. "Countries of the Region Approve Launching Negotiation of a Common Agreement on Rights of Access in Environmental Matters." Press release, 6 November 2014. Available at http://www.cepal.org/en/pressreleases/countries-region-approve-launching-^negotiation-common-agreement-rights-access, viewed 20 November, 2014.

EcoPeace / Friends of the Earth Middle East. *Environmental Peacebuilding Theory and Practice: A Case Study of the Good Water Neighbors Project and In Depth Analysis of the Wadi Fukin / Tzur Hadassah Communities.* January 2008.

Edwards, Rob. "World Summit Teeters on Brink of Failure." *New Scientist* 30 (August 2002). Available at http://www.newscientist.com/article/dn2744-world-summit-teeters-on-brink-of-failure.html, viewed 13 May 2013.

Environmental Politics 11, issue 1 (2002). Special edition on Green parties in Western Europe.

Excelle, Carole, and Consuela Fernandez. "Open Government Partnership: It's Time for Deeper Engagement with the Environment Sector." Blog post, World Resources Institute, 21 November 2013. Available at http://www.wri.org/blog/open-government-partnership-it%E2%80%99s-time-deeper-engagement-environment-sector, viewed 14 February 2014.

Extractive Industries Transparency Initiative. "Central African Republic." Available at http://eiti.org/CentralAfricanRepublic, viewed 7 August 2012.

Faramelli, Norman J. "Toying with the Environment and the Poor: A Report on the Stockholm Environmental Conference." *Boston College Environmental Affairs Law Review* 2, no. 3 (1972): 469–486.

Fiji Government, Strategic Framework for Change Coordinating Office. "PM's Office Partners with UNDP in Finding Solutions to Resource Based Conflicts." Available at http://www.sfcco.gov.fj/index.php?option=com_content&view=article&id=34:pms-office-partners-with-undp-in-finding-solutions-to-resource-based-conflicts&catid=32:header-stories&Itemid=68, viewed 12 August 2012.

Final Communiqué of the Asian-African Conference of Bandung, 24 April 1955. Available at http://www.bandungspirit.org/IMG/pdf/Final_Communique_Bandung_1955.pdf, viewed 20 December 2011.

Finnemore, Martha. *National Interest in International Society*. Ithaca, NY: Cornell University Press, 1996.

Finnemore, Martha, and Kathryn Sikkink. "International Norm Dynamics and Political Change." *International Organization* 52, no. 4 (Autumn 1998): 887–917.

Fischer, Alex, and Marc A. Levy. "Designing Environmental Restoration Programs in Politically Fragile States: Lessons from Haiti." In Carl Bruch, Mikiyasu Nakayama, and Ilona Coyle, eds., *Harnessing Natural Resources for Peacebuilding: Lessons from U.S. and Japanese Assistance*. Washington, DC: Environmental Law Institute, 2011.

Florini, Ann. "The End of Secrecy." *Foreign Policy* 111 (Summer 1998): 50–63.

Floyd, Rita. *Security and the Environment: Securitization Theory and US Environmental Security Policy*. Cambridge: Cambridge University Press, 2010.

Food and Agriculture Organization of the United Nations. "Countries Adopt Global Guidelines on Tenure of Land, Forests, Fisheries." Press release, 11 May 2012. Available at http://www.fao.org/news/story/en/item/142587/icode/, viewed 26 May 2013.

Food and Agriculture Organization of the United Nations. *Voluntary Guidelines to Support the Progressive Realization of the Right to Adequate Food in the Context of National Food Security*. Rome: FAO, 2005.

FoodFirst Information and Action Network. "FAO Tenure Guidelines a Modest Step, Governments Must Commit to Implementation." 15 May 2012. Available at http://humanrightshouse.org/Articles/18029.html, viewed 26 May 2013.

Forest Carbon Partnership Facility and UN-REDD Programme. "Guidelines on Stakeholder Engagement in REDD+ Readiness with a Focus on the Participation of Indigenous Peoples and Other Forest-Dependent Communities." 20 April 2012.

Foti, Joseph, with Lalanath de Silva, Heather McGray, Linda Shaffer, Jonathan Talbot, and Jacob Werksman. *Voice and Choice: Opening the Door to Environmental Democracy*. Washington, DC: World Resources Institute, 2008.

The Founex Report on Development and Environment. Adopted by the Founex Conference, 4–12 June 1971, Founex, Switzerland.

Fox, Jonathan. "Social Accountability: What Does the Evidence Really Say?" Global Partnership for Social Accountability and World Bank, September 2014, GPSA Working Paper No. 1.

Franze, Juliane, and Andreas Ciroth. "A Comparison of Cut Roses from Ecuador and the Netherlands." *International Journal of Life Cycle Assessment* 16, no. 4 (May 2011): 366–379.

Freedom House. *2014 Freedom in the World*. Available at https://freedomhouse.org/report-types/freedom-world#.VGo39sntoYQ, viewed 17 November 2014.

Friends Committee on National Legislation. *Central African Republic Crisis: Managing Natural Resources for Peace*. Washington, DC: FCNL, November 2014.

The Future We Want. Outcome document of the United Nations Conference on Sustainable Development, Rio de Janeiro, 19 June 2012. Available at http://www.un.org/en/sustainablefuture/index.shtml, viewed 14 July 2012.

Gage, Andrew, and Michael Byers. *Payback Time? What the Internationalization of Climate Litigation Could Mean for Canadian Oil and Gas Companies.* Ottawa: Canadian Center for Policy Alternatives, October 2014.

Gamble, John, Jr. "The Third United Nations Conference on the Law of the Sea and the New International Economic Order." *Loyola of Los Angeles International and Comparative Law Review* 6 (1983): 65–80.

Gibbs, David N. "Dag Hammarskjöld, the United Nations, and the Congo Crisis of 1960–1: A Reinterpretation." *Journal of Modern African Studies* 31, no. 1 (March 1993): 163–174.

Gibbs, David N. "Review: Misrepresenting the Congo Crisis." *African Affairs* 95, no. 380 (July 1996): 453–459.

Gleditsch, Nils Petter. "Armed Conflict and the Environment." In Paul F. Diehl and Nils Petter Gleditsch, eds., *Environmental Conflict.* Boulder, CO: Westview Press, 2001.

Gleick, Peter H. "The Human Right to Water." *Water Policy* 1, no. 5 (1998): 487–503.

Gleick, Peter H. "The Human Right to Water." Oakland, CA: Pacific Institute, 2007. Available at http://www.pacinst.org/reports/human_right_may_07.pdf, viewed 30 December 2011.

Global Centre for the Responsibility to Protect. "UN Security Council Resolutions Referencing R2P." Available at http://www.globalr2p.org/resources/335, viewed 10 February 2014.

Global Footprint Network. "Highlights of California's First Ecological Footprint Report." Available at http://www.footprintnetwork.org/en/index.php/newsletter/det/ca, viewed 30 December 2013.

Global Policy Forum. "NGO letter to the UN Secretary General's High-level Panel on Threats, Challenges and Change, October 11, 2004." Available at http://www.globalpolicy.org/security/natres/generaldebate/2004/1011highlevel.htm, viewed 10 February 2011.

Global Policy Forum. "NGO Proposals on Natural Resources and Conflict." Available at http://www.globalpolicy.org/component/content/article/198/40111.html, viewed 10 February 2011.

Global Policy Forum. "UN Reform." Available at https://www.globalpolicy.org/un-reform.html, viewed 1 December 2014.

Global Witness. *Coming Clean: How Supply Chain Controls Can Stop Congo's Minerals Trade Fueling Conflict.* London: Global Witness, May 2012.

Global Witness. *Deadly Environment: The Dramatic Rise in Killings of Environmental and Land Defenders.* London: Global Witness, 2014.

Global Witness. "Definition of Conflict Resources." Available at http://www.globalpolicy.org/component/content/article/198/40124.html, viewed 10 February 2011.

Global Witness. "Global Witness Open Letter to the UN Security Council, Regarding Conflict Resources and Peacekeeping in Liberia and the Democratic Republic of Congo." 18 March 2005. Available at http://www.globalpolicy.org/component/content/article/198/40117.html, viewed 10 February 2011.

Global Witness. *Lessons UNlearned: How the UN and Member States Must Do More to End Natural Resource-Fuelled Conflicts.* London: Global Witness, January 2010.

Gorbachev, Mikhail. Address to the Forty-Third Session of the United Nations General Assembly, 7 December 1988.

Government of Sierra Leone. *Biodiversity: Strategic Action Plan*, 2003. Available at http://www.cbd.int/countries/profile/default.shtml?country=sl#nbsap, viewed 2 January 2014.

Grove, Richard H. *Green Imperialism: Colonial Expansion, Tropical Island Edens and the Origins of Environmentalism*, 1600–1860. Cambridge: Cambridge University Press, 1995.

Gupta, Aarti. "Transparency under Scrutiny: Information Disclosure in Global Environmental Governance." *Global Environmental Politics* 8, no. 2 (May 2008): 1–8.

Gupta, Aarti, and Michael Mason, eds. *Transparency in Global Environmental Governance: Critical Perspectives*. Cambridge, MA: MIT Press, 2014.

Haas, Ernst B. *When Knowledge Is Power: Three Models of Change in International Organizations*. Berkeley: University of California Press, 1990.

Halle, Mark. "Life after Rio: A Commentary." International Institute for Sustainable Development, June 2012.

Harper, Krista, Tamara Steger, and Richard Filcak. "Environmental Justice and Roma Communities in Central and Eastern Europe." *Environmental Policy and Governance* 19, no. 4 (2009): 251–268.

Harsh, E. "Conflict Resources: From 'Curse' to Blessing." *Africa Renewal* 20, no. 4 (2007): 17.

Hartmann, Elizabeth. "Strategic Scarcity: The Origins and Impact of Environmental Conflict Ideas." PhD diss., London School of Economics, 2002.

Hawkins, Darren G., David A. Lake, Daniel L. Nielson, and Michael J. Tierney, eds. *Delegation and Agency in International Organizations*. Cambridge: Cambridge University Press, 2006.

Hazareesingh, Sandip. "Cotton, Climate and Colonialism in Dharwar, Western India, 1840–1880." *Journal of Historical Geography* 38, no. 1 (January 2012): 1–17.

Helm, Carsten, and Detlef Sprinz. "Measuring the Effectiveness of International Environmental Regimes." *Journal of Conflict Resolution* 45, no. 5 (2000): 630–652.

High-Level Panel on Threats, Challenges, and Change. *A More Secure World: Report of the Secretary-General's High-Level Panel on Threats, Challenges and Change*. New York: United Nations, 2004.

Hodgkinson, David, Tess Burton, Heather Anderson, and Lucy Young. "'The Hour When the Ship Comes In': A Convention for Persons Displaced by Climate Change." *Monash University Law Review* 36, no. 1 (2010): 69–120.

Homer-Dixon, Thomas F. "Environmental Scarcities and Violent Conflict: Evidence from Cases." *International Security* 19, no. 1 (Summer 1994): 5–40.

Hopwood, Bill, Mary Mellor, and Geoff O'Brien. "Sustainable Development: Mapping Different Approaches." *Sustainable Development* 13, no. 1 (February 2005): 38–52.

Horne, Ralph E. "Limits to Labels: The Role of Eco-labels in the Assessment of Product Sustainability and Routes to Sustainable Consumption." *International Journal of Consumer Studies* 33, no. 2 (March 2009): 175–182.

Hovi, Jon, Detlef Sprinz, and Arild Underdal. "The Oslo-Potsdam Solution to Measuring Regime Effectiveness: Critique, Response, and the Road Ahead." *Global Environmental Politics* 3, no. 3 (2003):74–96.

"How a Well-Intentioned U.S. Law Left Congolese Miners Jobless." *Washington Post*, 30 November 2014, A-1.

Human Development Report Office. Occasional Paper 2006/9. United Nations Development Programme, 2006. Available at http://hdr.undp.org/en/reports/global/hdr2006/papers/Mehta_L_rev.pdf, viewed 30 December 2011.

Human Rights and Environment: Stakeholder Input by the Dutch Section of the International Commission of Jurists (NJCM). June 2011.

Hurd, Ian. "Legitimacy and Authority in International Politics." *International Organization* 53, no. 2 (March 1999): 379–408.

"Indonesian-Swiss Country-Led Initiative on an Informal Process to Improve the Effectiveness of the Basel Convention." Presentation at the GEN Mission Briefing on the COP 10 of the Basel Convention, 14 September 2011, Geneva.

Informal Consultative Process on the Institutional Framework for the United Nations' Environmental Activities. Co-chairs' Options Paper, 14 June 2007.

Intergovernmental Panel on Climate Change. *Climate Change 2014 Synthesis Report: Summary for Policy Makers*. Geneva: IPCC, 2014.

International Court of Justice. *Reports of Judgments, Advisory Opinions and Orders: Case Concerning Armed Activities on the Territory of the Congo (Democratic Republic of the Congo v. Uganda), Judgment of 19 December 2005*.

International Covenant on Civil and Political Rights. Adopted and opened for signature, ratification, and accession by General Assembly resolution 2200A (XXI) of 16 December 1966. Entry into force 23 March 1976.

International Covenant on Economic, Social and Cultural Rights. Adopted and opened for signature, ratification, and accession by General Assembly resolution 2200A (XXI) of 16 December 1966. Entry into force 3 January 1976.

International Crisis Group. "Dangerous Little Stones: Diamonds in the Central African Republic." ICG Africa Report No. 167, 16 December 2010.

International Institute for Sustainable Development. "Summary of the 26th Session of the UN Environment Programme Governing Council/Global Ministerial Environment Forum: 21–24 February 2011." *Earth Negotiations Bulletin* 16, no. 89 (28 February 2011).

International Institute for Sustainable Development. "Summary of the Eighth Session of the UN General Assembly Open Working Group on Sustainable Development Goals: 3–7 February 2014." *Earth Negotiations Bulletin* 32, no. 8 (10 February 2014).

International Institute for Sustainable Development. "Summary of the Lima Climate Change Conference: 1–14 December 2014." *Earth Negotiations Bulletin* 12, no. 619 (16 December 2014).

International Institute for Sustainable Development. "Summary of the Sixth Session of the UN General Assembly Open Working Group on Sustainable Development Goals: 9–13 December 2013." *Earth Negotiations Bulletin* 32, no. 6 (16 December 2013).

International Institute for Sustainable Development. "The Twentieth Session of the Governing Council of the United Nations Environmental Programme." *Earth Negotiations Bulletin* 16, no. 6 (8 February 1999).

International Law Commission. *Fifth Report on the Protection of Persons in the Event of Disasters*. UN Document A/CN.4/652, 9 April 2012.

International Maritime Organization. "History of the IMO." Available at http://www.imo.org/About/HistoryOfIMO/Pages/Default.aspx, viewed 28 December 2011.

International Organization 54, no. 3 (Summer 2000). Special edition on legalization and world politics.

International Union for the Conservation of Nature and Natural Resources. *World Conservation Strategy: Living Resource Conservation for Sustainable Development*. Gland, Switzerland: IUCN, 1980.

Ivanova, Maria. "The Contested Legacy of Rio+20." *Global Environmental Politics* 13, no. 4 (November 2013): 1–11.

Jackson, Robert B., Stephen R. Carpenter, Clifford N. Dahm, Diane M. McKnight, Robert J. Naiman, Sandra L. Postel, and Steven W. Running. "Water in a Changing World." *Ecological Applications* 11, no. 4 (August 2001): 1027–1045.

Jacquet, Jennifer, John Hocevar, Sherman Lai, Patricia Majluf, Nathan Pelletier, Tony Pitcher, Enric Sala, Rashid Sumaila, and Daniel Pauly. "Conserving Wild Fish in a Sea of Market-Based Efforts." *Oryx* 44, no. 1 (January 2010): 45–56.

Jinnah, Sikina. *Post-treaty Politics: Secretariat Influence in Global Environmental Governance*. Cambridge, MA: MIT Press, 2014.

Johnson, Tana. *Organizational Progeny: Why Governments Are Losing Control over the Proliferating Structures of Global Governance*. New York: Oxford University Press, 2014.

Jolly, Richard, Louis Emmerij, and Thomas G. Weiss. *The Power of UN Ideas: Lessons from the First 60 Years*. New York: United Nations Intellectual History Project, 2005.

Jolly, Richard, Louis Emmerij, and Thomas G. Weiss. *UN Ideas That Changed the World*. Bloomington: Indiana University Press, 2009.

Kanie, Norichika. "Governance with Multilateral Environmental Agreements: A Healthy or Ill-Equipped Fragmentation?" In Lydia Swart and Estelle Siegal Perry, eds., *Global Environmental Governance: Perspectives on the Current Debate*. New York: Center for UN Reform Education, 2007.

Keck, Margaret, and Kathryn Sikkink. *Activists beyond Borders: Advocacy Networks in International Politics*. Ithaca, NY: Cornell University Press, 1998.

Knox, John H. "Linking Human Rights and Climate Change at the United Nations." *Harvard Environmental Law Review* 33 (2009): 477–498.

Koh, Harold Hongju. "Why Do Nations Obey International Law?" *Yale Law Journal* 106 (1997): 2599–2659.

Koivurova, Timo, Sébastien Duyck, and Leena Heinämäki. "Climate Change and Human Rights." In Erkki J. Hollo, Kati Kulovesi, and Michael Mehling, eds., *Climate Change and the Law*, 287–325. Dordrecht: Springer, 2013.

Krasno, Jean. "Former Secretary-General Kofi Annan: International Law and the Bully Pulpit in Norm Creation." Paper presented at the Annual Meeting of the International Studies Association, Montreal, March 2011.

Krasno, Jean. "The Founding of the United Nations: International Cooperation as an Evolutionary Process." Academic Council of the United Nations System, Occasional Paper no. 1, 2001.

Krummenacher, Heinz. "Economic and Environmental Early Warning for Confidence Building and Conflict Prevention." Discussion paper, OSCE-Chairmanship Workshop on Economic and Environmental Activities as Confidence-Building Measures, Vienna, 30 May 2011.

Kumar, C. Raj. "National Human Rights Institutions (NHRIs) and Economic, Social and Cultural Rights: Toward the Institutionalization and Developmentalization of Human Rights." *Human Rights Quarterly* 28, no. 3 (August 2006): 755–779.

Kumar, P., ed. *The Economics of Ecosystems and Biodiversity: Ecological and Economic Foundations*. Washington, DC: Earthscan, 2010.

Lang, Chris. "Discriminatory Forestry Regulations and REDD Projects in Indonesia." Posted to redd-monitor.org, 24 February 2012. Available at http://www.redd-monitor.org/2012/02/24/discriminatory-forestry-regulations-and-redd-projects-in-indonesia/

Le Billon, Philippe. "Natural Resources, Armed Conflicts, and the UN Security Council." Paper presented at the Seminar on Natural Resources and Armed Conflicts, United Nations Headquarters, New York, 21 May 2007.

Lehtonen, Matti. "Peacebuilding through Natural Resource Management: The UN Peacebuilding Commission's First Five Years." In Carl Bruch, Carroll Muffett, and Sandra S. Nichols, eds., *Governance, Natural Resources, and Post-conflict Peacebuilding*. New York: Routledge, 2015.

Lélé, Sharachchandra M. "Sustainable Development: A Critical Review." *World Development* 19, no. 6 (June 1991): 607–621.

Levin, Kelly, Benjamin Cashore, Steven Bernstein, and Graeme Auld. "Overcoming the Tragedy of Super Wicked Problems: Constraining Our Future Selves to Ameliorate Global Climate Change." *Policy Sciences* 45, no. 2 (2012): 123–152.

Levy, Marc A. "Is the Environment a Security Issue?" *International Security* 20, no. 2 (Fall 1995): 35–62.

Levy, Marc A., and Patrick Philippe Meier. "Early Warning and Assessment of Environment, Conflict, and Cooperation." In United Nations Environment Programme, *Understanding Environmental Conflict and Cooperation*, 38–47. Nairobi: UNEP and Washington, DC: Woodrow Wilson Center, 2004.

Lipschutz, Ronnie D. *When Nations Clash: Raw Materials, Ideology and Foreign Policy*. New York: Ballinger, 1989.

Litfin, Karen T. *Ozone Discourses*. New York: Columbia University Press, 1994.

Lohmann, Larry. "Whose Common Future?" *Ecologist* 20, no. 3 (May–June 1990): 82–84.

Maier, Jürgen. "18 Months after Rio+20—Did the Conference Have Any Impact at All?" *Future of Food: Journal on Food, Agriculture and Society* 1, no. 2 (Winter 2013): 119–121.

"Male' Declaration on the Human Dimensions of Global Climate Change." Adopted at Male', Republic of Maldives, 14 November 2007.

Malone, Linda A. "Green Helmets: A Conceptual Framework for Security Council Authority in Environmental Emergencies." William & Mary Law School, Faculty Publications, Paper 599, 1996.

Mani, Rama. "Peaceful Settlement of Disputes and Conflict Prevention." In Thomas G. Weiss and Sam Daws, eds., *The Oxford Handbook on the United Nations*. Oxford: Oxford University Press, 2007.

Manley, Michael. *The Poverty of Nations: Reflections on Underdevelopment and the World Economy*. London: Pluto Press, 1991.

Margulis, Lynn. *The Symbiotic Planet: A New Look at Evolution*. New York: Basic Books, 1999.

Martin, Adrian. "Environmental Conflict between Refugee and Host Communities." *Journal of Peace Research* 42, no. 3 (2005): 329–346.

Mathews, Jessica Tuchman. "Redefining Security." *Foreign Affairs* 68, no. 2 (Spring 1989): 162–177.

McAdam, Doug. *Political Process and the Development of Black Insurgency*, 1930–1970. Chicago: University of Chicago Press, 1999.

McCormick, John. *Reclaiming Paradise: The Global Environmental Movement.* Bloomington: Indiana University Press, 1989.

McInnes, Colin. "HIV/AIDS and Security." *International Affairs* 82, no. 2 (2006): 315–326.

Mehta, Lyla, ed. *The Limits to Scarcity: Contesting the Politics of Allocation.* New York: Routledge, 2010.

Mehta, Lyla, Gert Jan Veldwisch, and Jennifer Franco. "Introduction to the Special Issue: Water Grabbing? Focus on the (Re)Appropriation of Finite Water Resources." *Water Alternatives* 5, no. 2 (June 2012): 193–207.

Mertus, Julie A. *The United Nations and Human Rights.* London: Routledge, 2005.

Miles, Edward L., Steinar Andresen, Elaine M. Carlin, Jon Birger Skjærseth, Arild Underdal, and Jørgen Wettestad. *International Regime Effectiveness: Confronting Theory with Evidence.* Cambridge, MA: MIT Press, 2002.

Mining Working Group at the UN. "A Rights-Based Approach to Resource Extraction in the Pursuit of Sustainable Development." Advocacy brief, no date. Available at http://miningwg.com/resources-2/mwg-advocacy-brief/, viewed 1 December 2014.

Mitchell, Ronald B. *International Environmental Agreements Database Project (Version 2010.3).* Available at: http://iea.uoregon.edu/, viewed 9 August 2011.

Mitchell, Ronald B. "Problem Structure, Institutional Design, and the Relative Effectiveness of International Environmental Agreements." *Global Environmental Politics* 6, no. 3 (August 2006): 72–89.

Mitchell, Ronald B. "Regime Design Matters: Intentional Oil Pollution and Treaty Compliance." *International Organization* 48, no. 3 (Summer 1994): 425–458.

Morrow, Karen. "Rio+20: A Critique." *Journal of Human Rights and the Environment* 4, no. 1. (2013): 1–5.

Murphy, Craig N. *Emergence of the NIEO Ideology.* Boulder, CO: Westview Press, 1994.

Murphy, Craig N. *International Organization and Industrial Change: Global Governance since 1850.* Cambridge: Polity Press, 1994.

Murphy, Craig N. *The UN Development Programme: A Better Way?* Cambridge: Cambridge University Press, 2006.

Naidoo Kumi. Tweet via @kuminaidoo, 9:06 AM, 19 June 2012. Available at https://twitter.com/kuminaidoo/status/215113320632561664, viewed 1 December 2014.

Najam, Adil. "Developing Countries and Global Environmental Governance: From Contestation to Participation to Engagement. *International Environmental Agreements* 5, no. 3 (September 2005): 303–321.

National Intelligence Council. *The Global Infectious Disease Threat and Its Implications for the United States,* January 2000.

"Natural Resources Management in Post-conflict Countries." Online course available at http://stream.unitar.org/ptp/StartCourse/player.html, viewed 9 August 2012.

Nelson, Paul. *The World Bank and Non-governmental Organizations: The Limits of Apolitical Development.* New York: St. Martin's, 1995.

Newell, Peter. *Globalization and the Environment: Capitalism, Ecology and Power.* New York: Polity Press, 2012.

Newell, Peter. "New Environmental Architectures and the Search for Effectiveness." *Global Environmental Politics* 1, no. 1 (February 2001): 35–44.

Nixon, Edgar B., ed. *Franklin D. Roosevelt and Conservation, 1911–1945.* Vol. 2. New York: Franklin D. Roosevelt Library, 1957.

Non-Aligned Movement. The Declaration of the 3rd Summit of the Heads of State or Government of the Member Countries of the Non-Aligned Movement, issued on 8–10 September 1970. In Institute of Foreign Affairs, *Summit Declarations of Non-Aligned Movement* (1961–2009). Tripureshwor, Kathmandu: IFA, 2011.

North Atlantic Treaty Organization. "Topic: Environmental Security." Available at http://www.nato.int/cps/en/natolive/topics_49216.htm, viewed 26 July 2012.

"Observations by the United States of America on the Relationship between Climate Change and Human Rights." Comments submitted by the Government of the United States to the Office of the High Commissioner for Human Rights, no date.

Office of the Director of National Intelligence, Global Water Security. Intelligence Community Assessment ICA 2012-08, 2 February 2012.

Olagbaju, Folabi K., and Stephen Mills. "Defending Environmental Defenders." *Human Rights Dialogue* 2, no. 11 (2004): 32–33.

Oman, Natalie. "The Responsibility to Prevent: A Remit for Interventionism?" *Canadian Journal of Law and Jurisprudence* 22, no. 2 (2009): 335–380.

Open Working Group on Sustainable Development Goals. "Compilation of Goals and Targets Suggestions from OWG-10 in Response to Co-chairs' Focus Area Document dated 19 March, 2014." 19 April 2014.

Orellana, Marcos. "Statement to the UN Human Rights Council." Nineteenth Session, 1 March 2012.

Organisation for Economic Co-operation and Development. "Financing Water and Sanitation in Developing Countries: The Contribution of External Aid." Available at http://webnet.oecd.org/dcdgraphs/water/, viewed 25 November 2013.

Organization of American States. "Human Rights and Climate Change in the Americas." AG/RES.2429 (XXXVIII-O/08), adopted at the Fourth Plenary Session, 3 June 2008.

Paris, Roland. *At War's End: Building Peace after Civil Conflict.* Cambridge: Cambridge University Press, 2004.

Park, Jacob, Ken Conca, and Matthias Finger, eds., *The Crisis of Global Environmental Governance: Towards a New Political Economy of Sustainability.* London: Routledge, 2008.

Park, Jacob, Ken Conca, and Matthias Finger. "The Death of Rio Environmentalism." In Jacob Park, Ken Conca, and Matthias Finger, eds., *The Crisis of Global Environmental Governance: Toward a New Political Economy of Sustainability.* New York: Routledge, 2009.

Parson, Edward A. *Protecting the Ozone Layer.* New York: Oxford University Press, 2003.

Peacebuilding Centre. *Peace and Conflict Impact Assessment Handbook, Version 4.* Ottawa: Peacebuilding Centre, 2013.

Pearce, Fred. "Beyond Rio's Disappointment, Finding a Path to the Future." *Environment 360*, 28 June 2012. Available at http://e360.yale.edu/feature/beyond_rios_disappointment_finding_a_path_to_the_future/2547/, viewed 6 June 2013.

Peluso, Nancy Lee. "Coercing Conservation." In Ronnie D. Lipschutz and Ken Conca, eds., *The State and Social Power in Global Environmental Politics*. New York: Columbia University Press, 1993.

Peluso, Nancy Lee, and Michael Watts, eds. *Violent Environments*. Ithaca, NY: Cornell University Press, 2001.

Permanent Mission of Fiji to the United Nations. "Statement at the UN Security Council Debate on Women, Peace and Security (UNSCR 1325)." New York, 29 November 2012. Available at http://www.fijiprun.org/node/22, viewed 30 May 2013.

Permanent Mission of Germany to the United Nations. Security Council Presidential Statement, July 20, 2011.

Perrez, Franz Xaver. "The Relationship between 'Permanent Sovereignty' and the Obligation Not to Cause Transboundary Environmental Damage." *Environmental Law* 26, no. 4 (1996): 1207–1249.

Petition to the Inter American Commission on Human Rights Seeking Relief from Violations Resulting from Global Warming Caused by Acts and Omissions of the United States, 7 December 2005. Available at www.inuitcircumpolar.com/files/uploads/icc-files/FINALPetitionICC.pdf, viewed 25 November 2013.

Pillay, Navanethem. Open letter of Navanethem Pillay, High Commissioner for Human Rights, to UN member-states, 30 March 2012.

Pohl, Benjamin, Alexander Carius, Ken Conca, Geoffrey D. Dableko, Annika Kramer, David Michel, Susanne Schmeier, Ashok Swain, and Aaron Wolf. *The Rise of Hydro-diplomacy: Strengthening Foreign Policy for Transboundary Waters*. Berlin: Adelphi Research and Federal Foreign Office, 2014.

Price, Richard. "Reversing the Gun Sights: Transnational Civil Society Targets Land Mines." *International Organization* 52, no. 3 (Summer 1998): 613–644.

Prins, Gwyn. "AIDS and Global Security." *International Affairs* 80, no. 5 (2004): 931–952.

Rajagopal, Balakrishnan. "Human Rights and Development: Legal and Policy Issues with Special Reference to Dams." Contributing Paper, World Commission on Dams, no date.

Rajagopal, Balakrishnan. *International Law from Below: Development, Social Movements, and Third World Resistance*. Cambridge: Cambridge University Press, 2003.

Ramadhani, A. "Promoting Good Forest Governance for Sustainable Livelihood Improvement: A Tanzanian Example." *Unasylva* 234–235, no. 61 (2010): 54–59.

Raynolds, Laura T. "Fair Trade Flowers: Global Certification, Environmental Sustainability, and Labor Standards." *Rural Sociology* 77, no. 4 (December 2012): 493–519.

Redclift, Michael. "Sustainable Development (1987–2005): An Oxymoron Comes of Age." *Sustainable Development* 13, no. 4 (October 2005): 212–227.

Report of the Panel of Experts on the Illegal Exploitation of Natural Resources and Other Forms of Wealth of the Democratic Republic of the Congo. 2001.

Report of the United Nations Water Conference, Mar del Plata, March 14–25, 1977, UN Document E.77.II.A.12.

Rich, Bruce. *Mortgaging the Earth: The World Bank, Environmental Impoverishment, and the Crisis of Development*. Boston: Beacon Press, 1994.

Richardson, Dick, and Chris Rootes, eds. *The Green Challenge: The Development of Green Parties in Europe.* London: Routledge, 1995.

Rittel, Horst W. J., and Melvin M. Webber. "Dilemmas in a General Theory of Planning." *Policy Sciences* 4, no. 2 (1973): 155–169.

Rolnik, Raquel. Comments to the UN Human Rights Council, Eleventh Session, Panel on Human Rights and Climate Change. Geneva, 15 June 2009. Webcast available at http://www.un.org/webcast/unhrc/archive.asp?go=090615, viewed 25 May 2011.

Ross, Michael. "A Closer Look at Oil, Diamonds, and Civil War." *Annual Review of Political Science* 9 (2006): 265–300.

Ross, Michael. *The Oil Curse: How Petroleum Wealth Shapes the Development of Nations.* Princeton, NJ: Princeton University Press, 2012.

Rushton, Simon. "Framing AIDS: Securitization, Development-ization, Rights-ization." *Global Health Governance* 4, no. 1 (2010): 1–17.

Rutherford, Ken. "The Evolving Arms Control Agenda: Implications of the Role of NGOs in Banning in Antipersonnel Landmines." *World Politics* 53, no. 1 (October 2000): 74–114.

Sachs, Wolfgang. *Environment and Human Rights.* Berlin: Wuppertal Institute for Climate, Environment, Energy, 2009. Wuppertal Paper no. 137.

Sakharov, Andrei. Acceptance speech read by Elena Bonner Sakharova, Oslo, 10 December 1975. Available at http://www.nobelprize.org/nobel_prizes/peace/laureates/1975/sakharov-acceptance.html, viewed 1 August 2011.

Sale, Kirkpatrick. *The Green Revolution: The American Environmental Movement 1962–1992.* New York: Hill and Wang, 1993.

Salman, Salman M. A., and Siobhán McInerney-Lankford. *The Human Right to Water: Legal and Policy Dimensions.* Washington, DC: World Bank, 2004.

Schnurr, Matthew A., and Larry Swatuk, eds. *Natural Resources and Social Conflict: Towards Critical Environmental Security.* London: Palgrave Macmillan, 2012.

Schreurs, Miranda A. *Environmental Politics in Japan, Germany, and the United States.* Cambridge: Cambridge University Press, 2002.

Schrijver, Nico J. *Development without Destruction: The UN and Global Resource Management.* Bloomington: Indiana University Press, 2010.

Schrijver, Nico J. "Natural Resource Management and Sustainable Development." In Thomas G. Weiss and Sam Daws, eds., *The Oxford Handbook of the United Nations.* New York: Oxford University Press, 2007.

Schrijver, Nico J. "Natural Resources, Permanent Sovereignty Over." *Max Planck Encyclopedia of Public International Law.* Available at www.mpepil.com, viewed 24 June 2011.

Schubert S., and J. Gupta. "Comparing Global Coordination Mechanisms on Energy, Environment, and Water." *Ecology and Society* 18, no. 2 (2013): 22.

Secretary-General's High-Level Panel on UN System-Wide Coherence in the Areas of Development, Humanitarian Assistance, and the Environment. *Delivering as One: Report of the Secretary General's High-Level Panel.* New York: UN, 2006.

Security Council Report. "Special Research Report: Security Council Elections 2012." Available at http://www.securitycouncilreport.org/atf/cf/%7B65BFCF9B-6 D27-4E9C-8CD3-CF6E4FF96FF9%7D/special_research_report_elections_2012.pdf, viewed 30 May 2013.

Sen, Amartya. *Development as Freedom.* New York: Oxford University Press, 1999.

Sguaitamatti, Damiano A., Simon J. A. Mason, and Pilar Ramirez Gröbli, "Stepping Stones to Peace? Natural Resource Provisions in Peace Agreements." In Carl Bruch, Carroll Muffett, and Sandra S. Nichols, eds., *Governance, Natural Resources, and Post-conflict Peacebuilding.* New York: Routledge, 2015.

Shelton, Dinah. "Human Rights and Environment: Past, Present and Future Linkages and the Value of a Declaration." Paper presented at the High Level Expert Meeting on the New Future of Human Rights and Environment: Moving the Global Agenda Forward, Nairobi, 30 November–1 December 2009.

Shelton, Dinah. "Normative Hierarchy in International Law." *American Journal of International Law* 100, no. 2 (April 2006): 291–323.

Sierra Leone Truth and Reconciliation Commission. *Witness to Truth: Final Report of the Truth and Reconciliation Commission.* October 2004.

Silver, Cheryl Simon, with Ruth F. DeFries for the National Academies of Science. *One Earth, One Future: Our Changing Global Environment.* Washington, DC: National Academy Press, 1990.

Snow, David A., and Robert D. Benford. "Ideology, Frame Resonance, and Participant Mobilization." In Bert Klandermans, Hanspeter Kriesi, and Sidney Tarrow, eds., *International Social Movement Research*, 197–217. Greenwich, CT: JAI Press, 1988.

"Special Report: What Happened at Stockholm." *Bulletin of the Atomic Scientists* 28, no. 7 (September 1972): 16–29.

St. Clair, Asunción Lera. "Global Poverty and Climate Change: Towards the Responsibility to Protect." In Karen O'Brien, Asunción Lera St. Clair, and Berit Kristoffersen, eds., *Climate Change, Ethics and Human Security.* Cambridge: Cambridge University Press, 2010.

Stakeholder Forum for a Sustainable Future. *Review of Implementation of Agenda 21 and the Rio Principles: Synthesis Report.* January 2012.

"Statement on Behalf of the Group of 77 and China by Ambassador Peter Thomson, Permanent Representative of Fiji to the United Nations and Chairman of the Group of 77, at the Arria-Formula Meeting on the Security Dimensions of Climate Change." New York, 15 February 2013.

"State of Denial." *Sacramento Bee*, 27 April 2003.

Steinberg, Paul. *Who Rules the Earth?* New York: Oxford University Press, 2014.

Stern, Nicholas. *The Economics of Climate Change: The Stern Review.* Cambridge: Cambridge University Press, 2007.

Stokke, Olav S. *Disaggregating International Regimes: A New Approach to Evaluation and Comparison.* Cambridge, MA: MIT Press, 2012.

Strong, Maurice. "Message from Maurice Strong." In United Nations Environment Programme, *Multilateral Environmental Agreement Negotiator's Handbook.* Joensuu, Finland: University of Joensuu Department of Law, 2007.

Sustainable Development Solutions Network. *An Action Agenda for Sustainable Development: Report for the UN Secretary-General.* Revised version, 23 October 2013.

Swisspeace, Center for Security Studies, and Swiss Federal Institute of Technology Zurich. *Linking Environment and Conflict Prevention: The Role of the United Nations.* Zurich: Center for Security Studies; Bern: Swisspeace, 2008.

Szasz, Paul C. "Restructuring the International Organizational Framework." In Edith B. Weiss, ed., *Environmental Change and International Law.* Tokyo: United Nations University Press, 1992.

Tänzler, Dennis, Alexander Carius, and Achim Maas. "The Need for Conflict-Sensitive Adaptation." In Geoffrey D. Dabelko, Lauren Herzer, Schuyler Null, Meaghan Parker, and Russell Sticklor, eds., *Backdraft: The Conflict Potential of Climate Change Adaptation and Mitigation*. Washington, DC: Woodrow Wilson International Center for Scholars, 2013. Environmental Change & Security Program Report vol. 14, issue 2.

Themnér, Lotta, and Peter Wallensteen. "Armed Conflicts, 1946–2011." *Journal of Peace Research* 49, no. 4 (July 2012): 565–575.

Truman, Harry S. "Letter to William S. Paley on the Creation of the President's Materials Policy Commission." 22 January 1951. Available at http://www.presidency.ucsb.edu/ws/index.php?pid=13876#axzz1Q7Uh251p, viewed 23 June 2011.

Turco, R. P., O. B. Toon, T. P. Ackerman, J. B. Pollack, and C. Sagan. "Nuclear Winter: Global Consequences of Multiple Nuclear Explosions." *Science* 222, no. 4630 (23 December 1983): 1283–1292.

"UN Peacekeepers 'Traded Gold and Guns with Congolese Rebels.'" *Guardian*, 28 April 2008. Available at http://www.theguardian.com/world/2008/apr/28/congo.unitednations, viewed 1 December 2014.

Underdal, Arild, and Oran R Young, eds. *Regime Consequences*. Dordrecht: Kluwer, 2004.

United Nations. *Delivering as One: Report of the Secretary-General's High-Level Panel on UN System-Wide Coherence in the Areas of Development, Humanitarian Assistance, and the Environment*. 9 November 2006.

United Nations. "Greening the Blue." Available at http://www.greeningtheblue.org/, viewed 9 August 2012.

United Nations. "List of Peacekeeping Operations 1948–2013." Available at http://www.un.org/en/peacekeeping/documents/operationslist.pdf, viewed 20 November 2014.

United Nations. *Yearbook of the United Nations 1965*. New York: United Nations, 1965.

United Nations. *Yearbook of the United Nations*. Searchable database available at http://unyearbook.un.org/, viewed 16 June 2011.

United Nations Climate Change Secretariat. "UN Climate Change Conference in Warsaw Keeps Governments on a Track towards 2015 Climate Agreement." Press release, 23 November 2013.

United Nations Commission on Human Rights. *Human Rights and the Environment as Part of Sustainable Development: Report of the Secretary-General*. UN Document E/CN.4/2005/96, 19 January 2005.

United Nations Commission on Human Rights. Resolution 2004/17, 16 April 2004.

United Nations Committee on Economic, Social and Cultural Rights. *Substantive Issues Arising in the Implementation of the International Covenant on Economic, Social and Cultural Rights: General Comment 12*. UN Document E/C.12/1999/5, 12 May 1999.

United Nations Committee on Economic, Social and Cultural Rights. *Substantive Issues Arising in the Implementation of the International Covenant on Economic, Social and Cultural Rights: General Comment No. 14*. UN Document E/C.12/2000/4, 11 August 2000.

United Nations Committee on Economic, Social and Cultural Rights. *Substantive Issues Arising in the Implementation of the International Covenant on Economic, Social and Cultural Rights: General Comment No. 15 (2002): The Right to Water*, UN Document E/C.12/2002/11, 20 January 2003.

United Nations Conference on Environment and Development. Rio Declaration on Environment and Development. Adopted 14 June 1992, Rio de Janeiro, Brazil.

United Nations Conference on Sustainable Development. "Side Events at Rio." Available at http://www.uncsd2012.org/meetings_sidevents.html, viewed 28 January 2014.

United Nations Conference on the Human Environment. *Action Plan for the Human Environment.* Available at http://www.unep.org/Documents.Multilingual/Default.asp?DocumentID=97&ArticleID=1504&l=en, viewed 24 June 2013.

United Nations Conference on the Human Environment. Declaration of the United Nations Conference on the Human Environment. Adopted 16 June 1972, Stockholm, Sweden.

United Nations Convention on the Law of the Sea. Adopted by the Third United Nations Conference on the Law of the Sea, 10 December 1982, Montego Bay, Jamaica.

United Nations Department of Economic and Social Affairs. *Agenda 21.* New York: United Nations, 1992. Available at http://www.un.org/esa/dsd/agenda21/, viewed 26 December 2011.

United Nations Department of Economic and Social Affairs. *Back to Our Common Future: Sustainable Development in the 21st Century Project. Summary for Policy Makers.* New York: UNDESA, 2012.

United Nations Department of Economic and Social Affairs. *Review of Implementation of Agenda 21.* New York: UNDESA, 2012.

United Nations Department of Peacekeeping Operations. *United Nations Peacekeeping Operations: Principles and Guidelines.* New York: United Nations, 2008.

United Nations Department of Public Information. "Security Council Holds First-Ever Debate on Impact of Climate Change on Peace, Security, Hearing over 50 Speakers." Press release, 17 April 2007.

United Nations Development Group. "Natural Resource Management in Transition Settings." UNDG-ECHA Guidance Note, January 2013.

United Nations Development Group. "Thirty-Sixth Meeting of the United Nations Development Group, Thursday, 19 April 2007: Summary of Conclusions." Available at http://pcna.undg.org/index.php?option=com_docman&Itemid=15, viewed 7 August 2012.

United Nations Development Programme. "Human Security: Evaluation of UNDP Assistance to Conflict-Affected Countries. Case Study Sierra Leone." UNDP Evaluation Office, 2006.

United Nations Development Programme. "Promoting Rights and Access to Finance." Available at http://www.undp.org/localdevelopment/topic-promoting-rights-and-access-to-finance.shtml, viewed 25 May 2011.

United Nations Development Programme. "Strengthening Community Voices in Policy Processes." Available at http://www.undp.org/localdevelopment/topic-community-voices-in-policy-processes.shtml, viewed 25 May 2011.

United Nations Development Programme Sierra Leone. "Recovery for Development." Available at http://www.sl.undp.org/development.htm, viewed 30 August 2010.

United Nations Development Programme Sudan. "Reduction of Resource Based Conflicts among Pastoralists and Farmers." Available at http://www.sd.undp.org/projects/cp3.htm, viewed 12 August 2012.

United Nations Economic, Scientific and Cultural Organization. "The Biosphere Conference 25 Years Later." Available at http://unesdoc.unesco.org/images/0014/001471/147152eo.pdf, viewed 28 December 2011.

United Nations Economic, Scientific and Cultural Organization. "Timeline of IOC." Available at http://portal.unesco.org/science/en/ev.php-URL_ID= 8463&URL_DO=DO_TOPIC&URL_SECTION=201.htm, viewed 28 December 2011.

United Nations Economic, Scientific and Cultural Organization. "The World Heritage Convention." Available at http://whc.unesco.org/en/convention/, viewed 28 December 2011.

United Nations Environment Programme. *Desk Study on the Environment in Iraq.* Geneva: UNEP, 2003.

United Nations Environment Programme. *Desk Study in the Occupied Palestinian Territories.* Geneva: UNEP, 2003.

United Nations Environment Programme. "Disasters and Conflicts." Available at http://www.unep.org/disastersandconflicts/, viewed 20 November 2014.

United Nations Environment Programme. *Environment, Conflict and Peacebuilding Assessment: Technical Report.* Geneva: UNEP, 2010.

United Nations Environment Programme. *Environmental Assessment of Ogoniland.* Geneva: UNEP, 2011.

United Nations Environment Programme. "Environmental Cooperation for Peacebuilding." Available at http://www.unep.org/disastersandconflicts/ Introduction/ECP/tabid/105948/Default.aspx, viewed 23 December 2013.

United Nations Environment Programme. *From Conflict to Peacebuilding: The Role of Natural Resources and the Environment.* Nairobi: UNEP, 2009.

United Nations Environment Programme. *Global Environmental Outlook 4.* Nairobi: UNEP, 2007.

United Nations Environment Programme. *Global Environmental Outlook 5.* Nairobi: UNEP, 2012.

United Nations Environment Programme. *Governance for Peace over Natural Resources: A Review of Transitions in Environmental Governance across Africa as a Resource for Peacebuilding and Environmental Management in Sudan.* Nairobi: UNEP, 2013.

United Nations Environment Programme. *Greening the Blue Helmets: Environment, Natural Resources, and UN Peacekeeping Operations.* Nairobi: UNEP, 2012.

United Nations Environment Programme. "Integrating Environment in Postconflict Needs Assessments." UNEP Guidance Note, March 2009.

United Nations Environment Programme. *Livelihood Security: Climate Change, Migration and Conflict in the Sahel.* Nairobi: UNEP, 2011.

United Nations Environment Programme. "The New Future of Human Rights and Environment: Moving the Global Agenda Forward—High Level Experts Meeting." Available at http://www.unep.org/environmentalgovernance/ Events/HumanRightsandEnvironment/HighLevelExpertsMeeting/ tabid/2661/language/en-US/Default.aspx, viewed 26 May 2011.

United Nations Environment Programme. *Post-conflict Environmental Assessment: Côte d'Ivoire.* Nairobi: UNEP, forthcoming.

United Nations Environment Programme. *Protecting the Environment during Armed Conflict: An Inventory and Analysis of International Law.* Nairobi: UNEP, 2009.

United Nations Environment Programme. *Report of the Governing Council on the Work of its Second Session,* 11–22 March 1974.

United Nations Environment Programme. *Sierra Leone: Environment, Conflict and Peacebuilding Assessment. Technical Report.* Geneva: UNEP, February 2010.

United Nations Environment Programme. "UN-EU Partnership on Natural Resources, Conflict and Peacebuilding." Available at http://www.unep. org/dnc/Introduction/EnvironmentalCooperationforPeacebuilding/ OtherECPActivities/UNEUPartnership/tabid/54648/Default.aspx, viewed 10 August 2012.

United Nations Environment Programme. "UNEP and INTERPOL Assess Impacts of Environmental Crime on Security and Development." Press release, 6 November 2013.

United Nations Environment Programme. *UNEP Programme Performance Report for the 2010-2011 Biennium. Report of the Executive Director. Report No. 2: January–December 2010*. Nairobi: UNEP, 2011.

United Nations Environment Programme. *United Nations Environment Programme Annual Report 2013*. Nairobi: UNEP, 2014.

United Nations Environment Programme, Governing Council. *Nairobi Declaration on the State of Worldwide Environment*, 19 May 1982. UN Document UNEP/GC.10/ INF.5.

United Nations Environment Programme and United Nations Centre for Human Settlements. *The Kosovo Conflict: Consequences for the Environment and Human Settlements*. Geneva: UNEP and UNCHS, 1999.

United Nations Environment Programme, United Nations Entity for Gender Equality and the Empowerment of Women, United Nations Peacebuilding Support Office and United Nations Development Programme, *Women and Natural Resources: Unlocking the Peacebuilding Potential*. Nairobi: UNEP, 2013.

United Nations Environment Programme and United Nations Office of the High Commissioner for Human Rights. "High Level Expert Meeting on the New Future of Human Rights and Environment: Moving the Global Agenda Forward." Available at http://www.unep.org/environmentalgovernance/ Events/HumanRightsandEnvironment/tabid/2046/language/en-US/ Default.aspx, viewed 25 May 2011.

United Nations Framework Convention on Climate Change. "Declarations and Reservations by Parties—Kyoto Protocol: Nauru." Available at http://unfccc. int/kyoto_protocol/status_of_ratification/items/5424.php.

United Nations General Assembly. *Annual Report of the United Nations High Commissioner for Human Rights and Reports of the Office of the High Commissioner and the Secretary-General. Report of the Office of the United Nations High Commissioner for Human Rights on the Relationship between Climate Change and Human Rights*. UN Document A/HRC/10/61, 15 January 2009.

United Nations General Assembly. *Climate Change and its Possible Security Implications: Report of the Secretary-General*. Sixty-fourth session. UN Document A/64/350, 11 September 2009.

United Nations General Assembly. *Integrated and coordinated implementation of and follow-up to the outcomes of the major United Nations conferences and summits in the economic, social and related fields. Follow-up to the outcome of the Millennium Summit. Implementing the responsibility to protect. Report of the Secretary-General*. UN Document A/63/677, 12 January 2009.

United Nations General Assembly. "Letter dated 9 November 2006 from the Co-Chairs of the High-level Panel on United Nations System-wide Coherence in the areas of development, humanitarian assistance and the environment addressed to the Secretary-General." UN Document A/61/583, 20 November 2006.

United Nations General Assembly. *Report of the Office of the United Nations High Commissioner for Human Rights on the Relationship between Climate Change and Human Rights.* UN Document A/HRC/10/61, 15 January 2009.

United Nations General Assembly. *Report of the Open Working Group of the General Assembly on Sustainable Development Goals.* UN Document A/68/970, 12 August 2014.

United Nations General Assembly. *Report of the United Nations Conference on Environment and Development (Rio de Janeiro, 3–14 June 1992).* UN Document A/CONF.151/26. Vol. 4. 28 September 1992.

United Nations General Assembly. *Report of the World Conference on Human Rights.* UN Document A/CONF.157/24 (Part I), 13 October 1993.

United Nations General Assembly. Resolution 217(III) A, 10 December 1948.

United Nations General Assembly. Resolution 523, 12 January 1952.

United Nations General Assembly. Resolution 626, 21 December 1952.

United Nations General Assembly. Resolution 1314, 12 December 1958.

United Nations General Assembly. Resolution 1514, 14 December 1960.

United Nations General Assembly. Resolution 1803, 14 December 1962.

United Nations General Assembly. Resolution 2158, 25 November 1966.

United Nations General Assembly. Resolution 3281, 12 December 1974.

United Nations General Assembly. Resolution 37/7, 28 October 1982.

United Nations General Assembly. Resolution 38/161, 19 December 1983.

United Nations General Assembly. Resolution 53/242, 10 August 1999.

United Nations General Assembly. Resolution 54/175 of 17 December 1999.

United Nations General Assembly. Resolution 55/56, 1 December 2000.

United Nations General Assembly. Resolution 60/1, 24 October 2005.

United Nations General Assembly. Resolution 63/281, 11 June 2009.

United Nations General Assembly. Resolution 64/292, 28 July 2010.

United Nations General Assembly. *Sixty-Third Session, 85th Plenary Meeting. Agenda Item 107 (continued). Follow-up to the Outcome of the Millennium Summit. Draft Resolution (A/63/L.8/Rev.1).* UN Document A/63/PV.85, 3 June 2009.

United Nations General Assembly. *The Universal Declaration of Human Rights.* Resolution A/RES/217(III) A, adopted 10 December 1948.

United Nations General Assembly, Human Rights Council. *Annual Report of the United Nations High Commissioner for Human Rights and Reports of the Office of the High Commissioner and the Secretary-General. Report of the Office of the High Commissioner for Human Rights on the Relationship between Climate Change and Human Rights.* UN Document A/HRC/10/61, 15 January 2009.

United Nations General Assembly, Human Rights Council. Fifteenth Session, Agenda item 3. *Promotion and Protection of All Human Rights, Civil, Political, Economic, Social and Cultural Rights, Including the Right to Development. 15/ . . . Human Rights and Access to Safe Drinking Water and Sanitation.* UN Document A/HRC/15/L.14, 24 September 2010.

United Nations General Assembly, Human Rights Council. *Report of the Independent Expert on the Issue of Human Rights Obligations Relating to the Enjoyment of a Safe, Clean, Healthy and Sustainable Environment,* John H. Knox. Twenty-Third Session, Agenda item 3. UN Document A/HRC/25/5, 30 December 2013.

United Nations General Assembly, Human Rights Council. *Report of the Independent Expert on the Issue of Human Rights Obligations Relating to the Enjoyment of a Safe, Clean, Healthy and Sustainable Environment,* John H. Knox. Twenty-second session, Agenda item 3. UN Document A/HRC/22/43, 24 December 2012.

United Nations General Assembly, Human Rights Council. Twenty-Fifth Session, Agenda item 3. "Human Rights and the Environment." UN Document A/HRC/25/L.31, 24 March 2014.

United Nations General Assembly and United Nations Security Council. *Identical letters Dated 19 July 2010 from the Permanent Representatives of Ireland, Mexico and South Africa to the United Nations Addressed to the President of the General Assembly and the President of the Security Council.* UN Document A/64/868–S/2010/393, 21 July 2010.

United Nations General Assembly and United Nations Security Council. *Report of the Secretary-General on Peacebuilding in the Immediate Aftermath of Conflict.* UN Document A/63/881-S/2009/304, 11 June 2009.

United Nations General Assembly and United Nations Security Council. *Report of the Secretary-General on Peacebuilding in the Immediate Aftermath of Conflict.* UN Document A/64/866-S/2010/386, 16 July 2010.

United Nations Human Rights Council. *Analytical Study on the Relationship between Human Rights and the Environment: Report of the United Nations High Commissioner for Human Rights.* UN Document A/HRC/19/34, 16 December 2011.

United Nations Human Rights Council. Decision 19/10. "Human Rights and the Environment." 53rd meeting, 22 March 2012.

United Nations Human Rights Council. *Human Rights and Climate Change.* UN Document A/HRC/7/L.21/Rev.1, 26 March 2008.

United Nations Human Rights Council. *Report of the Special Representative of the Secretary-General on the Issue of Human Rights and Transnational Corporations and Other Business Enterprises, John Ruggie. Guiding Principles on Business and Human Rights: Implementing the United Nations "Protect, Respect and Remedy" Framework.* UN Document A/HRC/17/31, 21 March 2011.

United Nations International Strategy for Disaster Reduction. *Global Assessment Report on Disaster Risk Reduction.* Geneva: UNISDR, 2011.

United Nations News Center. "At World Economic Forum, Ban Ki-moon Pledges Action on Water Resources." January 2008. Available at http://www.un.org/apps/news/story.asp?NewsID=25398&Cr=davos&Cr1=#, viewed 1 March 2011.

United Nations News Center. "Ban Ki-moon Calls on New Generation to Take Better Care of Planet Earth than his own." 1 March 2007. Available at http://www.un.org/apps/news/story.asp?NewsID=21720&Cr=global&Cr1=warming, viewed 1 March 2011.

United Nations News Center. "Ban Ki-moon Warns That Water Shortages Are Increasingly Driving Conflicts." 6 February 2008. Available at http://www.un.org/apps/news/story.asp?NewsID=25527&Cr=water&Cr1, viewed 1 March 2011.

United Nations News Center. "Both Rich and Poor Have Clear Interest in Protecting Environment, Secretary-General Says." Press release SG/SM/8239 ENV/DEV/637, 14 May 2002.

United Nations Office of the High Commissioner for Human Rights. "A New Climate Change Agreement Must Include Human Rights Protections for All. An Open Letter from Special Procedures Mandate-Holders of the Human Rights Council to the State Parties to the UN Framework Convention on Climate Change on the Occasion of the Meeting of the Ad Hoc Working Group on the Durban Platform for Enhanced Action in Bonn (20–25 October 2014)." 17 October 2014.

United Nations Office of the High Commissioner on Human Rights. *Human Rights Council Panel Discussion on the Relationship between Climate Change and Human Rights: Summary of Discussions.* 15 June 2009.

United Nations Office of the High Commissioner for Human Rights. "What Are Human Rights?" Available at http://www.ohchr.org/EN/Issues/Pages/WhatareHumanRights.aspx, viewed 29 December 2011.

United Nations Office of the High Commissioner for Human Rights, UN Habitat, and World Health Organization. "The Right to Water." Fact Sheet No. 35. Geneva, August 2010.

United Nations Office of the High Commissioner for Human Rights, World Health Organization, Center on Housing Rights and Evictions, Center for Economic and Social Rights, and WaterAid. *The Right to Water.* Geneva: WHO, 2003.

United Nations Office of the Special Adviser on Africa. "Conference Report, UN Expert Group Meeting on Natural Resources and Conflict in Africa: Transforming a Peace Liability into a Peace Asset." Cairo, 17–19 June 2006.

United Nations Peacebuilding Commission. "Conclusions and Recommendations of the Second Biannual Review of the Strategic Framework for Peacebuilding in the Central African Republic." UN Document PBC/5/CAF/3, 18 November 2011.

United Nations Peacebuilding Commission. "Strategic Framework for Peacebuilding in the Central African Republic 2009–2011." UN Document PBC/3/CAF/7, 9 June 2009.

United Nations Security Council. 5663rd meeting, New York, Tuesday, 17 April 2007. *Agenda: Letter Dated 5 April 2007 from the Permanent Representative of the United Kingdom of Great Britain and Northern Ireland to the United Nations Addressed to the President of the Security Council (S/2007/186).* UN Documents S/PV.5663 and S/PV.5663 (resumption 1).

United Nations Security Council. 5705th meeting, New York, Monday, 25 June 2007. *Maintenance of International Peace and Security.* UN Documents S/PV.5705 and S/PV.5705 (resumption 1).

United Nations Security Council. 6587th meeting, New York, Wednesday, 20 July 2011. *Maintenance of International Peace and Security: Impact of Climate Change.* UN Documents S/PV.6587 and S/PV.6587 (resumption 1).

United Nations Security Council. 6982nd meeting, New York, Wednesday, 19 June 2013. *Maintenance of International Peace and Security. Conflict Prevention and Natural Resources.* UN Documents S/PV.6982 and S/PV.6982 (resumption 1).

United Nations Security Council. *Letter Dated 1 July 2011 from the Permanent Representative of Germany to the United Nations Addressed to the Secretary-General.* UN Document S/2011/408, 5 July 2011.

United Nations Security Council. *Letter Dated 12 April 2007 from the Chargé d'affaires a.i. of the Permanent Mission of Cuba to the United Nations Addressed to the President of the Security Council.* UN Document S/2007/203, 12 April 2007.

United Nations Security Council. *Letter Dated 16 April 2007 from the Permanent Representative of Pakistan to the United Nations Addressed to the Security Council.* UN Document S/2007/211, 16 April 2007.

United Nations Security Council. *Letter Dated 25 January 2007 from the Chairman of the Security Council Committee Established Pursuant to Resolution 1533 (2004) Concerning the Democratic Republic of the Congo Addressed to the President of the Security Council.* UN Document S/2007/40, 31 January 2007.

United Nations Security Council. *Letter Dated 5 April 2007 from the Permanent Representative of the United Kingdom of Great Britain and Northern Ireland to* the United Nations Addressed to the President of the Security Council, annex. UN Document S/2007/186, 5 April 2007.

United Nations Security Council. *Letter Dated 6 June 2007 from the Permanent Representative of Belgium to the United Nations to the Secretary-General*. UN Document S/2007/334, 6 June 2007.

United Nations Security Council. *Preventive Diplomacy: Delivering Results. Report of the Secretary-General*. UN Document S/2011/552, 26 August 2011.

United Nations Security Council. Resolution 255, 19 June 1968.

United Nations Security Council. Resolution 1459, 28 January 2003.

United Nations Security Council. Resolution 1509, 19 September 2003.

United Nations Security Council. Resolution 1562, 17 September 2004.

United Nations Security Council. Resolution 1625, 14 September 2005.

United Nations Security Council. Resolution 1706, 31 August 2006.

United Nations Security Council. Resolution 1756, 15 May 2007.

United Nations Security Council. Resolution 1854, 19 December 2008.

United Nations Security Council. Resolution 1856, 22 December 2008.

United Nations Security Council. Resolution 1896, 30 November 2009.

United Nations Security Council. Resolution 2117, 26 September 2013.

United Nations Security Council. *Statement by the President of the Security Council*. UN Document S/PRST/2007/22, 25 June 2007.

United Nations Security Council. *Third Report of the Secretary-General on the United Nations Mission in Sierra Leone*. UN Document S/2000/186, 7 March 2000.

United Nations Sub-Commission on the Prevention of Discrimination and Protection of Minorities. *Declaration of Principles on Human Rights and the Environment*, 1994. Available at http://www.environmentandhumanrights.org/resources/Draft%20Decl%20of%20Ppls%20on%20HR%20&%20the%20Env.pdf, viewed 2 June 2010.

United Nations System Task Team on the Post-2015 UN Development Agenda. *Realizing the Future We Want for All: Report to the Secretary-General*. New York: United Nations, June 2012.

United States House of Representatives, Permanent Select Committee on Intelligence and Select Committee on Energy Independence and Global Warming. *National Intelligence Assessment on the National Security Implications of Global Climate Change to 2030*. 25 June 2008.

UN-REDD Programme. *Fifth Consolidated Annual Progress Report of the UN REDD Programme Fund*, UN-REDD Programme Twelfth Policy Board Meeting, 7–9 July 2014, Lima, Peru.

van Dam, Chris. "Indigenous Territories and REDD in Latin America: Threat or Opportunity?" *Forests* 2 (2011): 394–414.

Vandemoortele, Jan. "Advancing the UN Development Agenda Post-2015: Some Practical Suggestions." Report submitted to the UN Task Force Regarding the Post-2015 Framework for Development, January 2012.

Vandemoortele, Jan. "The MDG Story: Intention Denied." *Development and Change* 42, no. 1 (January 2011): 1–21.

Vasak, Karel. "Human Rights: A Thirty-Year Struggle." *UNESCO Courier* 30, no. 11 (1977): 29–32.

Wapner, Paul. *Environmental Activism and World Civic Politics*. Albany: SUNY Press, 1996.

Wapner, Paul. "Politics beyond the State: Environmental Activism and World Civic Politics." *World Politics* 47, no. 3 (April 1995): 311–340.

Ward, Barbara, and Rene Dubos. *Only One Earth: The Care and Maintenance of a Small Planet*. London: Penguin, 1972.

"We Reject Redd+ in All Its Versions." Letter to the Governor of California (USA), Jerry Brown from activists in Chiapas, Mexico, April 2013. Available at http://www.redd-monitor.org/2013/04/30/we-reject-redd-in-all-its-versions-letter-from-chiapas-mexico-opposing-redd-in-californias-global-warming-solutions-act-ab-32/, viewed 20 May 2013.

"Web Gallery of Art: Tacca, Pietro." Available at http://www.wga.hu/frames-e.html?/html/t/tacca/philip4.html, viewed 1 February 2010.

Weinberg, Bill. "Mexico: Lacandon Selva Conflict Grows." *NACLA Report on the Americas* 36, no. 6 (May–June 2003): 26–47.

Weiss, Thomas, and Leon Gordenker, eds. *NGOs, the UN, and Global Governance*. Boulder, CO: Lynne Rienner, 1996.

Wikipedia. "Equestrian Statue." Available at http://en.wikipedia.org/wiki/Equestrian_statue, viewed 1 February 2010.

Wilde, Ralph, ed. *United Nations Reform through Practice*. Report of the International Law Association Study Group on United Nations Reform, December 2011.

Williams, Michael C. "Words, Images, Enemies: Securitization and International Politics." *International Studies Quarterly* 47, no. 4 (2003): 511–531.

World Bank. *The Human Right to Water. Legal and Policy Dimensions*. Washington, DC: World Bank, 2004.

World Commission on Environment and Development. *Our Common Future*. New York: Oxford University Press, 1987.

World Conservation Union. "Food Security: Making the Ecosystem Connections." Available at http://www.iucn.org/about/work/programmes/water/?12988/Food-Security-making-the-ecosystem-connections, viewed 20 May 2013.

World Health Organization. *Air Pollution: Fifth Report of the Expert Committee on Environmental Sanitation*. Geneva: WHO, 1958. WHO Technical Report Series, No. 157.

World Health Organization. *Handbook of Resolutions and Decisions of the World Health Assembly and the Executive Board*. Vol. 2: 1973–1984. Geneva: WHO, 1985.

World Health Organization. *Health Hazards of the Human Environment*. Geneva: WHO, 1972.

World Health Organization. *Human Rights, Health and Poverty Reduction Strategies*. Health and Human Rights Publications Series, Issue 5, 2008.

World Health Organization. *Research into Environmental Pollution: Report of Five Scientific Groups*. Geneva: WHO, 1968. WHO Technical Report Series, No. 406.

World Health Organization. *The Second Ten Years of the World Health Organization: 1958–1967*. Geneva: WHO, 1968.

World Health Organization. *The Third Ten Years of the World Health Organization: 1968–1977*. Geneva: WHO, 2008.

World Health Organization and UN-Water. *GLAAS 2010: UN-Water Global Annual Assessment of Sanitation and Drinking-water*. Geneva: World Health Organization, 2010.

World Health Organization and UN-Water. *GLAAS Report 2012: UN-Water Global Analysis and Assessment of Sanitation and Drinking Water*. Geneva: WHO, 2012.

World Health Organization and United Nations Children's Fund. *Progress on Sanitation and Drinking-Water: 2010 Update*. Geneva: World Health Organization, 2010.

World Resources Institute. *Closing the Gap: Information, Participation, and Justice in Decision-Making for the Environment*. Washington, DC: WRI, 2002.

World Wildlife Fund. "Conserving Freshwater Ecosystem Services." Available at http://wwf.panda.org/what_we_do/how_we_work/conservation/freshwater/ water_development/, viewed 20 May 2013.

Yale Center for Environmental Law and Policy and Center for International Earth Science Information Network. *Environmental Performance Index 2014*. Available at http://epi.yale.edu/epi/, viewed 14 November 2014.

Young, Oran R. "Effectiveness of International Environmental Regimes: Existing Knowledge, Cutting-Edge Themes, and Research Strategies." *Proceedings of the National Academy of Sciences* 108, no. 50 (December 13, 2011): 19853–19860.

Zarsky, Lyuba. "Stuck in the Mud? Nation-States, Globalization and Environment." In Ken Conca and Geoffrey D. Dabelko, eds., *Green Planet Blues: Environmental Politics from Stockholm to Johannesburg*, 82–93. 3rd ed. Boulder, CO: Westview Press, 2004.

INDEX

Page numbers followed by *t* or *f* indicate tables or figures, respectively. Numbers followed by n indicate notes.

India, 20, 37
    characteristics of, 104*t*
    climate diplomacy, 172–173, 187
    greenhouse-gas emissions, 203, 203*t*
    Indus Waters Treaty, 49
Indian Ocean, 81–82
indigenous peoples, 121, 124–125
Indonesia, 39, 170–171, 178, 225n55
Indus River, 115
Indus Waters Treaty, 49
Inter-American Commission on Human
    Rights, 143
intergovernmental organiza-
    tions (IGOs), 22, 25–26,
    107–108, 222n53
Intergovernmental Panel on Climate
    Change (IPCC), 47, 167
International Biological Program, 46
International Convention for the
    Prevention of Pollution from Ships
    (MARPOL Convention), 43, 46, 63
International Council of Scientific
    Unions (ICSU), 46
International Court of Justice (ICJ)
    (World Court), 17*t*, 41–42
International Covenant on Civil and
    Political Rights (ICCPR), 52, 126
International Covenant on Economic,
    Social, and Cultural Rights (ICESCR),
    52, 122, 126
International Criminal Court (ICC), 15, 41
International Day for Preventing the
    Exploitation of the Environment in
    War and Armed Conflict, 155–156
International Drinking Water Supply
    and Sanitation Decade, 135
international environmental law, 8–9,
    70–73, 79–88, 125
International Geophysical Year, 46
International Hydrologic Decade, 46
International Institute for Sustainable
    Development (IISD), 248n102
internationalism, liberal, 127
International Labour Organization
    (ILO), 16, 44, 47, 134
international law, 41–43
International Law Commission
    (ILC), 196
internationally shared watercourses,
    114–115, 206

International Maritime Organization
    (IMO), 46
International Monetary Fund (IMF), 25, 36
International Oceanographic
    Commission, 46
International Peace Academy, 163
International Union for Conservation of
    Nature (IUCN), 44, 227n94
International Union for the
    Conservation of Nature and
    Natural Resources (IUCN), 225n35
International Union for the Protection
    of Nature (IUPN), 44, 225n35
International Whaling Commission, 72
interventionism, 159
Inuit, 143
Inuit Circumpolar Council, 143
Iran, 38
Iraq, 40, 103, 104*t*, 180
Israel, 39, 48–49, 178
IUCN. *see* International Union for
    Conservation of Nature
IUPN. *see* International Union for the
    Protection of Nature
Ivanova, Maria, 190

Jamaica, 36
Japan, 36, 87, 170, 178, 203, 203*t*
Johnson, Tana, 22
Joint UN Programme on HIV/AIDS, 93
Jolly, Richard, 24, 39
jus cogens, 42, 224n28
justice, environmental, 125–126

Kanie, Norichika, 80
Katanga, 49–50
Kenya, 59, 104*t*, 204
Khmer Rouge, 160
Kimberley Process, 96, 162–164, 186
Knox, John, 132, 144–145, 240n94. *see*
    also Independent Expert on Human
    Rights and Environment
Korea, 38
Kosovo conflict, 178–179
Ksentini, Fatma Zohra, 128–129
Kyoto Protocol to the United Nations
    Framework Convention on Climate
    Change (UNFCCC), 83, 141, 144,
    169, 172, 199
Kyrgyzstan, 183

amendment rates, 83–84, 84*f*
  growth of, 62–63, 64*f*
  supraregional or global accords, 81,
    82*t*, 85
multistakeholder forums, 114
Murphy, Craig, 28
Myanmar (Burma), 104*t*, 178, 196

NAFTA. *see* North American Free Trade
  Agreement
*Nagoya Protocol on Access to Genetic
  Resources and the Fair and Equitable
  Sharing of Benefits Arising from their
  Utilization*, 83
Naidoo, Kumi, 10
Nairobi Declaration on the State
  of Worldwide Environment,
  67, 227n93
NAM, 37, 40
Namibia, 168
"naming and shaming" process, 162
NAS. *see* National Academy of Sciences
Nasser, Gamal Abdel, 38, 49
National Academy of Sciences (NAS)
  (US), 70
National Biodiversity Strategy Action
  Plan (Sierra Leone), 94
National Wildlife Federation
  (US), 71–72
NATO. *see* North Atlantic Treaty
  Organization
natural capital, 2
natural resources
  conflict resources, 160–161,
    166, 245n60
  lootable resources, 161
  peace resources, 166
  resource curse, 50–51
  resource wealth, 50–51
  scarcity of, 151–152, 154, 205
  shortages, 167
  strategic, 38
Natural Resources Defense
  Council, 72, 97
natural resources management,
  37–39, 113
  conflict prevention, 183
  and decolonization, 35–41
  exploitation, 162
  "good governance" of 215, 215*t*

law-and-development approach
  to, 166
national, 37–38
permanent sovereignty over,
  39, 42, 64
resource rights, 51–53, 64
sanctions, 161, 162*t*, 165
sovereignty over, 39
in transition settings, 180
and war, 148–188
Nauru, 144, 174
needs assessments, postconflict,
  179–180
neoliberalism, 69, 76–77, 139
Nepal, 104*t*
New International Economic Order
  (NIEO), 39–41, 43, 64–65,
  69, 224n30
new regionalism, 81–82
New Zealand, 87
NGOs. *see* nongovernmental
  organizations
NIEO. *see* New International
  Economic Order
Niger, 104*t*
Niger Delta, 98, 106, 109
Nigeria, 51, 98–99, 173, 202–203
Nile Basin Initiative (World Bank), 115
Nile River, 49
Nobel Peace Prize, 47, 51
Non-Aligned Movement, 173
nongovernmental organizations
  (NGOs), 23, 55, 72, 160, 163
North American Free Trade Agreement
  (NAFTA), 72
North Atlantic Treaty Organization
  (NATO), 150, 177, 184
Norway, 53, 142–143
nuclear winter hypothesis, 150

occupational health, 134
OECD. *see* Organisation for Economic
  Co-operation and Development
Office for Disaster Risk Reduction
  (UNISDR), 142
Office of the High Commissioner for
  Human Rights (OHCHR), 8–9, 119,
  121, 132, 136, 138–141, 143–144,
  146, 193–195, 194*t*
oil, 53, 161, 162*t*

Qatar, 164

R2P. *see* responsibility to protect
radicalism, 53
railroads, 38
Rajagopal, Ralakrishnan, 69
Ramsar Convention. *see Convention
    on Wetlands of International
    Importance, especially as Waterfowl
    Habitat*
Reagan, Ronald, 69
REDD. *see* Reducing Emissions
    from Deforestation and Forest
    Degradation in Developing
    Countries
REDD+, 142–143, 207
Redford, Robert, 97
Reducing Emissions from Deforestation
    and Forest Degradation in
    Developing Countries (REDD), 139,
    142, 206
reform debate, 4–7
reformism, 29
refugees, 222n53, 252n44
regionalism, new, 81–82
regional legal instruments, 131
regulations, 12–13, 108, 209
*Report on Peacebuilding in the Immediate
    Aftermath of Conflict* (UN
    Secretary-General), 158
Republic of the Congo, 49–51, 170
research, 154, 160–161
Resolution 53/242 (UN), 184
Resolution 63/281 (UN), 173
Resolution 65/283 (UN), 204
Resolution 523 (UN), 38
Resolution 1325 (UN), 204
Resolution 1625 (UN), 166–167, 204
Resolution 1803 (UN), 223n23, 224n27
Resolution 2158 (UN), 39–40
Resolution 3201 (UN), 224n27
Resolution 3281 (UN), 40,
    223n23, 224n27
resources. *see* natural resources
responsibility to protect (R2P), 159,
    195–197
Rhine River, 63
Rhodesia, 161
Rice, Susan, 172–173, 204
Right Livelihood Award, 111

rights
    civil rights, 25
    climate and, 140, 140f
    of countries, 52
    to development, 69–70
    environmental, 119–147, 193–197
    to food, 133–134
    human rights, 12, 56, 69–70,
        106–116, 119–147, 193–197
    indigenous people's rights, 121
    land rights, 121
    peace-and-rights practice, 205–212
    of peoples, 51–53
    property rights, 77, 107–108
    resource rights, 51–53, 64
    states' rights, 56
    UN principles on Business and
        Human Rights, 206
    water and, 136–137, 137f
    women's rights, 121
rights-based approach
    to climate change, 147
    to environmental governance,
        106–116, 121, 124–125, 127–129,
        193–197
    to health, 134
    to water, 134–137, 137f, 193
Rio+10 summit, 4
Rio+20 summit. *see* United Nations
    Conference on Sustainable
    Development
Rio Declaration on Environment and
    Development, 89, 136–137, 206
    Principle 10, 108
    principles addressing peace and secu-
        rity, 75–76, 75t
Rio Earth Summit. *see* United Nations
    Conference on Environment and
    Development (UNCED)
Rio model, 216
Road to Survival (Vogt), 48
Rolnik, Raquel, 147
Roma, 110
Rome Statute, 41
Roosevelt, Franklin, 48, 148
Rotterdam Convention. *see Convention
    on the Prior Informed Consent
    Procedure for Certain Hazardous
    Chemicals and Pesticides in
    International Trade*

World Health Organization (WHO), 2,
16, 44–45, 60, 77, 93, 129, 153
Expert Committee on Environmental
Sanitation, 45
*Human Rights, Health and Poverty
Reduction Strategies,* 134
and right to water, 136
World Heritage Convention, 46–47
World Meteorological Organization
(WMO), 47, 77
World Resources Institute (WRI), 72,
130–131, 142
World Summit on Sustainable
Development (WSSD), 80, 155

World Summit Outcomes
Document, 251n18
World Trade Organization (WTO),
5, 76–77
World Vision, 163
World Wildlife Fund (WWF), 66, 72, 97
WRI. *see* World Resources Institute
WSSD. *see* World Summit on
Sustainable Development
WWF. *see* World Wildlife Fund

Yearbook of the United Nations, 54
Yemen, 104*t*
Young, Oran, 85